Linguistics
FOR
DUMMIES®

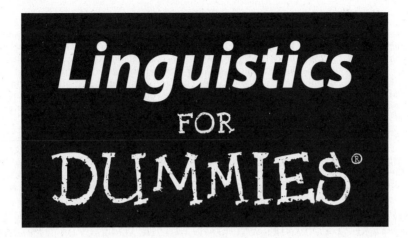

by Strang Burton, Rose-Marie Déchaine, and Eric Vatikiotis-Bateson

John Wiley & Sons Canada, Ltd.

Linguistics For Dummies®

Published by
John Wiley & Sons Canada, Ltd.
6045 Freemont Blvd.
Mississauga, Ontario, L5R 4J3
www.wiley.com

Burton, Strang

       Linguistics for dummies / Strang Burton, Rose-Marie Déchaine, Eric Vatikiotis-Bateson.

Includes index.

ISBN 978-1-118-09169-2

       1. Linguistics. 2. Language and languages. I. Déchaine,

Rose-Marie, 1960– II. Vatikiotis-Bateson, Eric III. Title.

P121.B87 2012   410   C2011-907371-4

ISBN 978-1-118-09169-2 (pbk); ISBN 978-1-118-10157-5 (ebk); ISBN 978-1-118-10158-2 (ebk); ISBN 978-1-118-10159-9 (ebk)

Printed in the United States

3 4 5 BRR 17 16 15

WILEY

About the Authors

Strang Burton (Ph.D. Linguistics, Rutgers University, 1995) is a linguist and multimedia developer specializing in documentation and re-vitalization work for severely endangered languages. Working with elders and community members to document the Upriver Halq'emeylem (Halkomelem) language, he contributes to a community-run language revitalization program, the *Stolo Shxweli Halq'emeylem Language Program*, at the Stolo Nation, in Chilliwack, British Columbia. He is a multi-media trainer and technical consultant for many endangered-language documentation projects and teaches linguistics and language documentation at the University of British Columbia and the University of Victoria.

Rose-Marie Déchaine (Ph.D. Linguistics, University of British Columbia, 1994) is a linguist who specializes in the formal analysis of language, with a focus on Native American and African languages. She is particularly interested in understanding how the languages of the world distinguish parts-of-speech and what this reveals about the relation between categorization and cognition. Her current research explores how gesture and speech are woven together in the course of performing language in communicative interaction. She teaches in the linguistics and cognitive systems programs at the University of British Columbia.

Eric Vatikiotis-Bateson (Ph.D. Linguistics, Indiana University, 1987) is Director of the *Cognitive Systems Program* at the University of British Columbia. He has developed experimental and analytic techniques for laboratory and field evaluation of communicative performance. Eric's empirical studies of the production, perception, and neural processing of multimodal speech focus on spatial and temporal coordination in spoken communication and musical performance at different scales ranging from conversation to ensemble performance to rock concerts.

Authors' Acknowledgments

Nothing worth doing is ever done alone. All three authors express their heartfelt thanks to the many people who provided (often lively and colorful!) advice, feedback and comments on different aspects of this book, including Peter Ackema, Outi-Bat-tel, Molly Babel, Eric Bakovic, Mauro Chiesa, Bryan Gick, Louis Goldstein, Laurence Horn, Ives Goddard, Lisa Matthewson, Shana Poplack, Bill Poser, Douglas Pulleyblank, Michael Rochemont, Philip Rubin, Hotze Rullmann, and Martina Wiltschko. We are deeply grateful to the Wiley editors — Robert Hickey and Laura Peterson Nussbaum — who patiently guided us through this project, and to Laurel Fais who assisted with the final revision of large chunks of the book. Too numerous to mention are the teachers who, in different ways, transmitted their passion for knowledge to each us. Our debt to them is the greatest, and this book is our way of carrying forward the rich intellectual traditions that they individually embody.

Publisher's Acknowledgments

We're proud of this book; please send us your comments at `http://dummies.custhelp.com`. For other comments, please contact our Customer Care Department within the U.S. at 877-762-2974, outside the U.S. at 317-572-3993, or fax 317-572-4002.

Some of the people who helped bring this book to market include the following:

Acquisitions, Editorial, and Vertical Websites

Acquisitions Editor: Robert Hickey

Project Editor: Laura Peterson Nussbaum

Production Editor: Lindsay Humphreys

Technical Editor: Steve Winters

Editorial Assistant: Jeremy Hanson-Finger

Cover Photo: © iStock / José Luis Gutiérrez

Cartoons: Rich Tennant (`www.the5thwave.com`)

Composition Services

Project Coordinator: Kristie Rees

Layout and Graphics: Carrie Cesavice, Joyce Haughey, Corrie Socolovitch, Laura Westhuis

Proofreaders: Laura Bowman, Susan Moritz

Indexer: Christine Karpeles

Figure Credits:

Fig 1-1: © International Phonetic Association; Figs 15-1 and 15-2: © 2011. Used with permission of Philip Rubin and Haskins Laboratories (www.haskins.yale.edu); Fig 16-2a: Reprinted from NeuroImage, 14(3), Pulvermuller, F., Kujala, T., Shtyrov, Y., Simola, J., Tiitinen, H., Alku, P., Alho, K., Martinkauppi, S., Ilmoniemi, R.I. & Naatanen, R., Memory Traces For Words As Revealed By The Mismatch Negativity (MMN), 607-616, Copyright (2001), with permission from Elsevier; Fig 16-2b: Lee Osterhout.

John Wiley & Sons Canada, Ltd.

Deborah Barton, Vice-President and Director of Operations

Jennifer Smith, Vice-President and Publisher, Professional & Trade Division

Alison Maclean, Managing Editor, Professional & Trade Division

Publishing and Editorial for Consumer Dummies

Kathleen Nebenhaus, Vice President and Executive Publisher

Kristin Ferguson-Wagstaffe, Product Development Director

Ensley Eikenburg, Associate Publisher, Travel

Kelly Regan, Editorial Director, Travel

Publishing for Technology Dummies

Andy Cummings, Vice President and Publisher

Composition Services

Debbie Stailey, Director of Composition Services

Contents at a Glance

Table of Contents

Introduction

· ·

*W*elcome to the world of language! It's a world that you already live in, but this book will give you tools that will help you see — and hear — language in all its wonder.

Language is connected to every aspect of what it means to be human: languages are spoken by everyone, everywhere. Language is the medium through which humans socialize with each other, barter and trade, teach and learn, lead and follow. Studying language can take you to the ends of the earth and back. It can also take you into the depths of a research lab or to the inner recesses of your own mind.

We, the three authors, are language geeks. We spend our waking hours thinking about language: how many different languages there are (6,000!), what they share in common, how they differ, how kids learn language, how humans perceive and produce language, how people make new words and sentences, how language expresses meaning, how people use language to communicate, how language is written down, how sign languages are organized, and on and on. We believe that language provides a window into the workings of the human mind, and that it's one of the most rewarding and fascinating things that anyone can study. And no, we're not crazy. We wrote this book because we want you to share the excitement and enchantment that we experience each time we learn something about human language.

Linguistics doesn't have all the answers about how language works, but you can use it to ask some very interesting questions: Where do accents come from? Why are computers amazing at chess but lousy at language? Why can kids soak up language like sponges but adults can't? How can sign language really be a language? How does rap ride the rhythm of language? Why do some languages end their sentences with a verb? Why are you able to recognize someone's voice at a loud party? What happens in your brain when you speak? Why is language always changing? How has writing changed the course of human history? Figuring out the answers to these questions — and a host of others — is what linguistics is all about.

About This Book

In this book, we introduce you to linguistics as the scientific study of language. While most linguistics books delve deep into a single facet of linguistics, we want to give you a taste of each of the four primary traditions in linguistics, focusing on what language is for (communication), how language works (pattern formation), what language reveals about the mind (cognition), and how written language shapes society (technology).

You don't have to read this book in order — feel free to just flip through and stop at whatever catches your interest. The chapters of Part II, however, have the real nitty-gritty work of linguistics and are a good base for the rest of the book. If you're not really sure what linguistics is, check out Chapter 1.

If you want to delve deeper on any topic, the Internet has loads of really good information on linguistics. Try searching on some of these key words: audio-visual speech, language accommodation, dialects, generative grammar, language revitalization, etymology, semiotics, discourse, sociolinguistics, language development, aphasia, Broca's area, Wernicke's area, neurolinguistics, computational linguistics, and, of course, just language!

Conventions Used in This Book

This book uses several symbols common in linguistics that you may not be familiar with. We provide a list here. If you come across a convention that you don't recognize, refer back to this list.

[ ] — We use square brackets to indicate the *phonetic* transcription of a particular sound, which includes all the information relevant for describing the sound. This symbol is used in phonetics, phonology, and morphology.

/ / — We use angle brackets when we want to set apart a single, distinct sound in a *phonemic* transcription of sounds. This indicates only those *distinctive* aspects of the sound that make a meaning difference. This symbol is used in phonetics, phonology, and morphology. (For a discussion on the difference between phonetic and phonemic transcription, see Chapter 4.)

* — We use an asterisk to indicate that a particular word or sentence is either not correct or doesn't exist in the language. In the context of word or sentence formation, it's called a *starred* form — speakers judge these forms to be *ill-formed*. In historical linguistics, this symbol indicates a *reconstructed* form — speakers of the modern language no longer use this form, but it used to be used.

— We use a hash-mark (or *pound sign*) to indicate that a word or sentence is not appropriate in a certain context. The form can be said, but not in the context under discussion. This symbol is used when looking at the meaning of language and how people use language in conversation.

What You're Not to Read

You'll get the core concepts and tools that you need to understand linguistics if you stick to reading the main text. For those who are gluttons for punishment, we've added some of the hoity-toity technical concepts and lingo that we linguists like to use. But you can skip anything highlighted with a *Technical Stuff* or a *Linguist Lingo* icon, and you will be none the worse for it. The sidebars provide background information that gives you a wider context for the discussion of the moment, but you can skip these, too.

Foolish Assumptions

Even though we, the authors, don't know you, we've made assumptions about the kind of person that you are. You're curious about language, you speak at least one language, and you can read English.

This book is for you if you have ever wondered why you have a hard time understanding your neighbor's foreign accent. Or if you've noticed that your dad uses funny old expressions that you'd never think of using. Or if you've been amused by an infant just beginning to make words. If you've ever thought about how you manage to speak and understand language and maybe been just a little curious about it, then this book is for you.

How This Book Is Organized

This book is divided into six parts that introduce you to linguistics as a discipline, the tricks of the trade for pattern analysis (how language works), the social dimension of language (what language is for), the cognitive dimension of language (what language reveals about the mind), and the technological dimension of language (how written language shapes society).

Part I: Looking at Language through the Lens of Linguistics

Part I introduces you to linguistics as the scientific study of language. We show you how linguists define *language,* how they use scientific methods to study it, and what linguists understand about how language is used as a system of communication.

Part II: The Building Blocks of Language

Part II shows you basic tricks of the trade for doing the pattern analysis that is the cornerstone of linguistic research — this is how language works. It introduces you to the units of structure that are the building blocks of language. We start with individual speech sounds and show you how they combine with each other to eventually form words and sentences and how these sentences are strung together to make meaning and conversation.

Part III: The Social Life of Language

Part III introduces you to the social dimension of language, which reflects the communicative function of language — this is what language is for. We show you how language varies across speakers and changes over time, how linguists compare the languages of the world to each other, how they trace language back to its earliest origins, how new languages are born, and how languages are lost.

Part IV: Your Brain on Language: Learning and Processing Language

Part IV introduces you to the cognitive and neural dimensions of language — this is what language reveals about the human mind and brain. We show you how children and adults learn language, how you perceive and produce spoken and signed languages, how language activates your brain, and ways things can go wrong.

Part V: Getting from Speaking to Writing

Part V introduces you to written language as a technological breakthrough and explores the impact it has on human society — this is what language does. We show you how different writing systems have developed, how writing a language down changes it, and how it changes you.

Part VI: The Part of Tens

Part VI gives you a glimpse of some of the crowning achievements of linguistics, unsolved problems, and possible career paths. We show you how linguists debunk popular misconceptions about language, we give you a bird's-eye view of unsolved problems in linguistics, and we clue you in to possible career paths in linguistics — just in case you're interested.

Icons Used in This Book

This icon highlights advice on how to apply key concepts.

This icon draws your attention to stuff that's worth remembering — don't skip these paragraphs!

This icon introduces information that delves into some of the more technical concepts and theories of linguistics. This is information that you can skip if you want to.

This icon introduces and defines specialized linguistic terms. It's the kind of information that will be helpful if you read other linguistics books — you can skip this if you want to.

Where to Go from Here

This book is designed so you can dive in and read any chapter in any order. Here are some suggestions for good places to begin:

- ✔ Want to join the circus and make funny sounds? Go to Chapter 3 on phonetics.

- ✔ Want to know how rhyming works? See Chapter 4 on phonology.

- ✔ Fascinated by words? Start with Chapter 5 on morphology.

- ✔ Like diagramming sentences? Chapter 6 is definitely for you.

- ✔ Driven mad by ambiguous sentences? Check out Chapter 7.

- ✔ Fascinated by the fine art of conversation? Go to Chapter 8.

- ✔ Accents are your thing? Go to Chapter 9 on language variation.

- ✔ Wondering where English comes from? See Chapter 10.

- ✔ Amazed at how many languages there are? Check out Chapter 11.

- ✔ Curious about the origins of human language? Begin with Chapter 12.

- ✔ Want to know how someone learns a language? Flip to Chapter 13.

- ✔ Befuddled by how you perceive sound? Start with Chapter 14.

- ✔ Wonder whether gestures add meaning to what people say? Go to Chapter 15.

- ✔ Want to see your brain on language? See Chapter 16.

- ✔ Wondering about writing systems? Chapter 17 is the place to go.

- ✔ Curious about the impact of writing on language? Tune in to Chapter 18.

Part I
Looking at Language through the Lens of Linguistics

The 5th Wave   By Rich Tennant

"I got a PhD in linguistics mainly because it just sounded so good."

In this part . . .

What do linguists do? You may have the impression that linguists are a kind of language police who check that everyone is using language in the right way. Far from it! By the end of this part, you'll know what linguistics is, what linguists do, and why and how they do it.

Chapter 1

Knowing a Language Versus Knowing What Language Is

*Y*ou probably take your ability to use language for granted. Imagine what your life would be like if you could no longer use language: no more chit-chats over a cup of coffee, no more friendly greetings or sad goodbyes, no more arguments with your friends about which sports team is best. You couldn't explain the symptoms of an illness to your doctor. You wouldn't be able to warn someone across the street of a looming danger. No more e-mails or text messages. Not only is human language important to us as humans, it's a uniquely human ability. It's also part of our genetic endowment. For both of these reasons — human language is unique and humans seem to be pre-programmed for it — the study of language *(linguistics)* lies at the center of efforts to understand the nature of what it is to be human. For more than 2,000 years, linguists have been trying to understand how language works, and that's what this book is about.

This chapter gives you a quick and dirty introduction to linguistics, introducing you to the defining traits of human language, showing you how linguists approach the study of language, and giving you a quick tour of the rules of the language game, the players, and what they need to know to play the game.

Uncovering the Traits of Language

Linguistics is the study of language; it's not the study of languages. What's the difference? Although linguists look at individual languages, when they do, they have the big picture in mind. Their goal is to understand the nature of human language. Individual languages are like different models of cars. For cars, each model varies according to engine size, wheelbase, transmission, and passenger capacity, but they all share a common set of traits. Same thing with languages — each language varies according to sound inventory, vocabulary, sentence patterns, and so on, but they all have a common set of traits. Most linguists agree that all human languages have the following six traits in common:

- Language is used to communicate.
- Language is composed of arbitrary signs.
- Language is hierarchically organized.
- Humans produce and perceive language using auditory, visual, and even tactile modalities.
- Language is unique to human beings.
- Humans are genetically endowed for language.

Individual linguists focus on specific language traits. A *functionalist* focuses on the communicative function of language. A *formalist* focuses on the organization of language. A *speech scientist* focuses on speech production and perception. A *gestural analyst* focuses on gesture production and visual perception. An *audio-visual analyst* focuses on the integration of speech with gesture and the integration of audition with vision. A *biolinguist* focuses on the biological foundations of language, while a *psycholinguist* focuses on the cognitive base of language.

Trait 1: Language is used to communicate

Language is used to communicate concepts and intentions. To do this, it uses a system of signs with assigned meanings that communicate messages from one person's mind to another. For example, when you say to your friend the words, "I'm going to pour a cup of coffee," your friend now knows that you're going to walk across the room to the coffee pot, grab a mug, and pour that brown liquid into the mug.

A *sign* is a discrete unit of meaning. A *convention* is a set of agreed upon norms. A *conventional sign* is one that all members of a language community agree to use with a certain meaning. For example, the word *cat* is a sign that members of the English language community agree, by convention, to use for those fluffy pets that go *meow*. The more general study of signs is called *semiotics,* and it applies to any system where organisms use signs to learn about and navigate their environment — it includes linguistic communication, but it also extends to animal communication as well as to the communicative use of signals from body posture, facial expression, and tone of voice.

Trait 2: Signs are arbitrary

In language, the association of a conventional sign with meaning is arbitrary. For example, to describe the domesticated, carnivorous, canine mammal valued for its companionship and ability to guard, guide, haul, herd, hunt, search, track, or rescue, individual languages use different words: English has *dog,* French has *chien,* Icelandic *hundur,* Japanese *inu,* Mandarin *gǒu,* and Swahili *mbwa.* There's no intrinsic relation between these conventional signs and the concept of this carnivorous mammal — rather, the relation is arbitrary. Sometimes you'll hear linguists say "language has an arbitrary sound-meaning relation." Concretely what this means is that there's no intrinsic relation between a particular set of sounds and a particular meaning. The sound-meaning relation differs from language to language: that's a fancy way of saying that different languages have different words to express the same concept.

Linguists call the lack of a connection between the form of a conventional sign and its meaning the *principle of arbitrariness*. See Chapter 2 for a discussion of arbitrariness. This is sometimes called *Saussurean arbitrariness,* after the Swiss linguist Ferdinand de Saussure, who drew attention to this aspect of human language.

Trait 3: Language is hierarchically organized

Language is composed of units that are assembled according to the rules of grammar. All languages systematically combine units to form larger units, arrange units in a particular order, and substitute units for each other.

Combining units to form larger units

Linguistic analysis identifies and assembles units of language and arranges them from smaller to larger:

- ✔ **Sounds:** These are the individual consonants and vowels of a language. For example, /p/, /t/, and /æ/ (this is the vowel of *hat*) are sounds of English.

- ✔ **Syllables:** Sounds combine to form syllables. For example, in English, /p/, /t/, and /æ/ can combine to form the syllables /pæt/, /tæp/, and /æpt/.

- ✔ **Words:** Syllables combine to form words. While some words are a single syllable *(pat, tap, apt)*, many words contain two or more syllables *(mo.ther, ba.by, pro.mo.tion, re.vo.lu.tion)*. (Here, the period (.) marks the syllable break.)

- ✔ **Phrases:** Words combine to form phrases. The word *the* combines with the word *dog* to form the phrase *the dog*.

- ✔ **Sentences:** Phrases combine to form sentences. The phrase *the dog* combines with the phrase *ran away* to form the sentence *The dog ran away*.

- ✔ **Groups of sentences:** The sentence *The dog chased the squirrel* can combine with the sentence *He didn't catch it*. You can do this in several ways, including simply stringing one sentence after the next or joining sentences with conjunctions like *but* or *and:*

  - *The dog chased the squirrel. He didn't catch it.*

  - *The dog chased the squirrel, but he didn't catch it.*

  - *The dog chased the squirrel, and he didn't catch it.*

Ordering units relative to each other

The relative ordering of sounds, words, and phrases can give different meanings.

- ✔ **Ordering sounds relative to each other:** The sounds /i/ and /t/ can combine with each other in one of two ways — /it/ 'eat' or /ti/ 'tea' — and each combination means something different.

- ✔ **Ordering syllables relative to each other:** The syllables /wi/ and /pi/ can combine in two ways — /wi.pi/ 'weepy' and /pi.wi/ 'peewee' — and each combination means something different.

- ✔ **Ordering words relative to each other:** The words *sea* and *blue* can combine in two ways, and each combination means something different. Compare the sentence ***Sea-blue** is my favorite color* to *The **blue sea** was visible from the road*. *Sea-blue* is a kind of blue, while *blue sea* is a kind of sea.

- ✔ **Ordering phrases relative to each other:** When forming a sentence, phrases such as *the dog* and *the squirrel* can be introduced either as the subject or the object. The sentence *The dog chased the squirrel* describes a situation that you're probably familiar with. But if you change the order of the two noun phrases, the meaning changes: *The squirrel chased the dog.*

- ✔ **Ordering sentences relative to each other:** *They bought a car and then they had an accident* means something quite different from *They had an accident and then they bought a car.* In the first situation, the car is damaged; in the second situation the car is new.

Substituting units for each other

Substituting one sound in place of another — or one word, phrase, or sentence in place of another — can also give different meanings.

- ✔ **Substituting sounds:** I don't mind if you /bu/ 'boo' me, just don't /su/ 'sue' me.

- ✔ **Substituting syllables:** Manufactured goods go in completely opposite directions depending on whether they are **im**.*port.ed* or **ex**.*port.ed*.

- ✔ **Substituting words:** Sometimes it doesn't make much difference if you *ask* for something or *request* it. But you'll get a whole different reaction if you *demand* it!

- ✔ **Substituting phrases:** Meeting a friend *on the beach* is very different from meeting *at the courthouse*.

- ✔ **Substituting sentences:** *Pass the salt, Could I please have the salt,* and *Do you think you might find a moment in your busy eating schedule to let someone else have some salt* all make the same request, but they range from informal to polite to sarcastic.

Syntagmatic relations refer to the relative order of elements in language; *paradigmatic relations* refer to the possibility of substituting one element for another.

Trait 4: Language is produced and perceived

Human languages are expressed using the human body. When you speak, you use your lungs, voice box, mouth, tongue, jaw, and even your nose. Of course, it doesn't stop there — you also move your head, do funny things with your eyebrows, wave your hands, and change your body posture. While these actions may accompany spoken language, in sign languages, the way you use your hands, face, and torso *is* the language.

In perceiving language you use your hearing and vision, and even touch, to take in the linguistic information coming your way. It helps that you are both a producer and a perceiver of language because you are constantly producing signals that have never been made before — you are not a robot and simply cannot do the same thing twice, but you have a good idea of what you need to do in order to be understood. And the shoe is on the other foot when you are the perceiver because you have to make sense of signals you've never encountered before, but your knowledge of what you would do guides your perception of novel language events.

Trait 5: Language is quintessentially human

What makes humans unique on the planet is their extraordinary ability to hang on in the face of ever-changing conditions. Language plays a key role in humanity's success and mirrors the malleable persistence of its users.

Language adapts to the needs of the language community. Those needs can be defined by physical geographic features (for example, a lot of names for fish, if you live on an island) and by evolving social structures (for example, stratified language styles for complex social hierarchies).

Language is interactive. What you say and how you say it is learned by experience and is guided by the need to communicate with others. When different languages come into contact with one another, they can get into a tug of war for dominance or they can compromise as happened with Anglo-Saxon and Norman French in 1066 after the Norman conquest of England.

Languages change constantly, but their overall evolution is slow and ponderous. Languages separated by vast geographic and temporal differences still reflect their common ancestry. The English of Shakespeare spoken in 1600 is very different in its pronunciation from modern English, but you can still read the language he wrote 400 years ago.

Trait 6: Language is genetic

All humans are born with a roughly equal capacity to acquire language. Evidence for this genetic, inborn, feature of language includes these facts:

✔ Language doesn't depend on intelligence: Someone with a severe cognitive impairment can still use language.

✔ The acquisition of language and speech is fast and easy for humans: Young children learn their mother tongue rapidly, from babbling at 6 months to speaking sentences by the age of three. Not even the most sophisticated computers today can learn to use language at anything like the level of a small child.

✔ In learning language, children everywhere follow the same sequence of steps, no matter which language they're learning or which cultural group or social class they belong to. And children acquire language much, much better than adults do.

The *innateness hypothesis* claims that humans are born with a genetically determined capacity for language. Many linguists, psychologists, and neuroscientists believe that children are genetically endowed with the capacity to acquire language — a learning ability that (like many genetically endowed behaviors) is largely lost after puberty. For details, see Chapter 13 on language learning.

Studying Language Scientifically

Over the last 25 centuries, linguists have developed an elaborate set of methods for studying language systematically and scientifically. These methods include tools for recording language and turning observations into appropriate data for studying the pattern and structure of specific languages. Comparison of different languages has shown how they interact, how they change through time, and how all languages, whatever their similarities and differences, have certain basic features in common.

In the modern era of linguistics, sophisticated technical and conceptual tools have become available for recording observations and testing hypotheses. Linguistics has adopted empirical techniques for analyzing large data sets, or *corpora,* and uses computational techniques to identify patterns in sound, the distribution and frequency of words, and the structure of phrases and sentences. Linguists have combined methods taken from mathematical logic, information theory, and cognitive psychology and applied them to the study of sound patterns *(phonology),* word formation *(morphology),* phrase structure *(syntax)* and systems of meaning *(semantics).*

The observations — called the *data set* — that linguists work with are generally drawn from one of three sources: a corpus, elicitation, or experimentation. A *corpus* is a recording of spontaneously produced language. An *elicitation* is a guided interview that elicits speaker judgments about well-formed and ill-formed expressions. *Experimentation* is conducted in a controlled laboratory setting and measures aspects of language perception and production as well as brain function related to language.

Playing the Language Game

As a language speaker, you're probably thinking that the things that linguists care most about — how to define language, how to uncover its traits, and how to study it scientifically — don't relate to your daily experience of language. But in order to be a successful speaker, you actually need to be a pretty good linguist, too. The difference between you and a linguist is that you play the language game on the fly, while a linguist sits down and tries to figure out all the invisible elements that make up the language game. In this book, we show you the language game rulebook, the players, the cognitive aspect of the game, and how writing language lets you play the language game over a longer stretch of time.

Abiding by the rulebook

If language is a game, then there have to be rules! Language rulebooks are all laid out in the same way. They include rules about the sound patterns of the language: This is the focus of *phonetics* (which looks at the basics of the production of speech sounds) and *phonology* (which looks at how speech sounds combine). They also include rules about how words are built (morphology), how sentences are structured (syntax), how meaning is composed (semantics), and how conversations are conducted (pragmatics).

But before you can read the language rulebook, you need to know the secret alphabet that linguists developed to help them study all the different sounds that languages make. Figure 1-1 lists all the symbols devised by the International Phonetic Association (IPA) to represent the 600 consonant sounds and the 200 vowel sounds that human languages make. Throughout this book, we refer to specific kinds of sounds: You can use this chart as a reference to see where these sounds fit into the larger set of human language sounds.

Don't worry if you don't have a clue what all those weird symbols in Figure 1-1 mean. Think of this chart as a chemistry table with all the elements listed, except that you're looking at sound elements rather than chemical elements. Chapter 3 introduces you to the principles of the IPA classification — after you read that chapter, this table will make more sense to you.

THE INTERNATIONAL PHONETIC ALPHABET (revised to 2005)

CONSONANTS (PULMONIC)

© 2005 IPA

	Bilabial	Labiodental	Dental	Alveolar	Postalveolar	Retroflex	Palatal	Velar	Uvular	Pharyngeal	Glottal
Plosive	p b			t d		ʈ ɖ	c ɟ	k ɡ	q ɢ		ʔ
Nasal	m	ɱ		n		ɳ	ɲ	ŋ	N		
Trill	ʙ			r					ʀ		
Tap or Flap		ⱱ		ɾ		ɽ					
Fricative	ɸ β	f v	θ ð	s z	ʃ ʒ	ʂ ʐ	ç ʝ	x ɣ	χ ʁ	ħ ʕ	h ɦ
Lateral fricative				ɬ ɮ							
Approximant		ʋ		ɹ		ɻ	j	ɰ			
Lateral approximant				l		ɭ	ʎ	ʟ			

Where symbols appear in pairs, the one to the right represents a voiced consonant. Shaded areas denote articulations judged impossible.

CONSONANTS (NON-PULMONIC)

Clicks		Voiced implosives		Ejectives	
ʘ	Bilabial	ɓ	Bilabial	'	Examples:
ǀ	Dental	ɗ	Dental/alveolar	p'	Bilabial
ǃ	(Post)alveolar	ʄ	Palatal	t'	Dental/alveolar
ǂ	Palatoalveolar	ɠ	Velar	k'	Velar
ǁ	Alveolar lateral	ʛ	Uvular	s'	Alveolar fricative

OTHER SYMBOLS

ʍ	Voiceless labial-velar fricative	ɕ ʑ	Alveolo-palatal fricatives
w	Voiced labial-velar approximant	ɺ	Voiced alveolar lateral flap
ɥ	Voiced labial-palatal approximant	ɧ	Simultaneous ʃ and x
ʜ	Voiceless epiglottal fricative		
ʢ	Voiced epiglottal fricative		Affricates and double articulations can be represented by two symbols joined by a tie bar if necessary. k͡p t͡s
ʡ	Epiglottal plosive		

VOWELS

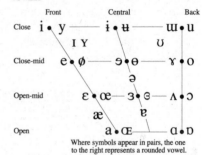

Where symbols appear in pairs, the one to the right represents a rounded vowel.

SUPRASEGMENTALS

ˈ	Primary stress
ˌ	Secondary stress ˌfoʊnəˈtɪʃən
ː	Long eː
ˑ	Half-long eˑ
˘	Extra-short ĕ
ǀ	Minor (foot) group
‖	Major (intonation) group
.	Syllable break ɹi.ækt
‿	Linking (absence of a break)

DIACRITICS

Diacritics may be placed above a symbol with a descender, e.g. ŋ̊

̥	Voiceless	n̥ d̥	̤	Breathy voiced	b̤ a̤	̪ Dental	t̪ d̪
̬	Voiced	s̬ t̬	̰	Creaky voiced	b̰ a̰	̺ Apical	t̺ d̺
ʰ	Aspirated	tʰ dʰ	̼	Linguolabial	t̼ d̼	̻ Laminal	t̻ d̻
̹	More rounded	ɔ̹	ʷ	Labialized	tʷ dʷ	̃ Nasalized	ẽ
̜	Less rounded	ɔ̜	ʲ	Palatalized	tʲ dʲ	ⁿ Nasal release	dⁿ
̟	Advanced	u̟	ˠ	Velarized	tˠ dˠ	ˡ Lateral release	dˡ
̠	Retracted	e̠	ˤ	Pharyngealized	tˤ dˤ	̚ No audible release	d̚
̈	Centralized	ë	̴	Velarized or pharyngealized	ɫ		
̽	Mid-centralized	e̽	̝	Raised	e̝ (ɹ̝ = voiced alveolar fricative)		
̩	Syllabic	n̩	̞	Lowered	e̞ (β̞ = voiced bilabial approximant)		
̯	Non-syllabic	e̯	̘	Advanced Tongue Root	e̘		
˞	Rhoticity	ɚ a˞	̙	Retracted Tongue Root	e̙		

TONES AND WORD ACCENTS

LEVEL			CONTOUR		
e̋ or ˥	Extra high		ě or ˥˩˦	Rising	
é ˦	High		ê ˥˩	Falling	
ē ˧	Mid		e᷄ ˦˥	High rising	
è ˨	Low		e᷅ ˩˨	Low rising	
ȅ ˩	Extra low		e᷈ ˧˦˧	Rising-falling	
↓	Downstep		↗	Global rise	
↑	Upstep		↘	Global fall	

Figure 1-1:
The International Phonetic Alphabet.

Getting along with other players

The language game has a lot of players, and wherever there are players, there's a pecking order. Although you may not be aware of it, as a player of the language game, you're always positioning yourself relative to other players. Maybe you're on an equal footing — for example, when you're talking to friends, you likely speak pretty informally. But if the other person has official status — like a colleague or a boss — you'll probably use more formal language. Or people from different places — say Australia versus Canada — might speak English differently. Such social differences lead to language variation. In addition, languages change over time, eventually leading to the development of new languages. And in comparing the languages of the world to each other, linguists find that, just as there are different personality types, there are different language types. The social force of language is also seen in the story of how human language first emerges, as well as in the regular ebbs and flows that account for the birth and death of individual languages.

Using your brain

Playing the language game not only involves knowing the rulebook and cooperating with other players but it also requires sophisticated cognitive skills. In learning language — whether as a child or later in life — you acquire knowledge of the rule systems that make your grammar work. And your day-in, day-out perception of language is based on your ability to integrate pattern detection, linguistic knowledge, and information screening. Likewise, your day-in, day-out production of language is based on your ability to transform your thoughts into words (for spoken language) or gestures (for signed language). And language literally lights up your brain! Linguists can now more accurately track the neural activity associated with language perception and production, and they're making mind-blowing discoveries.

Taking shortcuts with writing

Playing the language game can be exhausting — it's an activity that requires your full and immediate attention and participation. Long ago, humans invented a work-around to this problem: They started to use graphic symbols to represent the sounds of language. This technological breakthrough happened pretty recently, about 10,000 years ago. But even nowadays, most human languages — there are about 6,000 of them — don't have a written form.

Written language is a form of technology, and as with any other piece of technology, it allows humans to control and adapt to their environment. This is even truer today as people rely more and more on computer and Internet resources to communicate and obtain information.

Tuning In to Language: A Life-Changing Experience

Language defines who you are: It tells people where you come from, where you live now, how old you are, the kind of education you have, some pretty private things about your family history, your sexual persuasion, and who knows what else. What's more, your language broadcasts this information without any special help from you. Now, whether they notice or not, most folks get some information of this sort when they listen to others — yes, it's a form of stereotyping, but that doesn't mean it's wrong. Although it takes a lot of training and a good ear, experts can not only pull this kind of detailed information out of people's speech but also put it *into* people's speech and turn them into different people. This is exactly what voice coaches do for actors to give them new nationalities and new personalities. For example, Hugh Jackman is an Australian with the accent to match. Yet, with coaching he was able to deliver a believable performance playing the Canadian mutant orphan, Wolverine, in the *X-Men* movies.

Chapter 2

Communicating with Language: The Design Features

A ll human beings use language to communicate. Linguists call this the *communicative function* of language. And in the same way a car has design features that reflect its function as a vehicle for transport, human language has design features that reflect its function as a vehicle for communication. This chapter introduces you to these design features of human language.

Structuring the Ingredients of Communication

Whenever linguistic communication takes place, four ingredients are present: users, a message, a code, and a signal. In particular, *users* transmit *messages* to each other by *encoding* them into a *signal*. These four ingredients expand into the 14 design features listed in Table 2-1.

Table 2-1	Design Features of Human Language	
Ingredient	*Design Feature*	*Definition*
User	Specialized	Speech is specialized for communication.
	Interchangeable	Users send and receive messages.
	Sensitive to feedback	Users monitor and adjust their production as necessary.
	Interactive	Users learn language by interacting with other users.
Message	Meaningful	Language specifies meanings. (This is sometimes called *semanticity*.)
	Productive	Language creates new messages.
	Displaced from the here and now	Language talks about things that are located elsewhere in time and space.
Code	Discrete	Messages consist of smaller parts *(units)*.
	Arbitrary	There's no intrinsic (built-in) connection between the signal and the meaning it conveys.
	Hierarchical	Small units (individual sounds) combine to form larger units (words). (This is sometimes called *duality of patterning*.)
Signal	Modality-specific	Spoken language uses the airways to produce acoustic and visual signals, keeping the hands free for other tasks.
	One-to-many broadcast	One sender broadcasts speech signals to many receivers at the same time.
	Directional reception	Perceivers identify speech signals as coming from a single direction and source.
	Rapid fading	Speech signals disappear as soon as they are produced.

LINGUIST LINGO

Comparing communication systems

In the first half of the 20th century, Charles Hockett and other linguists of his day believed that a broad range of social and biological factors had to be considered in studying language. They studied human language by comparing it to other communication systems. Hockett first proposed the design features in Table 2-1 in the 1960s as a checklist for comparing human communication to other animal communication systems. All species need a certain level of communication to meet such basic needs as finding food and mates, negotiating territorial issues, and establishing pecking orders. While animal communication systems have some of the features listed in Table 2-1, human language is the only communication system that has all of them. In particular, productivity, hiearchical structure, and displacement are crucial features of human languages that aren't found all together in other communication systems.

In 1968, Hockett added three more design features intended to nail down what is specific to human language:

✔ *Prevarication* **(the ability to lie):** At the time, Hockett thought that only humans tell lies. But it turns out that primates such as *gibbons* (the smallest of the apes) and *guenons* (a small African monkey) are both capable of using messages to deceive. They can both manipulate the truth of one aspect of the immediate situation as a means to an end. For the guenon, it may be a way for an animal low on the pecking order to distract the higher-ranked animals momentarily from stealing his food. For the gibbon, the deception often may be part of a game, but with game-breaking, unpleasant consequences for the other party. We don't include it in the list in Table 2-1 because this feature has more to do with what we use language for than what language is.

✔ *Learnability* **(the ability to learn another language):** This is related to the fact that language is, in part, culturally transmitted: Humans learn language on the basis of interacting with other humans. Not only can they learn a first language, they can go on to learn other languages. Because the learnability feature is a by-product of social interaction, we don't include it as a separate feature in Table 2-1.

✔ *Reflexiveness* **(the ability to use language to talk about language):** This feature does seem to be specific to humans. In fact, this is what linguists do for a living. We don't include it in the list in Table 2-1 because, like prevarication, this feature has more to do with what we use language for than what language is.

Focusing on the Users

In approaching the puzzle of communication, one major piece that needs to be taken into account is the role of the users. In human language, users are interchangeable, sensitive to feedback, interactive, and specialized for language use.

Taking two to tango: Interchangeable

Communication requires both a sender and a receiver — this is the design feature of *interchangeability,* the ability that humans have to both send and receive messages. The sender and the receiver can even be the same entity — yes, you can talk to yourself — but the usual condition is for you to talk with someone else.

Not all communicative systems have users that are interchangeable. For example, when a hummingbird gets news of nutritious nectar from a nearby flower, the roles aren't interchangeable. The flower sends information to the hummingbird. And the hummingbird receives information from the flower. But they can't switch roles.

One-way versus two-way communication

Communication is a feature of all biological systems and can be defined as what happens when one organism (or part of an organism) stimulates a response in another organism (or part of an organism). This may be either a one-way process or a two-way process:

✔ **One-way communication:** For example, when a flower comes into bloom, its sight and smell informs the hummingbird that food is at hand. What makes it one-way communication is that the hummingbird doesn't transmit information to the flower.

✔ **Two-way communication:** For example, when dogs meet up on a walk, they go through an elaborate routine of sniffing each other, making sounds, wagging their tails, and even finding out who's boss. Both dogs are communicating their interest and receiving the interest of the other, so they have two-way communication.

Monitoring production: Sensitive to feedback

When you speak, you pay attention to what you are saying. You can hear yourself speaking. This provides you with *feedback* about what you are saying and how you are saying it. For example, you use feedback to adjust the volume and pitch of your voice, or even to choose different words (such as ones that are easier to hear in noise), to better fit the situation you're in. You also keep track of how well your words are expressing your meaning and you adjust both choice of words and their grammatical phrasing as you go along.

Learning from other users: Interactive

Human beings can't learn their first language in isolation, they need to *interact* with other speakers. That is, cultural transmission is crucial to acquiring language. As a child, you need other speakers to provide examples of how language is formed and used. You need names for objects and ways of talking about how they relate. As you get older, interaction becomes less about providing examples and more about communication, which is necessarily collaborative. Through interaction, you continue to learn new words and forms of expression and their context of use, and you learn about your relationship to your community.

Adapting real estate: Specialization for speech production and perception

Linguistic communication is a *specialized* behavior — you can't mistake it for anything else. Sound, the primary medium for linguistic messages, is produced by real estate adapted for sound production — the lungs provide the airflow that causes the vocal folds to vibrate for voiced sounds, and the vocal tract shapes speech sounds by positioning the lips, jaw, tongue, and uvula. Listeners use real estate adapted for hearing to perceive sound — this includes your outer ear, eardrums, auditory nerve, cochlea, and the auditory cortex. For the details of language perception and production, see Chapters 14 and 15.

Formulating the Message

When you construct a message, your linguistic knowledge gives you tremendous power to tell others about your world and to learn about theirs.

Making meaningful messages: Semanticity

You usually want your messages to be meaningful. That human language can convey meaning is the design feature of *semanticity*. Conveying meaning is also a fundamental aspect of animal communication systems. For example, when a *guenon* monkey squawks out an alarm call, the other guenons know what it means and even seem to have a dictionary of alarm calls that tells them whether they're running from a snake, a jaguar, or a hawk. This use of meaning to maintain a social structure is fundamental to all social animals. But this is nothing compared to the human ability to combine meaningful elements into a seemingly limitless number of grammatical structures with even greater complexity of meaning.

Creating new messages: Productivity

Humans' ability to quickly adapt to new situations has to do with your capacity to generate new descriptions and put new information into useable categories, more or less at the drop of a hat. This capacity to give names to new information is the design feature of *productivity*.

Linguistic productivity is closely tied to the human capacity to learn: Learning and productivity feed each other. What for the guenon monkey is probably just a list of alarm calls, for humans is a category of related meanings that can be readily updated and expanded. You can put all the things in your world that you consider dangerous or good into specific groups that share attributes. For example, you probably already have a mental list of things you know will kill you. You can add to that list as new things come along, and you can use your knowledge that there is such a list to go looking for more items to add to it! Using your ability to identify categories to group meanings and your ability to keep those categories open to receive new meanings is essential to human language. Some other animals — crows and chimpanzees — show remarkable categorization abilities, but this is rare and no other animal does it so often or with such sophistication as the human.

Talking about then, there, and them: Displacement

One of the crucial features of human language is the ability to talk about things that are not immediately present in time and space. Telling your friends what you did yesterday or what you plan to do tomorrow is trivial for you, but impossible for other animals. This is the design feature of *displacement*.

All human languages have ways of expressing spatial and temporal displacement from the here and now. Many languages put *inflection* on verbs to mark the *tense*, or relative time, of what is being said. English uses *-ed* on the end of regular verbs, such as *I park-ed the car*, to tell you that something has already happened. Because *where* and *when* are so important, languages tend to have many different ways to express spatial and temporal relations. For example, English uses *prepositions* — words like *on, about, over* — to specify spatial and temporal relations between things. You and a friend are talking at the beach, and you say *I'll see him on the train.* This is a statement about someone *(him)* displaced from you and your friend in both space *(on the train,* not the beach) and time *(will* indicates future time, relative to the "now" of your statement). English also uses adverbs, like *there* and *then,* to point the message away from the speaker in space and time.

If you can talk about what isn't here right now, how much of a stretch is it to talk about things that could be so, but aren't, or even things that couldn't ever be so? It's an impressive feat to generate meanings and refer to things and situations that don't exist and maybe could never exist! Think of literary fiction where authors create entire universes (in the case of science fiction) that are not possible but still make sense to you. The characters may have never existed, and the vehicles they ride around in operate on physical principles never seen in the real world, but these stories are interpretable because the author combines all these implausible elements into coherent, meaningful constructs.

The bee dance and displacement

The bee dance is a communicative act that a bee uses to inform other bees how far away and in what direction a source of food is relative to the hive, so this may be an example of *displacement*. However, that's about all the bee has to say on the topic and it is done using a strict formula: Specific postures and gestures explicitly define the orientation and distance of the food source the same way every time. You, on the other hand, can go on at great length about what type of food it is, whether or not it may be better to wait a couple of days before going after it, and what the terrain is like between here and there. So humans are still the champions at talking about *then* and *there*.

Working the Code

When you think of a code, you probably think of something like the Morse Code or a secret code. These codes simply change the form of a message, not its content. If you have the key to the code, you can recover the original message perfectly. But when linguists say that human language is a code, they have something more complex in mind — for them the linguistic code combines two monumental tasks:

✔ The linguistic code interacts with both speech perception and production — for perception the code converts information extracted from audible speech sounds and visible gestures into symbolic signs (words). For production, the code converts the signs into neuromotor plans for controlling the coordinated behavior of the lungs, vocal tract, and larynx. No simple translation exists between signs and what they stand for in perception and production. That is, you can't take a sign and recover the percept it signifies or all the sensory information that generated the percept.

✔ The linguistic code is a system of signs in which a sign's meaning is defined in terms of its relations with other signs. That is, the code is an active system. It has its own structure that makes signs meaningful and dictates how signs interpret perception and how they connect with plans to produce speech.

Three of Hockett's design features ensure extremely powerful and efficient coding devices in human language:

✔ **Discreteness:** The linguistic code divides up the continuous stream of sound and gesture, creating discrete bits of information that may be words, syllables, or even smaller bits, like individual sounds. For sign language, the linguistic code functions the same creating individual signs from the continuous stream of signed language.

✔ **Hierarchical organization:** The linguistic code assembles these discrete bits of information into larger units: sounds become syllables and words, words become phrases, and phrases become sentences and discourse.

✔ **Arbitrariness:** Sounds in language do not have intrinsic meaning; the relationship between the signs of a language and their meanings is arbitrary.

Swimming in the sound stream: Discreteness

Humans and other mammals have really great hearing. This excellent hearing means that you can detect small changes in sound incredibly rapidly. If you have a way to produce these rapid changes, you can pack a lot into the sound signal (for your listeners). But how? One of the oldest and most difficult questions facing people who study the sending and receiving of speech signals is this one:

> How do you put what you want to say into a stream of sound and be sure that it will make it across the gap between you and the person you are talking to?

The answer: You *encode* what you want to say by turning your thoughts into a linear sequence of small bits of sound chosen from a set that both you and your listener share. In and of themselves, these bits — we introduce them as *phonemes* in Chapter 4 — are meaningless. But you can string them together to form words and sequences of words that have meaning! The amazing thing about this story is that, if you look at the sound signal itself, you see a fairly continuous sound stream. Yet the listener is somehow able to process that stream and identify separate words and phrases within it. This is the design feature of discreteness: linguistic communication depends on individual units that you can't mistake for one another. These sounds are distinct because they *contrast* with one other — you know a sound is a [k] sound because it is none of the other 40 or so English sounds.

If linguistic tradition had been based on the *production* of speech rather than on perception, the concept of encoding would be very different. You never find discrete events in the vocal tract, where sounds are produced, that correspond to the discrete sequences you think you perceive. For example, the sound never stops, and the tongue, which shapes the sound, never stops moving in the utterance *Where were you a year ago?*

Coding efficiently: Hierarchical structure

One desirable feature of any code is to make efficient use of its elements through combination and recombination. Language does a remarkable job of this by working with a small number of contrastive sound units — less than 50 in the majority of the world's languages — and combining them to create a much larger set of meaningful *words*. This combination of basic (meaningless) units to form larger (meaningful) units exemplifies a coding process that uses the design feature of *hierarchical organization*.

The term *duality of patterning* is sometimes used to talk about the design feature of hierarchical organization. *Duality* refers to the fact that the same unit can be recycled. For example, the sound [p] occurs twice in the word *pup*. At one level of organization *(patterning)*, [p] is an individual sound that contrasts with other sounds. At another level of organization, the word *pup* contains two instances of the sound [p]. This design feature — which allows individual sounds to combine with each other to form larger units — is what sets human languages apart from other communication systems.

English has as many as 400,000 words, all created from sequencing a set of about 40 to 45 basic sounds. Of course, some words sound the same — they're *homophones* — so you have to put them into a larger sequence of words to tell them apart. This is a second level of hierarchical structure, where a large set of words can be combined into an almost infinite number of meaningful word-sequences or phrases.

What's interesting about both levels of combination — the sound-word and word-phrase combinations — is that not every imaginable combination of sounds is used in every language. No English words begin with the sound sequence /tl/ or /dl/, but /gl/ as in *glow* or /bl/ as in *blow* are okay. But the /tl/ sequence at the beginning of a word is okay in a language like Tlingit, spoken in the Pacific Northwest.

Linguists spend a lot of time trying to figure out how you use hierarchical organization to form larger units like words, phrases, and sentences. You'll see a lot of this in the chapters on morphology (Chapter 5), syntax (Chapter 6), and semantics (Chapter 7). But there's a further complication: The meanings of phrases, and even words, are partially determined by how you pronounce them, so you also have to consider how these patterns in pronunciation, or phonology (Chapter 4), work.

Associating sound with meaning: Arbitrariness

Another elegant feature of the linguistic code is that the association between a sequence of sounds and the meaning of that sequence is *arbitrary*. The arbitrariness of the sound-meaning relation is the design feature that explains why not all human languages combine sounds in the same way. For example, *dog* in English and *chien* in French both refer to the same set of animals that includes the *Chihuahua*. Or in different regions of North America, you will hear *soda, pop,* or *soda pop* for the same type of soft drink. Of course, due to a common ancestry or long association, different languages may have many words in common such as *warm* in English and German and *précis* in English and French.

Sound symbolism

Exceptions to arbitrariness at the sound-meaning level do exist. For example, in many languages, words with the vowel (phonetically transcribed as [i]) found in words like *wee*, *meek*, or *teeny weeny* mean something small.

These instances of *sound symbolism* are not well understood but may have to do with the iconic similarity of creating a small vocal cavity to make the /i/ vowel and the idea of smallness.

Working the Signal

To convey linguistic meaning from one person to another requires transmitting a physical signal of some sort. This means that producing and perceiving signals use one or more sensory modalities — for humans, these are sound, sight, and occasionally touch. But there are restrictions on broadcasting and receiving signals and on how long they persist in time.

Signaling in specific modalities

To talk to someone, you have to be able to communicate across the physical gap between you and the other person. You also want your communication to be efficient when necessary — it should not take ten minutes to call for help! Being able to communicate without having to stop doing whatever else you're up to is also important. So it's not surprising that humans, and a lot of other animals, use sounds produced in the throat for communication. Sound travels far and wide, it's fast and doesn't need daylight, and you can talk while you do other things — if you work it right, you can even talk while you eat.

Sound is a rich medium for encoding rapidly changing contrasts, which is necessary if you want to transmit a lot of information in a hurry. But you can use other signal media to transmit language. For example, if you've experienced *American Sign Language* (ASL) — used in and around hearing-impaired (deaf) communities — then you know how effective the visual medium can be for transmitting language. Using ASL doesn't have all the advantages of vocal communication because you have to use your hands to communicate in a well-lit place so your hand gestures can be seen.

When you speak, you often enhance the sound signal with visual or tactile signals in order to boost the transmission and reception of your intended message. For example, when two people talk, they may be able to see each other. This provides a useful channel for conveying additional meaning through hand gestures or facial gestures such as smiles, grimaces, and nods. Although these signals are different from the primary speech signal, they convey meaning.

That is, you can smile at someone without ever saying a word, and that is communication. And if you smile while scolding someone for a mistake they made, it changes the meaning of the message by taking the sting out of the words and providing unspoken reassurance that you still like them.

Broadcasting the signal: One-to-many

Many communicative interactions such as conversations are one-to-one — just you and another person. But in certain situations, like teaching school, giving a speech, or doing the weather on TV, one person communicates with many others at the same time. This is *one-to-many communication*.

Finding the source: Directional reception

Acoustically transmitted speech and visually transmitted sign language both exemplify the design feature of *directional reception.* The signal you produce goes off in all directions, but listeners know that it came from just you. They're able to pick out your speech sounds even when all the other sounds in the environment are getting in the way. This feature, also known as *auditory streaming,* is useful at parties where lots of people are talking at the same time and you're still able to know which snippets you're hearing belong to the guy you're talking to. This feature of directional reception works even when you don't understand the content of the signal. For example, someone speaking Laotian or some other unfamiliar language can still be singled out thanks to directional reception.

Speaking leaves no trace: Rapid fading

Whether or not you're in a hurry to get your message out to someone, there's a good physical reason for producing snappy messages. If you speak too slowly to someone, they may forget the beginning of the sentence by the time you get to the end of it. A problem with spoken communication — solved brilliantly by writing — is that speech signals occur in time, hang around just long enough to get processed, and then disappear without a trace.

The word *top* takes about a quarter of a second to say. The perceiver's *short-term* or *working memory* stores the word *top* for about 15 seconds. This is long enough for the brain to take in and process the sound stream for the word *top,* retrieve its word meaning, and then work out what it means in the context of the larger message. And then it's gone from memory, forever, because your brain extracts meaning from messages — it doesn't record them. And while you may remember the *content* of the message, the *signal* itself is lost in the mists of time.

Part II
The Building Blocks of Language

The 5th Wave

By Rich Tennant

"I've lived among them my entire life, and I can tell you, 'fetch,' 'roll over,' 'sit,' 'stay,' and 'bad dog,' is the extent of their vocabulary."

In this part . . .

One of the great discoveries of linguistics is that all languages use the same set of building blocks. All human languages have small units — speech sounds for spoken language and signed gestures for sign language — that combine with each other to form larger units like words, phrases, and sentences. No matter which language you speak (or sign), you know how to make speech sounds, combine sounds, make words and sentences, express meaning, and carry on conversation. That's what this part is all about.

Chapter 3

Building Sounds: Phonetics

A s humans, our fine-tuned machinery for speech production and perception has contributed as much to human development as the opposable thumb. It's hands-free, which means you can multi-task while you talk. You can send and receive complex messages while cooking dinner, riding a bike, or talking on your cell phone with lattes in each hand.

In this chapter, we introduce you to *phonetics,* the study of speech sounds. We show you what you do when you send and receive speech sounds, how sound production and perception work, and how you pluck meaning from the endless stream of human speech that surrounds you.

 Linguists write sounds phonetically using special symbols called the International Phonetic Alphabet (IPA), which are often the same as English alphabet symbols. Check out the full chart of IPA symbols in Chapter 1. We indicate the *phonetic transcription* of a sound with square brackets around the letters. So the phonetic transcription for the first sound in *big* is [b].

Defining Phonetics

Phonetics is the study of making and hearing speech sounds, and the linguists who work on phonetics are called *phoneticians*. The word *phonetics* is from the ancient Greek word *phōnē,* which means 'sound' or 'to speak'. Individual speech sounds, like [b] or [k], are called *phones*. The linguistic term *phone* is only distantly related to telephones, so please don't ask a phonetician to fix your cell phone!

Why phonetics matters

Researchers from many disciplines use the tools of phonetic analysis:

✔ Engineers use basic research in phonetics to develop natural-sounding speech synthesis, reliable automatic speech recognition, and automated translation systems. For example, those automated question-and-answer systems you run into on the telephone may be irritating when all you want to do is talk to a human. But, thanks to phonetic coding, their recognition and synthesis systems work pretty well. Also, years of research in acoustic phonetics has contributed to the efficient language-specific coding that allows thousands of digital cell phone users to place calls at the same time. (For more on the importance of efficient coding in human language, see Chapter 2.)

✔ Clinical researchers need tools from phonetics to understand and treat spoken language deficits that arise in childhood during development or later in life as the result of strokes, Parkinson's disease, and other conditions. For example, articulatory phonetics is used to assess disorders in sound production, known as *dyspraxia*. Phonetic transcription of acoustic recordings helps to diagnose developmental problems in language acquisition by children. Language processing disorders due to stroke and disease rely on perceptual phonetics to diagnose and locate the source of a dysfunction.

✔ Psychologists and neuroscientists integrate phonetics as a major part of their investigation of human cognition and the mind. They look at the role of memory and the effects of development and aging on speech processing, at how words and meanings are acquired, stored, retrieved, and lost, as well as at the multimodal motor and sensory channels of speech. Many of the same methods used in clinical research are used to explore human language processing. (For details on brain function and language, see Chapter 16.)

Phoneticians study speech sounds by looking at

✔ **Speech production:** *Articulatory phonetics* looks at how you make *(articulate)* speech sounds using your mouth, tongue, lips, and throat.

✔ **Sound waves:** *Acoustic phonetics* looks at the acoustic structure of the sound waves that travel between a speaker and a hearer.

✔ **Speech perception:** *Perceptual acoustics* looks at what you do to speech sounds when they reach your ears.

Whichever side of the problem phoneticians study, they have their work cut out for them. The production and perception of spoken language are perhaps the most complex skills humans have. The problems phoneticians encounter include the following:

✔ **Speech sounds don't come neatly packaged.** Acoustic analysis of speech is tricky. When you speak, you produce sound in a continuous and complex stream that contains all kinds of different frequencies and overlapping layers of information. To take apart and understand this stream of sound, your speech perception system needs to be a lean, mean, and extremely efficient analysis machine.

✔ **Speech is fleeting.** To make things more challenging for both you and the phonetician, speech sounds last only a fraction of a second and then — poof! — they're gone! You need to go super-fast to make (or hear) each sound and move on to the next one.

✔ **Speech articulators aren't visible.** You produce speech by moving different articulators — such as your tongue and your teeth — in different places at the same time. Moreover, most of your speech production machinery is hidden in your mouth. Just as it's hard for you to tell what's going on inside your mouth when you're talking, it's even harder for the phonetician, who has to find clever ways to see what's going on way back in your throat.

To tackle these problems, phoneticians use techniques that include

✔ **Phonetic transcription:** Before there were phonographs and tape recorders, phoneticians recorded speech sounds by hand using special alphabet symbols. Transcribing speech phonetically in this way allows linguists to accurately record any language or dialect.

✔ **Computer analysis:** Phoneticians use computer algorithms to analyze recordings of speech sounds. The computer analyzes the frequencies of the sound and reveals its acoustic properties, both quantitatively and graphically.

✔ **Ultrasound:** Ultrasound allows phoneticians to examine how speech is produced, especially in hard-to-reach places, like down in your throat.

✔ **Functional magnetic resonance imaging (fMRI) and electroencephalography (EEG):** Functional MRI and EEG recordings allow phoneticians to assess the brain function of people performing specific language tasks.

Getting to Know Your Speech Production System

Try a little exercise. First, breathe out. Feel the air flowing out of your lungs and up through your throat. Now say the word *tea* (which is transcribed phonetically as [ti]) and feel how your tongue first stops the airflow in your mouth for the consonant [t] and then lets it flow again while you reshape your mouth for the vowel [i]. You have just focused, in turn, on the three key steps for making most speech sounds:

1. **You force air out of your lungs and up through your throat.**

2. **You send air between your two vocal folds (also known as *vocal cords*) in your larynx located at the bottom of your throat.** Depending on the position of the vocal folds relative to each other, this airflow may cause the vocal folds to vibrate and produce sounds.

3. **You use your tongue, lips, and jaw to shape the airflow as it passes through your *vocal tract*.** Your vocal tract stretches from your larynx to your lips and (sometimes) to your nose.

In the following sections, we take you through this process in detail.

Using your lungs

Exhaling air from your lungs is the simplest way to make sounds. You take in a breath of air, creating pressure in your lungs, and then let the air flow out through your *trachea* (your windpipe), through the opening between the vocal folds, and finally through your lips or nose (or both). Sounds made this way are called *pulmonic sounds* (sounds produced by the lungs).

All spoken languages use pulmonic sounds. Most sounds are made using air *from* the lungs (called *egressive* sounds), but you can also make sounds while taking air *into* the lungs (*ingressive* sounds). You can even make speech sounds *without* using air from the lungs. To make these sounds, you create a low-pressure region in your mouth. When you release the suction, the flow of air into the low-pressure area makes a sound. An example is the clicking/clucking sound (phoneticians call this a *click*) that people make with their tongues when wagging their finger at you and saying *tsk tsk*.

We focus on pulmonic egressive sounds in this chapter because they account for the vast majority of the world's speech sounds.

Some languages use clicks to make speech sounds. To hear what this sounds like, check out the famous click song by singer Miriam Makeba. (Just search for "Makeba click song" on the Internet.)

Using your voice box

Your voice box *(larynx)* is located in your throat. The outside of the larynx consists of two *cartilages*, which are hard but not quite bone. One is the *thyroid* cartilage or your Adam's apple. The other is the *cricoid* cartilage, which contains your two vocal folds used to produce most of your speech sounds.

If you were to put a camera down your throat (not recommended, but you can find images and movies on the Internet), you'd find that your vocal folds look like corded bands of skin, hence the more common name *vocal cord*. The vocal folds are stretched across the opening of the trachea and are used to control airflow in and out of the lungs. The folds are attached to the thyroid cartilage at one end and to little triangular cartilages, called *arytenoids,* at the other end. The cricoid cartilage sits just below the thyroid cartilage and forms a protective ring around the vocal folds. Each fold gets its own arytenoid cartilage, which can be moved around by small muscles to change the position, tension, and length of the vocal folds. The opening between the folds, when there is one, is called the *glottis.* You do four main things with your vocal folds — referred to as *glottal states* — that are relevant to producing sounds (check out Figure 3-1 to see what these states look like):

✔ **You close your vocal folds tight and block the airflow.** Say *uh oh* over and over out loud. The separation you hear between *uh* and *oh* is caused by abruptly bringing your vocal folds together and holding them tightly closed for an instant. This is called a *glottal stop,* and the IPA symbol for it is [ʔ], a question mark with no dot.

✔ **You vibrate your vocal folds.** Say [z] as in *zoo,* and your vocal folds will vibrate. To feel the vibration, put your hand to your throat while saying [zzzz]. Do the same thing while saying [sssss], and you won't feel any vibration. This vibration is caused by your vocal folds popping open and closed as the air flows through the glottis. Vibrating sounds are called *voiced* sounds and include vowels and many consonants, like [z, m, b, g].

✔ **You hold your vocal folds open so air flows freely through them.** Say [s] as in *Sam* and the air flows freely through your glottis. Non-vibrating sounds are called *voiceless* and include consonants like [s, f, p, t].

✔ **You tighten your vocal folds, but hold them a little bit apart.** This causes turbulence in the airflow, which you can hear. Say [h] as in *ham,* and you'll be creating noisy turbulence with your vocal folds.

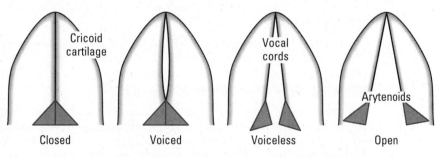

Figure 3-1:
The four main positions of the glottis/vocal folds.

Closed   Voiced   Voiceless   Open

To get a sense of your own speech production, say different sounds out loud. Use the IPA chart in Chapter 1 to work your way through the consonant and vowel sounds of your language. Start with consonants because they let you feel the contacts between your tongue, palate, teeth, and lips.

Messing with the airflow

After air comes up (for egressive sounds) through your vocal folds, it enters your throat *(pharynx)* and then your mouth *(oral cavity)* and possibly your nose *(nasal cavity)*. You then mess with the airflow by playing around with the position of your tongue, your jaw, and your lips.

Distorting the airflow: How it happens

Changing how air moves through the vocal tract allows you to produce different sounds. Phoneticians call these different ways of manipulating airflow *manners of articulation*. The six most common ones are

- **Stops:** These completely stop the airflow. For example, to make [p], you stop the airflow at your lips. To make [t], you stop the airflow at the *alveolar ridge* (the ridge just behind your upper teeth).

- **Fricatives:** These constrict the airflow to create friction. For example, to make [f], you create friction between your lip and teeth. To make [s], you create friction between your tongue and the alveolar ridge (near where you make [t]).

- **Nasals:** These let air flow only through your nose. For example, to make [m], you stop airflow at the lips while air is going out through the nose. To make [n], you stop airflow at the alveolar ridge while air is going out through the nose.

- **Approximants:** These constrict airflow only a little bit. For example, to make [w], you constrict the lips slightly and raise the back of the tongue a little. To make [j] as in the first sound in *yes,* you constrict your vocal tract near the front of the palate, but air still flows quite freely.

- **Affricates:** These make a stop and *then* a fricative. The first sound in *church* is the affricate [tʃ], which you make by combining [t] as in *tea* and [ʃ] as in *ship*.

- **Vowels:** These let air flow freely, but you change the sound by changing the shape of the vocal tract with the tongue.

Distorting the airflow: Where it happens

In addition to a manner of articulation, consonant sounds have a *place of articulation.* This is the location in your mouth where you mess with the airflow. Figure 3-2 shows you the vocal tract with all the places of articulation. The most common places of articulation when speaking English are

- **Bilabials:** These involve bringing the lips together — [p, b] and [m].

- **Labiodentals:** These involve touching the lower lip against the upper teeth — [f] in *fink* and [v] in *victory*.

✔ **Interdentals:** These involve sticking the tongue tip between the teeth — [θ] the first sound in *think* and [ð] the first sound in *then*.

✔ **Alveolars:** These involve the front of the tongue and the bony *(alveolar)* ridge behind the teeth. This is a popular place to make speech sounds — [t, d, s, z, n, l] are just a few.

✔ **Palatals:** These involve bringing the tongue close to the *hard palate* (the hard surface surrounded on three sides by your upper teeth). *Palato-alveolar* sounds are made at the front of the palate, a bit behind the alveolar ridge — / ʃ / in **sh**ip, / j / in **y**es, /ɲ/ in ca**ny**on.

✔ **Velars:** These are made further back, at or near where the *soft palate* begins. Run your finger backwards along the roof of your mouth, and you should be able to feel where the soft palate begins. This is where you make [k] and [g]. If you have a mirror, you can see the soft palate extend all the way back to that flap of skin (the *uvula*) that you see hanging down when you say [aaaaa]. This entire region is called the *velum*.

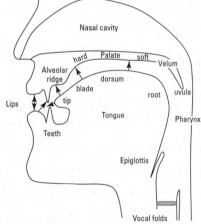

Figure 3-2: The major vocal tract structures (arrows indicate the six main places for consonant articulation).

Your full name, please

A full description of a speech sound describes the airflow mechanism, the state of the vocal folds, the manner of articulation, and the place of articulation. Here's the full description of the consonant [p]:

[p] = *pulmonic-egressive voiceless bilabial stop*

[p] requires air pressure from the lungs (pulmonic-egressive), no vocal fold vibration (voiceless), and stopped airflow using both lips (bilabial stop). Because English uses only pulmonic egressive sounds, however, phoneticians often simplify the description to *voiceless bilabial stop.*

Combined with air from your lungs and maybe vocal fold vibration, these places of articulation allow you to say anything you want — whether scolding your dog or ordering a pizza.

Creating Consonants

In order to say a consonant, you have to make three choices along the way:

1. **Choose one of the five main manners of articulation for a consonant: stop, fricative, nasal, approximant, or affricate.**

2. **Choose one of the six main places of articulation: bilabial, interdental, labiodental, alveolar, palatal, or velar.**

3. **Choose vocal fold vibration (voiced) or no vocal fold vibration (voiceless).**

Setting aside a few complications that we deal with as we go along, that's pretty much how you produce all your consonant sounds.

Stopping the airflow

You can briefly stop the airflow at three places of articulation to get the following *voiceless stops* (no vocal fold vibration):

- ✔ **[p]:** Stop at both lips (voiceless bilabial stop)
- ✔ **[t]:** Stop at the alveolar ridge (voiceless alveolar stop)
- ✔ **[k]:** Stop at the soft/hard palate border (voiceless velar stop)

Some dialects of English have replaced the alveolar *t* in the middle of words like *kitten* and *button* with the glottal stop: [kʰɪʔən] and [bʌʔən].

In English, each voiceless stop has a voiced counterpart:

- ✔ **[b]:** Stop at both lips (voiced bilabial stop)
- ✔ **[d]:** Stop at the alveolar ridge (voiced alveolar stop)
- ✔ **[g]:** Stop at the soft/hard palate border (voiced velar stop)

Phonetically, voicing is the *only* difference between the pairs [p]/[b], [t]/[d], and [k]/[g] — they are otherwise identical in place and manner.

Some languages use other places to make more stops. For example, many languages make stops back near the uvula. This is where Arabic makes the final consonant of *Iraq*, which is a uvular stop written phonetically as [q].

Making noise

If you let air flow freely through the vocal folds, but constrict it at various places of articulation so that you create friction, you get a *voiceless fricative:*

- **[f]:** Friction between lips and teeth, as in *fit* (voiceless labiodental fricative)
- **[θ]:** Friction between tongue and teeth, as in *think, thin,* and *thistle* (voiceless interdental fricative)
- **[s]:** Friction at the alveolar ridge, as in *sit* (voiceless alveolar fricative)
- **[ʃ]:** Friction at the front of the palate, as in *ship* and *show* (voiceless palato-alveolar fricative)

Each voiceless fricative has a *voiced fricative* counterpart, identical in place and manner:

- **[v]:** Friction between lips and teeth, as in *vim* (voiced labiodental fricative)
- **[ð]:** Friction between tongue and teeth, as in *then* and *those* (voiced interdental fricative)
- **[z]:** Friction at the alveolar ridge, as in *zoo* (voiced alveolar fricative)
- **[ʒ]:** Friction at the front of the palate, as in the last sound in *rouge* (voiced palato-alveolar fricative)

Other languages make fricatives at different places. For example, if you make a [k], but lower the tongue slightly while still holding it at the same place of articulation, you get a continuous sound with friction that the IPA represents with [x] (voiceless velar fricative). This is the sound you hear at the end of German pronunciations of *Bach,* and it used to be a sound in English. Ever wonder why *night* and *knight* are spelled with a *gh?* The *gh* represented the [x] fricative, but it stopped being used somewhere along the way. Hebrew and Arabic make the fricative further back, at the uvula (voiceless uvular fricative), represented with a big X, like this: [χ]. Voiced versions of [x] and [χ] and fricatives are also made at the palate. Check out Chapter 1 for more IPA symbols; and visit the IPA website for sound samples.

Many people have a hard time with the voiceless fricative [θ] of *thistle* and its voiced counterpart, the [ð] of *this.* Say the following pairs out loud: **th**igh vs. **th**y, sheath vs. sheathe, and teeth vs. teethe. For each pair, the first word has the voiceless fricative ([θ]), the second has the voiced fricative ([ð]).

The voiceless palato-alveolar fricative [ʃ] is common in English and is usually written *sh* (*ship, should, shall, sham*). The voiced version [ʒ] occurs in the middle and at the end of some words, as in *version* and *rouge,* but never starts a word. In contrast, French starts words with this sound all the time: *genre, je,* and *Jacques.* Why French allows this and English doesn't is a problem relating to the sound sequences *(phonotactics)* permitted by each language. (For discussion of phonotactics, see Chapter 4.)

Going nasal

When you make a speech sound, air usually passes through your oral cavity and comes out of your mouth only. But you can also direct the flow of air through your nose, making a *nasal* sound.

To get the air to come out of your nose, you lower your velum. This opens up your nasal cavity and lets the air out through your nostrils (so long as you don't have a head cold, in which case nasals don't work so well). Of course you can let air out through your nose and mouth at the same time: This makes a nasalized vowel sound.

Nasal consonants are made by closing the mouth at specific places of articulation and opening the velum. The resulting nasal consonants are called stops because the oral cavity is closed, but air still flows out through the nasal cavity. English has three nasal consonants:

- ✔ **[m]:** Stop at both lips, airflow through nose, as in the last sound in *bam* (voiced bilabial nasal stop)

- ✔ **[n]:** Stop at the alveolar ridge, airflow through nose, as in the last sound in *ban* (voiced alveolar nasal stop)

- ✔ **[ŋ]:** Stop at soft palate (velum), airflow through nose, as in the last sound in *bang* (voiced velar nasal stop)

The hooked [ŋ] nasal is the hardest to get a handle on. It's almost always written *ng* in English, but [ŋ] is a single sound. If you're having trouble getting a sense of how it's different from the others, say the sequence *bam, ban, bang*. On the third one, you may feel the back of your tongue raise up and close off the airflow at the back of your palate.

Other languages have nasals in a few other places, the most common being a nasal made right at the roof of the mouth (at the hard palate), which is symbolized [ɲ] in the IPA for the nasal sound in the Spanish words *Niña and cañon,* borrowed into English as *canyon.*

Languages hardly ever have voiceless nasals. That's because, without voicing, you don't get a nasal sound that anyone can hear clearly. For nasals, phoneticians often skip the bit about voicing because they know nasals are usually voiced. So they describe [m] as a *bilabial nasal stop*.

Making the smooth sounds

You make an approximant sound by narrowing the vocal tract at a place of articulation, but not closing it enough to produce friction or to stop the airflow. The term *approximant* comes from Latin *approximare,* which means *come near to.* These sounds flow smoothly and have a note-like quality. English has four of these sounds:

- **[ɹ]:** This is the English *r* as in *Robert* and *Roger.* It's usually made by bunching the front part of your tongue up near your palato-alveolar region, but without getting close enough to create friction. Linguists call it a *palato-alveolar approximant,* but because of its smooth sound, they also sometimes call it a *liquid* sound. [ɹ] is also a *retroflex* sound because it involves curling back or bunching up the tongue towards the palato-alveolar region. [ɹ] is voiced in English except when clustered with voiceless consonants as in *spray* and *tray.*

The IPA symbol for English *r* is an upside-down 'r,' [ɹ]. When representing English, linguists often simplify and write [r], but the IPA uses the [r] symbol for the trilled r-sound made at the alveolar ridge, as in the Italian word *terra.* Words written with *r* in different languages are made in many different ways. For example, in some varieties of French and German, the r-sound is a uvular trill, symbolized as [ʁ].

- **[l]:** This is the English *l* as in *lip* and *lead.* It's made by pressing the tip of your tongue against the alveolar ridge or your front teeth and then lowering one or both sides of the tongue to let air flow out. Linguists call this an *alveolar lateral approximant* or, because the air flows smoothly, a *lateral liquid.* [l] is usually voiced in English, except when it follows a voiceless consonant as in *splay* and *clay.*

Many languages make a lateral sound that's voiceless. The IPA symbol for a voiceless lateral fricative is an *l* with a squiggle through it, like this: [ɬ]. Try whispering your [l] and you come close to the [ɬ] sound in Welsh names like *Lloyd Llewellyn.* Those double *l*s are voiceless [ɬ].

- **[w]:** For most English speakers, this is the first sound in *way* and *weird.* You make it by closing the lips slightly and raising the back of your tongue high. Linguists call this a *labiovelar.* [w] flows very smoothly, so you'll sometimes see it called a *labiovelar glide* or a *semi-vowel.*

You probably say the same sound, [w], for both *witch* and *which.* But some speakers start the word *which* with a voiceless frication, so that it comes out as [hw]. This is a holdover from an older form of English; nowadays, most English speakers say *wh-words* with plain [w].

- **[j]:** This is the first sound in English in *you* and *yelp.* You make it by raising the center of the tongue close to the palate. Linguists call this a *palatal approximant.* [j] also flows very smoothly, so you'll sometimes see it called a *palatal glide* or a *semi-vowel.*

Combining sounds

Sometimes two sounds stick together and act like a single sound, occurring in positions where normally only one consonant can fit. In English, these combo sounds involve a stop released directly into a fricative. This is called an *affricate*. English has two combo sounds:

- ✔ **[t]+[ʃ] = [tʃ]:** This combination is usually written *ch* in English, as in *chip, Chinese,* and *chow-chow.* It's not official IPA, but many linguists represent it with [č].

- ✔ **[d]+[ʒ] = [dʒ]:** This combination is usually written *j* in English spelling, as in *judge, jug,* and *jujubee.* Again it's not official IPA, but many linguists represent this with [ǰ].

Other languages have different combos. German combines [p] with [f] in words like *Pferd* (horse). Setswana, spoken in Botswana, combines [t] with [s] in words like *tse-tse* (the fly that causes sleeping sickness).

Vocalizing Vowels

Before ultrasound and other imaging tools provided easy viewing of the tongue during speech, phoneticians described vowels in terms of the position of the tongue — its relative height and *backness* in the mouth — and its rigidity or tension:

- ✔ **Relative backness of the tongue in the mouth.** There are three basic tongue positions: You push your tongue to the front of your mouth, you leave it in the middle, or you push it to the back.

- ✔ **Relative height of the tongue in the mouth.** There are three basic positions: Your tongue is high, in the middle, or low in your mouth.

- ✔ **Relative rigidity of the tongue muscles.** There are two basic states: Your tongue is rigid *(tense)* or relaxed *(lax).* Figuring out whether your tongue is tense or lax is not so obvious. If you need to know whether a vowel is *tense* or *lax,* check if that vowel can end a word. In English, only tense vowels can end a word. This is about as good a definition of what *tense* means as any. The actual definition of tenseness depends on things like the sound-wave frequencies and the position and shape of the root of the tongue.

When ultrasound came on the scene and let phoneticians look at the tongue surface while you talk, they found that the tongue often isn't where the traditional description says it should be when you're saying a particular vowel. In fact, different tongue positions can result in the same vowel sound, which throws a wrench into using tongue position to classify vowels. It turns out that what actually distinguishes vowels from each other are the distinct acoustic patterns and, more specifically, the frequency differences.

But those old phoneticians had good ears and identified and classified the vowels correctly for the most part. High vowels usually do have a high tongue height, and back vowels usually do use more of the back of the tongue. So linguists still use the tongue position as a way to classify vowels. Figure 3-3 shows how both the tongue position *(articulatory)* and acoustic classifications match up for the standard American English vowels.

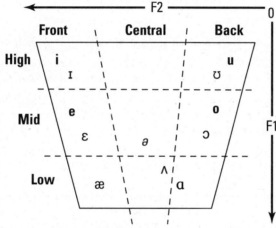

Figure 3-3: Standard American English vowels plotted articulatorily and acoustically.

The front vowels

If you start with the vowel in *seed,* extend the vowel, and slowly lower your jaw to say the vowel in *sad,* you will run through the full front-vowel series in English, in this order:

- ✔ **[i]:** High front tense vowel, in *eat, each, meet, see*
- ✔ **[I]:** High front lax vowel (lax version of [i]), in *it, itch, mitt, sit*
- ✔ **[e]:** Mid front tense vowel, in *ate, ache, mate, say*
- ✔ **[ɛ]:** Mid front lax vowel (lax version of [e]), in *wet, etch, met, said*
- ✔ **[æ]:** Low front (lax) vowel, in *mad, sad, lad, had* (English has no low front tense vowel.)

The lax vowel [I] still counts as *high,* even though it's not as high as [i]; lax vowels are usually a little lower than their tense counterparts. Similarly, [ɛ] (the lax counterpart of [e]) is mid, though it's a little lower than its tense counterpart.

If you're learning French or German, then you want to practice rounding your front vowels. For example, say [i] (as in *see*) and round your lips; you'll make something like French *sud* ('south') or German *süss* ('sweet'). This vowel is a *high front tense rounded vowel* transcribed as [y]. Say [e], then round your lips, and you'll make [ø], also a vowel found in French and German.

The back vowels

English back vowels (made with the back of the tongue) include the following five:

- ✔ **[u]:** High back tense round vowel, sound in *oops, ooze, suit, too*

- ✔ **[ʊ]:** High back lax round vowel (lax version of [u]), sound in *should, would, could, hook, shook*

- ✔ **[o]:** Mid back tense round vowel, sound in *oats, O's, soak, so*

- ✔ **[ɔ]:** Mid back lax round vowel (lax version of [o]), occurs only in some varieties of English, including the New York and New Jersey pronunciations of the words *coffee* and *caught*

- ✔ **[ɑ]:** Low back tense vowel, sound in *sod, cod*, and for some dialects, *saw, law* (There's no lax counterpart of [ɑ] in English.)

Remember that lax vowels are a little lower than their tense counterparts, so the lax vowel [ʊ] still counts as high, even though it's not as high as [u]. And [ɔ] (the lax counterpart of [o]) is mid, though it's lower than its tense counterpart. If you place your hand under your jaw and say *soup* ([u]) and then *sop* ([ɑ]), you'll feel that your jaw drops a lot from the high back [u] to the low back [ɑ] vowel.

Back vowels can have unrounded counterparts — English doesn't, but other languages do. Take an [u], and un-round your lips; that makes [ɯ], a *high back tense unrounded* vowel. This is the first vowel in the Japanese word *sushi*.

The nothing vowels

Phoneticians describe *schwa* [ə] as the sound you make when you aren't trying to say anything. Relax your jaw and let your tongue rest neither high nor low and neither front nor back — now make a vowel sound. It's a common vowel in languages like English that produce sequences of alternating long *(stressed)* and short *(unstressed)* syllables. In English, schwa appears only in unstressed syllables and especially when you talk fast. Some examples are [ðə.'ti] (the tea), ['sei.tən] (satan), ['maɹ.vəl] (marvel), and ['kæ.nə.də] (Canada).

The vowel [ʌ] is a lot like schwa, but it can stand alone in a stressed syllable. Most speakers of English say [ʌ] as in *hut, cut, sun, fun,* and *muck.* It's both lower and further back in the mouth than schwa.

The moving vowels

Say the [ɑ] vowel as in *hop.* Now extend it into a big, long vowel [ɑɑɑɑɑɑɑɑɑ]), and then move to [e] as in *say* and stop. Try it again [ɑɑɑɑɑɑɑɑe]. Faster now: [ɑɑɑɑe], [ɑɑe], [ɑe]. If you don't emphasize the [e] too much (just sort of go toward the position for it), you'll end up saying the vowel in the words *mine, I,* and *sigh.*

This kind of vowel is made by moving from one vowel to another. Linguists call these combinations of vowels *diphthongs.* English has three major diphthongs:

- ✔ **[ɑe]:** This is the dipthong you just said in *mine, I,* or *sigh.*

- ✔ **[ɔe]:** Moving from [ɔ] (the vowel in New Jersey *coffee*) towards, but not quite reaching, the mid front [e] as in *shape.* This is the diphthong in *soy, coy,* and *ploy.*

- ✔ **[ɑʊ]:** Moving from [ɑ] up to high back, near [ʊ] as in *shook.* This is the diphthong in *loud, cow,* and *sow.*

Some transcriptions use [I] as the endpoint for the first (as in *mine*) and second (as in *soy*) diphthongs: [ɑI] and [ɔI]. But most people end these diphthongs with [e].

If a vowel is written with a colon after it, like [i:], the colon tells you that the vowel is long. English has long and short versions of every vowel: compare [bi:d] *(bead)* and [bit] *(beet).* In English, length is most obvious for tense vowels like [i]. But other languages use vowel length to change meaning; in such languages, vowel length is *contrastive.* See Chapter 4 for more on contrasting sounds.

Hearing Sound Waves

The most accessible way to classify speech sounds precisely is by their physical sound waves — or *acoustics.* It's not as intuitive as the traditional articulatory method that refers to the position of the tongue and other articulators, but acoustic phonetics provides a more manageable description of vowels and consonants. Phoneticians measure three dimensions of speech sounds: their *time,* their *frequency,* and their *amplitude.* In this section, we show you how frequency and amplitude combine to create acoustic patterns that change through time.

You make a sound the same way no matter how the linguists classify it. But acoustic phoneticians describe the process a bit differently. Here's how they look at it:

1. **You create a sound source using one or both of the following mechanisms:**
   - Periodic vibration of the vocal folds
   - Non-periodic turbulent noise resulting from airflow through a narrow constriction
2. **You filter the periodic or non-periodic sound source with the vocal tract to shape the frequency and amplitude of the signal into a particular speech sound.**

Creating periodic vibration

Most of the speech sounds you make — all of your vowels and at least half of your consonants — are voiced. Voicing happens when air passing through the glottis causes the vocal folds to vibrate *periodically* (open and close rapidly at a steady rate). In particular, air pressure differences interact with the physical dimensions of your vocal folds.

Putting the pressure on

For air to flow through the glottis, there must be a difference in air pressure above and below the glottis — between the lungs and vocal tract. This is why you can't produce voicing for very long with your vocal tract closed — oral stops like [b] and [d] can't be voiced for more than an instant. On the other hand, with the nasal cavity open, you can produce stops like [m] and [n] until you need to take another breath of air.

Applying string theory to speech sounds

The periodic vibration of the vocal folds in voiced speech sounds is similar to the vibration of a guitar or piano string. The rate or *frequency* of vocal fold vibration depends on three physical properties:

- **Length:** The shorter the vocal folds, the faster they vibrate.
- **Mass:** The thinner the vocal folds, the faster they vibrate.
- **Tension:** The tighter the vocal folds, the faster they vibrate.

You can't control the mass of your vocal folds — you work with what you've got — but you can control the length and tension to a certain extent by using the muscles in your larynx to stretch or relax the vocal folds.

Faster vibrations are perceived as higher pitch, and slower vibrations are perceived as lower pitch.

Women's vocal folds vibrate faster than men's because they're shorter and lighter. The vibration rate for guys slows down at puberty, dropping from 180 to 200 vibrations or cycles per second (written in Hertz as 180 to 200 Hz) to 100 to 125 Hz, because their folds get longer and heavier when their thyroid cartilage grows (that's how boys end up with an Adam's apple).

Harmonizing speech sounds

Given a certain length, mass, and tension, a perfect string would vibrate at just one frequency: This is known as the *fundamental frequency* or *F0* for short. But vocal folds and guitar strings aren't perfect, so when they vibrate, they generate other frequencies that are even multiples of their F0. These multiples are called *harmonics* and are, in musical terms, one octave apart just like the two E-strings on a guitar.

Your vocal folds produce a lot of harmonics. The left side of Figure 3-4 shows a harmonic progression for vocal fold vibration beginning with F0 and going up to higher frequencies. Notice how the harmonics get smaller in *amplitude* (loudness) as they go up in frequency. Even though higher harmonics have a smaller amplitude, these frequencies give your voice the rich quality everybody hears.

The F0 for adult men is about half that of women: While men's vocal folds typically vibrate 100 to 125 times per second, women's folds vibrate 200 to 250 times per second. This difference in F0 makes a big difference for the harmonics. For example, if a man's F0 is 100 Hz, the man's harmonics will be at 200, 300, 400, and so on. On the other hand, if a woman's F0 is 200 Hz, her harmonics will be at 400, 600, 800, and so on, with the gaps between harmonics twice as big as those of men. That's one reason why men's voices sound richer and carry over longer distances.

Creating non-periodic sounds

You get sound by moving air quickly enough to get it to complain. All the sounds you make when you speak are caused by moving air quickly through a narrow opening. This is true of periodic and non-periodic sounds. What makes the non-periodic sounds special is that they generate vibrations at all kinds of crazy frequencies. This is because the airflow becomes *turbulent* — which is a polite way of saying that the airflow is chaotic and crazy — before it generates vibration. Languages use two basic types of non-periodic sound:

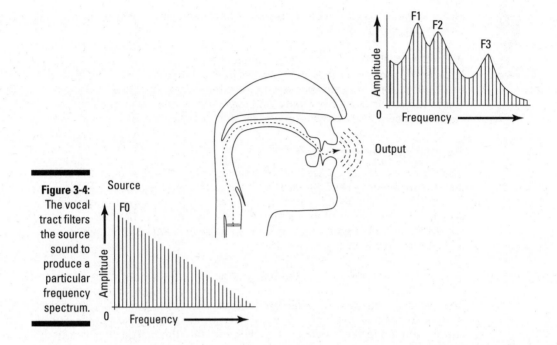

Figure 3-4:
The vocal tract filters the source sound to produce a particular frequency spectrum.

✔ **Fricatives:** These sounds occur when air is channeled through a narrow opening and then becomes turbulent when it exits the channel. This is what happens in the palato-alveolar area where you make [ʃ, ʒ], at the teeth for [θ, ð], and between the lips and the teeth for [f, v]. What makes alveolar [s, z] so loud is that you aim the air channeled by your tongue so that it crashes into your upper front teeth.

✔ **Clicks:** These are created by creating a hard closure, like your lips held tightly together or your tongue pressed up against the roof of your mouth, and then suddenly pulling the relevant articulators apart. This causes a local vacuum, which fills up with air so fast that it makes a noise. Babies start in on the lip smacking at an early age and soon discover the tongue clicks as well.

Because non-periodic sounds generate such a broad range of frequencies, the amplitude of any one frequency is quite small. This means no harmonics are generated and interaction with the vocal tract is weak. (For the frequency spread of [f] and [s], see Figure 3-5.)

Filtering source frequencies

Without modification, the sound your vocal folds make is a weak, dull buzzing sound. Just as you do with an electric guitar, you need to amplify your vocal fold vibrations. But that's not all: You also need to shape the source frequencies in order to create different sounds. Your vocal tract does both of these jobs at the same time: It *filters* the source frequencies, amplifying some harmonics, suppressing some, and leaving others unchanged.

Your vocal tract doesn't produce new frequencies; you work with what your vocal folds send up. How you position your tongue, lips, jaw, and velum adjusts the shape of your vocal tract, which, in turn, determines which frequencies come out of your mouth and how loud they are. Your oral and nasal cavities filter the source signal, *resonating* with some frequencies and so amplifying them, while toning down other frequencies, as you can see in the output sound on the right side of Figure 3-4. The resulting pattern of frequencies and amplitudes, which looks a bit like mountain peaks, defines the *frequency spectrum* of a sound.

Acoustic string instruments use a resonator to make the sounds louder. Guitars, violins, and cellos have their strings vibrate over a hole in a box, while the piano has its strings *in* the box. Different sizes, shapes, and materials affect how a resonator behaves. Lower sounds need bigger boxes — compare the violin and the double bass. You can check this out for yourself by blowing air across the opening of different size bottles and comparing the sounds. Your vocal tract is a resonator, but it's way more complicated than violins and bottles — you change the way the vocal tract affects different sound frequencies by changing its shape, size, and soft tissue properties. That's how you get the amazing variety of speech sounds you can make.

Where Figure 3-4 tells a sound's frequency story for one brief instant in time, Figure 3-5 shows you the frequency-amplitude spectrum while the words *feed* and *seed* are said. Linguists call this a *spectrogram*. In Figure 3-5, the different amplitudes are indicated by the darkness of the graph: Higher amplitude frequencies are darker.

Most of the important frequencies in speech occur between 50 Hz and 5,000 Hz. Fundamental frequency (F0) is at the bottom of the graph, but when it comes out of the mouth its amplitude is small, so it can be hard to see. More important are the darkish bands that appear at higher frequencies during the production of vowels (as well as during sounds like /l/ and /r/, although you can't see that example here). These bands — called *formants* — combine specific frequencies with high amplitude, just like the mountain peaks in Figure 3-4 which show peaks of amplitude for specific frequencies. The formants in Figure 3-5 (the dark bands with the white line running through their middles) are at typical frequencies for the vowel [i] of *feed* and *seed*.

The upper panel of Figure 3-5 gives the most common view of acoustic signals — this is generally the first thing a phonetician will show you. Known as the *audio* or *amplitude* waveform, this way of representing the acoustics is useful for examining how the total amplitude of the speech signal changes through time. This is not so easy to see in the spectrogram where amplitude at any given moment is distributed over a range of frequencies. In particular, the audio waveform shows the big difference in loudness between [f] and [s] much more clearly than the spectrogram.

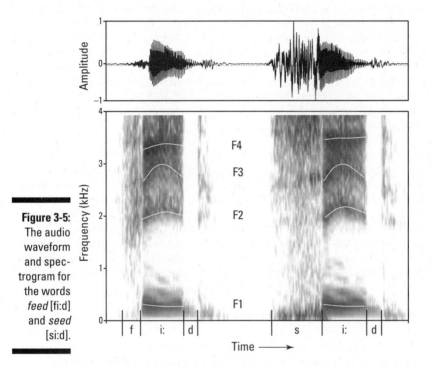

Figure 3-5: The audio waveform and spectrogram for the words *feed* [fi:d] and *seed* [si:d].

Perceiving vowels

By changing its shape, the vocal tract creates distinct patterns of resonating formant frequencies (F1, F2, F3) for each vowel, and you use these frequency values to identify vowels. In fact, you can classify the vowels using only the first two formant frequencies, F1 and F2:

- ✔ If the first formant (F1) of a vowel has a relatively *low frequency,* this corresponds to the traditional description of a vowel as *high.* A high F1 corresponds to a *low* vowel.

- ✔ If the second formant (F2) of a vowel has a relatively *high frequency,* this corresponds to the traditional description of a vowel as *front.* A low F2 corresponds to a *back* vowel.

Using acoustic formants to classify vowels is more accurate than using tongue position because acoustic classification is *quantitative* (based on measurements), while the original articulatory description was *qualitative* (based on observation). But they tell a similar story, as you can see back in Figure 3-3, which plots Standard American English vowels with both the acoustic and articulatory methods.

Perceiving fricatives

While vowels, approximants, and nasals use the vocal tract to shape the rich, periodic vibration of the vocal folds into formant bands, fricatives mainly contain non-periodic sound, also called *noise,* generated in the upper vocal tract. We say mainly because if you voice a fricative, you have two sound sources: one non-periodic sound produced at the place of articulation for the fricative and a periodic sound from the vocal folds.

So what's the technical definition of *noisy?* Noisy sounds are non-periodic; they generate vibrations over a wide range of frequencies, distributing their energy (corresponding to amplitude) too broadly for there to be harmonics — that is, each frequency gets about the same amount of energy. So, even when the vocal tract shape generates formant bands, the signals at those frequencies will barely have enough amplitude to make a difference — for example, note how weak the formants are for the [s] of *seed* in Figure 3-5. To differentiate between different kinds of fricatives, phoneticians look at

- ✔ **Frequency range:** If you look at the regions of the spectrogram in Figure 3-5, the frequency ranges corresponding to [f] in *feed* and [s] in *seed* are different; you see more grey shading at lower frequencies for [s] than for [f]. You can't see it in Figure 3-5, but the [s] noise becomes louder at about 5,000 Hz (5 kHz).

- ✔ **Duration:** It takes less time to say the [f] in *feed* than the [s] in *seed.*

- ✔ **Voicing:** Fricatives can be voiced or voiceless. Voicing doesn't change the frequency range of the frication noise, but it does add the periodic sound of the vocal fold vibration.

Except for the voiceless glottal fricative [h], all English fricatives and affricates come in voiceless and voiced pairs: [f, v], [θ, ð], [s, z], [ʃ, ʒ], [č, ǰ], where the first sound of each pair is voiceless.

Perceiving stops

Stops are funny things. While you sometimes can hear the vibration of the vocal folds during a voiced stop, you never hear a voiceless stop until it's released.

So how are you able to identify stop sounds? It works like this: As a speaker releases the stop to make a vowel, the stop's place of articulation specifies a particular vocal tract shape that determines the resonance for the initial vowel sound and the starting frequency of the vowel's formant resonances. You can see this in Figure 3-6 for different consonant+vowel combinations, like [bi, ba, bu]. The vocal tract shape changes between the release of the consonant and the following vowel, especially when the tongue is involved for both sounds. This initial change in formant value is called the *formant transition*. Figure 3-6 shows stylized formants where there is a sharp bend between the formant transition (between the consonant release and the beginning of the vowel) and the formant frequency for the rest of the vowel. In real speech, formants change more smoothly.

Figure 3-6: First and second formant transitions for [bi, ba, bu] and [di, da, du].

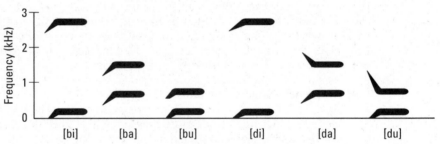

Chapter 4

Putting Sounds Together: Phonology

*Y*ou can produce and recognize at least 40 individual speech sounds, and that's cool. But to speak — and understand — a language, you need to know more than sounds in isolation: You need to be able to combine speech sounds into meaningful sound patterns.

The folks who try to understand how speech sounds combine are called *phonologists,* and their sub-branch of linguistics is *phonology.* In this chapter, we show you how sounds are segmented from the continuous stream of speech, how they contrast, how they fit together, how they form syllables, and how they carry melody.

Phoneticians and phonologists study speech sounds, but they party in different ways. *Phoneticians* sit around in lab coats, looking at ultrasound videos of the larynx on a smartphone — they're into the physics and physiology of speech sounds. (For more on phonetics, see Chapter 3.) *Phonologists* puzzle over how sounds combine: You'll find them playing word games, doing crosswords, or setting up a Scrabble board (yes, at a party!).

Segmenting the Speech Stream

If you've ever learned a language as an adult, you know how, at first, the new language just sounds like a blur. Then, you begin to be able to pick out smaller, distinct pieces — words, perhaps — and then even smaller pieces as you learn to identify the individual sounds. This ability is called *segmenting the speech stream*. After you can identify individual sound segments, you're unstoppable because you can now begin to combine those discrete segments into complex words and, with some grammatical knowledge, combine words into meaningful phrases and sentences. How you actually learn to segment the speech stream is one of the big questions of language acquisition (for more on this, see Chapter 13).

The power of a phoneme

Every language has a small set of sounds that are different from each other in an important way — they not only sound different, but if you use one in place of the other in a sound sequence such as a word, the meaning of the word changes. So, [bi:t] *beet* is not the same as [bi:m] *beam.* The *t* and *m* contrast with each other, both in the way they sound and in the effect they have on the meaning of the sequences they're in. Linguists call these contrasting sounds *phonemes* and mark them off with *angle slashes* /.../. Linguists say that two sounds are *phonologically distinct* only if substituting one for the other changes the meaning of a sequence. If substituting the sounds doesn't change the meaning of the sequence, they are considered non-contrastive or different pronunciations of the same unit of sound. For example the vowel /i/ in *beat* is a plain old vowel — the air goes through your mouth when you make it (it's *oral*). But the /i/ in *beam* is nasalized, meaning that air flows out through your nose and mouth when you make it because it's just before a nasal consonant /m/. Making an oral /i/ in *beam* won't give a different meaning to the word *beam,* just a funny pronunciation. Oral vowels and nasal vowels are non-contrastive in English.

The small size of a language's set of contrastive sounds makes the job of learning and using them manageable. Whether speaking or listening to language, you need to be able to identify a sound not only by what it is, say, a /b/, but also by what it's not — namely, none of the other 40 or so sounds in the language. Finally, as members of the set of distinct sounds you use to produce meaningful messages, contrastive sounds aren't just noises you make, they signal differences in meaning.

The combinatorial power of language

You may be wondering why we think that combining contrastive sounds together is so cool. It's cool because you combine signs to create more signs that carry meaning, such as words. To see how this works, try out these two thought experiments:

> ✔ **Thought experiment 1:** Suppose you can't combine sounds with each other. Then the largest unit of meaning you can ever have is a single sound like the /ʌ/ of the article in the phrase *a potato,* but you can never have *potato.* If you have 40 contrastive sounds — about the number of distinct speech sounds in English — that gives you only 40 distinct words: /u/, /m/, /d/, and so on. You might get a decent shopping list, but you'd never get directions to the store.

> ✔ **Thought experiment 2:** Suppose you can combine 40 sounds together into sequences and assign meanings to these combinations: /m/+/ʌ/+/d/ becomes /mʌd/ *mud.* Or turn them around to get /dʌm/, the first syllable of *dummies.* Now you've got enough new combinations — words, prefixes, suffixes — for a good Stephen King novel or the full version of the Oxford English Dictionary (whichever is longer).

The ability to string signs together to make new signs gives humans a huge leg up over other animals, who are stuck at the 40 word level. The fancy term for this ability to combine sounds is *combinatorial power.*

Contrasting Sounds with Each Other

Contrastive sounds or phonemes allow you to distinguish words from one another. For example, the words *bead* and *beet* are written phonemically as /bid/ and /bit/, where only the final phonemes /d/ and /t/ differ. Compare *bead* and *bid,* transcribed phonemically as /bid/ and /bɪd/. These words differ only in their vowels — /i/ and /ɪ/. *Thin* and *tin* contrast their initial phonemes: /θɪn/ and /tɪn/. These phonemes are all part of the set of English phonemes. Each of the 6,000 or so human languages has its own distinct set of phonemes. In this section, we show you how to tell which sounds are contrasting and which ones aren't and how phonemes differ in other languages.

We use square brackets […] for the *phonetic transcription* of any sound, whether contrastive or not. We use angle brackets /…/ just for the *phonological transcription* of phonemes — in other words, only for sounds that can signal a difference in meaning. Linguists sometimes call the phonetic transcription *narrow* and transcription that focuses only on sounds that can change meaning *broad.*

Setting aside sounds that don't contrast

Some sounds, even though you can hear them distinctly, don't make a difference in meaning when you substitute them for each other: Linguists call them *non-contrastive* sounds and they bring the total number of sounds in English to a lot more than 40. That's because you can pronounce each English phoneme in usually two or more ways — there are at least two kinds of /p/, a bunch of /t/ sounds, two different /l/ sounds, and several versions of each vowel. These differences in pronunciation are subtle and usually depend on how they are used. For example, the phoneme /g/ is pronounced as a stop sound (technically a voiced velar stop) in words like /tæg/ *tag* (see Chapter 1 for a list of all the phonetic symbols and Chapter 3 for a description of voicing, stops, and fricatives). The same /g/ phoneme in the middle of *dagger* is often pronounced with continuous frication (technically as a voiced velar fricative, which is represented in a narrow phonetic transcription as [ɣ]). Because these two non-contrastive variants of /g/ occur in different places, it's easy not to notice the difference. As far as distinguishing meaning is concerned, the two versions of /g/, called *allophones,* both belong to the phoneme /g/. Because they occur in different places, they are said to be in *complementary distribution.*

Sometimes, though, you pronounce a phoneme differently for no apparent reason at all, even if it's in the same position in a word. In Canada, for example, the words *Don* and *dawn* can be pronounced with the same sounds as in [dɑn] for both words — words that sound the same are *homophones.* But Canadians can also pronounce *Don* as either [dɑn] or [dɔn]. The two vowels sounds [ɑ] and [ɔ] are contrastive in other contexts, but not here because they don't cause a difference in meaning. When two sounds can be used in the same context without changing meaning, linguists say they're in *free variation.*

Identifying phonemes with the minimal pair test

The best way to tell whether two different sounds are phonemes or only allophones is to look for *minimal pairs.* Minimal pairs are sound strings that differ by just a single sound but have different meanings. Take a look at the minimal pairs in Table 4-1. As the phonetic description shows, each pair of words differs only in one segment: one is voiceless and the other is voiced. Note that you can't rely on English spelling to indicate different phonemes because sometimes English spells the same phoneme in different ways, as you can see with the final vowel phoneme in *thigh* vs. *thy* and *sue* vs. *zoo.* (For details on the phonetic description of the individual sounds, see Chapter 3.) The minimal pairs in Table 4-1 show that voicing is contrastive in English: Whether a sound is voiceless or voiced makes a difference in meaning.

Table 4-1	English Voicing Contrast in Minimal Pairs	
Minimal Pair	*Phonetic Description of Contrasting Segments*	
pill – bill [pɪl] – [bɪl]	/p/ voiceless bilabial stop	/b/ voiced bilabial stop
till – dill [tɪl] – [dɪl]	/t/ voiceless alveolar stop	/d/ voiced alveolar stop
kill – gill [kɪl] – [gɪl]	/k/ voiceless velar stop	/g/ voiced velar stop
file – vile [faɛl] – [vaɛl]	/f/ voiceless labiodental fricative	/v/ voiced labiodental fricative
thigh – thy [θɑe] – [ðɑe]	/θ/ voiceless interdental fricative	/ð/ voiced interdental fricative
sue – zoo [su] – [zu]	/s/ voiceless alveolar fricative	/z/ voiced alveolar fricative

The minimal pair test is the best test for finding the phonemes of a language.

John Higgins has a website for English minimal pairs, *Minimal Pairs for RP:* `http://myweb.tiscali.co.uk/wordscape/wordlist`. RP stands for *Received Pronunciation* or the Queen's English, which is still used by BBC (British Broadcasting Corporation) announcers.

Drilling down to morphemes

Although all the examples of minimal pairs in Table 4-1 were distinct words, sometimes it's not always clear what counts as a word. And sometimes you can have a sound sequence that carries meaning but isn't a word. For example, the suffix *-ed* at the end of the word *played* isn't a word on its own, but it carries the meaning that an action happened in the past. So when phonologists are identifying sound contrasts, they don't limit themselves to words; they also look at these smaller meaningful sound sequences, which are called *morphemes*. Here's what you need to know about morphemes:

- **A morpheme is a unit of meaning.** If you string sounds together and the string has a meaning, a linguist calls this meaningful unit a *morpheme*. (For more on morphemes, see Chapter 5.)

- **Some words consist of a single morpheme.** The word *bag* has three sounds /bæg/, but it's not divisible into smaller meaningful units. Like a one-horse town, it's a one-morpheme word.

- **Some words contain multiple morphemes.** The word *unconsciousness* has three morphemes: the prefix *un-*, the root *conscious,* and the suffix *-ness.* Each part is a meaningful unit.

- **Contrast is defined in terms of morphemes.** By comparing morphemes to each other, phonologists identify the contrastive sounds — the phonemes — of a language.

- **When you combine morphemes, their sounds can change.** For example, the sound used for the English plural ending changes depending on the word it is added to — it is /z/ in *dogs,* but /s/ in *cats.* By observing how the pronunciation of morphemes changes when they combine, phonologists identify the phonological rules of a language.

Finding sound contrasts and distinctive features

The minimal pair test lets you discover the set of contrasting sounds or phonemes for a language. But the phonologist's job is not just to identify lists of phonemes, it's also to understand how languages organize those phonemes into sound patterns. For example, why is *input* made of the two morphemes /ɪn/ and /pʊt/ and pronounced [ɪmpʊt] instead of *[ɪnpʊt]? You know it must have something to do with context because /ɪn/ is pronounced [ɪn] in words like *inactive* and *intact.* You can probably guess at least part of what's going on here: The nasal /n/ changes to [m] because you're closing your lips in anticipation of saying the bilabial [p]:

> An alveolar nasal /n/ changes to a bilabial nasal /m/ before a bilabial consonant.

Linguists spotted this process ages ago and named it *assimilation* — one thing becoming like another, in this case, a bilabial. But descriptions like this are haphazard and work only for obvious patterns. What the linguists really needed was a more detailed and systematic understanding of contrastive sounds that would help them not only understand easily observed patterns but also predict less obvious or impossible patterns. So, in the early 1950s, three of the most famous guys working on language — Roman Jakobson, Gunnar Fant, and Morris Halle — did something really smart. They took what they knew about the acoustics and articulation of sounds and devised a system of sound attributes or features that would thoroughly describe any speech sound and would identify the subset of *distinctive features* that uniquely distinguishes each phoneme from all others in a particular language. For example, a distinctive feature of an English phoneme could be whether it's voiced or not.

Descriptive features are all the things you can use to describe a sound. *Distinctive* features are the smaller set of features needed to identify contrastive sounds, or *phonemes*. Phonologists often ignore the descriptive features — like whether or not vowels are nasalized in English — when they don't need them to specify phonemic contrasts. But phonologists and engineers working on computer-based recognition and synthesis of speech have discovered that these non-contrastive descriptive features are important for modeling sound patterns and making them sound natural.

The list of features these guys came up with set the stage for modern phonology and is particularly appealing because it's *binary.* That is, every feature is either present (+) or absent (–); for example, a phoneme can't be "sort of" voiced — it either is voiced or it isn't. This means that phonemes can be uniquely identified according to a checklist of simple yes/no questions. Take a look at the partial list of distinctive features for English phonemes in Table 4-2.

Table 4-2   Distinctive Feature Checklist for English

Feature	Yes	No
Are the vocal folds vibrating?	[+voice]	[–voice]
Is the airflow continuous?	[+continuant]	[–continuant]
Is air coming through the nose?	[+nasal]	[–nasal]
Is it a vowel, or vowel-like?	[+vocalic]	[–vocalic]
Is the vowel high?	[+high]	[–high]
Is the vowel back?	[+back]	[–back]
Is the vowel low?	[+low]	[–low]
Is the vowel tense?	[+tense]	[–tense]
Does the vowel have rounded lips?	[+round]	[–round]
Is it a consonant, or consonant-like?	[+consonantal]	[–consonantal]
Is the tongue tip raised?	[+coronal]	[–coronal]
Is there contact at or in front of the alveolar ridge?	[+anterior]	[–anterior]
Is there high frequency noise?	[+strident]	[–strident]
Is the sound bilabial?	[+bilabial]	[–bilabial]

You can use checklists like this to find the unique set of distinctive feature values for each phoneme in a language. But the much more important value of this approach is that it helps you understand *how* phonemes differ from one another systematically. In particular, you use your knowledge of which features make a critical difference between some phonemes, but not others, to group them into *sound classes* such as consonants, vowels, fricatives, stops, bilabials, alveolars, and so on (if you have no idea what we're talking about here, flip to Chapter 3 real quick). Here's a small example.

You can use your checklist of features to discover that the three phonemes /p/, /b/, and /m/ form a unique subset or sound class in English — they're the only phonemes with the feature [+bilabial].

Okay, now how can you distinguish /p/, /b/, and /m/ from one another? All three phonemes are [+bilabial], but /b/ is [+voice], while /p/ is [–voice], so voicing distinguishes /b/ from /p/. And while /b/ and /m/ are both [+bilabial, +voice], /m/ is also [+nasal], so nasalization distinguishes /m/ from /b/.

- ✔ /p/ is [+bilabial, –voice, –nasal].
- ✔ /b/ is [+bilabial, +voice, –nasal].
- ✔ /m/ is [+bilabial, +voice, +nasal].

You can play this game out to discover all sorts of things about the sound classes of English. For example, each major place of articulation (bilabial, alveolar, velar) has at least two oral (one voiced and one voiceless) and one nasal stop consonant. You can then compare this to what other languages do and discover certain natural classes that all languages share, such as consonants and vowels, voiceless and voiced consonants, stops and fricatives, and so on.

The exact set of phonemes and subsets of sound classes may vary — that is, after you know what's possible, you'll find that languages have *gaps* in their inventories. (For discussion of gaps in sound systems, see Chapter 11.)

Contrasting sounds in other languages

Phonological contrasts are language-specific — a pair of sounds can be contrastive in one language, but not in another. In this section, we walk you through two examples: English to Korean and English to Hindi.

Hearing the difference in English and Korean: /l/ and /r/

English /l/ and /r/ are contrastive sounds — for example, *lip* /lɪp/ versus *rip* /rɪp/, or *deal* /dil/ versus *dear* /dir/. You can easily think of many more minimal pairs with /l/ and /r/ in English.

In Korean, however, [l] and [r] aren't contrastive. Speakers of Korean can say both sounds, but they don't use them to distinguish meaning. Korean speakers also hear [l] and [r] as the same sound. That's the reason why, when learning English, Korean speakers have trouble distinguishing *rip* and *lip* or *far* and *fall*. The Korean writing system even writes [l] and [r] with one symbol: ㄹ.

/l/ and /r/ differ from each other with respect to one distinctive feature: /l/ is [+lateral], but /r/ is [–lateral]. Lateral sounds allow air to flow over the sides of the tongue.

So [l] and [r] exist in Korean, but they aren't contrastive. How do Korean speakers decide when to say [l] and when to say [r]? It works like this:

- ✔ **Koreans pronounce ㄹ as [l] when it's syllable-final.** For example, *Seoul* is pronounced [səul] in Korean. The word for *barber* in Korean is [ipalsa] — the *syllable breaks* (shown by periods) are [i.pal.sa], which puts [l] at the end of the second syllable.

- ✔ **Koreans pronounce ㄹ as [r] when it's syllable-initial.** For example, *ruby* is pronounced [rubi] in Korean.

The split between [l] and [r] is systematic, predictable, and completely unnoticed by Korean speakers. That's what it's like when two sounds are non-contrastive: The difference fades into the background.

Blowing hot air: p and pʰ

The phoneme /p/ can be pronounced in two different ways. In English, when /p/ starts a syllable, it's followed by a puff of air, called *aspiration*. The IPA symbol for aspiration is a raised h, so you can phonetically transcribe words like *puff* and *apart* as [pʰʌf] and [ə.pʰɑrt]. But /p/ is also pronounced without aspiration in words like *topgun,* where /p/ comes at the end of a syllable. In these cases, you transcribe the /p/ with plain old [p] — [tɑp.gʌn]. You can check this difference for yourself by holding your fingers in front of your lips as you say these words. Because the difference between [pʰ] and [p] in English is predictable by its position in a syllable, they're allophones of /p/ and do not contrast. However, this difference is contrastive in other languages.

For example, Hindi, a language spoken in Northern India, uses /p/ or /pʰ/ in the same positions to distinguish different words. That is, Hindi /pʰ/ isn't the result of some process that predicts aspiration in certain places and no aspiration in others; it's a contrastive sound, and you find minimal pairs like those in Table 4-3. The Hindi writing system recognizes the difference and writes the two sounds differently: प for unaspirated versus फ for aspirated.

Table 4-3	Hindi Aspiration Contrast		
Minimal Pair	*Translation*	*Phoneme Transcription*	*Phonetic Description*
[pəl]	'moment'	/p/	unaspirated voiceless bilabial stop
[pʰəl]	'fruit'	/pʰ/	aspirated voiceless bilabial stop
[pal]	'to take care of'	/p/	
[pʰal]	'knife blade'	/pʰ/	

Wondering where the puff of air for /pʰ/ comes from? When you make a /p/, you stop the airflow through your mouth by closing your lips. You can now let air pressure build up in your vocal tract so that when you release the /p/, it makes a nice puff. Or you can release the airflow before the pressure builds up. What determines your choice is complicated. For example, in English, you get aspirated [pʰ] at the beginning of a *stressed* syllable, but [p] at the beginning of an *unstressed* syllable. This is because a stressed syllable is bigger in every way than an unstressed one — in English stressed syllables are louder, longer in duration, and have higher rates of vocal fold vibration than unstressed syllables containing the same segments. You can check this for yourself: If you put your hand in front of your mouth as you say the word *poppy*, transcribed phonetically as [pʰɑ.pɪ], you should feel only one air puff.

How do you know when two vowels contrast?

Finding minimal pairs doesn't work only for consonants — you can also use them to figure out whether vowels contrast. Take this small sample of words in Akan, a language spoken in Ghana, West Africa. The words in the following table show that regular vowels contrast with nasal vowels in Akan. If you're not sure what a nasal vowel is, say *ma* and sustain the vowel — *maaa*. The air flows through your nose for the [m] and keeps going through your nose while you produce the vowel [ɑ]; so the vowel is nasal. Compare this with *taaa*. If the vowel sounds different, it's because air doesn't flow through your nose for *ta*.

Akan minimal pair	*Meaning in English*
[nsa] – [nsã]	'hand' – 'liquor'
[ka] – [kã]	'bite' – 'to speak'

Aspiration applies to all English voiceless stops, so /p, t, k/ are pronounced [pʰ, tʰ, kʰ] in stressed syllable-initial position. Aspiration on voiceless stops is distinctive in Hindi, so Hindi has six voiceless contrasting consonants: /p, pʰ, t, tʰ, k, kʰ/. Hindi even has something like aspiration on voiced stops — involving a special state of the glottis and transcribed as /bʰ, dʰ, gʰ/ (for discussion of glottal states, see Chapter 3).

Fitting Sounds Together with Phonological Rules

Each language, and each dialect of a language, has rules that adjust the pronunciation of sounds when they're strung together. For example, in North American English, if /t/ occurs between two vowels in a word like *butter*, /t/ changes to a short sound similar to /d/. Linguists call this a *flap* because it involves a quick flap of the tongue against the alveolar ridge behind your teeth. But not all English speakers do this. Speakers of Cockney English pronounce the /t/ of *butter* as a glottal stop that sounds like a catch in the throat.

In this section, we show you examples of sound-changing rules — what phonologists call *phonological rules* — and how these rules lead to different accents.

Uncovering pronunciation rules in English

You probably aren't aware that you're an avid user of phonological rules. You follow them subconsciously, not even noticing you're doing so. Here are some of the things that you, as an English speaker, do when you combine sounds:

- Anytime you pronounce /p, t, k/ — these are the voiceless stops — at the start of a word, you aspirate them [pʰ], [tʰ], [kʰ].

- When you say a vowel in a syllable containing an initial voiceless consonant, you shorten it: *pad, tap,* and *tab* are examples.

- You actually start words that are written with a vowel at the beginning with a consonant: the glottal stop. So the word *at* comes out as [ʔæt].

- When you say an /l/ after a vowel, you probably say it with the back of your tongue raised toward the velum as for /k/. Try saying *ball* to check this out. Linguists call this a *dark l* and use the symbol [ɫ].

✔ You always nasalize vowels near the nasal consonants /m, n, ŋ/. You might nasalize vowels elsewhere, but this varies among speakers and is heard as a nasal twang.

Tracking sound-changing rules in dialects

Different dialects usually have different phonological rules — this is a major reason people have different accents. Understanding these rules is useful for anyone interested in learning to copy accents.

Detecting a Cockney accent: 'ello 'ello 'ello

Cockney is a British dialect of English, originally from the East End of London. Speakers of Cockney English have the following phonological rules:

✔ **Delete /r/ at the end of a word (or syllable).** The word *fur* is pronounced [fə] — the /r/ isn't pronounced. This is a rule of deletion as /r/ is present in the underlying form of *fur*. You can tell that /r/ is still there because, if you add a suffix, /r/ shows up — *furry* is pronounced [fəri] in Cockney, as in most dialects of English.

✔ **Turn /t/ into a glottal stop.** This is a Cockney specialty and now popular with many non-Cockney younger people in Britain. When /t/ is at the end of a syllable or between stressed and unstressed vowels, it becomes a glottal stop [ʔ]. For example, *bat* in Cockney is [bæʔ] and *butter* comes out as [bʌʔə].

✔ **Turn word-initial [h] into a glottal stop.** A distinctive Cockney touch, this rule turns *ham* into [ʔæm]. Notice that, combined with the previous rule, this rule makes *hat* into [ʔæʔ]: All the consonants in the word change to glottal stops!

✔ **Turn /θ/ into /f/.** The Cockney for *toothbrush* is [tʊfbrʌʃ]. Replacing the /θ/ with the /f/ is popular as far away as California. This sound rule may have a perceptual basis, as the difference between [θ] and [f] is difficult to hear. (For discussion of speech perception, see Chapter 14.)

Speaking like a German: Ve heff vater

Germans make consonants voiceless at the end of a syllable in some contexts and always at the end of a word. Because this rule is so consistent, it gets a name: *German final-devoicing*. If a German speaker tries to say the English word *have*, it comes out [hɛf] — the /v/ becomes [f] because it's at the end of the syllable (and word, in this example). Similarly, if they try to say *sees*, which we say [siz], /z/ turns into [s] and it comes out [sis]. Even though Germans say voiced sounds like /v/ and /z/ elsewhere, they devoice them at the end of a word/syllable. Final devoicing of consonants is a phonological rule for Germans, and English listeners use it to identify the German accent.

Word-final devoicing predicts the set of sound changes in German in Table 4-4. Note that in the plural, the consonant becomes voiced again, because it's no longer the final sound. The forms for 'bed' and 'guess/bet' end in voiceless consonants anyway, so devoicing doesn't affect them.

Table 4-4	Examples of German Final Devoicing		
English	*German Root*	*Singular*	*Plural*
'sieve'	/zib/	[zɪp]	[zibə]
'hero'	/hɛld/	[hɛlt]	[hɛldən]
'bed'	/bɛt/	[bɛt]	[bɛtən]
'guess/bet'	/tɪp/	[tɪp]	[tɪpən]

Identifying Canadian vowels: "Oot" and "aboot", eh?

All speakers of English — no matter what their dialect — say the vowel of the word *how* like this: [aʊ]. However, in Ontario, Canada, many speakers, especially older ones, use the diphthong [ʌʊ] instead of [aʊ] before certain voiceless consonants. Linguists call this rule *Canadian raising.* (Some speakers in Virginia do this too, but no one pays much attention to this phenomenon there.) Table 4-5 gives examples for this variant of Canadian English.

Table 4-5	Canadian Raising of /aʊ/ before Voiceless Sounds		
Word	*US and English (UK)*	*Canadian*	*Compare*
how	[haʊ]	[haʊ]	same
now	[naʊ]	[naʊ]	same
brown	[braʊn]	[braʊn]	same
about	[əbaʊt]	[əbʌʊt]	different
couch	[kaʊtʃ]	[kʌʊtʃ]	different
house	[haʊs]	[hʌʊs]	different
to house (verb)	[haʊz]	[haʊz]	same
mouth	[maʊθ]	[mʌʊθ]	different
to mouth (verb)	[maʊð]	[maʊð]	same

/aʊ/ is a moving vowel — linguists call it a *diphthong* — that starts with the vowel [ɑ] as in *car* and moves to the high back region, where we say [ʊ] as in *put.* The Canadian variant, /ʌʊ/, starts with the vowel in *cut.* (For more discussion of diphthongs, see Chapter 3.)

Grouping Sounds into Syllables

As you speak, you group sounds into syllables. To get a sense of what a syllable is, tap your finger as you say a long word, like *lollapallooza*. You'll find yourself dividing it up into five groups, probably like this: [lo.lə.pə.lu.zə]. Those groups are *syllables*. Syllables are a basic unit of speech perception and production — they reflect the fact that sounds are both perceived and produced in time. (For discussion of the perception and production of syllables, see Chapters 14 and 15.) To paraphrase Woody Allen, syllables are nature's way of keeping everything from happening at once.

Although the IPA marks syllable breaks with a period (.), as in *lo.lla.pa.lloo. za,* some folks mark syllable breaks with a hyphen, as in *lo-lla-pa-lloo-za*. We follow the IPA convention and reserve hyphens for marking morpheme boundaries. (For more on morphemes, see Chapter 5.)

Defining the syllable

All phonologists agree that syllables exist, but no two phonologists agree on the definition of a syllable. Here's the one that we use: A *syllable* is the smallest unit of sound that can be pronounced all by itself. Phonologists describe syllables in terms of sequences of consonants (C) and vowels (V). In English, the smallest syllable contains a single sound: either a single vowel (V) (for example, the /ə/ or /e/ you use to pronounce *a* in *a pen*) or a consonant that can be *sustained* (stretched out), such as the nasals /m, n/ and the liquids /l, r/ (for example, in *reader* the final /r/ forms a syllable by itself). In general, phonologists treat vowels as the heart of the syllable: If you have a vowel, you have a syllable, and all syllables have something vowel-like in them. Consonants like /d/ or /b/ can't be a syllable by themselves — if you say /d/ out loud and think it is a syllable, you are probably giving it a vowel and pronouncing it not [d] but [dʌ]. Thus the vowel is the core element of the syllable — the *nucleus*. Consonants that begin a syllable are part of the *onset*: An onset can contain one or more consonants. And consonants that end a syllable are part of the *coda* (an Italian word that means 'end') — a coda can contain one or more consonants.

You can sustain fricatives like /s/ and /z/, but English doesn't make linguistic use of this possibility. But in Blackfoot, an Algonquian language spoken in southern Alberta and northern Montana, /s/ can be a syllable by itself, which linguists call a syllabic /s/.

English is unusual in allowing very large syllables. Check out Table 4-6 to see just how long they can get. How a language structures syllables, also known as its *phonotactics,* determines the set of permissible phoneme combinations. Similarly, words are made of syllables, so the set of possible syllables determines the forms of possible words in a language. Phonologists identify this set of possible syllables by seeing how many consonants can start a syllable, how many can end it, and what kinds of vowels the language has. If you hear someone talking about *syllabic phonology,* they're talking about this stuff.

Table 4-6	**Examples of Monosyllabic Words in English**						
Orthography	*a*	*be*	*ebb*	*but*	*skit*	*desk*	*skimp*	*skrimped*
Transcription	[ʌ], [e]	[biː]	[ɛb]	[bʌt]	[skɪt]	[dɛsk]	[skɪmp]	[skrɪmpt]
Syllable Structure	V	CV	VC	CVC	CCVC	CVCC	CCVCC	CCCVCCC

If you see a CVCV string, how do you break it down into syllables? Each vowel forms the nucleus of a syllable, but where does the middle consonant go? Do you syllabify the string as CV.CV or as CVC.V? Here's a tip: Assume it's CV.CV because languages prefer CV syllables to all other forms. For example, the English word *hobo* (a guy who rides the rails) syllabifies as *ho.bo*, not as **hob.o*.

Syllables and sound patterns

Scat singing, a precursor to *doo-wop* and *hip hop,* uses nonsense syllables to improvise melody and rhythm. The syllable a singer uses is a matter of personal style: Betty Carter uses soft-tongued sounds (liquids) like [lu.i.u.i.la.la]. Sarah Vaughan plays on the difference between continuants and stops, as in [ʃu.du.ʃu.bi.u.bi]. Disney films use nonsense syllables in many of their musicals: think *Mary Poppins* and *supercalifragilisticexpialidocious* ([su.pəɹ.kæ.lɪ.fræ.jɪ.lɪs.tɪk. ɛk.spɪ.æ.lɪ.do.ʃəs]), *Song of the South* ([zɪ.pɫ.di.du.dɑ]), and *Cinderella* ([bɪ.bɪ.di.bɑ.bɪ.di.bu]). Musicologists call nonsense syllables used for singing *non-lexical vocables.* Languages that use this technique include Blackfoot and Plains Cree (Algonquian languages spoken in the northern Plains of Canada and the United States), Irish and Scots Gaelic (where the technique is called *puirt à beul),* Appalachian English (in a musical form called *eefing),* and Hebrew (with religious music called *nigun).* Syllables also play an important role in language acquisition: All human infants — no matter which language they learn — go through a babbling stage where they practice producing syllables (for some babble on babbling, see Chapter 13).

Syllabifying affects sound-changing rules

For many phonological rules, you need to know the position of a sound segment in a syllable in order to know whether the rule applies. Because a syllable has three parts — onset, nucleus, and coda — there are phonological rules that apply to each part. In fact, most of the rules we've shown you in this chapter apply only if the segment occupies a particular position in the syllable.

✔ **Phonological rules that care about the onset:**

- Korean speakers pronounce ㄹ as [r] in the onset position.

- English speakers pronounce the voiceless stops /p, t, k/ as aspirated [pʰ, tʰ, kʰ] in the onset position.

- English speakers insert a glottal stop [ʔ] onset before vowel-initial words.

- Cockney English speakers pronounce /h/ as [ʔ] in the onset position.

✔ **Phonological rules that care about the nucleus:**

- English speakers pronounce a vowel as nasalized when there's a nasal consonant nearby, especially one that follows the vowel in the coda.

- English speakers shorten the long vowels if the coda contains a voiceless consonant — compare [biːd] and [bit].

- The Canadian raising rule changes the diphthong [aʊ] to [ʌʊ] when the coda consists of certain voiceless consonants. (For examples, see Table 4-5.)

✔ **Phonological rules that care about the coda:**

- Korean speakers pronounce ㄹ as [l] in the coda position.

- English speakers pronounce /l/ as [ɫ] in the coda position.

- Cockney English speakers delete /r/ in the coda position.

- Cockney English speakers pronounce /t/ as [ʔ] in the coda position.

- German speakers devoice consonants in the coda position.

Some phonological rules care about the entire syllable. For example, phonologists assign stress to vowels because that's where it is easiest to hear differences. The amount of aspiration you give the initial voiceless stops /p, t, k/ is also related to stress in English. See the section "Stressing out in English" for more on what stress is and how it works.

Linguists rank sounds according to how sonorant (loud) they are: Vowels are the most sonorant, stops the least, and other sounds fall in between — Vowels > Liquids > Nasals > Fricatives > Stops. Phonologists use this *sonority hierarchy* to explain which kinds of sound segments can function as the nucleus, onset, or coda in a particular language. Individual languages have different phonotactic constraints on syllable structure and these interact with sonority.

Syllabifying in different languages

All languages group sounds into syllables, but how they make syllables differs. In some languages, you're allowed at most one consonant (C) and one vowel (V), making the maximum syllable size CV. This is true of Hawaiian (a Polynesian language) and Yorùbá (a Niger-Congo language spoken in Nigeria). This constraint on syllable size severely restricts word form. The two languages solve this problem in different ways.

Hawaiian words often consist of long CVCVCV units, as in [hu.mu.hu.mu.nu.ku.nu.ku.a.pu.a.ʔa] 'trigger fish', which breaks down as:

[hu.mu.hu.mu] ('triggerfish') + [nu.ku] ('snout') + [nu.ku] ('blunt') + [a] ('modifier') + [pu.a.ʔa] ('pig') → "triggerfish with a snout like a pig."

Yorùbá keeps its words short: Verbs are CV (/*ri*/ 'see'), while most nouns are V.CV (/e.sɛ/ 'hippopotamus'). Most languages allow bigger syllables than Hawaiian and Yorùbá, but many don't go bigger than CVC and often limit the coda that ends a syllable to just one or two types of consonant. Languages also differ in what they permit as the nucleus of the syllable. For example, Blackfoot, spoken in southern Alberta and northern Montana, allows /s/ as a syllable nucleus.

Grouping syllables with rhythm

How many feet do you have? If a phonologist asks you this, they're asking about how you group your syllables together into rhythmic units called *feet*. If you hear someone mention *metrical phonology,* they're talking about rhythm.

English often groups its syllables into pairs and emphasizes or *stresses* the second one. This results in a (ba BOOM) pattern.

(ba **BOOM**) (ba **BOOM**) (ba **BOOM**)

(The **'mouse**) (ran **'up**) (the **'clock**)

(I'd **'like**) (to **'catch**) (the **'bus**)

Counting syllables in poetry

Have you ever wondered why poetry needs to be read out loud to be fully appreciated? That's because poets use stress rules to create special sound effects. The same rules of rhythm that apply to ordinary spoken language apply to poetry. Take a look at the following extract of a poem entitled *The Tyger*, written by William Blake. These lines use the trochaic BOOM ba pattern: a stressed syllable followed by an unstressed syllable. When phonologists analyze the stress system of a language, they often turn to poetry because the regular patterns used by poets provide evidence for the organization of syllables into larger units, such as metrical feet.

('**Ty**.ger) ('**Ty**.ger) ('**bur**.ning) '**bright**

('**In** the) ('**fo**.rests) ('**of** the) '**night**

But you can also stress the first syllable of each pair of syllables. This gives a (BOOM ba) pattern:

(**BOOM** ba) (**BOOM** ba) (**BOOM** ba) **BOOM**

('**Twin** kle) ('**twin** kle) ('**li** ttle) '**star**

('**Tell** me) ('**why** you) ('**don't** a) '**gree**

The (ba BOOM) pattern is an *iamb*, and the (BOOM ba) pattern is a *trochee*. A trochee and an iamb are two examples of meters or syllable groupings. For a survey of different metrical types, see the website of Michael J. Cummings: http://www.cummingsstudyguides.net/xmeter.html.

Stressing out in English

The thing about stress in English is that it allows you to play with and complicate the rhythm in various ways at the same time. For example, the word *alienation* basically follows the (BOOM ba) pattern, where the final /n/ in /ʃn/ is syllabic:

(**BOOM** ba) (**BOOM** ba)

['e. lɪ.ɪə 'ne. ʃn]

The word contains two (BOOM ba) groups, each beginning with a stressed syllable: the first and the fourth. (Stress is marked by an apostrophe.) But, typical of words imported from Latin by way of French, the two stressed syllables are slightly different in how stressed they are — you probably say this word with slightly more stress on the fourth syllable. This is the most stressed syllable in the word, so it gets *primary stress*. The first syllable [e] then gets *secondary stress*. What about the other syllables? If you pay close attention, you can probably tell that the second syllable [lɪ] is ever so slightly more stressed than either the third or fifth syllable. This one gets *tertiary stress,* while the third and fifth syllables are unstressed. As an English speaker, you've learned these patterns so well that you can usually get the stress pattern right even on words you encounter for the first time in print. Finally, the stress patterning of words like *alienation* interacts with other rhythmic factors at the sentence level. For example, when you want to emphasize something or make it clear that you bought "THIS book," not "some OTHER book," you manipulate the stress patterning of all the syllable elements.

Entire books have been written about English stress rules, but here we give you some basic rules for word-level stress:

- **One word has one main stress.** If you hear two main stresses, then there are two words. (Longer words have secondary stress, but it's smaller than the main stress.)

- **Stress the first syllable of a bi-syllabic noun or adjective.**

     'pre.sent, 'ex.port, 'chi.na, 'ta.ble

     'slen.der, 'cle.ver, 'ha.ppy

- **Stress the second syllable of a bi-syllabic verb.**

     pre.'sent, ex.'port, de.'cide, be'gin

- **Stress the second-to-last syllable for words with *-ic, -sion, -tion*.**

     ge.o.'gra.phic, ge.o.'lo.gic, te.le.'vi.sion, re.ve.'la.tion

- **Stress the third-to-last syllable for words with *-cy, -ty, -phy, -gy, -al*.**

     de.'mo.cra.cy, de.pen.da.'bi.li.ty, pho.'to.gra.phy, ge.'o.lo.gy

- **Stress the first member of a compound noun or the second member of a compound adjective or verb.**

     Compound noun: *'black-bird*

     Compound adjective: *good-'loo.king*

     Compound verb: *ov.er-'look*

Playing with Melody

Languages have melodic patterns that indicate whether someone is making a declaration, asking a question, reciting a list, or calling attention to something. Linguists call the study of such melodic patterns the study of *intonation.* In English, questions and statements have different melodic patterns and therefore different intonation. If you ask a yes/no question, the pitch of your voice goes up at the end of the sentence. If you say the exact same words as a statement, your pitch goes down at the end. The intonation pattern for lists is different again: There is rising intonation on each item, except the last item, which has falling intonation — the fall on the last item signals that the list is done. The IPA marks rising intonation with a diagonal arrow rising left-to-right [↗] and falling intonation with a diagonal arrow falling left-to-right [↘]. Table 4-7 gives examples of English intonation.

Table 4-7	Examples of English Intonation	
Example	*Intonation*	*Type*
You're the boss? [↗]	rising	question intonation
You're the boss. [↘]	falling	declarative intonation
I'll have coke[↗], fries[↗], and a burger[↘].	rise, rise, fall	list intonation

Many languages have similar intonation patterns — rise on questions and within lists, fall on statements and at the end of lists — but these aren't universal. Some languages, like Chickasaw (a language from the southeastern U.S.) fall on yes/no questions and rise on statements. And some English speakers in the North of Britain fall on yes/no questions, too. Another example is *upspeak* (also called *uptalk*), which has become widespread in North American English, especially among younger speakers. In *upspeak,* statements, phrases, and even individual words end with a rising intonation.

Using tone to create word meaning

Many languages in Asia and Africa are *tone* languages. Tone languages use pitch to contrast meanings at the word level. *Pitch* is a perceived property of sound based mainly on a speaker's rate of vocal fold vibration and to a lesser extent on loudness. You perceive higher rates of vocal fold vibration and greater loudness as being higher in pitch. For example, in Mandarin (the official language of China), the same syllable can have four meanings, depending just on the pitch pattern. That is, pitch is contrastive at the word level! Check out this example using the syllable /ba/:

- /ba/ with high pitch = 'scar'
- /ba/ with low pitch = 'target'
- /ba/ with rising pitch = 'cymbal'
- /ba/ with falling pitch = 'dam'

Chapter 5

Building Words: Morphology

*B*y the time you're two, you absorb words at a rate of one every two hours — you clock 12 words a day, 84 words a week. When you start school, you're packing 13,000 words. At your high school graduation, you have 60,000 under your belt. If you're a champion Scrabble player, you top out at 120,000. But that's nothing compared to the total number of words in English, which is estimated to be around a quarter of a million. Yup, that's right: 250,000 distinct words. And if distinct meanings are counted, the total is more like three quarters of a million: 750,000 words! You can master 60,000 words — the average vocabulary size of an adult — and yet, according to studies on information processing, you can't accurately remember a list that has more than seven items. What gives? Your ability to learn and maintain such a large vocabulary reflects a combination of skills unique to human beings. You're incredibly good at vocal mimicry — this allows you to learn a large number of distinct words. You have stable long-term memory — this allows you to remember a large number of words. But here, we're going to focus on how you use efficient rules for word-formation, which allows you to form new words at the drop of a hat. In this chapter, we give you a glimpse of the intricate word-formation system, called *morphology,* that underlies your talents as a wordsmith.

Minding Your Morphemes

A *word* is a freestanding unit of meaning, and a *morpheme* is single unit of meaning. Every word has at least one morpheme. For example, words such as *cat, walk,* and *tall* are words that contain a single unit of meaning. But some words have more than one morpheme. For example, the words *cats, walked,* and *tallest* each contain two units of meaning: *cats* is *cat* plus the plural suffix *-s; walked* is *walk* plus the past tense suffix *-ed; tallest* is *tall* plus the superlative suffix *-est.* The goal of morphology is to find minimal units of meaning — morphemes — and to understand how these units combine to form words. All languages distinguish two basic types of morphemes:

- ✔ A *free morpheme* is a unit of meaning that can stand by itself — for example, *cat, walk,* and *tall.*

- ✔ A *bound morpheme* is a unit of meaning that can't stand by itself — for example, the *-s* of *cats,* the *-ed* of *walked,* and the *-est* of *tallest.*

To find units of meaning, linguists use a simple procedure: They compare related forms. For example, to determine how many units of meaning — how many morphemes — are contained in *hardness,* a morphologist goes through the following steps:

1. **Select related forms for comparison.** To find a related form for *hardness,* look for other words that have the same units of meaning. You could look at other words that contain the morpheme *hard,* which happens to be an independent word (a free morpheme) — *harden, hardship,* and *hardy.* Or you could look at words that contain the morpheme *-ness,* which can't stand by itself (it's a bound morpheme) — *kindness, baldness,* and *weirdness.*

   So suppose your comparison sets are

   Set A: { ***hard**ness,* ***hard**en,* ***hard**ship,* ***hard**y* }

   Set B: { *hard**ness**, kind**ness**, bald**ness**, weird**ness*** }

2. **Identify similar parts and their meaning.**

   Set A has in common the unit *hard,* which is associated with the quality of being rigid, firm, unyielding, or resistant to pressure.

   Set B has in common the unit *-ness,* a suffix that attaches to adjectives to form nouns that refer to the quality of the adjective. For example, *hardness* refers to the quality of being hard.

3. **Divide the forms into parts, according to what they have in common, and indicate the division with a hyphen.**

   Set A: { ***hard**-ness,* ***hard**-en,* ***hard**-ship,* ***hard**-y* }

   Set B: { *hard-**ness**, kind-**ness**, bald-**ness**, weird-**ness*** }

Morphologists use hyphens to mark boundaries between morphemes — these are called *morpheme boundaries.* The morpheme breakdown of *hardness* is *hard-ness.*

To establish the morpheme inventory of a language, you need to know how sounds *(phonemes)* combine to form minimal units of meaning *(morphemes)* — this is the study of *morpho-phonology. Morpho-syntax* studies how morphemes combine to produce complex words. *Morpho-semantics* studies how morphemes combine to produce new meanings. And many morphemes add shades of meaning that can only be understood if you look at the larger context — this is the study of *morpho-pragmatics.*

Discovering the Architecture of Words

A word is a house: It has a foundation, which supports a main area, and then some extensions. Houses are built according to different architectural styles — same thing with words. The foundation of any word is the root upon which it's based. All words have at least one root, and some words have more than one. The *root* of the word is its core element of meaning. For example, the root of the word *cats* is *cat;* the root of *wonderful* is *wonder.* Compound words such as *bluebird* and *tabletop* each have two roots.

After you've uncovered the foundation of a word — its root — you can turn to its extensions. These are the elements that alter the basic meaning of the root. The following sub-sections show you some of the many ways languages add extensions to the foundational root of a word.

Picking a word-building method

Languages use two building techniques to add extensions to their roots: concatenation and non-concatenation.

Concatenation is the brick-and-mortar approach, where one extension is added at a time. This is like adding another floor to a house. English often uses this building technique by adding an affix to a root, for example, *music* can be extended to *musical* by adding the suffix *-al.* Concatenation extends the root in one of five ways:

- ✔ *Prefixing* attaches a bound morpheme before the root. Examples: **un**button, **dis**respect, **re**cover
- ✔ *Suffixing* attaches a bound morpheme after the root. Examples: teach**er**, cover**able**, judg**ment**
- ✔ *Infixing* attaches a bound morpheme inside the root. Examples: saxo-**ma**-phone, sy-**IZ**-rup
- ✔ *Circumfixing* wraps a bound morpheme around the root. Older forms of English used **a**-...-**ing** as a circumfix, as in *time is **a**-fly**ing**.*
- ✔ *Compounding* extends the root by adding another root. For example, the root *bird* combines with roots like *black*, *blue*, and *song* to form the compounds *blackbird*, *bluebird*, and *songbird.*

When morphemes combine, they "stick together" — this is called *agglutination.* But in some languages a morpheme fuses two bits of meaning; this is called *fusion.* For example, French *du,* which means 'of the', fuses 'of' and 'the'. (See Chapter 11 for a discussion of agglutination and fusion.)

Non-concatenation is the second building method and it weaves the extension into the root. This method is not used in English, but is important in Semitic languages, such as Arabic. Words are formed by weaving in a vowel pattern on a root that is, by itself, unpronounceable. For example, in Modern Standard Arabic, words referring to the notion of writing all involve the *k-t-b* root, interleaved with vowel patterns: *katab* 'to write', *kaatab* 'to correspond with someone', *kitaab* 'a book'.

Non-concatenative morphology is also called *discontinuous morphology* or *introflection*. The non-concatenative morphology found in Semitic languages is called *root and pattern morphology*. Semitic languages include Amharic, Arabic, Aramaic, Hebrew, and Triginya — they're part of the Afroasiatic language family. For a discussion of language families, see Chapter 10.

Adding grammatical information with inflectional affixes

Inflectional affixes provide grammatical information about the word they attach to:

- For verbs, they provide information about time (linguists call this *tense,* such as the English past *-ed*), possibility (linguists call this *mood*), and the internal structure of an event (linguists call this *aspect,* such as the English progressive *-ing*).

- For nouns, they provide information about case, *number* (singular versus plural), and *gender* (masculine versus feminine).

- For adjectives, they provide information about the degree to which an adjective holds. This includes the comparative (the *-er* of *taller*) and the superlative (the *-est* of tall-*est*).

Inflectional affixes don't change the basic meaning of the word they attach to, and they never change the category of the word — in other words, they can't change a verb into a noun or vice versa. Each of the major grammatical categories — verbs, nouns, and adjectives — is associated with a set of inflectional morphemes. English has seven inflectional suffixes, which you can see in Table 5-1, a small number compared to other languages. To figure out how to identify the category of a word, see Chapter 6.

Table 5-1		Inflectional Morphemes in English	
Attaches to	*Morpheme*	*Marks*	*Examples*
Verb	*-ed*	Past tense	*walked, talked, buzzed, wanted*
	-s	3rd person singular	*walks, talks, buzzes, wants*
	-ing	Progressive aspect	*walking, talking, buzzing, boating*
	-en	Perfect aspect	*seen, broken, fallen*
Noun	*-s*	Plural	*boys, girls, matches, cups*
Adjective	*-er*	Comparative	*taller, shorter, wider, longer*
	-est	Superlative	tall**est**, short**est**, wid**est**, long**est**

Inflection and grammatical categories

Inflectional affixes only combine with certain categories, so they're handy to have around if you want to figure out the category of a word. To see this, take a look at the following sentence:

The gostak distims the doshes.

This sentence contains words you've never seen before: *gostak, dosh,* and *distim.* Even if you don't know what these words mean, you know that whatever *gostak* and *dosh* are, they're things of some sort, and that whatever *distim* is, it's an action of some sort. The information that you're using to figure this out partly relies on your knowledge of English inflectional morphology. The suffix *-s* marks third person singular on verbs *(distims)* and plural on nouns *(the doshes).* You also use your knowledge of grammatical categories and word order. For example, the determiner *the* only introduces nouns, such as **the** gostak and **the** doshes. And

English word order is Subject-Verb-Object — that tells you that the gostaks (whatever they are) are doing something to the doshes (whatever they are). What you did with the sentence *The gostak distims the doshes* is what kids do day in and day out when they learn a language. (See Chapter 13 for how kids learn language.)

This sentence — coined in 1903 by Andrew Ingraham and discussed by C. K. Ogden and I. A. Richards in their 1923 book *The Meaning of Meaning* — has gone viral. Science fiction fans will know the story by M. Breuer entitled "The Gostak and the Doshes." Music buffs will have heard Hiawatha's three movement sonata called "The Gostak Distims the Doshes": Movement I is "Doshes"; movement II is "Distimming"; movement III is "The Gostak." And gamers will know the interactive fiction game "The Gostak," written by C. Muckenhoupt.

English uses a third *s* morpheme to mark possession in expressions like *Lucy's book*. Notice that possessor *s* is spelled with an apostrophe: This indicates it's a *clitic*. Clitics, like affixes, are bound morphemes. But while affixes attach to words, clitics attach to phrases. (See Chapter 6 for a discussion of phrases.) You can see the difference by comparing the position of the plural *-s* suffix with the possessor *'s* clitic. Plural appears on the noun *(the queen**s** of England)*, while the possessor appears on the noun phrase *(the queen of England**'s** reign)*.

Creating new words with derivational affixes

A *derivational affix* combines with a root to form a new word. The combination always involves a change in meaning and often involves a change in word category. (For discussion of categories, see Chapter 6.) English derivational affixes can be prefixes, suffixes, or infixes.

Barging in at the beginning

Derivational prefixes are classified according to the category of the new word they create or *derive*. Although they change the meaning of the word they attach to, most English prefixes don't change the category of the word they attach to:

- **Prefixes that derive verbs by attaching to verbs:** *co*-ordinate, *mal*nourish, *de*-link, *dis*agree, *em*power, *mis*inform, *pre*-qualify, *re*act, *un*button

- **Prefixes that derive nouns by attaching to nouns:** *arch*-rival, *anti*virus, *fore*sight, *post*-election, *mid*life, *ex*-colleague, *mini*market, *ultra*sound, *pro*-democracy, *step*sister, *vice*-president

- **Prefixes that derive adjectives by attaching to adjectives:** *a*moral, *im*possible, *pan*-Canadian, *un*equal

Some prefixes are written with a hyphen, and there's no rhyme or reason to it. This is where the English writing system and linguists part company: a morpheme breakdown always puts a hyphen between a prefix and the root.

Tagging on at the end

Derivational suffixes are classified according to the category of the word that they derive and which category they attach to:

- **Suffixes that derive verbs by attaching to:**

    Nouns: *origin**ate**, class**ify**, symbol**ize***

    Adjectives: *hard**en**, intens**ify**, special**ize***

- ✔ **Suffixes that derive nouns by attaching to:**

    Nouns: *neighbour**hood**, despot**ism**, rac**ist**, orphan**age**, prison**er**, robb**ery***

    Verbs: *annoy**ance**, rebell**ion**, contain**ment**, steer**age**, teach**er**, assembl**y***

    Adjectives: *modern**ism**, formal**ist**, southern**er**, honest**y***

- ✔ **Suffixes that derive adjectives by attaching to:**

    Nouns: *hood**ed**, metall**ic**, spac**ious**, heart**y***

    Verbs: *read**able**, restrict**ive**, advis**ory***

    Adjectives: *green**ish**, dead**ly***

Affixes can be verb-forming, noun-forming, or adjective-forming. Linguists who focus on parallels between building words and sentences give affixes a grammatical category. For them, verb-forming affixes are verbs, noun-forming affixes are nouns, and adjective-forming affixes are adjectives.

Building words with several layers

Just as a building can have several stories, a word can have several layers by adding multiple affixes to the root:

- ✔ **Addition of several prefixes:** *reunbutton (**re-un**-button), disempower (**dis-em**-power)*
- ✔ **Addition of several suffixes:** *classifier (class-**ifi-er**), restrictiveness (restrict-**ive-ness**)*
- ✔ **Addition of prefixes and suffixes:** *unequality (**un**-equal-**ity**), declassify (**de**-class-**ify**), unlockable (**un**-lock-**able**)*

Morphologists get excited about words that have both prefixes and suffixes because they reveal the architecture of word-building. Take another look at *unequality, declassify,* and *unlockable*. Sometimes the prefix attaches first, sometimes the suffix:

- ✔ **Prefix attaches first:**

    Unequality: Attach *un-* to *equal* to form *unequal*. Then attach *-ity* to *unequal* to form *unequality*. The reason the prefix must attach first is that *un-* doesn't attach to nouns — there are no words like **unconstitution* or **unintelligence*. But *un-* can attach to adjectives — there are words like *unconstitutional* and *unintelligent*.

    Unlockable: Attach *un-* to the verb *lock* to form the verb *unlock*. Then attach *-able* to the verb *unlock* to form the adjective *unlockable*. Derived in this way, *unlockable* means 'able to be unlocked'.

> ✔ **Suffix attaches first:**
>
> *Declassify:* Attach *-ify* to the noun *class* to form *classify.* Then attach *de-* to the verb *classify* to make the verb *declassify.*
>
> *Unlockable:* Attach *-able* to the verb *lock* to form the adjective *lockable.* Then attach *un-* to the adjective *lockable* to make the adjective *unlockable.* Derived in this way, *unlockable* means 'not able to be locked'.

Unlockable can be built in two ways: [[unlock]-able] is 'able to be unlocked', while [un-[lockable]] is 'not able to be locked'. Linguists call this *structural ambiguity* — the same form has two structures, each with a different meaning. This reflects the design feature of *duality of patterning,* discussed in Chapter 2.

Making new words with compounds

If two roots combine, as in *bluebird,* linguists call this a *compound* or a *root compound.* Most English compounds show a pattern that morphologists call the *righthand head rule.* It goes like this: If the first word is of category X and the second of category Y, then the compound is of category Y. (X and Y stand for the major grammatical categories: verb, noun, adjective, and preposition.) The *head* determines the category of the compound — so Y is the head. The rule can be written as X + Y → Y. Table 5-2 gives examples.

Building long words

Antidisestablishmentarianism — one of the longest English words — is a 19th-century political movement opposed to the disestablishment of the Church of England. The Duke Ellington song *You're Just an Old Antidisestablishmentarianismist* goes one better. Here's how this word is built:

Establish
dis-establish   to reverse the action of establishing
disestablish-**ment**   result of disestablishing
disestablishment-**arian**   supporter of disestablishment
disestablishmentarian-**ism**   practice of disestablishmentarians
anti-disestablishmentarianism   opposition to disestablishmentarianism
*antidisestablishmentarianism-**ist***   someone who opposes disestablishmentarianism

Table 5-2			**Compound Formation in English**			
X + V → V				**X + N → N**		
X	Y = Verb	Compound = Verb	X	Y = Noun	Compound = Noun
Noun	spoon	feed	to spoon-feed	Noun	foot	ball	a football
Verb	stir	fry	to stirfry	Verb	rattle	snake	a rattle-snake
Adjec-tive	dry	clean	to dry-clean	Adjec-tive	blue	bird	a bluebird
Prepo-sition	over	look	to over-look	Prepo-sition	under	dog	an under-dog

Morphologists call headed compounds *endocentric compounds.* Headed compounds pass the "is a" test: "[X Y] is a kind of Y." For example, *spoonfeeding* is a kind of *feeding*, a *football* is a kind of *ball*, to *overlook* is a kind of *looking*. But some compounds don't have a head, and so don't pass the "is a" test. For example, *paleface* isn't a kind of face, but refers to a person with white skin. Similarly, *skinhead* isn't a kind of head, but refers to someone who has shaved their head. Compounds that lack a head are called *exocentric compounds.*

Squeezing in between

Infixes are common in languages like Tagalog, where, for example, the affix *-um-* is inserted inside the word: from *píilit* 'effort', the addition of the infix *-um-* forms *p-úm-iilit* 'one who is compelled', English does have a few infixes. These include Homer Simpson's *-ma-* infix (Cana-**ma**-da) and the *-IZ-* infix of rap and hip-hop music (sy-**IZ**-rup). In terms of their meanings, Homeric *-ma-* indicates an ironic attitude, while *-IZ-* is a mark of "insider" identity in hip-hop and rap. Where you put an infix depends on syllable count and word stress. For this reason, linguists who want to understand the connection between morphology and phonology find infixes super-cool.

With Homeric *-ma-* infixation, named after Homer Simpson, *-ma-* is sandwiched between the first metrical grouping of syllables (linguists call this a *foot*) and a following syllable. In the following examples, syllables are marked off with a period (.), and the foot is marked with parentheses. With two-syllable words, an extra syllable is added:

(*'live.ly*)	(*'li.va*)-**ma**-(*ly*)
(*'mu.sic*)	(*'mu.sa*)-**ma**-(*sic*)
(*'Ca.na*)(*da*)	(*'Ca.na*)-**ma**-(*da*)
(*'sa.xo*)(*phone*)	(*'sa.xo*)-**ma**-(*phone*)
(*'te.ri*)(*to.ry*)	(*'te.ri*)-**ma**-(*to.ry*)
(*a.la*)(*'ba.ma*)	(*a.la*)-**ma**-(*'ba.ma*)
(*hi.ppo*)(*'po.ta*)(*mus*)	(*hi.ppo*)-**ma**-(*'po.ta*)(*mus*)

Hip-hop *-IZ-* infixation is used in rap and hip-hop music. With one-syllable words, *-IZ-* is inserted after the first consonant or consonants of the syllable (if there are any), but before the syllable nucleus.

at	*IZ-at*	/'ɪ.zæt/
work	*w-IZ-ork*	/'wɪ.zork/
dream	*dr-IZ-eam*	/'drɪ.zim/

With two-syllable words, *-IZ-* is inserted before the stressed vowel, and stress is put on the second-to-last syllable. (*-IZ-* infixation with words that have more than two syllables is rare.)

'sol.diers	*s-IZ-oldiers*	/sɪ.'zol.dʒərs/
ex.'change	*ex.ch-IZ-ange*	/eks.'tʃɪ.zendʒ]

A tale of two vocabulary sets

English has two vocabulary sets, and each has different morphological and phonological rules. (Flip to Chapter 4 for more on phonological rules.) How did this happen? Well, it goes back to the Norman conquest of England in 1066. At that time, the people living in England were Germanic-speaking Anglo-Saxons. The Norman kings introduced French words into spoken English (for example, *manual*) — linguists call these French imports the *Latinate lexicon*. By some estimates, over 60 percent of the vocabulary of modern-day English is from the Latinate lexicon. But English also retained its original Anglo-Saxon vocabulary, and to this day, the most frequent words (for example, *hand*) are from the Anglo-Saxon lexicon. While the Anglo-Saxon vocabulary is used more in spoken English, the Latinate vocabulary — also called the learned vocabulary — is used more in written English. Another language with two vocabulary sets is Japanese: One lexicon is native Yamato-Japanese, and the other is Sino-Japanese, with words borrowed from Chinese.

English expletive infixation: @$#%!

English can use an *expletive* — a profane or taboo word — as an infix. You probably do this in the company of friends (but likely not when your mom's around). In North American English, the most common expletive infix is the infamous f-word (as in *abso-@$#%-ing-lutely*). The British English counterpart is *bloody* (as in *abso-**bloody**-lutely*). Expletive infixes mark surprise and are put before the syllable with primary stress. They can occur inside words, as in *al-X-mighty*, *disa-X-greeable*, *fan-X-tastic*, and *propa-X-ganda*. (Replace X with your favorite expletive: Go ahead, try it!) Expletive infixes also occur inside phrases: *the @$#%ing boss, all X over, all to X pieces, I beg your X pardon, brand X new, too X excited.* Because expletives occur inside words and phrases, some linguists classify them as *par-entheticals*, rather than infixes. (For discussion of what counts as a phrase, see Chapter 6.) But many linguists use the term *expletive infixation.*

English infixes indicate the speaker's attitude — linguists call them *evaluative affixes.* So how do evaluative affixes relate to inflectional and derivational affixes? Well, they're in a grey zone. Strictly speaking, an evaluative affix doesn't change the meaning of the word it attaches to, so it's not a deriva-tional affix. But it does add a nuance of meaning by providing information about the speaker's state of mind. Like inflectional affixes, evaluative affixes don't change the category of the word they attach to. But while inflectional affixes express a grammatical category (like tense or gender), evaluative affixes don't add grammatical features. And when they're suffixes, evaluative morphemes attach after derivational morphemes, but before inflectional ones.

Classifying Morphemes by Pronunciation

Morphology meets up with phonology in an area of study called *morpho-phonology.* Sometimes, one morpheme can have two or more phonological forms — in other words, the same morpheme can be pronounced in different ways but still have the same meaning. These different forms are called *allomorphs.*

The English past tense morpheme (the *-ed* suffix in *walked*) has several allo-morphs. It is pronounced [əd] after the alveolar stops [t, d]; [t] after voice-less stops like [p]; and [d] everywhere else. If you say the verbs in Table 5-3 by themselves and then in the past tense, you'll hear the difference between the three allomorphs.

Table 5-3		English Past Tense Allomorphs		
Verb Root		*Past Tense Verb*		*Morphology*
bat	[bæt]	batted	[bæ.təd]	[bæt -əd]
add	[æd]	added	[æ.dəd]	[æd -əd]
map	[mæp]	mapped	[mæpt]	[mæp -t]
mob	[mɑb]	mobbed	[mɑbd]	[mɑb -d]
sew	[so]	sewed	[sod]	[so -d]

The English plural morpheme (the *-s* suffix in *cats*) is pronounced [əz] after sibilants (sounds like [s]); [s] after all voiceless stops; and [z] everywhere else. If you say the nouns in Table 5-4 by themselves and then in the plural form, you'll hear the difference between the three allomorphs.

Table 5-4		English Plural Allomorphs		
Noun Root		*Plural Nouns*		*Morphology*
bus	[bʌs]	buses	[bʌ.səz]	[bʌs -əz]
match	[mætʃ]	matches	[mæ.tʃəz]	[mætʃ -əz]
mop	[mɑp]	mops	[mɑps]	[mɑp -s]
mob	[mɑb]	mobs	[mɑbz]	[mɑb -z]
toe	[to]	toes	[toz]	[to -z]

Just as affixes can have allomorphs, so too can words. For example, many English words change their form by changing the vowel. Linguists call this *vowel ablaut*. English vowel ablaut marks past tense on verbs and plural on nouns:

- **English past tense formed by vowel ablaut:** *ride/rode, freeze/froze, speak/spoke, steal/stole, sing/sang*

- **English plurals formed by vowel ablaut:** foot/feet, goose/geese, louse/lice, man/men, mouse/mice, tooth/teeth

If an affix has different allomorphs, this is *affixal allomorphy* — this is what happens with English past tense ([-əd], [-d], [-t]) and plural ([-əz], [-z], [-s]). If a word has different allomorphs, this is *stem allomorphy* — this is found with the alternation between *index* and *indic-es*.

Navigating the Morphology Maze

You can venture into any language and drill down to find morphemes. To show you how to do this, we use examples from Biblical Hebrew, but we could select any language. Follow us into the morphology maze. After you come out the other side, you'll be able to pick apart words in any language.

Contrasting form and meaning

The first step to picking out morphemes is to look at related forms that express different meanings. Linguists do this by using the criteria of *phonological relatedness* — two forms are related if they contain the same or similar sequence of sounds. With this in mind, look at the following forms from Biblical Hebrew:

> *zəkartíihuu* 'I remembered him'
>
> *zəkartíihaa* 'I remembered her'
>
> *zəkartíikaa* 'I remembered you (singular masculine)'

Now let's go to town with the compare-and-contrast method.

1. **Select related forms for comparison.**

   zəkartíihuu, zəkartíihaa, zəkartíikaa

2. **Identify the parts and their meaning.**

   zəkartii 'I remembered', *-huu* 'him', *-haa* 'her', *-kaa* 'you (singular masculine object)'

3. **Divide the forms into parts.**

   zəkartíi-huu, zəkartíi-haa, zəkartíi-kaa

Biblical Hebrew is the archaic form of Hebrew used in the Bible. In the examples, ə is the vowel of *the*, *i* is the vowel of *read*, *u* is the vowel of *boot*, and ʃ is the first consonant sound of *ship*. A doubled vowel *(uu, aa)* indicates a long vowel, an acute accent (ˊ) indicates stress, the dot below ṭ indicates an ejective, and *q* is a uvular stop. See Chapter 1 for details about phonetic symbols.

Getting to the stem

Now expand your data set to include the following examples and apply the compare-and-contrast method.

zəkarnúuhuu 'we remembered him'

zəkarnúuhaa 'we remembered her'

zəkarnúukaa 'we remembered you (singular masculine object)'

zəkartáanii 'you (singular subject) remembered me'

qəṭaltíihuu 'I killed him'

qəṭalnúuhuu 'we killed him'

ʃəmartáahaa 'you (singular subject) guarded her'

1. **Select related forms for comparison.**

   z**əkar**núuhuu, z**əkar**núuhaa, z**əkar**núukaa, z**əkar**táanii

   q**əṭal**tíihuu, q**əṭal**núuhuu

   ʃəmar**táa**haa, zəkar**táa**nii

   ʃəmartáa**haa**, zəkarnúu**haa**

2. **Identify the parts and their meaning.**

   From before, you know -huu 'him', -haa 'her', and -kaa 'you, singular masculine object'. Now you can add the following to your list:

   zəkar, 'remembered', qəṭal 'killed', ʃəmar 'guarded', -tii 'I', -nuu 'we', -taa 'you, singular subject'

3. **Divide the forms into parts.**

   zəkar-núu-huu, zəkar-núu-haa, zəkar-núu-kaa, zəkar-táa-nii

   qəṭal-tíi-huu, qəṭal-núu-huu

   ʃəmar-táa-haa

You're now getting a fuller picture of the pronoun suffixes:

		Singular		*Plural*	
Subject	1st person	-tii	'I'	-nuu	'we'
	2nd person	-taa	'you'		
Object	1st person	-nii	'me'		
	2nd person, masculine	-kaa	'you'		
	3rd person, masculine	-huu	'him'		
	3rd person, feminine	-haa	'her'		

The verbal forms you've identified are zəkar 'remembered', qəṭal 'killed', and ʃəmar 'guarded'. If you pay attention to the meaning of the morphemes, you'll notice a pattern. The verb morpheme is first. Then comes the subject suffix — this is the person doing the action. Last is the object suffix — this is the person to whom the action is being done. So the general pattern is [verb-subject-object]. With this, you can now build words that express meanings you haven't seen before, such as 'I remembered you', 'You killed him', 'We guarded her'.

1. **Find the morphemes for the verbs.**

   'remembered' *zəkar*

   'killed' *qəṭal*

   'guarded' *ʃəmar*

2. **Add the subject and object suffixes using the [verb-subject-object] pattern.**

   'I remembered you (singular, masculine)' *zəkar-tíi-kaa*

   'You killed him' *qəṭal-táa-huu*

   'We guarded her' *ʃəmar-núu-haa*

This is the cool thing about morphology: After you figure out the patterns, you can make new words!

Finding invisible meanings

This next example puts a monkey wrench in the [verb-subject-object] pattern:

   zəkaaróo 'he remembered him'

You can be confident that *zəkaar* means 'remembered'. But what about what's left over, the *-oo?* If you only have this example, you can't tell what's going on. The mystery gets cleared up if you look at verbs that have only a subject, like the following:

   zaakártii 'I remembered'

   zaakárnuu 'we remembered'

   zaakár 'he remembered'

Applying the compare-and-contrast method gives you the following results:

1. **Select related forms for comparison.**

   zaakár**tii*, ***zaakár**nuu*, ***zaakár

2. **Identify the parts and their meaning.**

   zaakar 'remembered', *-tii* 'I', *-nuu* 'we'

3. **Divide the forms into parts.**

   zaakár-tii, zaakár-nuu, zaakár

This confirms what you already know: *-tii* is 'I', and *-nuu* is 'we'. It also adds two other forms for 'remembered': *zəkaar* and *zaakar*. And it reveals what marks the Hebrew form for 'he': nothing! Linguists call this a *null morpheme*, and they use the null sign (∅) to indicate its presence. You can now solve the puzzle of *zəkaaróo* 'he remembered him'. The pattern for verbs with a subject and an object is [verb-subject-object]. If you put this together with the fact that 'he' is a null morpheme, then you get the following morpheme breakdown: *zəkaar-Ø-óo*. So this means that *-óo* stands for 'him'. Notice that you now have two forms (allomorphs) for 'him': *-óo* and *-huu*.

The alternation between the two forms for 'him' in Biblical Hebrew is determined by the placement of stress (marked with an acute accent). A third person singular object is pronounced *-óo* if it bears stress and as *-huu* if it doesn't.

Digging out the root

Your morphological analysis has identified three verb forms: *zəkar* 'remembered', *qəṭal* 'killed', and *ʃəmar* 'guarded'. Now take a closer look at the arrangement of the vowels:

1. **Select related forms for comparison.**

   zəkar, qəṭal, ʃəmar

2. **Identify the parts and their meaning.**

   ...-ə...-a-... 'past'

   z-...-k-...-r 'remember'

   q-...-ṭ-...-l 'kill'

   ə...-m-...-r 'guard'

3. **Divide the forms into parts.**

   z-ə-k-a-r, q-əṭ-a-l, ʃ-ə-m-a-r

The compare-and-contrast method leads to a surprising conclusion: Hebrew verb stems subdivide into sequences of consonants and vowels. But the consonants are not next to each other and neither are the vowels! You might think that we've taken a wrong turn. But take a look at the following nouns and apply the compare-and-contrast method:

   zookéer 'one who remembers'

   qooṭéel 'killer'

   ʃooméer 'watchman'

1. **Select related forms for comparison.**

    zookéer, qootéel, ʃooméer

2. **Identify the parts and their meaning**.

    …-oo-…-ée-… 'someone who does an action'

    z-…-k-…-r 'remember'

    q-…-ṭ-…-l 'kill'

    ʃ-…-m-…-r 'guard'

3. **Divide the forms into parts.**

    z-oo-k-ée-r, q-oo-ṭ-ée-l, ʃoo-m-ée-r

This confirms that consonants and vowels function as separate units of meaning in Biblical Hebrew. The pattern that you've uncovered is an example of *non-concatenative morphology*, where words are formed by imposing a vowel pattern on a root that is, by itself, unpronounceable.

Tallying up the morpheme inventory

Updating the morpheme inventory, you can see that you're dealing with roots, an inflectional morpheme (past tense), a noun-forming derivational morpheme, and pronouns.

The roots, past tense, and noun-forming element are non-concatenative morphemes:

✔ **Root consonantal pattern:**

   z-k-r 'remember', *q-ṭ-l* 'kill', *ʃm-r* 'guard'

✔ **Inflectional vowel pattern:**

   -ə-a- 'past'

✔ **Derivational vowel pattern:**

   -oo-ée- 'someone who does an action'

The pronouns are concatenative morphemes, as the following table shows.

		Singular		*Plural*	
Subject	1st person	*-tii*	'I'	*-nuu*	'we'
	2nd person	*-taa*	'you'		
	3rd person, masculine	*-Ø*	'he'		
	3rd person, feminine	*-at*	'she'	*-uu*	'they'
Object	1st person	*-nii*	'me'		
	2nd person	*-kaa*	'you'		
	3rd person, masculine	*-huu, -oo*	'him'		
	3rd person, feminine	*-haa*	'her'		

Words matter to everyone

Words are a basic unit of organization, so the study of words connects to many research areas:

✔ **Search engine designers:** Google, one of the most successful search engines ever designed, uses morphology to extract information from text. When expanding to other languages, Google hit a wall with languages that have complicated words, like Finnish or Japanese. So they turned to morphologists to help them find a solution. Using a technique called *morphological stripping* (get your mind out of the gutter!), morphologists provide a morpheme breakdown of long words, which allows them to find the root of a word. After that's done — and it's no simple matter — the search engine takes over and tracks the occurrence of the root across various texts.

✔ **Advertisers:** Advertising language — be it for shampoo, pharmaceuticals, or sports shoes — uses words that pack a punch. For example, the soft drink *7-up* and the car *Renault* were marketed as the *Uncola* and the *Uncar*. These words stick in your mind because *un-* doesn't usually attach to nouns. Normally, *un-* attaches to adjectives (**un**happy) or verbs (**un**do).

✔ **Speech language pathologists and audiologists:** Speech impediments often involve difficulties in retrieving a word, pronouncing it, hearing it, or understanding it. Because word-level knowledge is a bottleneck for the rest of grammar, speech language pathologists and audiologists need to know a lot about morphology to develop effective interventions.

Chapter 6

Creating Sentences: Syntax

• •

In This Chapter

▶ Generalizing sentence structure

▶ Discovering grammatical categories

▶ Moving beyond templates

▶ Generating new sentences

▶ Working with phrases

• •

*Y*ou can string together your vocabulary — about 60,000 words — to create not thousands, not millions, but *billions* of sentences, at potentially infinite levels of complexity. Cool. But how do you know *how* to put words together like this? Take a simple example. How is it that you know that the subject noun precedes the verb in most sentences *(Alice left),* and you also know that this generalization doesn't hold in commands *(Leave, Alice!)?*

You know how to build sentences because you've subconsciously learned a powerful set of rules and patterns for combining words. Linguists call this set of rules and patterns *syntax.* People who study syntax, *syntacticians,* try to figure out exactly what these rules and patterns for sentence-creation are.

We show you how syntacticians study the human creative power to produce sentences. We give you a glimpse of how words divide into word classes called "grammatical categories" and how these categories allow you to make generalizations about sentence patterns. Then we show you an even more powerful kind of sentence-building that fully captures your enormous and, in principle, infinite capacity for creating sentences.

Unlocking Sentence Structure: The Secret of Syntactic Generalization

Syntactic analysis involves more than just listing the sentences of a language. Syntacticians aim to understand the *types* of sentences that are possible in each language in order to make generalizations about how words combine to form sentences. So how do you state generalizations about word order? The first, and in some ways still the most important, step in answering this question was discovered in ancient India by a man named Yāska. His insight that words group into classes, called *grammatical categories,* has been passed down, with additions, through Greek grammarians. You're familiar with them from grade school as *noun, verb,* and *adjective.* What may surprise you is how important these grammatical categories are for doing syntax and why.

Listing has its limits: Why generalization is necessary

It's helpful, in understanding what syntacticians do, to consider why they *can't* do syntax without abstract generalizations. Why not just look at which word combinations occur and make a list of them? After all, in principle, all the *words* in a language can be listed: The Oxford English Dictionary comes close to this. So why don't linguists make a similar *dictionary of sentences* and have that as their account of syntax? Linguists don't list sentences for at least three good reasons:

✔ **There are just too many sentences to list.** The 20-volume Oxford English Dictionary, the work of generations of scholars, holds about 250,000 words. But a full listing of the well-formed *sentences* of English (or any language), even those within the capacity of one ordinary person, easily runs into the *billions.* And for the full language, the list would be *infinite.*

✔ **Speakers know more than lists.** Syntacticians try to account for the unconscious knowledge of sentence-formation of speakers like you. If you learned sentence patterns by memorizing a list of sentences, then you'd have to *hear* each sentence before you could *say* it. But that's not what happens: You produce and understand a great many new sentences that you've never heard before. That shows you're not memorizing a list, so no list can represent what you know as a speaker.

✔ **Syntax follows patterns.** The way words are organized into sentences isn't random. If you look at the sets of words {*Lucy, Sue, Mary*} and {*walked, smiled, ran*}, you'll find that the words in the first set (the names) always come before the words in the second set (the verbs). There's a pattern here, a generalization. But how do linguists capture and explain this general pattern? Listing sentences reveals the general patterns, but it doesn't explain them.

What syntacticians need are tools that capture generalizations that overcome the limitations of listing. Their goal is to describe huge numbers of sentences in a few simple statements in a way that captures the patterns of word combinations that appear in sentences.

Teachers are from Venus, linguists are from Mars

It may surprise you that syntacticians consider sentences from non-standard dialects, like the two sentences below, to be *well-formed* and *grammatical*:

> *Alice seen Mary in the park.* (Grammatical, to a syntactician)

> *Man, I just ain't got no money!* (Grammatical, to a syntactician)

To a syntactician, *well-formed* or *grammatical* means that the sentence follows the patterns and rules for sentence-building of a particular variety of English. So long as the sentences are something native speakers say, whether they speak a standard or a non-standard variety, linguists will say, "Well, that's a grammatical sentence in the syntax of that dialect." In other words: If people say it, syntacticians don't judge it as wrong.

The only sentences that a syntactician calls *ill-formed* or *ungrammatical* are ones like the following, which *no* native speaker regardless of dialect says (* indicates ungrammaticality):

> * *Saw Alice park Mary in the.* (Ungrammatical, even to a syntactician)

> * *No money man just haven't I got.* (Ungrammatical, even to a syntactician)

When you first start studying syntax, the way syntacticians use the terms *grammatical* and *ungrammatical* is confusing. That's because you're probably used to teachers telling you that sentences like the first pair, though used by many speakers, are bad, ungrammatical, or ill-formed. This is because your teachers have a different goal from syntacticians: Your teachers want you to learn to use a certain standard dialect of English, and they're teaching you to avoid non-standard dialects. Your teachers have a *prescriptive* approach, whereas syntacticians, who want to describe and understand all dialects, have a *descriptive* approach.

Categorizing leads to generalized templates: Yāska's insight

Yāska, a Sanskrit scholar who lived in India around 500 BCE, was one of the first people to understand what was needed to make syntactic generalizations. His insight was to recognize that words divide into groups — word classes — or what we call today *grammatical categories*.

For example, Yāska recognized that there was a distinction between the following two grammatical categories, given with English examples:

✔ **Category A:** Yāska called these *nāma;* we call them *nouns.*

{*Alice, Bill, Doug, Eduardo, Fred, Janice, Juan, Lothario, Pim, Sue*}

✔ **Category B:** He called these *ākhyāta;* we call them *verbs.*

{*cried, fled, giggled, hid, ran, sighed, smiled, snickered, called, walked*}

Grammatical categories make it possible to state generalizations about word order. For example, *Category A* comes before *Category B* or, using the modern terms, [Noun Verb]. This generalization describes a large number of sentences. So if each of the ten words from Category A combines with one word from Category B, say *walked,* this gives the ten following sentences:

{*Alice walked, Bill walked, Doug walked, Eduardo walked, Fred walked, Janice walked, Juan walked, Lothario walked, Pim walked, Sue walked*}

Continuing in this, way, we'd get 90 more sentences just with this small vocabulary!

Adding just one verb to this list adds another ten sentences. If you know 1,000 verbs and 1,000 nouns, you could make, using the [Noun Verb] template, 1,000,000 two-word sentences (that's 1,000 x 1,000!). Add more categories, more templates, and more vocabulary, and you see how a few simple generalizations can describe a huge number of sentences. Crucially, these templates depend on categories as tools to make general statements. And that's how Yāska's insight makes syntactic generalizations possible.

Later scholars — especially the grammarian Dionysius and the philosophers Plato and Aristotle — introduced the eight grammatical categories: *noun, verb, participle, interjection, pronoun, preposition, adverb* and *conjunction.* Modern syntax recognizes a slightly different set of categories and a much richer way of stating generalizations about them. But it all begins with the recognition that categories are a key part of every language's organization.

Grammatical categories are also called *word classes* and *parts of speech.*

Putting words together to make a large number of meanings — precisely what grammatical categories and generalizations based on them accomplish — is a distinguishing feature of human language. Check out Chapter 2 for more on this property called *duality of patterning.*

Discovering the Atoms of Syntax

Without grammatical categories there can be no syntax. But how do linguists *discover* what the grammatical categories of a language are, and which words belong to which category? Though it's clear that words *do* divide into different categories for the purposes of sentence-building, English words don't come stamped with their grammatical category: There's no name-tag on the word *man* that says, "Hi, I'm in the category *noun!*"

Testing for categories

You can find all sorts of ways to classify words in a language — you could categorize words for blue things or words for tall things. But for the purpose of sentence-building, only a small number of distinctions are relevant. Children learning, and linguists describing, language use a combination of three criteria to recognize grammatical categories within a language: morphology, distribution, and meaning.

Testing for grammatical category with morphology (affixation)

Some *affixes* (units of meaning that attach to a word) can attach to certain types of words, but not to others. For example, words like *walk* or *smile* occur with a past-tense suffix *(walked, smiled),* but words like *and* or *Fred* don't (you can't say **anded,* or **Fredded*). By this criteria, linguists conclude that *walk* and *smile* belong to the same grammatical category and that *and* and *Fred* aren't in this category.

An *affix* is a unit of meaning that can't stand by itself — like *-ed* that marks past tense in English. Affixes that attach to the end of the word are called *suffixes.* See Chapter 5 for info on different kinds of affixes.

Probing for grammatical category using position (distribution)

You can recognize grammatical categories based on where words fit into a sentence — this is the *syntactic context* of the word. For example, only a small set of words (including *a* and *the*) can precede a noun at the start of a sentence (filling the blank in sequences like __ *man left*). So words like *a* and *the* belong to the same grammatical category. Linguists call this a *distributional test* because it's based on where different types of words are distributed in positions throughout the sentence.

Using meaning as a test of grammatical category

It's possible to find criteria based on *meaning* that group words into grammatical categories. For example, *Bill* and *Mary* are both names directly referring to individuals in the world, and these words are always part of one grammatical category (nouns) in English and many languages. Some caution is required with meaning-based criteria for categories because often the definition of a category doesn't capture all the words that actually go in the category, but combined with other tests, this test can be part of recognizing a grammatical category.

Evidence that linguists work with

To show that certain word orders are possible (or impossible) in a language, syntacticians look for particular types of sentences. Syntacticians work with two kinds of evidence:

✔ **Positive evidence:** If a linguist finds a sentence in a newspaper or hears someone say a sentence in conversation, linguists say that there's *positive evidence* that this type of sentence is possible (grammatical) in the language. Large collections *(corpora)* of natural speech and writing are available on the Internet now, and many linguists search these collections to look for positive evidence about sentence structure.

✔ **Negative evidence:** Some linguists look for linguistic data by making up their own example sentences and asking native speakers whether it sounds like a possible or impossible sentence in their language. This is called eliciting *speaker judgments.* If the speaker answers, "Oh, that's not how anyone could say it in our language," then the evidence is called *negative evidence.*

Most syntacticians consider both positive *and* negative evidence as important data and are as likely to ask a speaker for their judgments as to search a corpus.

Identifying nouns

In English, the grammatical category of *noun* can be identified with morphological, distributional, and meaning-based criteria.

Morphological criteria to test for nouns

The English plural ending *-s* divides words into two groups: nouns and non-nouns.

✔ **Nouns can occur with the plural suffix *-s:*** *angel/angels, cola/colas, action/actions, strength/strengths, other/others.*

✔ **Non-nouns can't occur with the plural suffix *-s:*** *terribly/*terriblies, that/*thats, some/*somes, the/*thes, tall/*talls.* (We use * to mark the impossible forms.)

The plural test works best with *common nouns.* Proper nouns, such as *Bill* or *London* don't usually have plural forms because they're used as unique names for one individual. But in certain uses proper nouns can take the plural. For example: *I know several Bills* or *There are two Londons: one in England and one in Ontario, Canada.*

English has two *-s* suffixes. One marks plural on nouns: *angel**s**.* The other is found on *verbs* and marks agreement with a third person singular subject, as in *He shoot**s**! He score**s**!* Only nouns take plural *-s;* only verbs take third person subject agreement *-s.* Watch out for this distinction by looking at what *-s* means. To see how *-s* fits into English morphology, see Chapter 5.

Distributional evidence for nouns

Let's suppose you have independent evidence for the grammatical categories of *verb* and *determiner:* You know that the verb category includes words like *is* and the determiner category includes words like *a* or *the*. This is very helpful because it turns out that only nouns *fit* between a determiner and a verb to form a sentence. For example:

> ✔ **Nouns can fit between a determiner and a verb in the frame**
>
> > [The _____ is great] { *angel, cola, action, strength, other* }
>
> ✔ **Non-nouns can't fit between a determiner and a verb in the frame**
>
> > [The _____ is great] { *terribly, *that, *some, *the, *tall* }

The words that fit in the first bullet take the plural ending; the words that *don't* fit don't take the plural ending. So, if you know which words are determiners and verbs, you can construct frames to identify the words that fit between them.

If the frame [*The ___ is great*] creates a sentence with a wacky meaning, like *The strength is great,* just switch to other words. So long as a determiner comes before it and a verb after it, the tested word must be a noun. So you can show that *strength* is a noun from *His strength is inspiring,* if you independently know that *his* is a determiner and *is* is a verb.

The frame [determiner ___ verb] only identifies *common nouns*, a sub-category within the broader grammatical category of nouns. It doesn't work with proper names, such as *Alice* or *London*. That's because English proper names don't allow determiners before them. But linguists can use other distributional tests to show that proper names are nouns.

Adjectives can fit between the determiner and the noun. The frame [The first _____ is great] only allows nouns. This doesn't interfere with the noun test, but you may notice adjectives popping up when you test for nouns.

Meaning-based criteria for nouns

Though the plural and distributional tests work well for identifying the noun class, you may be more familiar with a meaning-based definition, probably from grade-school: A noun is a *person, place, or thing*. This definition is partly right, but it's not general enough to describe the entire category. It's partly right because it's true that words for people, places, and things do pattern (according to the other tests) as nouns. Children may well use this fact as a guide in learning the syntax of their language as they try to find the grammatical category for new words.

However, many words that pattern as nouns according to morphological and distributional criteria don't refer to a person, place, or thing. For example, the following words are all nouns, but none of them are persons, places, or things: *depth, gender, defeat, frailty, continuation, irony, party,* and *golfing.* The moral of the story is that meaning-based criteria for identifying nouns must be used with caution.

Sub-categories of nouns

Each grammatical category also has *sub-categories.* Sub-categories of nouns include the following:

- ✔ *Common nouns* occur with determiners before them, or they have a plural form, for example *the dog/the dogs, the cat/the cats.*

- ✔ *Proper nouns* don't normally occur with determiners before them in English (**the Janice*) or have a plural form (**the Bills*).

- ✔ *Pronouns* don't occur with determiners in English, but do have plural forms: first person (singular *I;* plural *we*), second person (singular *you;* in some dialects plural *y'all*), and third person (singular *he/she/it;* plural *they*).

Each type of noun has a different distribution, mostly because of differences with respect to determiners. But all nouns can be the subject noun preceding the verb.

Recognizing verbs

You can easily spot the grammatical category *verb* through a simple morphological test, along with distributional criteria. However, meaning-based criteria don't work well for verbs.

Morphological criteria for verbs

English past tense is an affix that divides words into two groups: certain words, verbs, can occur with past tense forms, but other words can't. This is a distinguishing property of the grammatical category of verbs:

- ✔ **Verbs can occur with the past tense suffix** *-ed: demonstrate/demonstrated; deliver/delivered; sigh/sighed; laugh/laughed*

- ✔ **Non-verbs can't occur with the past tense suffix** *-ed: terribly/*terriblied; that/*thated; some/*somed; the/*thed; tall/*talled*

Distributional evidence for verb

If you have evidence for the grammatical category *noun,* you can find positional patterns that identify verbs. In English, only verbs come after a noun to form a sentence. (Here we use the pronoun *You* as the noun.)

✔ **Verbs can form a sentence with a preceding noun in the frame**

[You _____] { *demonstrate/demonstrated, deliver/delivered, sigh/sighed, laugh/laughed* }

✔ **Non-verbs can't form a sentence with a preceding noun in the frame**

[You _____] { **terribly, *that, *some, *the, *tall* }

If you use a third person pronoun *(she* or *he)* preceding the verb in these frames, the verb takes the third person subject ending *-s,* but only in the present tense *(She demonstrates, He delivers).* In English, the ability to take third person agreement is another morphological characteristic of verbs.

Meaning-based evidence for verbs: Use with extreme caution

Using meaning-based criteria to identify the grammatical category verb can lead you in the wrong direction. You're probably familiar with definitions of a verb as an *action word.* While it's true that many words for actions are verbs, the action-word definition has two serious problems:

✔ Many words that describe actions or events are nouns according to morphological and distributional criteria. For example, *action, activity, leaving, smiling, kissing, party,* and *explosion* are all nouns.

✔ Some words, which pattern as verbs by the morphological and distributional criteria, don't describe actions or events. For example, *to despise, to fear, to love,* and *to loathe* are all states of being.

For these reasons, morphological and distributional tests are more reliable ways to recognize verbs.

Subcategories of verbs

Linguists categorize three kinds of verbs according to the number of nouns the verb occurs with:

✔ **Ditransitive verbs:** Some verbs require two nouns after them. *Give* is an example of a ditransitive verb in English: **Alice gave, *Alice gave Mary, *Alice gave the book, Alice gave Mary the book.*

✔ **Transitive verbs:** Some verbs strictly require one noun after them. Examples of strictly transitive verbs are rare in English but include verbs like *admire (*Alice admires, Alice admires courage)* and *despise (*Alice despises, Alice despises broccoli).* Some verbs are optionally transitive: They can but don't need to be followed by a noun. For example, *Alice ate* and *Alice ate supper.*

✔ **Intransitive verbs:** Many verbs don't require anything after them — linguists call these *intransitives*. Intransitive verbs can't be followed by another word or phrase. *Smile* is an intransitive verb (*Alice smiled,* **Alice smiled Lucy*) as is *laugh* (*Alice laughed,* **Alice laughed Lucy.*)

The distinction between ditransitive, transitive, and intransitive verbs isn't very important for describing syntax in English. That's why linguists simply talk about the category of *verb*. But these subcategories are important in describing syntactic patterns in other languages.

Linguists say things like "This verb subcategorizes for a noun." This means that the verb requires a noun after it. This use of *subcategorizes* comes from the notion that transitive verbs are a subcategory within the larger verb class.

Finding other grammatical categories

Linguists group grammatical categories into two broad classes: lexical categories and functional categories. Each group of categories has characteristic morphological, distributional, and meaning-based properties. Here we focus on their distributional and meaning-based properties.

Categories in other languages

Distributional tests identify categories in all languages, but they don't always work the same way.

✔ **Some languages have *name-tags* on their words.** In Yorùbá, spoken in West Africa, it's easy to tell verbs and nouns apart. Verbs are a single syllable and consist of a consonant-vowel (CV) sequence. Nouns are two or more syllables, and most consist of a vowel-consonant-vowel sequence (VCV). So it's easy to identify verbs and nouns in this language: of obvious help to children and handy for linguists.

✔ **Some languages mark plurality on verbs.** Plural-marking doesn't work as a test for nouns in all languages. For example, in Squamish, a language spoken on the northwest coast of North America, both nouns and verbs can be pluralized. A pluralized noun indicates that several objects of the same kind are around. A pluralized verb indicates that several actions of the same kind are around.

✔ **Some languages mark tense on nouns.** Tense-marking doesn't work as a test for verbs in all languages, For example, in Halkomelem, just next door to Squamish, past tense is found on both verbs and nouns. Past tense on a verb indicates that the action occurred sometime in the past. What about past tense on a noun? That indicates that the noun no longer exists or that it's broken.

The other lexical categories: Adjectives and adverbs

Lexical categories are open-class categories: You can add new words to the category. The number of lexical categories in languages is limited — besides *nouns* and *verbs*, *adjectives* and *adverbs* are the only other two.

- **Adjectives:** In English, only adjectives occur in the frame

    [determiner ___ noun] as in [*the **happy** man*]

    Examples include *happy, sad, tall,* or *hungry. Adjectives* are modifiers that describe properties of the following noun.

- **Adverbs:** In English only adverbs occur in the frame

    [determiner noun verb ___] as in [*The man ran **quickly***]

    Examples include *quickly, happily, sadly,* and *well. Adverbs* modify the verb.

Adverbs often end in *-ly* in English, but this isn't always the case. There's also dialect variation in which words can be used as adverbs in English: some speakers say *The man ran good,* using *good* as an adverb as well as an adjective.

Functional categories

Functional categories are few in number but carry much of the weight of syntax. They include determiners, complementizers, and conjunctions. Linguists call these smaller, less variable categories *closed-class categories* because languages don't generally add (or lose) words in these categories.

- **Determiners:** Also called *articles,* these precede a noun (or an adjective-noun sequence), and fit into frames:

    [__ (Adjective) Noun] as in [***the** (tall) man*]

    Examples include *a, the,* and sometimes *this* and *that* (*this* and *that* also function as nouns). Determiners fix the reference of the noun (see Chapter 8 for discussion of how this works). Quantifiers like *each* and *every* are also part of the determiner class, and they have special semantic properties that are discussed in Chapter 7.

- **Complementizers:** These words that can occur before an embedded sentence, as in the frame *John will say _____ [Mary left].* Words that fit here include *if, whether,* and a version of *that* (*that* is also used as a noun and a determiner).

- **Conjunctions:** Also called *coordinators,* these include *and, or,* and *but.* Their syntactic distribution is special: They unite two words or phrases of the same category, as in:

    [Noun + Noun] John and Mary

    [Verb + Verb] walk and sing

    Conjunctions can also unite sentences (*John smiled and Mary laughed*) and other units within sentences.

Mr. In-Between: Prepositions

Prepositions have meaning-based properties that single them out as special: They name locations *(on, in, over, under, beside)* or paths *(to, from, through, around, up, down)*. For locative prepositions, a good test is to use a sentence frame like this:

[John kissed Mary ____ the bed]

Words like *in, on, at, over, under, beyond* fit in this frame, but not verbs, nouns, adjectives, or other grammatical categories. In terms of the distinction between open-class and closed-class categories, prepositions fall in the middle. Unlike verbs, nouns, adjectives, and adverbs — which number in the thousands — there are about 70 or so prepositions in English. But they form a much larger class than determiners and complementizers, which can be counted off on the fingers of your hand. Linguists continue to debate which side of the fence prepositions sit on: Are they lexical categories (likes verbs, nouns, adjectives, and adverbs) or are they functional categories (like determiners and complementizers)?

Prepositions can be transitive or intransitive. For example, **I looked at* can't be used as a full sentence in English because *at* is a transitive preposition: It requires a noun after it, as in *I looked at Alice.* Other transitive prepositions include *of* and *into.* Intransitive prepositions don't require anything after them. For example, you can say *I looked over* or *I looked over the bridge* — the object noun that gets looked over is optional. Other intransitive prepositions include *in* and *up.*

Holding Infinity in the Palm of Your Hand: Recursive Generative Rules

In 1957, the linguist Noam Chomsky found a new way to generalize the way grammatical categories combine — using the tool of *generative rules* — which was far more efficient in describing how people create sentences than the templates that linguists had been using before. Generative rules allow for *recursion,* a potentially infinite pattern of looping, where parts of sentences repeat. We show you how generative rules — and especially recursive generative rules — capture the power of syntax.

In describing sentence patterns, linguists use abbreviations. The abbreviations are pretty obvious: N = noun; V = verb; ADJ = adjective; ADV = adverb; P = preposition; DET = determiner; COMP = complementizer; S = sentence.

Pushing category templates to their limit

To understand the power of generative rules, it's helpful to push the limits of the template approach. Take a look at Table 6-1. Suppose you want to describe English syntax using only templates. You start off with the [N V] template in the first section of the table — this captures a large number of well-formed English sentences. But if we add determiners (which we have to because common nouns require them), then we need more templates, including (but not limited to) those in the second section. With a decent vocabulary, these templates can describe several million sentences. But what about adjectives? We need templates for them, too, including (but again not limited to) those in the third section of the table.

Table 6-1						**Templates Reveal Patterns**	
	Template						*Example*
1			N	V			*Alice sighed.*
2	DET		N	V			*The rabbit sighed.*
	DET		N	V	N		*The rabbit saw Alice.*
	DET		N	V	DET	N	*The girl saw the rabbit.*
3	DET	ADJ	N	V			*The white rabbit left.*
	DET	ADJ	N	V	N		*The white rabbit saw Alice.*
	DET		N	V	DET	ADJ	N	*The girl saw the white rabbit.*

You're now in a heap of trouble — as you try and work through the other lexical categories, you'll find the templates get longer, and longer, and more complicated. And — as a fatal blow to the template approach — consider what happens in patterns like those in Table 6-2, where sentences contain other sentences. Not only do sentences that contain other sentences get long and complex, it seems like we can always, if we want, make the sentence a little longer. Though you'd eventually run out of breath, nothing in the syntax stops you from adding another [N V] to continue the sentence! Patterns like these make templates look not just unwieldy, but impossible: Grammatical categories are great, but we need to do something besides just list them.

Table 6-2	Sentences Contain Other Sentences								
Pattern	**Template**								**Example**
S	N	V							Alice sighed.
[S [S]]	N	V	N	V					Lucy said Alice sighed.
[S [S [S]]]	N	V	N	V	N	V			Lucy thinks Alice said Mary smiled.
[S [S [S[S]]]]	N	V	N	V	N	V	N	V	Lucy thinks Alice said Mary thinks Ed left.

Repeated looping isn't uncommon in regular speech: If you're a fan of the TV show *Friends,* for example, you may recall Episode 5.17, which contains quite a long run: *They're trying to mess with us? They don't know that we know they know we know!*

You may find the infinitely looping pattern better with the complementizer *that* introducing each sentence, as in *Lucy said that Alice sighed.* The complementizer is allowed, but not required, in these sentences. In a templatic approach, the complementizer is simply added to the template: [N V COMP N V]. But the problem of infinitely long sentences is still there.

For a long time, nobody knew how to solve this problem. Linguists resigned themselves to jotting down only simple generalizations like "the noun precedes the verb in a two-word sentence." But nobody, even though grammatical categories were all known and recognized, was able to tackle anything like the full complexity of human syntax. Nobody, that is, until Noam Chomsky and his *recursive generative rules.*

Making mobiles: Recursive generative rules

To help you get the hang of building sentences with recursive generative rules, we're going to ask you, for a moment, to set aside language. Imagine that you work at a mobile factory, where you make mobiles to dangle over babies' cribs. (Bear with us: What you learn at the mobile factory will help you to understand the nuts and bolts of syntactic theory.)

Starting work at the mobile factory: Day 1

On your first day on the job, your boss takes you to your workstation, which has a desk, an instruction book, and three buckets. One bucket contains hooks in the shape of S. Another bucket contains N-shapes that you can hang from the hook with a bit of string. And the third bucket contains V-shapes that you can also hang from the hook.

The boss explains that every mobile has to start with a hook (S) and that the Ns and Vs have to hang in certain ways. You get a book of instructions that tells you how to make two kinds of mobiles:

S → N V

S → N V N

The first instruction tells you to make a mobile that looks like Figure 6-1a, and the second a mobile that looks like Figure 6-1b. You spend the rest of the day building one or the other shape. A nice lady with a cart comes by every now and then to refill your buckets of hooks, Ns, and Vs whenever you get low on them. Not a hard job!

Figure 6-1: Basic shapes made with generative rule instructions.

(a) 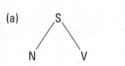 (b)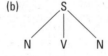

Getting promoted at the mobile factory: Day 2

Your second day the boss sees that you've figured out how to assemble simple mobiles. So he promotes you and brings over a bucket of shapes that look like Ds and a couple more instructions added to your list:

S → N V

S → N V N

S → D N V

S → D N V D N

Wow! Two more mobile shapes! You catch on quick, and soon you're switching easily between four different kinds of mobiles. But by the end of the day, you feel somehow . . . limited. You know you could do more, and working with just four shapes is stifling your creative potential.

Making infinite mobiles: Day 3

On your third day, seeing how fast you catch on, your boss promotes you again — a big promotion, this time. "I'm going to add just *one* more instruction to your rule-book," he tells you with a mysterious look. "It will give you the power to create an *infinite* variety of mobiles!" That sounds crazy. How could adding *one* rule add an infinite variety of mobiles? Curious and skeptical, you open up the new rule book. It's almost the same as before — just one extra rule has been added, down at the end:

$$S \rightarrow N\ V$$

$$S \rightarrow N\ V\ N$$

$$S \rightarrow D\ N\ V$$

$$S \rightarrow D\ N\ V\ D\ N$$

$$S \rightarrow N\ V\ S$$

At first, you're not sure how to use the new rule. It lets you hang a hook from another hook? Then you start to get it: You can use the S → N V S rule first to get a shape like that in Figure 6-2a and then expand on that with any of the other S rules, as in Figures 6-2b and 6-2c. Cool. That *does* add some variety! As you experiment further, you see that you can use the S → N V S rule once and then use that same instruction again, to hang off the embedded S, as in Figure 6-2d. And you can keep on applying the rule as many times as you want. The boss was right, that rule does create an endless variety of mobile shapes!

  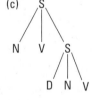 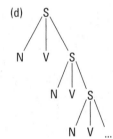

Figure 6-2:
Recursive
rule applica-
tion with S
rule.

Applying your mobile factory experience to sentences

The mobile factory rules are *generative rules*. They combine items together to generate shapes — or combine words together to generate sentences. If your rules are *recursive* (which means you can reapply them again and again to the same sentence), the resulting loop generates an infinite variety of combinations, all following a few simple patterns.

Your experience at the mobile factory has laid the groundwork for the infinite looping that we find in sentences like *I said (that) you said (that) she said (that) he said (that)*. . . . All you need to do is interpret the rulebook from the mobile factory as the symbols of syntax: S stands for *sentence*, N for *noun*, V for *verb*, and D for *determiner*. Take a look at Figure 6-3, which predicts both correct English word order and the potentially infinitely looping patterns we observe in English sentences.

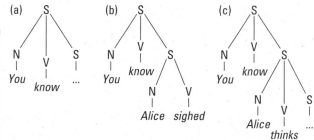

Figure 6-3:
Recursive
rule applica-
tion with S
rule, applied
to words.

Exactly how to formulate the full set of generative rules is a complex problem. In large part, modern syntactic theory is an attempt to solve this
problem. But even very basic generative rules like the ones given here demonstrate Chomsky's key insight into syntax: It boils down to the repeated
application of recursive generative rules. Templates, though they reveal the
pattern, have no way of making a generalization about recursion.

Linguists call the structures created by generative rule application *syntactic
trees* or *tree structures.*

The rule S → N V S, though it captures the infinite potential for looping sentences, does not in itself allow for the complementizer *that,* as in *You know
that Alice thinks that . . .* This can be handled by adding a rule of the form S →
N V COMP S.

Working with Bigger Chunks of Structure: From Words to Phrases

Generative rules produce intermediate branches within the syntactic tree.
As Figure 6-3 shows, when we use generative rules to make *You know Alice
sighed,* the sentence *Alice sighed* forms a separate branch within the tree
structure, labeled S. You may wonder: Does this kind of intermediate unit
ever play a role in syntax or is it just an accidental byproduct of the method
for describing word order? These intermediate levels of structure *do* indeed
play a role in syntactic description. In fact, syntacticians find it useful — in
terms of simplifying the system and capturing generalizations about word
order — to add even *more* units of structure, including branches that they
label NP (noun phrase), VP (verb phrase), and many others. Syntacticians
call these intermediate branchings *phrases.* We show you some of the power
that these phrasal units bring to syntactic description.

Assembling nouns into larger units: The noun phrase

Syntacticians working with nouns and their modifiers posit an NP unit, which combines DET, ADJ, and N into an intermediate branch.

To see why this unit of structure is useful, let's look at a system *without* an intermediate NP level and try and extend it to cover all the uses of DET, ADJ, and N in simple sentences. With no NP level, to combine DET, ADJ, and N, you need the set of rules in the following table, plus at least five more rules for sentences like *The tall man saw the tall woman*.

Rule	*Example*
S → N V	*Alice fainted.*
S → DET N V	*The rabbit left.*
S → DET ADJ N V	*The white rabbit left.*
S → N V N	*Alice saw Lucy.*
S → N V DET N	*Alice saw the rabbit.*
S → N V DET ADJ N	*Alice saw the white rabbit.*
S → DET N V N	*The man saw Mary.*

That's a lot of rules. Worse, it includes repetition of the same sequences — N, DET N, and DET ADJ N keep occurring in the same places — without recognizing the pattern. Whenever a noun is possible, a determiner or an adjective is also possible. That's where phrasal units like noun phrases (NPs) come in. Instead of introducing N, DET N, and DET ADJ N with separate rules, you introduce NP as a unit and then have separate rules for how NP expands. See how much simpler the rule system becomes:

What the rule does	*Rule*
Introduce NP	S → NP V
	S → NP V NP
Expand NP	NP → N
	NP → DET N
	NP → DET ADJ N

Creating a sentence requires two rule applications — one for S and one for NP — but the rule system is much simpler. And we can simplify it even more if we recognize that an NP always contains a noun and that determiners and adjectives are optional elements within the NP. Optional elements are enclosed in parentheses: For example, (DET) indicates that DET can be there or not. With the optional notation, the rules reduce to *two* general rules:

What the rule does	*Rule*
Introduces NP	S → NP V (NP)
Expands NP	NP → (DET)(ADJ) N

This rule system is small, but it generates all the sentences noted at the beginning of this section. (You can verify this if you try building sentences yourself.) The rule system is also general and expresses the basic pattern: Where there is an N, it's also possible to have DET N or DET ADJ N. And there's even *more* value: The NP unit captures two other properties of DET ADJ N sequences:

✔ **Substitution:** A pronoun like *it* can substitute for N, for DET N, or for DET ADJ N. For example, consider this conjoined sentence:

> I saw *the big dog*, and Lucy saw *it* too.

Here the pronoun *it* substitutes for three words: *the big dog*. That's DET, ADJ, *and* the N. If pronouns substitute for units, then the NP unit explains exactly why this is possible. The pronoun *it* substitutes for a whole NP. But if there's no NP unit, then it's harder to explain what *it* substitutes for.

✔ **Movement:** Instead of *I love doughnuts,* many (though not all) speakers can also say *Doughnuts, I love!* This is a special variation on the basic word order for sentences, and linguists treat this as a kind of movement of an element to the beginning of a sentence. But what's the unit that moves? It's not just a noun: If there's a determiner or adjective modifying the noun, these move too: *These doughnuts, I love!* or *Fresh doughnuts, I love!* This is simple to describe if we have an NP: Move the NP unit to the front. But without this phrasal unit, it's harder to describe or understand what's going on.

For these reasons, you'll find an NP unit in every syntactician's toolkit. And though the details of individual rules differ across languages, you'll find evidence for NPs as a phrasal unit in every language.

The NP that occurs *before* the verb in the rule S → **NP** V (NP) is the *subject NP*. The *subject* is whichever NP occupies this position in the structure.

Grouping verbs into larger units: The verb phrase

Another common unit of structure that syntacticians use is the *VP* for *verb phrase*. The VP unit consists of the verb itself and a subsequent NP and can be generated by a rule system like the following:

What the rule does	*Rule*
Expands S	S → NP VP
Expands NP	NP → (DET)(ADJ) N
Expands VP	VP → V (NP)

This VP rule explains a couple of important ways in which the V and a following NP act as a unit:

✔ **Substitution:** In English, VPs can be replaced by *did*. For example, in the first sentence below, *did* substitutes for the verb *left,* and in the second, *did* substitutes for the verb and the following NP *(kissed the baby).* This pattern is easy to describe and understand if there's a VP unit: *did* substitutes for the VP unit. But without a VP unit, it's much harder to explain what *did* substitutes for.

> Alice *left*, and Lucy *did* too.

> Alice *saw the rabbit*, and Lucy *did* too.

✔ **Movement:** Verbal elements can move to the beginning of a sentence, as you can see in the two example sentences below. In the first sentence, it may seem that just the verb moves to the beginning of the sentence. But notice that in the second sentence, where the verb is followed by a NP, it moves along with the verb. This pattern is easy to describe and understand with the VP unit: Move the VP unit to the front. But without a VP unit, it's harder to describe what's going on.

> I said I would *leave,* and *leave* I will!

> I said I would *finish the book*, and *finish the book* I will!

Embedded sentences are also introduced by the VP rule. Along with VP → V (NP), there's also VP → V S. If we add in complementizers like *that,* we'll need a rule of the form VP → V (COMP) S.

When a NP occurs *after* the verb and within the VP, syntacticians call that NP the *object* or the *object of the verb.* If the verb is an action word, the object will be the person or thing to whom the action is done. But not all verbs describe actions, so to a syntactician, the *object NP* is whichever NP is introduced by the VP rule, as in VP → V (NP). Embedded sentences generated by rules like VP → V (S) also count as a kind of object.

Rules such as "move NP to the beginning of a sentence" or "move VP to the beginning of a sentence" are called *movement transformations.* Syntacticians use generative rules to build syntactic trees and use movement transformations to move words and phrases after they've been generated. So *generative grammar* is also called *transformational generative grammar.*

Putting together other phrasal units

It's something of an industry for syntacticians to look for and find (and then argue over) phrasal units. Some other common phrasal groupings include the following:

- ✔ **ADJP (adjective phrase):** Adjectives can be modified by words that indicate the degree to which the adjective holds. For example, *very, somewhat,* and *really* are degree words (though they may also have other uses). Degree words form a unit with the adjective: In *Alice saw a very big rabbit, very big* forms an ADJP unit, containing the degree word *very* and the adjective *big.*

- ✔ **ADVP (adverb phrase):** Adverbial phrases also occur with degree modifiers like *very,* as in *Alice followed the rabbit very happily.* Again, syntacticians find evidence that *[very happily]* forms a unit within the sentence, which they call *ADVP.*

- ✔ **PP (prepositional phrase):** A preposition P and a following NP form a PP unit (yes, it's pronounced *pee-pee*). So in *Alice played with the rabbit, with the rabbit* forms a PP unit.

ADJP, ADVP, and PP units simplify the rule system. The categories grouped by the phrases [DEG ADJ], [DEG ADV], and [P NP] behave as units with respect to distribution, substitution, and movement. If you add phrase-structure rules for ADJP, ADVP, and PP, you need to modify the other rules to accommodate them:

What the rule does	Rule
Expands S	S → NP VP
Expands VP	VP → V (NP)(ADVP)
Expands NP	NP → (DET)(ADJP) N
Expands ADJP	ADJP → (DEG) ADJ
Expands ADVP	ADVP → (DEG) ADV

There's no final list of generative rules for English. Syntacticians constantly find evidence for new and different kinds of phrasal structures, even for well-studied languages like English.

Combining phrases with each other: The "and" hat trick

One special kind of phrase structure arises with conjunctions like *and* and *or.* Conjunctions combine words of any grammatical category, and they also combine phrases of any category, including NP and VP. As Table 6-3 shows, we could add a separate conjunction rule for each word-level category and for each phrase-level unit in order to accommodate conjunctions.

Table 6-3		Accommodating Conjunctions
	Conjunction Rule	*Example*
Word-level conjunction	N → N Conj N	*Mary had the chicken and fish.*
	V → V Conj V	*Fred yawned and stretched.*
	ADJ → ADJ Conj ADJ	*Mary is a beautiful and intelligent lady.*
	P → P Conj P	*The kids ran up and down the stairs.*
Phrase-level conjunction	NP → NP Conj NP	*Mary saw the cat and the little dog.*
	VP → VP Conj VP	*Mary fed the cat and watered the plants.*
	S → S Conj S	*Bill went home and Mary stayed out.*

The rules in Table 6-3 (and others to handle phrases like ADJP, ADVP, and PP) describe the patterns of conjunctions. But they miss a generalization: *Any* two items can be conjoined, so long as they're in the same category. Why not just come out and say that? That's what syntacticians do with the generalized conjunction rule:

X → X Conj X

where X stands for any word or phrase of the same type

And with just that one rule — so long as you use the same lexical category or phrase for both instances of X — you can capture all the different uses of conjunctions. Cool!

Conjunctions can be used as a test to reveal phrasal units. You can conjoin [*the cat*] and [*the little dog*] because both are NPs. Similarly, conjunctions can be used to test for *all* phrasal categories (VP, AJDP, ADVP, PP).

The universal grammar hypothesis

Every language is unique in certain ways. And yet, all languages have fundamental properties in common. When syntacticians push beyond superficial differences, they find that the principles of categorization and phrase-building are the same in every language — although languages differ on the surface, all languages build sentences using the same set of tools. Some linguists hold that this similarity reflects a structure common to all human language. They call this *universal grammar* or *"UG"* (say the letters *u* then *g* — don't pronounce it like *ugh!*). Proponents of universal grammar — most famously Noam Chomsky — argue that humans are born with an ability to learn and create language, guided by the innate UG system. (For discussion of how humans learn language, see Chapter 13.) Syntacticians, more so than other types of linguists, are attracted to the UG hypothesis because syntax clearly shows universal patterns.

Chapter 7

Making Sense of Meaning: Semantics

Around 370 BCE, the Greek philosopher Plato sat down with members of his academy for a special meeting. "I want us to figure out the meaning of just one word: the word *man,*" he told them. After a long and heated debate, the gang found something that seemed to work. *Man,* they decided, means a *featherless biped.* Imagine their consternation, then, when a rival philosopher showed up at the Academy waving around a squirming, freshly plucked chicken. "Behold, Plato's man!" chortled the cheeky fellow. Chastened, the group went back to the drawing board, and eventually Plato found a new and much better meaning for the word *man*, one that touches on the essence of what it means to be human: *man,* he decided, is a *being in search of meaning.*

Plato and his group were engaged in *semantics:* the study of how humans search for and find meaning in language. And as the chicken incident shows, semantics is a deep and challenging subject — so much so that 23 centuries later people are still trying to understand how meaning works. Not only linguists and philosophers but also psychologists, social theorists, literary critics, mathematicians, and logicians all continue to look — from sometimes radically different perspectives — for the meaning of *meaning*.

In this chapter we give you a rundown of some of the different linguistic approaches to semantics, but we focus on an approach focused on truth and reference to the world, called *formal semantics.* This approach — pioneered by Richard Montague and Barbara Partee in the 1970s — adopts a structural account of meaning (based on syntax), where elements combine with each other to form larger units of meaning. Formal semantics is not the only modern theory of meaning, but it is our personal favorite, and certainly one of the most influential modern approaches to meaning. It has lead to many discoveries about how natural language "builds meaning," and we introduce you to some of them here.

Looking for Meaning in Different Ways

To be meaningful, words and phrases must be *about* something: Without a symbolic connection to something else, a word or a phrase is just a sound wave. That *something* that the word or phrase represents, points to, and symbolizes, is its *meaning*:

Word/Phrase → [something]

Linguists usually agree on that much. Where linguists part company, though, is in *where* they look for the *something*:

- ✔ Certain linguists (lexicographers, the ones who write dictionaries) locate meaning in *dictionary definitions*.

- ✔ Other linguists, as well as some philosophers and psychologists, locate meaning in the *mind* — in how language connects to ideas and concepts.

- ✔ Most linguists look for meaning in the connections between language and the *world* — the things, events, and facts that words refer to. This is called a *referential approach* to meaning. Formal semanticists, the group we study most closely in this chapter, fall into this group.

None of these approaches is best or more right — they just look at different aspects of meaning and try to understand different things. So before we dive into formal semantics, we start with a whirlwind tour of the other main approaches to meaning.

Finding meaning in the dictionary

Lexicographers create dictionary definition *meanings* by studying books, newspapers, and transcripts of everyday conversation. Modern lexicographers don't try to determine the correct meaning for a word, they just look at ordinary usage and summarize it with paraphrases and (in the best dictionaries) examples of sentences from books or other sources. For a lexicographer, the meaning of the word *dog,* for example, corresponds to a paraphrased definition in a book. Figure 7-1 illustrates four different approaches to finding the meaning of *dog.* Figure 7-1a shows the lexicographic meaning.

Lexicographic meanings have a lot of practical uses, but dictionary definitions can't be *all* there is to meaning. That's because you can't define *all* words using just *other* words without eventually running into circular definitions. At some level, meaning must involve connections between language and something other than language. For this reason, most linguists try to go beyond dictionary accounts of meaning — though dictionaries are important records of how people use words.

Figure 7-1:
Different
linguistic
approaches
to finding
the meaning
of *dog*.

The dictionaries that lexicographers create are sometimes called *lexicons*. But the term *lexicon* can mean both a *printed dictionary* and the *mental dictionary* of information that you store in your brain when you learn a new word. *Lexical semanticists* study this mental dictionary, looking for underlying features of meaning that items in the mental lexicon share, looking at connections between them, and figuring out how this influences other parts of grammar.

Finding meaning in concepts and ideas

Linguists who take a psychological approach to semantics look for the meaning of a word in the mind. This approach associates a meaning with a mental picture, so that the word *dog* points to the picture of a dog that you have in your head, like the cheery chap in Figure 7-1b.

You probably do have a mental image and other sensory associations with many words, but the basic mental image model is too simple — for example *dog* refers to a bunch of very different-looking creatures, and we probably all have slightly different images in our minds. Because of this, linguists (as well as philosophers and psychologists) who explore the psychological basis of meaning often frame their discussion in terms of *mental representations*. These are internal mental symbols that represent reality or other forms of mental activity associated with a word. Some linguists have also explored the use of basic features that combine together to create complex meanings — for example, in defining *woman* as [+human, +female, +adult, they try to show how word meanings can be understood in terms of combinations of these features. Whichever approach you take, there definitely *is* a mental component to meaning, and that's what these linguists look for. (See Chapter 16 for more info on language and cognition.)

Finding meaning in the world

Referential semanticists look for meaning in connections between words and things in the external world. The referential approach focuses on a simple question: How does language connect to and make true (or false) statements about the world? And how do the individual words, which have their own meaning, combine together to make these true (or false) statements?

In a simplistic theory of meaning, the word *dog* would point to a real flesh and blood dog in the actual world, like the Fido in Figure 7-1c. But most formal semanticists today would argue that common nouns like *dog* actually have a more complex referential meaning: *Dog* (even without the plural marker added!) points not to one dog but to a whole set of creatures, united by some shared property even though they are not identical, like the pack in Figure 7-1d.

Cognitive grammar and prototype meanings

Cognitive grammar looks for meaning in terms of links to concepts. One important area of research in the cognitive grammar framework started with the work of a linguist named Eleanor Rosch and her colleagues. They found that the concepts associated with a word, such as *dog* or *bird,* seem to have different degrees of membership: some things are *prototypical examples* of the concept, others are more peripheral or less typical examples. They found several ways in which the prototypical items were more central to the concept:

- Speakers recognize prototypical items fastest as a member of a group: When identifying items that match the word *bird*, they recognize a robin faster than a penguin.

- Speakers name prototypical items first when asked to come up with examples: When asked for examples of a bird, they name *robin* before *penguin.*

- When they've just heard the word for the general concept, they're faster at word-recognition tasks with prototypical members than with others: After hearing the general term *bird*, they identify two instances of the word *robin* as matching faster than two instances of the word *penguin.*

To cognitive grammarians, these results suggest that the concepts that words point to have internal structure: In measurable ways, some items are central, core elements of the concept, while other items are more peripheral examples of the concept. But results like this may simply show that people are faster with more familiar terms. And critics of the theory wonder whether a mother is more of a *female* than an actress, or whether 3 is more of an *odd number* than 79. But regardless of critics, the experiments do reveal something about how people organize concepts.

Finding meaning in social interactions

Some linguists locate meaning in *social structures* — in how language is used to mark and negotiate social relationships between speakers. For example, certain words and phrases are important not in terms of what they say literally but in terms of the social meaning that they carry. This includes the use of *honorifics* (to address someone of higher social status), taboo words, racial epithets, or choosing to use a fancy word like *prevaricate* instead of a regular word like *lie*. Social factors are an important part of how language *means*. The study of social meaning in linguistics connects to pragmatics and sociolinguistics, which are discussed in Chapters 8 and 9.

Linguists use the term *referent* to talk about the thing in the world that a word or phrase represents. The word *extension* is sometimes used the same way. *Denotation* can also be used for the referent, but it's sometimes used for the concept or idea associated with the word. *Connotation* is used for the feelings or other associations that go along with a word, in addition to its basic literal meaning.

Modeling Meaning with Reference, Composition, and Truth

Formal semantics tries to understand how language relates to and makes meaningful statements about the world. But the goal is broader than just trying to find a referent for each word: Formal semanticists want to understand the creative power of words in *combination* — how the meanings of words fit together in various orders to make new statements. Formal semanticists tackle this problem by asking three questions:

- ✔ **What do individual words mean?** Because formal semanticists take a referential approach, this question comes down to this: What things (or events, or properties, or locations) in the world do nouns, verbs, adjectives, and prepositions point to?

- ✔ **How do you combine word meanings to make statements about the world?** Because you combine individual words creatively to make all sorts of statements, there must be general principles you use to build complex meanings. So what do these principles — which formal semanticists call *the principles of semantic composition* — look like? And how do you use these principles to build and understand complex meanings?

✔ **How does the truth (or falsity) of a statement follow from principles of composition?** To know the meaning of a statement, you need to know the circumstances under which it would be true or false. You may not know *if* the statement is true or false, but you must have a rough idea of what would *make* it true or false. For this reason, formal semanticists are interested in the *truth* side of meaning. Their central goal is to have explicit steps that predict whether a statement is true or false, under certain conditions in the world, just from individual word meanings and general principles of semantic composition.

In the following sub-sections, we walk you through a simple framework that a formal semanticist may use to explore the basic interpretations of nouns and verbs and then show you how this framework helps you make sense of problems like logical connectives, quantifiers, and tense.

Stumbling upon meaning

Formal semantics started out as an abstract study of meaning by logicians and mathematicians. In its early days (back at the start of the 20th century), the theory wasn't focused on understanding features of languages — logicians and mathematicians were actually trying to understand the foundations of mathematics by exploring how mathematical proofs (which used reasoning in ordinary language) worked. To their own surprise, formal semanticists ended up with insightful analyses of tricky parts of meaning in human language, too. Among other things, the work of formal semanticists has shed light on three particular areas of the search for meaning:

✔ **Logical terms in language:** Formal semantics is good at helping us understand words that make logical connections like *not*, *and*, and *if . . . then*. Of course, this is because the first formal semanticists were *logicians* — and they did a nice job.

Logical connectives are words that connect sentences to each other so that the truth-value of the compound sentence depends on the truth-value of the original sentences. Various English words and word-pairs are used as logical connectives, and they're associated with different kinds of logical relations: *and* (conjunction), *or* (disjunction), *either . . . or* (exclusive disjunction), *implies* (implication), *if . . . then* (implication), *if and only if* (equivalence), *only if* (implication), *just in case* (equivalence), *but* (conjunction), *however* (conjunction), *not both* (negative conjunction), *neither . . . nor* (negative disjunction), *not* (negation).

✔ **Quantifiers:** Interpreting phrases like *no men, two men,* and *some men* (linguists call these *quantified noun phrases*) is tricky because it's not always easy to find any specific set of individuals who the phrases refer to — sometimes it's no individuals, sometimes it's a group but a group which can shift with each use of the phrase (as in *two men lived, but two men died*).

✔ **Tense:** The interpretation of past and future and other ways of expressing time in language has fascinated linguists for many centuries, and formal semantics gives us new ways of understanding how past, present, and future markers contribute systematically to the meanings of sentences, in particular by showing how you can understand them in terms of interpretations at ordered moments in time.

Formal semanticists use the term *composition* when talking about how two words combine to make larger meanings. For example, when the words *Lucy* and *walks* combine to make the larger meaningful statement *Lucy walks,* they call that *composition of meanings* or *semantic composition.*

Simplifying the world to study meaning

Semanticists test the word-meanings and compositional rules that they propose by examining how language relates to the world. But they don't want to deal with the *whole* world, in all its complexity and messiness. Like physicists who ignore air pressure in exploring a theory of gravity, formal semanticists focus just on what's important to test their theory of meaning. They want the simplest way possible to check, in an abstract way, whether they've understood how words add up to meaningful statements.

To keep things simple, then, formal semanticists test their accounts of meaning against extremely simplified *imagined worlds,* which they call *models.* Models are little sketches on paper consisting of a few individuals, their properties, and whatever else is relevant to the question at hand. These models can be as simple as the sketch in Figure 7-2. The individuals in our model are labeled with lowercase letters a, b, c, and d. Models also normally include a few properties that these individuals have, which are marked with capital letters P, Q, R, S. More complex models may include relationships between individuals, moments in time, and other elements — but always at the level of a simplified abstract sketch of a little world.

Here we test our accounts of meaning against just one model, the one in Figure 7-2. Doing that much demonstrates how the basic approach works. But a good theory of formal semantics accounts for meaning and composition in a much stronger way: Accounts of meaning are tested against all possible models. Of course that's much harder and requires more elaborate models than the one in this chapter.

A model in formal semantics is like a simplified imagined world, but don't confuse a *model* with a *possible world,* which is a technical device in formal semantics that refers to a possible arrangement of individuals and properties. Complex models may contain various possible worlds, each of which represents a possibility within the model. Models containing possible worlds are pretty cool and are used to test sentences with modals (words like *would, should*).

Figure 7-2:
A formal
semantics
model.

a, b have property *P*
c, d have property *Q*
a, c have property *R*
b, d have property *S*

Much of formal semantics, and everything we talk about in this chapter, focuses on statements — sentences that say something that is potentially true or false — that are tested against models. For this reason, this approach is often called *truth-conditional semantics* or *model-theoretic semantics*. But some formal semanticists work on questions, which are neither true nor false.

Models as your math teacher would want them

Formal semanticists would definitely be more popular if they used cartoons to describe their models, but in the interest of being taken seriously, they prefer to use math-like notations. So here is what the model in Figure 7-2 would look like in a formal semantics textbook:

✔ D = {*a, b, c, d*} (D stands for *domain of individuals*)

✔ Properties = *P, Q, R,* and *S*

✔ *P(a)* is true, *P(b)* is true, *P(c)* is false, *P(d)* is false

✔ *Q(a)* is false, *Q(b)* is false, *Q(c)* is true, *Q(d)* is true

Semanticists don't draw pictures of the individuals or the properties; they just throw some letters on a page. When they say *P(a)* is true, that means *a* has the property *P*; they need to say it like that because they don't have pictures to illustrate that the *a* guy is smiling (property *P*).

Finding meanings for nouns and verbs

When choosing which words to examine in their model world, formal semanticists start with just a few representative nouns and verbs or other words,
rather than the whole dictionary. They then see whether they can uncover
a general account of meaning for that small vocabulary set, which they call
a *language fragment*. Of course, they can always add more vocabulary items,
which increases the complexity of the problem. But you have to start somewhere, and semanticists always start with something simple.

We're going to start out investigating language in our model with just a few
proper names and a few verbs:

> **Nouns:** Arnold, Beth, Chris, Denise

> **Verbs:** is smiling, is frowning

To keep things simple, we treat *is* and the marker *-ing* as if they were part of
the verb: *is smiling* and *is frowning* are actually *verb phrases*. *Is* is a helping
verb that marks present tense, and *-ing* marks an ongoing action. (For more
on verb phrases, see Chapter 6.)

Our first pass at finding the meaning of these proper names is *names refer
to individuals in the world*. So we can say that *Arnold, Beth, Chris,* and *Denise*
each refer to a real individual in our model in Figure 7-2.

> **Arnold** $\rightarrow a$
>
> **Beth** $\rightarrow b$
>
> **Chris** $\rightarrow c$
>
> **Denise** $\rightarrow d$

Because it's a made-up model, all we're doing is testing whether or not
it's plausible for the meaning of names to refer to individuals in the world.
(Which name goes with which individual in the model is something we make
up for the test.)

Semanticists use a few different notations to mark that a word *points to* an element in the model. They may use an arrow (*Beth* $\rightarrow b$), as in the main text, or
they may use double brackets, like this: [[*Beth*]]=*b*.

Now, what about the verbs *is smiling* or *is frowning?* Semanticists identify the
meaning of a verb with a *property*. Here, a *property* is something that holds (is
true) or not for the individuals in the world. With that understanding of property, each verb can be understood as picking out one of the properties in the
world. In our simplified model, the verbs have meanings like this:

> **is smiling** $\rightarrow a$, *b* (those individuals with property *P*)

> **is frowning** $\rightarrow c$, *d* (those individuals with property *Q*)

Formal semantics and real-world knowledge

Formal semanticists don't care which name goes with which individual in the model or which verb goes with which particular property: They want to test the *general* plausibility of associating names with individuals, verbs with properties, and so on. But in your real use of language, these little details matter a lot. So, even though the general account of what words refer to may be reasonable, it's still fair to ask: How do real speakers of a real language figure out which individual each name points to? And how do they figure out which property each verb points to?

Formal semanticists put these questions aside, and just say "well, somehow the word points to these things in the world, and we take it from there." Their strategy is to try and make progress by simplifying the problem and focusing just on one aspect of meaning — in this case, the problem of what things the words refer to (however you learn that) and how the referential aspects of the meaning combine. Psychological theories of meaning and formal semantics are not incompatible. Ultimately a full theory of meaning will account for *both* sides of the problem.

P and *Q* each describe a property that is true of some individuals in our world. The idea is that verbs describe things that individuals are doing or that are true of individuals.

Using the compositional rule for nouns and verbs

Finding clearly defined meanings for words is good, but something important is still missing. A *compositional rule* describes how the meanings of the words *combine*. For our model, one general compositional rule looks like this:

> *Where a sentence consists of the elements Noun Verb, the meaning of the sentence is true only if the Noun refers to one of the individuals with the property described by the Verb.*

With the meanings assigned to the words in the previous section, this compositional rule correctly and explicitly predicts a meaning — specifically, a value of true or false, relative to any model — for all the possible sentences in our language fragment. For example, the words in *Arnold is smiling* are predicted to be true in our model in Figure 7-2:

- ✔ **Arnold** refers to an individual **a** (we assigned this meaning to *Arnold*).

- ✔ **is smiling** refers to the individuals with property **P** (we assigned this meaning to *is smiling*).

- ✔ **Arnold is smiling** is true only if **a** is one of the individuals **a** or **b**.

    a obviously is one of the individuals **a** or **b**, so the sentence is predicted to be true — relative to that model and with the word meanings as we've assigned them.

This is all pretty abstract and rather obvious, of course, but it's getting the results that formal semanticists want. The word-meanings are reasonable, and the compositional rule combining them predicts what seems to be the right result: The sentence is predicted to make a true statement relative to the world of the model. This suggests that this general approach to meaning and composition is at least on the right track. Follow these same steps with other sentences, like *Beth is frowning* or *Chris is smiling,* and the system correctly predicts the truth-value (true or false) for each one. And — most importantly — if you switch to different models, where the individuals are arranged differently, the correct meaning is still predicted for each one (as long as the models are explicit and each word is assigned a referent in the model).

Now, it is a little strange for a sentence like *Arnold is smiling* to *mean* true or false. How can the meaning of a sentence be a truth-value? And it would be strange if you looked at only one model. But the meaning of *Arnold is smiling* is true or false for *any* model that you can make, not just in the model in Figure 7-2. Because it works across a set of models, expressing which ones it is true in and which ones it is false in, our compositional rule captures, in a general way, the full set of circumstances where a sentence is true, as well as the full set of circumstances where it's false — a reasonable, if quite abstract, way of explaining at least a major part of what it means.

In the nouns we've looked at so far, we've used only proper names, not common nouns like *dog, cat,* or *woman.* Common nouns have a more complex interpretation because they don't point to a single individual in the world. Formal semanticists treat common nouns as pointing to *(denoting)* whole *groups* of individuals (technically sets of individuals).

Our basic formulation of semantic composition works only for sentences consisting of the sequence *Noun Verb;* obviously we need to account for the composition of *all* kinds of words. But most formal semanticists believe there actually is just *one* significant compositional rule that combines *all* words together. They call this general compositional rule *function application.* The idea behind function application is that whenever any two words combine, one is a *function* (something that determines a predictable result for each input) and the other is the input to that function.

Capturing Complex Meanings

With its focus on meaning as truth, formal semantics excels at describing how meaning works with certain kinds of truth-related words, including negation (words like *not*), conjunction (words like *and*), and quantifiers (words like *every, no,* and *some*).

Going into reverse with negation

At a basic level, negation is quite straightforward in formal semantics: *not* is a word that attaches to a sentence and reverses its truth value. If the basic sentence is true, *not* makes it false. If the basic sentence is false, *not* makes it true. For example, if *Arnold is frowning* is false on any model (as in Figure 7-2), *Arnold is not frowning* is predicted to be true on the same model.

Negation can be written as the formula *not(S) is true if and only if S is false,* where *S* is the noun verb sentence. Though this formula is simple, it can be tricky to calculate the meanings directly off of sentence structure because the negative marker *(not)* appears between the subject and the verb, at least in English *(Arnold is **not** smiling)*. To get the negative to combine with a whole sentence (which it needs to, by this definition), semanticists put the negative element at the front of the sentence — ***not**(Arnold is frowning)*. Note that negation isn't always as simple as just having one negative element that reverses truth values. For example, some languages, such as French, use two negative elements together: *ne…pas*, as in *Arnold **ne** sourit **pas*** (which means 'Arnold is not smiling').

Conjoining with 'and' and 'or'

If you take two sentences and join them together with *and*, then they're true if both sentences are true. On the other hand, for two sentences joined with *or* to be true, at least one (and possibly both) of the component sentences has to be true. (This is called the *inclusive or* — there's also an *exclusive or* which we mention in the next paragraph.) For example, *Arnold is smiling and Beth is smiling* is true in the model shown in Figure 7-2 because both the sentences it contains are true. *Arnold is frowning or Chris is smiling* is false because both sentences are false.

And and *or* do more than combine two sentences into one, however. They can also combine names as in *Alice and Lucy are smiling*. Linguists have noticed that there's another version of *or*, too, which they call *exclusive or*. *Exclusive or* is true only if one or the other (but *not* both) of the sentences are true. This occurs in English sentences like *You can have fries or you can have salad with your order* — as anyone who goes to a restaurant knows, that doesn't mean you can have both.

Hanging out in groups with quantifiers

Consider the following words with *no: no-one, nothing, no woman, nobody*. These are words that, by their meaning, don't refer to any individuals (or groups of individuals) in the world. So what do they mean and how are they interpreted? Welcome to the wacky world of *quantifiers!*

The element *no* in words like *nothing* and *nobody* is a type of morpheme that quantifies or tells us something about the number of elements being talked about. Other quantifiers include *every*, *some*, and *most*. The quantities these words indicate are not specific, so figuring out an exact meaning for sentences containing quantifiers is a tough problem. One of the biggest triumphs of formal semantics was to find a solution to this problem.

The first step of the solution is to treat the meanings of verbs (and verb phrases) as referring to a group of individuals who share a certain property. The second step, which may be a little surprising, is to treat common nouns, like *man, woman,* and *dog,* in the same way — as if they, too, refer to groups of individuals who share a certain property. So going back to Figure 7-2 again, you can assume the following meanings for the common nouns *man* and *woman:*

> **man** $\rightarrow$ **a, c** (individuals with property R)
>
> **woman** $\rightarrow$ **b, d** (individuals with property Q)

Note that these forms don't have the plural marking, just *man* and *woman* — technically, a noun denotes a group (or set) whether it is plural or not.

With this understanding of noun meaning, it's fairly easy to characterize the meaning of sentences containing quantifiers:

- ✔ **Every:** *Every man is smiling* is true only if the group of people to whom *is smiling* refers contains the whole group of people that *man* refers to, as in Figure 7-3a. Thus this sentence is correctly predicted to be false in the model sketched out in Figure 7-2.

- ✔ **At least one:** *At least one man is smiling* is true only if the group of people who *is smiling* has an overlap greater than 0 with the group of individuals that *man* refers to, as in the relation in Figure 7-3b. This is predicted, again correctly, to be true in the model in Figure 7-2.

- ✔ **No:** *No man is smiling* is true only if the group of people *is smiling* refers to is entirely distinct from the group of people that *man* refers to, as in the relation in Figure 7-3c. Again, for the model in Figure 7-2, you get the right prediction that it should be false.

Notice how this approach entirely avoids questions like, "What individual does *no man* refer to?" In formal semantics, *no man* (like *every man* or *at least one man*) doesn't directly refer to *any* individual. Rather, in this approach, for sentences with quantified noun phrases, the relation is between two groups of individuals — this sweeps away centuries of confusion (including yours, right?)!

When talking about a collection of individuals, linguists use the term *set,* as in "*dog* refers to a set."

 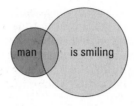 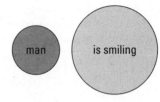

(a) Every man is smiling. (b) At least one man is smiling. (c) No man is smiling.

Moving through time with tense

Humans are concerned with what's happening now (the present), what happened before now (the past), and what'll happen after now (the future): These are tense distinctions. Tense fits quite nicely into formal semantics models. All you have to do is soup up the model so that a sentence is true or false relative to a model at a particular time. To do this, you expand the models and make some clarifying assumptions. Here's how to start:

- ✔ Introduce a set of *moments of time* into the model. For example, assume three moments, represented with little **t**s, and labeled $t_{YESTERDAY}$, t_{NOW}, and $t_{TOMORROW}$.

- ✔ Set the model up so that each sentence is true relative to each moment of time, rather than (as in the simpler model) simply true or false for the whole model. For example, *Beth smiling* may be true at t_{NOW}, but false at $t_{YESTERDAY}$ and at $t_{TOMORROW}$. In this way, each sentence can have a different truth value at each moment of time.

- ✔ Represent moments as sequenced to capture the fact that moments of time come in a specific *order*. You can do it like this, where the symbol "<" indicates temporal ordering:

  $$t_{YESTERDAY} < t_{NOW} < t_{TOMORROW}$$

After moments have been assigned an order, a basic account of the meaning of tense is easy to put together:

- ✔ **Past tense sentences:** If, in the model, Beth smiled yesterday, then the sentence *Beth was smiling* is true at the moment of speech t_{NOW} if the following two points are true:

  - There is some *other* moment **t** where the person Beth refers to is one of the individuals smiling.

  - **t** precedes t_{NOW} in the sequence of moments ($t < t_{NOW}$).

✔ **Future tense sentences:** If, in the model, Beth will smile tomorrow, then the sentence *Beth will be smiling* is true at the moment of speech t_{NOW} if the following two points are true:

- There is some *other* moment **t** where the person Beth refers to is one of the individuals smiling.

- **t** follows t_{NOW} in the sequence of moments ($t_{NOW} < t$).

✔ **Present tense sentences:** If, in the model, Beth is smiling at the moment of speech, then the sentence *Beth is smiling* is true at the moment of speech t_{NOW} if the following point is true:

- The person Beth refers to is one of the individuals smiling at the moment of speech t_{NOW}.

Even though we don't go into the details of semantic composition for tense, formal semanticists using this approach always ensure that the meanings they propose are compositional.

Time travel: The displacement property

Displacement is a design feature of human language that allows humans to talk about things that are not in the here and now. (For more on other design features, see Chapter 2.) For example, tense points to past or future events — this is called *temporal displacement.* You also distinguish *here* and *there,* and so can refer to locations that aren't in their vicinity. You can be in your home in Vancouver and talk about your friend Beth in Edmonton, and say: *Beth is in Edmonton.* This is *locative displacement.* Humans also talk about situations that aren't in the actual world, using modal expressions like *could, would,* and *might,* as in *Beth might be in Edmonton.* This is *modal displacement.*

Chapter 8

Using Language in Conversation: Pragmatics

In This Chapter

▶ Using language in context

▶ Cooperating in a conversation

▶ Making things happen with words

▶ Pointing to the world around you in conversation

*Y*ou talk to people about stuff — this is conversation. You talk to friends about a movie you saw. You talk to neighbors about the upcoming election. You talk to your boss about a raise. In this chapter, we give you the lowdown on *pragmatics* — how you make a conversation work, how you use language to change the world, and how you relate what you say to the surrounding context.

Defining Pragmatics: Utterances in Context

You have conversations with your friends that flow smoothly. You're in sync and on the same wavelength, and you know where the other person's coming from. You walk away feeling that you communicated successfully. But what exactly makes a conversation work? Well, when communication takes place, four ingredients are present: a message, a code, a signal, and participants. (These are all design features of human language — check out Chapter 2 for more.) In this chapter, we're looking at the last ingredient, the interaction between a speaker and a hearer.

Pragmatics is the branch of linguistics that looks at what you actually say: your *utterances*. Linguists study how what you say relates to the communicative situation or *context* you're in and how the context can be changed by what you say — all in order to find the rules that you, as a speaker, use when talking to other people.

Pragmatics comes from Greek *pragmatikos*. The word stem *pragmat-* means 'deed'. Pragmatics looks at the deeds of language: utterances. Linguists who study pragmatics are called *pragmaticists*.

Pragmatics in the large sense can be traced to two sources. The work of the philosophers Paul Grice (on the logic of conversation) together with J. L. Austin and John Searle (on speech acts) is the basis of *formal pragmatics*. The work of sociologist Harvey Sacks (on talking as social interaction) is the basis of *conversation analysis*.

Making Conversations Work

Conversations, which are where people do most of their talking, involve (at least) two people: a *speaker* and a *listener*. Linguists also use the terms *addressee* or *hearer* for listener. In order to make conversation work, though, the speaker and listener have to cooperate with each other in ways you may not think of.

Writing is an extension of oral communication. See Chapter 18 for a discussion of how writing and speaking influence one another.

Making basic conversation

As a speaker, you need to figure out how informal conversation works before you can successfully engage in other types of communicative social interaction, such as giving oral presentations, delivering speeches, or negotiating a complicated contract. Here are some reasons why conversations may be the most basic form of human communicative interaction:

- ✔ Conversation is the most common form of interaction. If you keep track of the interactions you have in a day, you'll see most are conversations.

- ✔ Conversation is the first form of communication that you're exposed to as a child and is key to your social development. Your introduction to language is through conversation: Adults don't recite lists of words to you, they engage you in conversation. And conversation is a social activity: You can't have a conversation by yourself.

- ✔ Conversation is the oldest form of linguistic communication. People conversed with each other in informal conversation — both in terms of the history of society and the indiviudal — before they used devices such as speeches and lectures.

- ✔ Conversation is the default form of human communication: Communicative behavior in specialized social institutions narrows down the range of conduct found in ordinary conversation.

Signed conversations follow the same principles as spoken ones. Check this out the next time you're around deaf people who are talking with their hands.

Finding what makes a conversation tick

In a successful conversation, participants cooperate to pursue topics of mutual interest that support common goals. People who study conversations classify them according to what they're about (the *topic*), what they're for (the *goal*), and how they're managed (the *strategy*).

- ✔ **Selecting a conversational topic:** A conversation has a theme. These themes fall into two categories: *person-centered talk* (about oneself or others) and *world-centered talk* (about ideas or facts). These topics don't exclude each other, and people often combine them.

- ✔ **Pursuing a conversational goal:** The two main goals of conversation are to exchange information and to establish or maintain social bonds. If you do both at the same time, then you're an excellent conversationalist.

- ✔ **Managing a conversational strategy:** Your conversational strategy is the nuts and bolts of what you, as a conversational agent, do to develop the topic you've selected and to achieve your desired goal. There are two simple, but far-reaching, conversational strategies: Make the best contribution you can and make it at the best time.

When you argue with someone — linguists call this an *adversarial conversation* — you still play by the rules of the conversation game. You argue about something (that's the topic), you have a goal in mind (to win the argument), and you have a strategy (to reason or plead with the other person — or if you're really desperate, to shout them down).

Cultural differences affect how conversations work, which has lead to a field of study called *cross-linguistic pragmatics*. See Chapter 11 for examples of how languages can differ in their use of pragmatic strategies.

Making the best contribution you can

In interacting with other people, you follow certain social conventions: You don't slam doors in people's faces, you're quiet when other people are sleeping, you tip at least 15 percent, and you don't face strangers in an elevator. You also observe social conventions when you're in conversation with someone. Suppose it's your turn to talk and the pressure is on to keep the conversation rolling. How do you do this? Linguists believe that, in such contexts, what you say is governed by the social convention of cooperation: You try to make the best contribution to the conversation that you can. Paul Grice calls this the *cooperative principle* and describes it this way:

Make your conversational contribution such as required, at the stage at which it occurs, by the accepted purpose or direction of the talk exchange in which you are engaged.

The cooperative principle determines a code of conduct, which boils down to four *conversational maxims:* Be as truthful, informative, relevant, and clear as the situation warrants. These maxims go a long way in explaining why so much of what you mean is not in what you actually say (your utterances) but in what you leave unsaid.

A *maxim* is a succinct formulation of a rule of conduct. Individual maxims sometimes conflict — this is called *maxim clash.*

Being truthful: The maxim of quality

Try to say things that are true. The maxim of quality often comes up in situations where you have to assess someone's performance. You must be truthful: You can't exaggerate their good qualities or underplay their weak points. The following scenario is adapted from a real-life situation (no, it doesn't involve any one of the three co-authors):

> An instructor received a request from a student for a "strong letter of recommendation." The student was fine in class but didn't participate much and was a bit of a pest about his papers. All the instructor could honestly say about this student was: "this student worked and improved."

Anyone reading a letter that says "this student worked and improved" infers, on the basis of the maxim of quality, that the student doesn't have the qualities of a good student. If he did, then those qualities — such as being curious, engaging, helpful, stimulating, hardworking, and thoughtful — would have been mentioned. Paul Grice discusses a similar example: "Jones has beautiful handwriting and his English is grammatical." The maxim of quality allows you to infer that Jones isn't the sharpest knife in the drawer.

Being informative: The maxim of quantity

Say neither too much nor too little: supply only the information that's required. John Stuart Mill — the British philosopher — stumbled across this maxim of quantity back in 1865. He observed that if you say to someone "I saw some of your children today," the person you're talking to infers that you haven't seen *all* of their children. If you had seen them all, you would have said "I saw all your children today" (or even "I saw your children today"). The word *some* gives too little information if, in fact, you saw all the children.

What counts as informative isn't determined in an absolute fashion but is different in different contexts.

Being relevant: The maxim of relevance

Say things that are relevant to the topic. The following joke plays on the fact that the candidate tries — unsuccessfully — to make the promise relevant:

> Candidate: *If you vote for me, I'll build a bridge.*
>
> Listener: *But we don't have a river.*
>
> Candidate: *I'll dig a river and then build the bridge.*

Being clear: The maxim of manner

Be brief: Get to the point quickly and straightforwardly and avoid ambiguous or obscure expressions. The *Plain English Campaign* — formed by folks who are fed up with unclear language — champions this maxim. They target long-winded statements and make suggestions about how to say things directly and succinctly. Here are some "before" and "after" examples:

- ✔ **Before:** "High-quality learning environments are a necessary precondition for facilitation and enhancement of the ongoing learning process."

  After: "Good schools help kids learn."

- ✔ **Before:** "If there are any points on which you require explanation of further particulars, we shall be glad to furnish such additional details as may be required by telephone."

  After: "Call us if you have any questions."

Following the four conversational maxims — be truthful, informative, relevant, and clear — doesn't mean that you always blurt out what you're thinking. Rather, in line with your conversational goals — which are to exchange information and establish social bonds — you'll be as truthful, informative, relevant, and clear as you can be. For example, in a conversation with your friend Bob, you may notice that he's made a factual error about who won the gold medal in downhill skiing at the last Winter Olympics. But you may choose not to correct Bob because you know he's thin-skinned about such things. This is an example of how the exchange of information can take second place to the desire to maintain a social bond. Conversational maxims often bend to the context of the conversation.

Meaning more than you say

In Lewis Carroll's *Alice in Wonderland*, the March Hare tells Alice she should say what she means, and Alice replies that she always means what she says. But as the Mad Hatter points out, the two are very different things. "Saying what you mean" is tricky because what you communicate is more than what you literally say. And "meaning what you say" is a challenge because what you mean is more than the conventional meanings of the words. Here's where the cooperative principle comes in handy. If you assume that people are trying to be truthful, informative, relevant, and clear, then you can draw inferences based on what they say. In the following exchange, although Lucy doesn't actually say so, Sandra infers that because Lucy has to work, she can't attend the party.

> Sandra: *Are you coming to the party on Friday?*
>
> Lucy: *I work the evening shift that night.*

The listener assumes that Lucy's cooperative: Her answer is taken to be truthful, informative, relevant, and clear. Therefore, Lucy's working the evening shift is relevant to whether she can attend the party. Because she can't be in two places at the same time, it follows that if she works on Friday, she can't attend the party on Friday. This type of inferential reasoning is an example of what linguists call *conversational implicature*.

In conversation, your ability to make inductive inferences allows you to interpret utterances beyond their face value. Conversational implicature allows a speaker to mean more than they say and allows a listener to understand more than what is said. A big part of your communicative exchanges with other people rely on your joint ability to make such inferences.

In any conversation, there's a speaker and a hearer. Speakers *implicate:* They mean more than what they say. Hearers *infer:* They understand more than what is said.

Pragmaticists typically work with a more technical definition of conversational implicature. It goes something like this: A speaker conversationally implicates a proposition by observing the cooperative principle *(cooperative presumption),* believing the proposition *(determinacy),* and believing that the hearer can determine the speaker's belief *(mutual knowledge).*

Making timely contributions

When you're in a conversation with someone, how do you know when it's your turn to talk? You, as a conversational agent, solve this problem with your conversation partners by regulating the sequence of your interaction and by adhering to strict rules for selecting the current speaker.

Conversational analysis studies language use in social contexts and is used in anthropology, linguistics, communication studies, cognitive science, electrical engineering, robotics, and sociology. *Sociolinguistics* focuses on variations in the use of language and their sociological determinants (see Chapter 9 on language variation). *Sociology of language* considers language use in relation to large-scale social processes.

Pragmatic deficits

Linguists call the ability to have conversations *pragmatic competence*. But sometimes, the skills that make conversation possible go wonky — psycholinguists and neurolinguists call this a *pragmatic deficit*. Conditions with pragmatic deficits include the following:

✔ **Autism and Asperger's Syndrome:** Individuals affected by these developmental disorders have a hard time understanding how context shapes meaning. This makes them interpret utterances literally, which makes it really difficult for them to understand non-literal utterances such as idiomatic expressions, jokes, metaphor, or irony.

✔ **Schizophrenia:** Individuals with schizophrenia experience a disintegration of thought processes called *formal thought disorder*, which makes their language — both spoken and written — gibberish. It's called a thought disorder because their language is assumed to reflect their thinking. They may be difficult to understand because they don't stay on topic or are so long-winded that they lose track of the conversation. Schizophrenics often violate conversational maxims, such as the maxims of quantity, relation, and manner, and find it hard to convey irony. Formal thought disorder also means schizophrenics have a hard time modulating loudness, pitch, and speech rate — their non-verbal communication is awkward. They may use inappropriate words or sentence structures or be unable to follow an ongoing conversation.

✔ **Right Hemisphere Dysfunction (RHD):** RHD is a form of *aphasia* (disruption of language production or perception) arising from damage to the right hemisphere of the brain, usually as a result of a stroke or injury. (See Chapter 16 for more on aphasia.) People with RHD have difficulty with ambiguity and inferential reasoning and their utterances are irrelevant or tangential. They also have difficulty understanding non-literal utterances that involve idioms, sarcasm, or irony.

Threading together a conversation

Human beings organize their conversations in a sequential fashion. It's like a chess game: Each player knows where their pieces are on the board and keeps track of the moves that come before and the moves that come after. Folks who do conversational analysis call the turns that people take *actions* and distinguish between *current action* (whoever's talking now), *next action* (whoever talks next), and *preceding action* (whoever talked before). In conversation, these actions connect with one another in the following ways:

✔ **The current action projects the next action.** The current speaker lays the groundwork for what the next speaker will say.

✔ **The current action addresses the previous action.** The current speaker acknowledges what the previous speaker said and indicates understanding of what was said.

It's the connection between previous action, current action, and next action that gives a conversation its continuity and characteristic thread. If you fail, when it's your turn to hold the floor, to both acknowledge the previous action and anticipate the next action, the conversation will come to a screeching halt.

Some first actions make certain kinds of next actions relevant; linguists call these *adjacency pairs*. For example, asking a question is an action that makes the action of answering relevant: The question-answer sequence is an adjacency pair. And making a statement can elicit disbelief *(No way!)*, endorsement *(Yeah, I know what you mean)*, or simply acknowledgement *(Mm-hmmm)*. These are all adjacency pairs.

Repairing a conversation

When you talk, you sometimes get things wrong: You may mispronounce a word, choose the wrong word, or put the words together in a way that doesn't make sense. This is when you go to the repair shop. Just as speakers and listeners cooperate to maintain a conversational thread and to decide whose turn it is to speak, they also cooperate with each other to repair conversations. The repair can be initiated by the speaker *(self-initiation)* or by the listener *(other-initiation)* and can be carried out by the current speaker *(self-repair)* or by the listener *(other-repair)*. Just as there are rules for deciding whose turn it is to speak, there are rules for deciding who initiates and carries out the repair. Self-initiation is preferred, as is self-correction. This means that the rules are ordered as follows:

1. **Self-initiation:** The current speaker initiates the repair within the conversational turn.

   Self-repair: If possible, the speaker corrects what he or she has just said, correcting the form or content of what they said. When self-repairing, speakers often recycle part of an utterance by repeating a part of what they've just said. For example, in the following utterance, the speaker self-repairs, going back to *if* in order to fix the *if* clause that got cut off at the beginning of the utterance: "*Let see if — before I go back and look at the solution — if I can...*"

Other-repair: If the speaker doesn't self-repair, then the listener volunteers a correction. Depending on the role of the listener, other-repair can be focused on form or content. Form-focused other-repairs are common in language teaching: If the speaker uses an incorrect grammatical form, then the listener may offer a repair. Content-based other-repairs are used if the listener corrects the speaker in order to keep the conversation on-track. For example, a listener may jump in to make a correction such as, "*No, Alice couldn't have been at that meeting; she was away on holiday then.*"

2. **Other-initiation:** If neither the current speaker nor the current listener initiates the repair within the conversational turn where the problem occurs, then the listener can initiate the repair after the transition point that makes him or her the new speaker, thus beginning a new cycle of opportunities for self-repair and other-repair.

Generally, when speakers make errors in a conversation, they are the first to notice and the first to make the correction. But different contexts are associated with different repair strategies. If you don't know the person you're talking to well, repairs are more likely to be about form; if you're more familiar with the other person, repairs are more likely to be about content. Also, the better the person you're talking to knows you, the more likely they are to initiate and carry out a repair.

Selecting a speaker

Although you may not be aware of it, your participation in a conversation is guided by a strict set of speaker-selection rules. This is how it works:

1. **Allocate a turn.** Initiate a turn by selecting a speaker. This gets the conversation started (and keeps it going): Someone steps up to the plate.

2. **Get to a transition point.** After the conversation has begun, there'll be a point — called a *turn constructional unit* — when it's possible, but not necessary, to switch to another speaker. For listeners, paying attention to the speaker's syntax is important in predicting transition points, with completion of a sentence — the basic unit of syntax — being the most obvious turn-taking point. But even more important is *prosody,* where a combination of the speaker's speech rate, loudness, and pitch signals a transition point. In English, a turn constructional unit is usually associated with a falling intonation.

3. **At the transition point, decide whether to choose a new speaker.**

   • **Choose a new speaker.** This is done in one of two ways:

   Current speaker selects next speaker. The current speaker can do this verbally or with a gesture such as a gaze.

   Next speaker self-selects. Any participant in the conversation can choose to be the next speaker. Now go back to Step 1.

   • **Don't choose a new speaker.** This has two outcomes:

   Current speaker continues to hold the floor; go back to Step 1.

   Current speaker stops talking. The conversation comes to an end.

Saying It Makes It So

You use language to make things happen in the world: You ask someone for directions or invite them to a party. You make an appointment with the dentist or order take-out food. Linguists call these things *speech acts.* Speech acts include statements, questions, promises, orders, and so on. And if you have authority, you can do special things with words: name a ship, pronounce someone man and wife, declare someone innocent, or award a penalty to the Canucks. Table 8-1 lists some of the most common speech acts.

Talking with computers

Some linguistic researchers are marrying speech act theory with conversation analysis to create *artificial dialogue systems*. A dialogue system is what *computational linguists* design in order to get humans and computers talking to each other. These systems are useful for two reasons. First, as scientific applications, human-computer dialogue systems allow linguists to test their understanding about how conversations are structured. Second, as practical applications, human-computer dialogue systems use spoken language as an interface.

Table 8-1	Types of Speech Acts	
Type	**Description**	**Example**
Assertive	Speaker commits to the truth of the statement.	I **affirm** that…, I **believe** that…, I **conclude** that…
Directive	Speaker tries to make hearer do something.	I **ask** you to…, I **beg** you to…, I **challenge** you to…, I **command** you to…, I **dare** you to…, I **invite** you to…, I **request** you to…
Commissive	Speaker commits to a course of action.	I **guarantee** that…, I **pledge** that…, I **promise** that…, I **swear** that…, I **vow** that…, I **undertake** to…, I **warrant** that…, I **want** to…
Expressive	Speaker expresses attitude.	I **apologize** for…, I **appreciate** that…, I **congratulate** you on…, I **deplore** that…, I **detest** that…, I **regret** that…, I **thank** you for…, I **welcome**…, I'm **glad** that…
Declarative	Speaker alters external condition of object.	I now **pronounce** you man and wife, I **sentence** you to life in prison, I **name** this ship the Black Pearl, I **declare** you innocent of the charges.

Linguists and philosophers debate how many types of speech acts there are and how best to analyze them. Here we focus on figuring out which speech acts are appropriate in which contexts. To be appropriate — or *felicitous*, as we linguists call it — in an utterance context, a speech act must meet certain conditions. Linguists call these *felicity conditions*. Using the speech acts of requesting and promising as examples, here are the four felicity conditions that linguists use to probe for differences between speech acts.

The # notation indicates that an utterance isn't appropriate in a certain context. Linguists call such utterances *infelicitous*.

- **Getting the context right:** The *propositional content condition* requires the meaning of the utterance — its propositional content — to be compatible with the context. For example, the propositional content of a request and a promise differ:

  - A request is about a future act by the hearer: When you say, *"Would you close the door, please?"* this is about a future action of the person you're talking to. It makes no sense to request something that's already been done: #*Please close the door (that you already closed)*.

  - A promise is about a future act by the speaker: When you say, *"I promise to close the door,"* this is about your future action. You don't promise to do something you've already done: #*I promise to close the door (that I already closed)*.

- **Having appropriate beliefs:** *Preparatory conditions* are the beliefs that a speaker must have prior to the utterance.

  - In making a request, the speaker believes that the hearer can reasonably fulfill the request and that the hearer wouldn't do it without being asked. You wouldn't say: #*"I know you're in Europe, but can you help me clean the house?"* (the hearer can't do the requested act) or #*"Do you mind breathing?"* (you breathe without being asked).

  - In making a promise, the speaker believes that the hearer desires the promised act. A teacher won't tell a group of parents, #*"I promise to fail all of your children,"* because the teacher isn't likely to believe that parents want their kids to fail.

    In English, the verb *promise* is also used to make threats. So in a situation where parents haven't paid their kids' school fees, a teacher could say, *"If you don't pay your fees by next week, I promise to fail all of your children!"*

- **Meaning what you say:** The *sincerity condition* requires that the speaker is serious.

  - In making a request, the speaker really wants the hearer to perform the requested act. You don't say: #*Get lost; have some soup*.

  - In making a promise, the speaker really means to fulfill the promise. You don't say, #*I'll pick you up after school,* when you know you'll be in a meeting downtown instead.

- **Having the right intention:** The *essential condition* requires that the speaker have a certain intention in mind when making the utterance.

  - A request is an attempt by the speaker to get the hearer to do something. When a martyred mother says, #*I really wish you'd clean up after yourself* as she picks up her daughter's dirty clothes from the floor, it doesn't work as a request because the mother doesn't intend it as a request (she knows it's hopeless).

- A promise is a commitment by the speaker to do something. If you take a cynical view of politicians, you may think that their promises aren't felicitous. Although they may mean them at the time, they don't really intend to fulfill them; they just intend to get elected.

It may seem to you that linguists assume that people live in a fairytale world: always saying the right thing, always meaning what they say, always having a purpose to what they say, and having full knowledge of the relevant facts. But we all have conversations where inappropriate things are said, where people don't mean what they say, where they have purposeless conversations, and where they don't have full knowledge of the relevant facts. The idealized scenarios of speech act theory can be used as a baseline to assess people's actual behavior in communicative exchanges. Communication does in fact work better if people's utterances match up with the world in a systematic fashion. For example, some researchers combine speech act theory with probability theory to determine the likelihood of someone behaving in an ideal fashion.

Situating a Conversation

Whenever you say something — whenever you make an utterance — you're saying it to someone about something, and you're saying it at a particular place and time for a particular reason. For example, suppose you want to buy a new bicycle and you go to your local bike shop to look around. The salesperson approaches you and you ask:

> *"Why is this bicycle over here so expensive? And why is that one over there so much cheaper?"*

In this context, you use the words *this* and *that* as well as *here* and *there* to indicate where the bicycles are relative to your location. *Deictics* are the words that you use to point to things in the world around you: They include personal pronouns *(I, me, my, mine, you, your, yours)*, demonstratives *(this, that)*, articles *(the)*, and adverbs specifying location and time *(here, now)*.

Deixis is the process of pointing at something. *Deictics* are the words used for pointing. The *deictic center* or *origo* is the person from whose perspective the pointing takes place.

Using language in different contexts

Humans can use language appropriately across a broad range of situations. Linguists call these situations *contexts* and classify them according to a number of characteristics. When looking at the context of an utterance, here are some of the major distinctions to keep in mind:

✔ **Discourse context:** This is any utterance before and after the utterance under consideration. This is important for knowing how and when to use pronouns such as *she* or *he*. (This is also called the *linguistic context*.)

✔ **Narrow utterance context:** This includes those aspects of the immediate situation in which the utterance is made. Every utterance is associated with (at least) four parameters: it is said by a certain speaker, at a certain a place, at a certain time, in a certain world.

✔ **Broad utterance context:** This includes non-linguistic social and cultural information, including:

- **The physical context:** For example, whether you're in an orderly peacetime situation or in a state of war.

- **Shared beliefs about how the world works:** Be it physical laws (there is gravity), moral laws (killing is wrong), or economic laws (distributing wealth is good).

- **Speaker's intentions and actions in the conversation:** To convince someone of their point of view, to obtain information from someone, or to alert someone to new information.

✔ **Interactional context:** This includes the non-linguistic aspects of the social interaction. You interact differently with someone in a face-to-face conversation than you do talking on the phone.

Connecting semantics to pragmatics

For many semanticists, the meaning of a sentence is defined in terms of the conditions that make the sentence true (see Chapter 7 for how formal semanticists do this). If you say, "That dog is a Blue Merle Collie," this sentence is true if:

✔ There's an entity that fits your description of a dog — this meaning is contributed by the noun *dog*.

✔ The dog is perceivable to you and to the person that you're talking to in the utterance situation. That's the meaning contributed by the demonstrative determiner *that*.

✔ The dog has the properties of being genetically a collie, having a merle color combination (solid base color and lighter patches), and having black as the base color with lighter blue/grey patches. (For dog-breeders, "blue" is any color with a black undertone to it.)

✔ The sentence is true at the moment of utterance; in other words, it's in the present tense. That's the meaning contributed by the verb *is*.

Even a simple sentence like "*That dog is a Blue Merle Collie*" has aspects of its meaning that are context-sensitive, in particular the demonstrative *that* (which points to a specific, *perceivable* dog in the utterance situation) and the helping verb *is*, which links the sentence to the time of speaking (the *utterance time*).

Utterance context is of interest to philosophers, psychologists, anthropologists, sociologists, computer scientists, and literary scholars. Because each discipline uses different terms to describe context, sometimes it's hard to see the links between the disciplines. For example, literary scholars call the broad utterance context the *setting*, and computer scientists call it *background knowledge*. But if you can figure out the characteristics of the context they're looking at, it doesn't really matter what label they use.

Shaping meaning with context

Semanticists study meaning, and pragmaticists try to understand how context affects meaning: Not surprisingly, they sometimes look at the same problems. *Formal pragmatics* looks at how context and meaning influence each other. Semanticists and pragmaticists investigating these problems focus on expressions whose meaning is partly determined by context — linguists call them *context-sensitive expressions*.

Indexicals like *me*, *here*, *now* get all their meaning from the utterance situation. *Me* refers to the speaker, *here* to the utterance location, *now* to the utterance time. Their meaning is determined by the narrow utterance context.

Demonstratives (this, that, these, those) and third person pronouns *(she/her, he/him, they/them, it)* do two things:

- They point to things: **this** book on the table, **that** book on the floor, **her** over here, **him** over there. Used in this way, their meaning is determined by the narrow utterance context and is often accompanied by a pointing gesture.

- They refer to the previous utterance, so their meaning is determined by the discourse context. In the following examples, the demonstrative *that film* gets its reference from *Pirates of the Caribbean,* and *she* gets its reference from *Lucy.*

  *I saw Pirates of the Caribbean with my nephew. He loves **that film**.*

  *Lucy loves her pet rabbit. **She** dotes over it.*

Indexing the utterance context

What do *I*, *here*, and *now* refer to? They refer to three parameters that accompany every utterance. Every utterance is said by someone (the *speaker*), at a certain place (the *location*), at a certain time (the *time*). The trick with words like *I*, *here*, and *now* is that they have no fixed reference. Rather, what they refer to shifts according to the context: *I* refers to the *utterance speaker,* likewise *here* and *now* refer to the *utterance location* and *utterance time*. (See Chapter 7 for discussion of reference.) For example, suppose you say:

"I saw the Canucks win last night."

The *I* refers to the speaker, in this case you. If someone other than you says the same sentence, then *I* refers to that speaker (and not to you). Linguists say that the pronoun *I* — and also *me*, *we*, *us* — is a context-sensitive *speaker indexical*.

Pointing to the physical context with demonstratives

The meaning of a demonstrative — forms such as *this* or *that* — is partly determined by the narrow utterance context. Speakers use demonstratives to point at what they're talking about — metaphorically or literally. In doing this, they highlight the actual physical context of the utterance, triggering the pragmatic process of reference fixing. In English, *this* (and its plural counterpart *these*) picks out entities that are nearer to the speaker, while *that* (and its plural counterpart *those*) fixes the discourse reference on entities that are farther from the speaker. Take the following example, where both Lucy and the saleswoman are discussing the same watch.

Lucy: *Could I look at that watch near the display over there?*

Saleswoman: *Do you mean this watch here?*

Lucy: *Yes, that watch.*

Matching utterances to the world: Direction of fit

Speech acts can be assessed by how well the utterance matches the way the world is. Speech act theorists call this *direction of fit*, and they distinguish four cases:

✔ **Matching the utterance to the world: word-to-world fit.** Assertions such as "*Barack Obama is the president of the United States*," have a word-to-world fit. To make an assertion is to be committed that the propositional content corresponds to an actual state of affairs in the world. Notice that you can, in the long run, turn out to be mistaken about some of the assertions that you make. This happens a lot with politicians.

✔ **Matching the world to the utterance: world-to-word fit.** Orders, requests ("*Would you put the garbage out?*"), promises ("*I promise to be on time*"), and desires ("*I want to meet the Prime Minister*") require a world-to-word fit. For these speech acts to work,

the world must change to fit the propositional content.

✔ **World-to-word-to-world fit.** Declarations such as "*I now pronounce you man and wife*" do double duty: The utterance itself changes the world. Achieving a successful fit with these speech acts is a two-step process. First, the world changes to fit the propositional content: The fact that two people can fit the condition of being married is world-to-word. This creates a state of affairs where the word — the pronouncement of marriage — now fits the word to the world.

✔ **Presupposing a fit between utterance and world.** Expressive speech acts presuppose success of fit. For example, the utterance "*I'm glad that Barack Obama is the president of the United States*" presupposes a successful word-to-world direction, namely that Barack Obama is the president of the United States.

From Lucy's vantage point, the watch is relatively far from her, so she uses the demonstrative *that*. From the saleswoman's vantage point, the watch is relatively close to her, so she uses the demonstrative *this*.

Connecting to the discourse context with pronouns

The meaning of a third person pronoun — forms such as *he*, *she*, or *it* — is partly determined by linguistic context. In particular, a pronoun is often connected to someone mentioned in an earlier utterance. Suppose you're at a café with Sandra who sees your mutual friend Lucy across the room and exclaims:

> "*Oh look! There's Lucy; she hasn't been here in ages!*"

In discourse terms, Sandra's exclamation contains three utterances — marked off above by the semi-colon and the two exclamation marks. The pronoun *she* in the third utterance refers back to the person *Lucy*, first mentioned in the second utterance. Of course, part of the meaning of a pronoun is independent of context. For example, *she* is an animate female, *he* is an animate male, and *it* is an animate or inanimate entity where gender is not an issue. That's why linguists say that pronouns are context-sensitive: Some of their meaning resides in their form, and some of their meaning comes from their context of use.

Drawing on common ground

To get the ball rolling in a conversation, you need to figure out what you have in common with the person you're talking with. When you do this, you're finding what pragmaticists call a *common ground*. If you know the other person well — for example, a friend, relative, or colleague you interact with regularly — you take the existence of a common ground for granted and jump right in. For example, suppose you walk into a room and say:

> *The dog ran away.*

The English definite article *the* marks that something is in the common ground. *The* introduces the *presupposition* that there exists a dog that's known to you and the listener. You can introduce a presupposition in many ways. Words that do this are called *presupposition triggers* and include

- **Definite determiners:** *The dog ran away.* Presupposition: There exists a dog.

- **Possessive case** *'s: Lucy's dog is big.* Presupposition: Lucy has a dog.

- **Factive verbs such as** *realize: Lucy realized that she made a mistake.* Presupposition: Lucy made a mistake.

- **Change-of-state verbs such as** *stop: Lucy stopped running marathons.* Presupposition: Lucy used to run marathons.

- **Iteratives like *again*:** *Lucy is late **again**.* Presupposition: Lucy has been late before.

- **Temporal clauses *before, after,* and *when*:** ***Before*** *we visited Amsterdam, we were in Paris.* Presupposition: We visited Amsterdam.

- **Cleft sentences introduced by *It was…* or *It is…*:** ***It was*** *Lucy that won the race.* Presupposition: Someone won the race.

- **Comparisons and contrasts:** *Lucy's **a better swimmer than** Sandra.* Presupposition: Sandra's a swimmer.

- **Counterfactual conditionals introduced by *if*:** ***If*** *Ed **had** gone, we'd have seen him.* Presupposition: Ed didn't go.

Part III
The Social Life
of Language

The 5th Wave   By Rich Tennant

RICHTENNANT

Oh, no. It's Dougie Prescott. This guy is terrible at small talk.

In this part . . .

Language is fundamentally social — it's one of the most important tools that human beings have to interact with each other. Language not only communicates thoughts and ideas, it also communicates which part of society a person belongs to. In this part, we explain how linguists understand the ways that language varies and changes, how they compare the (6,000!) languages of the world to each other, and what they've discovered about where human language comes from, how new languages are born, and why some languages die out.

Chapter 9

Living with Language Variation: Sociolinguistics

*T*he way you talk reflects where you were born, where you live, what you do for a living, and who you hang out with. The study of how such social factors are mirrored in your language is called *sociolinguistics*. We show you what sociolinguists have found out about how you, as a social animal, use language as a social tool.

Sociolinguistics looks at how social structure affects language use, and so is related to pragmatics or how people make conversations work (see Chapter 8 for more on this). *Sociology of language* focuses on how linguistic usage shapes social dynamics. *Linguistic anthropology* focuses on how language shapes cultural identity, organizes belief systems, and sustains worldviews.

Using Language As a Social Tool

Suppose you're talking to someone and they interrupt to tell you that what you've just said isn't "proper English." If your speech is corrected — or if you correct someone else's speech — what's at stake is a *norm*. Norms are rules — explicit or implicit — that a group uses to govern its values, beliefs, attitudes, and behaviors. Different groups have different values — what's okay in one group won't be okay in another group. Applied to language, this means that different groups have different linguistic values.

Winning out over other dialects

The way you talk isn't the same as the way you write. In societies where language is written down, the *standard* form of the language is the written language. The standard form of any language lives side-by-side with other language varieties — linguists call these varieties *non-standard*.

- ✔ The standard variety of language is prestigious, schools teach it, and being able to speak it gives you power. Sounds like anyone with any sense would speak the standard variety! Actually, in any society, only a minority speak the standard. Sociologists call this minority the *elite* — they include professionals like teachers, professors, lawyers, doctors, and business leaders. If you know someone who speaks this way — or if you speak this way — then they (or you) probably sound stuffy and bookish.

- ✔ The non-standard variety is spoken by down-to-earth sensible types like plumbers, electricians, oil-rig workers, cafeteria workers, hotel maids, and janitors. This way of speaking isn't prestigious, the school system ignores it, and speaking it doesn't give you more power. If you know someone who talks this way — or if you do — then they (or you) probably sound like a regular good old guy (or gal).

No matter which language you speak, you bounce back and forth between using standard and non-standard varieties of your language. Every speaker does this. Which variety you use in what situations depends on many social factors.

For linguists, the terms *standard* and *non-standard* carry no value judgment about quality. A standard variety of a language isn't better than a non-standard variety — they're just different. What determines whether a variety is selected as the standard? A combination of social, economic, and historical factors — and these can all change over time.

Maintaining "top dog" status

In places where people speak two or more languages, one language is usually dominant in the public sphere. But how does a language or language variety get to be top dog? It's like being a movie star — the more exposure you get, the more recognition you get. Top dog status is awarded to the language or language variety that gets the most airtime, has the most perks, and is most useful to social climbers.

For sociolinguists, a *dominant language* is the one used by government. Many situations of language context involve complex situations of language usage. For example, one language is used for administration, another at school, another in the streets, and yet another at home.

Getting airtime in the linguistic marketplace

If groups that speak different languages are in contact over a long period of time, they compete over which language or language variety is used in public. Linguists call this competition the *linguistic marketplace*. Table 9-1 gives examples of how contact creates a linguistic marketplace where one variety — or one language — is top dog.

Table 9-1	The Linguistic Marketplace	
Competition	*Nature of Contact*	*Example*
Language varieties compete with each other	Continuous residency on same territory	United Kingdom: Standard British English competes with non-standard varieties
	Speaker groups settle onto same territory	United States: Standard American English competes with non-standard varieties
Languages compete with each other	Continuous residency on same territory	France: French competes with Breton
		Spain: Spanish competes with Basque
	Speaker groups settle onto same territory	Canada: English competes with French
		United States: English competes with Spanish

Giving perks to some speaker groups

Some people are more equal than others. Folks who speak the standard language variety have a head start. Put plainly: It doesn't hurt to be born on the right side of town. This is an example of *social alignment*. And while some groups have privileges, others are subject to *social exclusion*. It's like not being picked for the high school basketball team — some groups don't get to participate in certain activities. Strange as it may seem, language does both of these things: It promotes alignment *and* exclusion. Sound contradictory? Here's how it works:

- ✔ Speakers of a non-standard variety (or a non-dominant language) are more likely to have lower levels of education and less-skilled jobs. They have more problems getting adequate healthcare, they're under-represented in media and politics, and they're over-represented in prisons.

- ✔ Speakers of a standard variety or a dominant language are in sync with mainstream society. They're more likely to have higher levels of education and high-skilled jobs. They have better access to healthcare, and they're generally over-represented in media and politics.

If the story ended there, the world would be unfair and dreary. In the words of David Hume, "life would be nasty, brutish, and short." But human beings also use the social tool of language in creative ways to strengthen their identity.

Groups who speak a non-standard variety (or a non-dominant language) can exclude outsiders on the basis of language. They can use language to create social alignment and strengthen group identity within their speech community. See Chapter 12 for a discussion of how this interacts with language maintenance and revitalization.

Social climbing with language

Whenever you meet a new person, you make judgments about the kind of person they are the minute they open their mouth. Your judgments are often unconscious and automatic — you can't stop yourself from doing this. (Even if you're a trained linguist!) This judging is something that all language users do: They assign a positive or negative social value to a language variety (or a language), which transforms language into a powerful social tool. This is something that humans *do to* language. And after humans shape language into a social tool, they then cleverly use it to position themselves in the social pecking order.

✔ **At an individual level,** speakers use the standard variety (or dominant language) to advance socially and economically. In the film *My Fair Lady*, Henry Higgins teaches Eliza Doolittle standard British English, enabling her to acquire a higher social standing. This is an example of how language promotes social mobility. Even if someone is born on the "wrong side of the tracks," they can improve their social and economic status by mastering the standard variety or dominant language. Indeed, the education system is based on the belief that teaching the standard variety (or dominant language) levels the playing field.

✔ **At a societal level,** the use of language as a social tool involves setting out rules for spoken and written language. This includes rules for spelling and for what counts as standard language, a process of prescriptive grammar (see Chapter 6 for discussion of the difference between prescriptive and descriptive linguistics).

Speakers belong to a *speech community,* defined as a group of people who use language with each other in a unique and mutually accepted way. A speech community consists of the *social networks* that tie together individual members of the community and affect the speech patterns of community members. Networks differ according to the degree of interaction between members. In a *tight network,* all members interact with one another. In a *loose network,* individuals interact with a subset of the entire community. In a *multiplex network,* individuals move back and forth across several networks.

A short history of sociolinguistics

Sociolinguistics emerged as a subfield in the 1970s and combines three research threads:

- **Historical linguistics** studies how language changes over time. It grew out of the discipline of *philology* (the study of ancient texts) and emerged in the late 1700s as an attempt to reconstruct pre-historic languages (see Chapter 10 for a discussion of language change). In gathering evidence for language change, one of the things that historical linguists do is look at different dialects of the same language.

- **Sociology** analyzes modern society. It emerged as an academic discipline in the late 1800s in response to rapid changes in technology and society. It is associated with the work of Emile Durkheim (on industrialization and the social division of labor), Karl Marx (on capitalism), and Max Weber (on efficiency and the protestant work ethic).

- **Structural linguistics** focuses on the structural analysis of language. It emerged in the early 1900s and views language as a formal system defined by structural features universal to all languages. European structuralism is associated with Ferdinand de Saussure, Roman Jakobson, and Nikolai Trubetzkoy. American structuralism is associated with Leonard Bloomfield and Zellig Harris. Noam Chomsky's generative grammar (discussed in Chapter 6) is an outgrowth of European and American structuralist linguistics.

Sociolinguists adopt and extend methods from these three disciplines — the notion of variation from historical linguistics, the idea of social structure from sociology, and the concept of rules of language structure from structural linguistics and generative grammar. Two pioneers in this area are William Labov in the United States and Basil Bernstein in the United Kingdom.

Observing Language Variation

You often have conversations with people that you perceive as having an accent. But then they probably think that you have an accent. Who's right? Is the other person speaking with an accent or are you? Well, in reality, you both are. This is an important insight of linguistics: No two people speak in exactly the same way. In looking at what makes people sound different from each other, linguists have discovered that

- **Language variation is pervasive.** Language is in a constant state of flux. It's impossible for you to say the same thing twice in exactly the same way: This is because the physics of speech production is variable (see Chapter 15 for more on how you produce speech).

- **Language variation is systematic.** Your speech doesn't vary just any which way. Rather, your speech variation follows a system of rules, which makes language variation systematic. Sociolinguists try to uncover the system of rules that allow you, as a speaker, to decide how to say what in a certain social context.

Linguists compare speakers with each other and identify which aspects of their speech are the same and which show variation. This involves looking at *linguistic variables* — those aspects of speech that vary — including phonetic, phonological, lexical, syntactic, semantic, and pragmatic variables. (See Chapters 3 through 8 for info about each of these areas.)

Linguists classify linguistic variables into three types. *Linguistic indicators* are perceivable to the speaker and mark social differences. *Linguistic markers* aren't perceivable to the speaker but mark social differences and style shifts. *Linguistic stereotypes* are perceivable to the speaker and mark social differences and style shifts.

Pronouncing things differently: Phonetic and phonological variation

An Australian English speaker may pronounce the word *bed* as [bɪd] (to rhyme with *bid*), while a North American English speaker pronounces it as [bɛd]. Such differences reflect *phonetic* and *phonological variation*. At first, these differences can throw you off, but speakers usually quickly adjust to differences in each other's speech patterns.

For examples of different varieties of English spoken in the United Kingdom, see the British Library website *Sounds Familiar* (www.bl.uk/learning/langlit/sounds/).

Using different words: Lexical variation

Different varieties of the same language can use different words for the same thing: Linguists call this *lexical variation*. This can happen in two ways. Speakers can have twin words for everything, or they can use different forms of the same word.

Doubling up: Lexical doublets

Some vocabulary items are associated with particular social groups. For example, your doctor may say *ulnar nerve* where you'd say *funny bone* — this is an example of lexical variation based on occupation. Your grandmother may say *chesterfield,* and you'd say *couch* — this is an example of lexical variation based on age. A feminist cousin may say *humankind,* while you'd say *mankind* — this is an example of lexical variation involving politics. All languages have lexical variation, but some languages have it more than others. For example, French is notorious for having hundreds of word-pairs, called *lexical doublets*. The two words mean the same thing, but one is a standard form used in more formal situations and the other is used in more casual situations. For example, car is either *automobile* or *bagnole:* The first is high-falutin', the second is plain-jane. And dear to every French person's heart are discussions about food. Here too, there are doublets. To eat is *manger* or *bouffer;* the first action takes place at a high-end restaurant, the second at a fast-food joint. As for the obligatory walk after their meal, there is *se balader* and *se promener,* both mean 'to walk'. The first is breezy and light-hearted, the second is serious and sedate.

French doublets come from the same vocabulary set but are used in different social situations. This differs from English, which, for historical reasons has two vocabulary sets — the *Latinate lexicon* (for example, *mutton* and *pork*) and the *Anglo-Saxon lexicon* (for example, *sheep* and *pig*). For info on the origin and usage of these two vocabulary sets in English, see Chapter 5.

Using different forms of the same word: Morphological variation

The standard English past tense of the helping verb *to be* uses two forms — *was (I was happy)* and *were (We were happy, You guys were happy, They were happy)*. Many regional varieties of English simplify this and use only one of the two forms. For example, in the United Kingdom, speakers in northern England and the Midlands have a tendency to use *were* in all persons, while speakers from the Southeast tend to use *was* in all persons. Table 9-2 spells out this example of *morphological variation*. In contexts where the standard variety is appropriate, speakers switch to the standard English pattern. And in contexts where the regional variety is more suitable, speakers switch to that variety.

Table 9-2	Morphological Variation with the Verb Was/Were		
	Standard English	*Northern England & Midlands*	*Southeast England*
1st person singular	*I* **was** *sad*	*I* **were** *sad*	*I* **was** *sad*
1st person plural	*We* **were** *sad*	*We* **were** *sad*	*We* **was** *sad*
2nd person (singular or plural)	*You* **were** *sad*	*You* **were** *sad*	*You* **was** *sad*
3rd person singular	*She* **was** *sad*	*She* **were** *sad*	*She* **was** *sad*
3rd person plural	*They* **were** *sad*	*They* **were** *sad*	*They* **was** *sad*

For examples of speakers using different forms of the past tense English helping verb, see www.bl.uk/learning/langlit/sounds/regional-voices/grammatical-variation/.

Putting sentences together differently: Syntactic variation

Syntactic variation happens when speakers use different rules for forming sentences. For example, the French spoken in Montreal differs from standard French in its syntax. Montrealers use different helping verbs, have a different way of making the future tense, and chain sentences together differently:

- **Helping verb *être* 'to be':** To say 'I fell', the standard form is *Je **suis** tombé,* literally 'I am fallen', with the helping verb 'be'. The Montreal variety of French uses the helping verb *avoir* 'have': (*J'**ai** tombé,* literally 'I have fallen', with the helping verb 'have'.

- **Future tense:** The standard variety uses a future tense suffix on the verb: *Je tomberai* 'I will fall'). The Montreal variety of French uses the helping verb 'go' (*Je **vais** tomber* 'I'm gonna fall').

- **The subordinating conjunction *que* 'that':** To introduce a subordinate clause, the standard variety requires *que: Je pensais que c'était bien* 'I thought that it was good'). The Montreal variety can omit it: *Je pensais c'était bien* 'I thought it was good'.

Montreal French speakers use both the standard and non-standard (Montreal French) forms. Which form they select depends on the social context: Standard forms are more likely to be used in formal situations (talking to an employer); non-standard forms are more often used in casual conversation (joking around with friends).

Montreal French is a form of Laurentian French — also known as Québécois French — spoken along the Laurentian River valley in Canada, as well as in Ontario and western Canada. The other variety of French spoken in Canada is Acadian French, mostly spoken in New Brunswick, Nova Scotia, Prince Edward Island, the Saint John River valley in northern Maine, as well as the Magdalen Islands and Havre Saint-Pierre in the Gulf of Saint Lawrence. Acadian French is related to the Cajun French spoken in the state of Louisiana.

Expressing meaning differently: Semantic variation

Semantic variation occurs when two language varieties use the same form but with a different meaning. An example is the use of the quantifier *beaucoup* 'many' in European and Québécois French. In both varieties, the quantifier can be separated from the noun it modifies — linguists call this *quantification-at-a-distance*. The following example illustrates this type of quantification:

> *J'ai* **beaucoup** *vu de films.*
>
> I have many seen of the films
>
> 'I saw many films'

Both varieties use quantification-at-a-distance for multiple events as in the previous example. Seeing many films implies several events of film viewing. But Québécois speakers can also use quantification-at-a-distance with single events. The following example — which involves a single event of finding — is fine in Québécois French, but *not* in European French:

> *J'ai* **beaucoup** *trouvé de pièces d'or.*
>
> I have many found of the pieces of gold
>
> 'I found many pieces of gold'

When a sentence is possible in one variety but ungrammatical in another variety, linguists put a percentage mark at the beginning of the sentence to indicate the variation in grammaticality: *%J'ai beaucoup trouvé de pieces d'or.*

Using context differently: Pragmatic variation

Pragmatic variation arises when speakers use different forms in the same context. For example, the French equivalent of the question 'When are you coming?' can be expressed in several ways. French speakers have three ways of formulating a question, according to whether they want to sound like an upper class speaker, like a working class speaker, or neutral between the two:

- Upper class: *Quand venez-vous?*, literally 'when come you?'

- Working class: *Quand que vous venez?*, literally 'when that you come?'

- Neutral: *Quand est-ce que vous venez?*, literally, 'when is it that you come?'

Sociolinguists use the term *social stratification* to talk about differences that reflect distinctions in social class.

Social class groups members of a society according to how much social and political power they have. Three widely recognized class divisions are *upper class, middle class,* and *working class* (also called *lower class*). In terms of language use, members of the working class use the non-standard variety more often, while members of the middle and upper classes use the standard variety more often. The twist is that middle-class speakers use the standard variety more often than upper-class speakers. This is because middle-class speakers are more likely to use the standard variety as a tool for social advancement — they're social climbers! But all speakers use standard and non-standard varieties; they simply differ in how much, and in which contexts, they use the two varieties.

Searching for language variation

Sociolinguists use different ways of collecting data that allow them to measure how linguistic and social factors affect one another. The most common forms of data collection are surveys, interviews, and polls.

- **Surveys** date back to the late 19th century. Linguists specializing in dialect variation — called *dialectologists* — traveled throughout the rural areas of Europe and America to record differences in pronunciation, grammar, and the lexicon. Questionnaires probe directly for dialectal forms: They're very detailed and can take several days to complete. Surveys continue to be used to make dialect maps that indicate the geographical boundaries (called *isoglosses*) of sounds, grammatical structures, and words.

- **Interviews** probe indirectly for target forms. This technique controls for differences between casual and careful speech by asking subjects to participate in different production tasks such as reading out loud, answering formal questions, and participating in casual conversation. In addition, subjects are asked to listen and evaluate speech samples that have the linguistic variables being studied — this is called a *subjective reaction test*. Linguists then compare what informants say about others' usage (during the reaction test)

and their own usage (during the structured interview) with their actual usage.

- **Polling** is used for large-scale data collection. Subjects provide information about pronunciation and vocabulary by answering fill-in-the-blank questions such as "*Does the ending of AVENUE sound like ___you or ___oo?*" The Internet is really useful for polls. Other techniques include *telephone polling* and *in-person anonymous polling*, which use *unelicited data* (data the researcher observes) or *elicited data* (data volunteered in response to questions posed by the researcher).

When choosing the actual participants for surveys or interviews, sociolinguists use several different sampling techniques to make sure that the data they collect is representative and unbiased:

- **Random sample:** Everyone in the group has an equal chance of being selected.

- **Judgment sample:** Subjects are selected according to a set of criteria, such as age, gender, class, and education. The researcher sometimes also judges which subjects have which criteria. This type of sampling is often used in sociolinguistic studies.

- **Stratified sample:** Subjects are selected from a random sample on the basis of specific characteristics.

Investigating Why Language Varies

Social factors such as where you're from, how old you are, whether you're male or female, and what you do for a living influence your speech pattern. You can also alter your *speech style* in different situations — your ability to adapt your talking style according to the situation you're in is what makes you socially adaptive. Taken together, social factors and speech style shape the way that you talk.

Constructing linguistic identity

You're a social animal, and your way of talking reflects your social identity: where you come from, as well as your age, class, gender, and occupation. Linguists call these *social variables*.

Location, location, location!

Dialect variation is linguistic variation based on the social variable of location. If you have friends or relatives from Newfoundland, you know that Newfoundlanders (also called Newfies) have a distinctive way of talking. Newfoundland is the oldest English colony in Canada, and its English derives from two settler communities — one from southeast Ireland and the other from southwest England. The uniqueness of Newfoundland English reflects three factors:

- **Geographical isolation:** Newfoundland is an island, so Newfoundland English was isolated from the rest of North American English from the late 1600s through the mid-20th century.

- **Political independence:** Newfoundland didn't join Canada until 1949, and so had little truck with the mainland until then. Its variety of English has always been distinct from the variety of English spoken in the rest of Canada.

- **Continuous contact with Irish and British English:** Until the early 1800s, Irish and British fishermen would seasonally fish off the coast of Newfoundland, keeping speakers from the Old World and New World in continuous contact.

Newfoundland English differs from Canadian English in various ways:

- **Phonology:** [t] and [d] replace the fricatives that begin *think* and *this*, which come out as *tink and dis*. The last consonant of *killed* is pronounced [t], so it comes out as *kill't*. And [d] replaces the [z] of *wasn't* and *isn't*, so the Newfie pronunciation is *wadn't* and *idn't*.

- **Lexicon:** *Ye*, a special form of the second plural pronoun, replaces *you*. Where a Canadian English speaker says *Did **you** see Lucy?*, a Newfie says *Did **ye** see Lucy?*

- **Syntax:** Newfoundland English uses *after* for prospective actions and resultant states. Where an inland Canadian English speaker says *He wants to eat his dinner*, a Newfie says *He's **after** his dinner*. And Newfie English marks habitual actions with *do:* where a Canadian English speaker says *He's always tired after work*, a Newfie says *He **does** be tired after work.*

Glimpsing language change in progress

Language variation and change are connected. Language variation occurs if a speaker uses different variants in different social contexts. Language change occurs if, over time, one variant replaces another variant (see Chapter 10 for more on language change). Linguists can see language change as it's happening — this is *change in progress* — by attending to language variation. In particular, linguists can detect which features are being lost, maintained, or introduced by looking at

✔ **Variation across generations of speakers.** By sampling speaker groups at regular age intervals — for example 20-, 40-,

and 60-year-olds — linguists observe which parts of the grammar are undergoing change. Studies using this technique are called *apparent-time studies*. *Real-time studies* return to speakers at regular intervals, for example every 10 years. If the same speakers are involved, it's a *panel study*. If different speakers are involved, it's a *trend study*.

✔ **Variation in speech style.** To get a snapshot of linguistic change in progress, linguists look at casual speech, which functions as an "early detection system" for language change.

The generation gap: Young versus old folk

You probably hear people around you use the word *like* to introduce a quotation, as in the following example:

> I'm **like** "No way!", and she's **like** "Yes way!"

Depending on your age, this may be something that you say. Linguists think that this *like* originated in California. It's now used throughout English-speaking North America and has even spread to England and other English-speaking countries. Several sociolinguistic studies have found that this use of *like* shows an age-related distribution, with younger speakers more likely to use it than older speakers. This is an example of age-based pragmatic variation.

Warring classes: Underdog versus top dog

In November 1962, William Labov conducted a now-famous anonymous in-person poll to track variation in New York City English. Labov selected three stores with different markets:

✔ High-end market: Saks 5th Avenue

✔ Mid-range market: Macy's

✔ Budget market: S. Klein

Approaching employees in each store, he asked the location of departments on the fourth floor — he wanted to hear the employees say the phrase *fourth floor* because New York City English speakers vary according to whether they pronounce /r/ in these words. After the initial question, which Labov expected the employees to answer in casual speech, he then elicited careful repetition of *fourth floor* by pretending to mishear the first response. This allowed Labov to see whether a store's market niche (and the employees' speaking style) was related to *r*-pronunciation. This is what he found:

- ✔ **Speech style:** Careful repetition always increased *r*-pronunciation.

- ✔ **Linguistic features:** The word-final [r] of *floor* was kept more often than the [r] of *fourth*.

- ✔ **Class:** More people at the high-end and mid-range stores used [r]. About one-third of the employees at the high-end and mid-range stores kept [r], but only one-fifth of the employees at the low-end store kept it.

- ✔ **Age and class:** Controlling for age, middle social groups adapted their pronunciation more than the higher and lower social groups. Older employees used *r*-pronunciation less in the high-end store (Saks) but more in the mid-range store (Macy's); the budget store (S. Klein) had no age difference.

If only class is considered, employees at the high-end and mid-range stores behave the same way — about one-third of them keep [r]. But if both age *and* class are factored in, then the *social climbing* aspect of language use is more visible. Older employees at the mid-range store keep [r] *more than* the older employees at the high-end store do! What gives? Why are employees at the mid-range store (Macy's) pronouncing [r] more that the high-falutin' employees at Saks. Sociolinguists think that this is because middle-class speakers are more anxious about their social standing and so are more likely to use the standard as a tool for social advancement. And if you're already the top dog — like the Saks employees — you don't care so much about the standard.

The battle of the sexes: Women versus men

Do women and men talk differently? Before answering this, we need to be clear about the difference between *gender* and *sex:*

- ✔ **Gender** is a social role associated with feminine versus masculine behavior.

- ✔ **Sex** is a trait associated with the biological difference between female (two X chromosomes) and male (X and Y chromosome).

Most human females behave in a feminine way and most human males behave in a masculine way. Of course, it's always possible for a female to adopt masculine behavior, for example, a *butch chick*. And it's possible for a male to adopt feminine behavior — for example, an *effeminate man*. So *women's speech* is the speech of females who have adopted a feminine social role; *men's speech* is the speech of males who have adopted a masculine social role.

Some languages have different forms for men and women, so pinning down how women's and men's speech differs is easy. Here are some examples:

- ✔ **Phonological difference:** In Atsina, an Algonquian language that used to be spoken by the Gros Ventre in Montana, women had palatalized velar stops, but men had palatalized dental stops. The female word for 'bread' was *kjatsa*, the male word was *djatsa*.

- ✔ **Lexical difference:** In casual Japanese, for 'I' a woman says *watasi,* but a man says *boku*. And women often add *wa* to the end of their sentences. So, for 'I will go back', a woman says *watasi kaeru wa;* a man says *boku kaeru*. And in Dyirbal, an Australian aboriginal language, all speakers use the same everyday language (Guwal), but a different language (Dyalnuy) is used by a woman speaking in the presence of her father-in-law or by a man speaking in the presence of his mother-in-law. This in-law language has the same phonology and syntax as Guwal, but it has a completely different vocabulary.

- ✔ **Morphological difference:** Yanyuwa, an Australian aboriginal language, has distinct dialects for women and men. All speakers use the base forms *(roots),* but women and men use a different set of prefixes on nouns, verbs, and pronouns.

For languages like English, the differences between female and male speech are more elusive. In response to the first wave of modern feminism, research in the 1970s and 1980s focused on uncovering differences between male and female speech. But the more they looked, the less they found! After a lot of prodding and poking around, linguists concluded that men and women — at least in English-speaking countries such as Australia, Canada, New Zealand, the United States, and the United Kingdom — use the same linguistic features but differ in the contexts and extent to which they use them. This results in subtle, but systematic, gender-based tendencies. The ones that come up the most often are

- ✔ **Conversational goal:** Women use conversation to reinforce social bonds by using compliments *(What a gorgeous dress!)* and praise *(You're so smart!)*. Men focus on exchanging information: They issue statements *(The Alberta economy is heating up)* and challenge the statements of others.

- ✔ **Conversational content:** Women talk about how they *feel (*linguists call this *affective content);* men talk about what they *do*.

- ✔ **Conversational flow:** Women manage conversational flow by asking questions, encouraging others to speak, and being inclusive — they focus on building cooperation and rapport. Men often seek to dominate and control the interaction: They do this by interrupting, challenging, disputing, protesting, and, if all else fails, ignoring the other person.

Sociolinguistic studies looking at pronunciation and lexical differences in men's and women's speech find that women *lead* linguistic innovation and change. What does this mean? Well, if a linguistic feature is introduced into a speech community — a different rule of pronunciation *(tomato* versus *tomahto)* or a new expression *(no problem* versus *no worries)* — the change is usually introduced by women. Exactly why this is so isn't clearly understood.

Correlating social and linguistic variables

After a social variable has been identified, sociolinguists try to see whether it correlates with a linguistic variable. They do this by matching social variables with linguistic variables and checking to see how they affect one another. These are the variables they work with:

- **Social variables:** Location, age, gender, class, occupation, and ethnicity

- **Linguistic variables:** Phonetic, phonological, lexical, morphological, syntactic, semantic, and pragmatic

One goal of sociolinguistic research is to identify which social variables correlate with which linguistic variables. For example, the social variable of location (where someone lives) can correlate with speaker variation in phonetics, phonology, morphology, syntax, semantics, or pragmatics, and so on for each of the other social variables. In principle, for a given language (or variety), sociolinguists evaluate all the logically possible correlations of social and linguistic variables. In practice, until recently, sociolinguistic research has focused on phonetic, phonological, and lexical variations. That's because these differences are the easiest to observe and measure. Recent work looks at syntactic, semantic, and pragmatic variations more systematically.

If you're trying to figure out where a sociolinguistic study fits into the larger picture, use the list of social and linguistic variables previous to get a sense of which part of the pie the study is looking at.

Projecting your style

If you're at a party with friends, you speak pretty casually. But if you're making a presentation to the members of the board, you use more formal language. Linguists call these different ways of talking *speaking styles*. The speaking style that you adopt reflects three factors:

- How you adapt your way of speaking to the social context
- The efforts you make to accommodate your audience
- How you define your role as a speaker

Being a linguistic shape-shifter

Sociolinguists have discovered that the speech style that you use in casual speech — that's when you're not monitoring yourself — reflects your social class. And whatever your social class, you use the same style-shifts as speakers from other social classes, but not to the same degree.

Shifting speech style isn't just a matter of switching from speaking the standard variety to speaking the non-standard variety. Whatever is your normal way of speaking is the baseline — sociolinguists define this as the way you speak when you're relaxed. Depending on your social class, your relaxed speech style may be more like the standard variety or more like the non-standard variety or somewhere in between. For example, the linguistic baseline of Prince William is not the same as the one for British blues singer Adele. But both of them use the same set of style-shifting devices. The only difference lies in how often they use them. This discovery has changed how teachers approach language instruction in the school system. For example, rather than correcting speech style differences — which aren't *wrong* to begin with — teachers help students understand which speech styles are appropriate in which situations.

Style-shifting devices make use of all the language-related social variables that speakers have at their disposal. For example, speakers can play around with regional differences; for example, a Canadian English speaker may say "zee" instead of "zed" for the letter *z* when speaking to someone from the United States. Speakers play with differences in phrasing and intonation, as well as vocabulary differences related to social variables like occupation, gender, age, and so on.

Talking to your audience

Most people adapt their speech style to their audience. For example, lawyers use a different speech style in a courtroom than they would when going out to celebrate a win. In this way, speech style has social meaning because some topics connect with certain settings and audiences:

Addressing your audience

Your interaction with audience members reflects four factors: physical presence, your awareness of them, whether you address them, and your effort to include them. Here are five audience scenarios:

✔ **Addressees** are physically present. As a speaker, you're aware of them, you address them directly, and you make an effort to include them. Visually, you do this by checking to see that they're paying attention. Verbally you check in with them to see if they're following what you're saying (with phrases such as "*What do you think?*" or "*Is that so?*"). You use language that emphasizes inclusion (for example, by using the first person plural pronoun *we* and trying to find topics of mutual interest).

✔ **Auditors** are also physically present. As a speaker, you're aware of them, and though

you don't address them directly, you do include them in your audience.

✔ **Overhearers** are physically present. As a speaker, you're aware of them, but you neither address them directly nor include them in your audience. You basically ignore them and don't adjust your speech style to them.

✔ **Eavesdroppers** are physically present, but the speaker is unaware of them so of course can't address them or include them in the audience.

✔ **Referees** are a virtual audience: Even though they're not physically present, the speaker is aware of them, addresses them, and includes them. Social media forums are an example of a virtual audience. (Check out Chapter 18 for more on how the Internet changes the way people communicate.)

✔ **Social context determines your speaking style.** When you shift styles, you respond to your social environment by taking into account the presence and response of your audience. You can even create a social environment by addressing a virtual audience.

✔ **Your audience determines your speaking style.** Everybody wants to be loved! Your desire to gain the approval of your audience affects your speech style.

Audience-design shifting describes your ability to adjust your speaking style to your audience. *Speaker-design shifting* describes how you balance your desire to project your identity against your desire to connect with your audience. When a speaker identifies with a group that isn't present, linguists call this *initiative style-shifting*; the absent group is called a *referee group*.

Playing your role as a speaker

As a speaker, you play a role with respect to your audience; this is your *role relation*. When shifting styles to play a role, you use one of two strategies:

✔ **You shift your style away from your audience.** You can imitate a dialect that isn't part of your everyday conversation or your audience's — linguists call this *dialect-performance*. You may do this to express solidarity with the group that's associated with that dialect or *sociolect* (the speech variety linked with social features such as age, class, gender, and occupation). Linguists call this *divergent linguistic behavior*.

✔ **You shift your style towards your audience.** An example of this is when language teachers accommodate their speech to the level of their students. Linguists call this *convergent linguistic behavior*.

A *lect* is a variety of speech. The speech variety of a single individual is an *idiolect*. A *dialect* is the speech variety of a regional area. A *sociolect* (also called *social dialect*) is the speech variety linked with social features such as age, class, gender, and occupation. A *genderlect* is the speech variety associated with gender — for example, linguists compare the female genderlect with the male genderlect.

Variationist analyses focus on the linguistic variables associated with speaking styles. In anthropological linguistics, speaking styles are part of the *ethnography of communication*, which looks at how ways of speaking reflect social structures.

Chapter 10

Finding Family Relations: Historical Linguistics

*L*anguages, like siblings, often resemble other languages from the same language family. For example, you as an English speaker say *mother* while a German speaker says *mutter*. For 'cheese', the French have *frômage*, and the Italians have *formaggio*. For 'woman', Plains Cree has *iskwêw* and Ojibwe has *ikwe*. For 'sea', the Māori have *tai*, and the Hawaiians have *kai*. These similarities reflect the fact that these pairs of languages are related. *Historical linguists* use a form of linguistic archeology called the *comparative method* to figure out how languages are related to each other and how they change over time. In uncovering historical connections between languages, linguists make discoveries not just about the history of languages but also about the history of humankind.

Uncovering Family Ties

You speak Modern English. Modern English descends from Early Modern English (the language of William Shakespeare), which descends from Middle English (the language of Geoffrey Chaucer), which descends from Old English (the language of *Beowulf*). These are distinct historical stages of the same language. What was there before Old English? To answer this question historical linguists focus on two observations:

✔ Languages change.

✔ Some languages resemble other languages.

In this section, we show you how linguists uncover language change and how this helps them understand how human languages are related to one another.

To hear what English sounded like 1,000 years ago, search for the Lord's Prayer in Old English. Don't worry if you can't understand it. Only 10 percent of Modern English words existed in Old English, though many common vocabulary items, like *father* and *our,* are still around.

Linguists distinguish *languages* from *dialects*. Languages aren't mutually intelligible. Dialects tend to be mutually intelligible — speakers of two dialects can usually understand one another, but not always. Suppose one dialect, call it B, is mutually intelligible with two other dialects, A and C. Depending on the way they differ from one another, dialects A and C may be so different that they are no longer mutually intelligible. For example, dialects of Cree are like this: Their differences form a *dialect continuum* that stretches geographically from the foothills of the Rockies all the way to the eastern seaboard. Moving from west to east, each dialect-pair is mutually intelligible, but speakers of the westernmost dialects don't understand speakers of the easternmost dialects. Linguists use dialects to study change in progress (see Chapter 9 for examples of dialect variation).

Identifying related languages

To identify related languages, linguists use a method of analysis called the *comparative method,* which involves three steps:

1. **Find related words.**

2. **Establish sound correspondences.**

3. **Establish correspondences between words.**

Historical linguists use the term *proto-language* to talk about ancestral languages, but they use this term in two different ways. A proto-language can be the real language from which related languages descend. Or it can be the ancestral language that historical linguists predict existed through reconstruction.

Finding related words

The first step is to assemble a list of words with similar meaning. Certain vocabulary areas tend not to change much over time — they include terms for kinship *(father, mother, sister, aunt),* people, pronouns *(I, you, he, she, they),* numbers, body parts, animals, agriculture, natural features, and directions. Adjectives describing mental and physical attributes, as well as verbs describing mental and bodily functions, construction, fabrication, motion, and rest, are also stable. These stable vocabulary items usually make it easier to find related words *(cognates)* in other languages and so figure out whether languages are historically connected. But rare words are useful, too, because they may preserve features found only in certain dialects or languages. In the end, historical linguists work with whatever words they find and try to recover the most information they can from them.

Just because two languages share vocabulary doesn't mean they're related. The similarities may be because of borrowings through language contact. To figure out whether a word is a borrowing, linguists use historical records — this allows them to date when a word appears on the scene.

Establishing sound correspondences

By comparing basic words with similar meaning, linguists can see whether sounds match up with one other. If sounds regularly match up, linguists call this a *sound correspondence*. For example, in comparing Māori and Hawaiian, two languages that belong to the Polynesian language family, linguists consider forms like those in Table 10-1.

Table 10-1	Sound Correspondences in Māori and Hawaiian				
	t/k Correspondence		*r/l Correspondence*		
	'sea'	'one'	'five'	'enter'	'three'
Māori	tai	tahi	rima	uru	toru
Hawaiian	kai	kahi	lima	ulu	kolu

Linguists can reconstruct the sounds of the ancestral language by observing sound correspondences in the daughter languages. For example, everywhere that Māori has /t/, Hawaiian has /k/. And everywhere that Māori has /r/, Hawaiian has /l/. But which sounds are older? By comparing other Polynesian languages — including Tongan, Niuean, Samoan, Takuu, and Tahitian — linguists have reconstructed proto-Polynesian as having */t/ and */l/. (Linguists use the asterisk * to mark that these were the sounds in the proto-language.) This means that Hawaiian innovated /k/ and Māori innovated /r/.

Linguists then check that the reconstructed sounds are plausible, by ensuring that they're consistent with what linguists know about sound change. Three kinds of sound change are possible:

✔ **A sound can replace another sound.** Hawaiian /k/ replaces proto-Polynesian /t/; Māori /r/ replaces proto-Polynesian /l/. Both of these changes, t>k and l>r, are consistent with what phonologists know about sound rules — stop consonants often replace other stop consonants (/t/ and /k/ are stops), and approximants often replace other approximants (/l/ and /r/ are approximants). See Chapter 3 for a description of different kinds of sounds.

✔ **A sound can be lost.** While the proto-Polynesian form for 'sea' is *tahi*, Māori has *tai* and Hawaiian has *kai*. So in both these languages, /h/ was lost between vowels. Linguists symbolized this as h>Ø. ("Ø" is the symbol for null.)

✔ **A sound can be introduced.** For example, Māori introduced /w/ before words that begin with /h/, so proto-Polynesian *hati* 'break' changed to Māori *whati*.

Linguists use a lot of jargon for describing sound change. Here are some of the more commonly used terms. A sound replacing another sound includes *assimilation* (a sound becoming more like neighboring sounds), *dissimilation* (a sound becoming less like neighboring sounds), and *metathesis* (two sounds switching places). A sound being lost includes *elision* (the loss of an unstressed sound), *aphaeresis* (the loss of initial sounds), *syncope* (the loss of medial sounds), and *apocope* (the loss of final sounds). A sound being introduced includes *epenthesis* (introduction of a sound between two adjacent sounds), *prothesis* (addition of a sound at the beginning of a word), *tonogenesis* (syllables start to carry distinctive pitch), and *nasalization* (the pronunciation of a vowel as nasalized).

Establishing correspondences between words

After sound correspondences are found, historical linguists turn their attention to the forms of words. They find regular patterns in how the form of a word in related (daughter) languages is related to the form of that same word in the ancestral (mother) language. For example, the word 'tooth' is *dent* /dã/ in French, *dente* /dentsi/ in Portuguese, *dente* /dente/ in Italian, and *diente* /diente/ in Spanish. These four languages are Romance languages that derive from Latin. But the Latin word for 'tooth' is *dens* /dens/, so it's not obvious how the daughter languages came to have the forms they do. However, linguists are pretty sure that the form in spoken Latin (called *Vulgar Latin*) was */dente/ which dropped the final *m* of accusative *dentem*. Linguists reconstruct */dente/ as the intermediate form that is the basis for modern-day Romance forms.

> */dente/ > Spanish /diente/
>
> */dente/ > Portuguese /dentsi/
>
> */dente/ > Italian /dente/
>
> */dente/ > French /dãnt/ > /dãn/ > /dã/

Understanding why language changes

Each of the four periods of English — Old English, Middle English, Early Modern English, and Modern English — has its own different grammar — a different rule system. Some of the rules have remained constant through each reincarnation of the language, but other rules change. Several factors cause these changes in a language, from kids introducing new lingo to neighboring languages lending some new words.

Learning a language changes it

Each generation changes the language it speaks. Always. From the first caveman kids on down to today, each generation of learners changes the language of their parents. Kids don't learn a grammar directly, like you may as an adult learner of a second language — they construct it from what they hear. In general, kids construct different grammars from the ones their parents (and the larger speech community) are using. Like continental drift or climate change, language change doesn't look like much from the perspective of one lifetime: You and your parents can still talk to each other. Sort of. But across 10 to 12 generations, the changes add up: A few hundred years is enough to create different varieties of a language. A thousand years — or sometimes much less — is enough to create a new language.

When children learn a first language, linguists call this *first language acquisition* or L1 acquisition. See Chapter 13 for a discussion of the stages that kids go through when learning a language.

Pecking orders change a language

Groups set themselves apart by how they dress, what they eat, and how they talk — this is called *social differentiation*. Language is part of the package. Linguistically, you set yourself apart in many ways: with your vocabulary (in your use of slang or specialized terms), your pronunciation (in your dialect), and in how you use morphology and syntax. Such socially based differences contribute to language change.

Talking changes a language

Humans talk pretty fast, and this often means that individual sounds are crowded out. Fast speech facilitates processes like assimilation, dissimilation, syncope, or apocope. Over time, these processes can lead to major and relatively permanent changes in the sound system.

Does sound change happen for a reason?

Historical linguists feel better about an analysis if they can find a reason for the change. But sometimes, there's no good reason for sound changes — they just happen. A sound change that "just happens" is an *unconditioned sound change*. A sound change that occurs for a reason is a *conditioned sound change*.

- **Unconditioned sound change:** All instances of a sound undergo the change. For example, the switch that Hawaiian made from /t/ to /k/ applied across-the-board to all proto-Polynesian /k/ sounds. By the time Europeans came into contact with Hawaiian, no /t/ sounds were left. Another example is English words like *beet* and *seek*. Today these words have the vowel represented in the IPA as /i/. But originally these words had a long version of a different vowel, represented in the IPA as /e/, as in modern English *say* or *pay*. What happened was that around Shakespeare's time, long /e/ turned into /i/, which is the vowel used today in *beer* and *see*. But English spelling reflects the older pronunciation, as a long /e:/ (actually close to the IPA). Similar changes happened to many other vowels — the vowel in *boot* was originally long /o/, which changed around the same time into /u/. Again, the spelling reflects the older form.

- **Conditioned sound change:** The sound change applies only under certain conditions. For example, a consonant may change only if it occurs before a certain vowel.

Semantic drift changes a language

Word meaning also changes over time; linguists call this *semantic drift*. For example, the English word *nice* used to mean *stupid* — but its meaning drifted over time into something positive. Similarly, *deer* used to mean any four-footed animal, but the meaning gradually shifted to the particular species it refers to today.

Cozying up to other languages changes a language

Speakers of different languages come into contact through commerce, migration, or war. When this contact extends over a period of time, some individuals learn the other language — either as adults or as kids. The adults learn it as a second language, while the kids become fully bilingual. In such situations of sustained contact, languages borrow sounds, words, and constructions from each other. For example, as a result of the Norman Conquest in 1066, English took in a lot of borrowed words from French. (See Chapter 5 for the effects this had on the English vocabulary.)

Sharing language traits

Languages often resemble one another — that's just a fact. And some languages are more similar to each other than others. But these similarities occur for several different reasons — some languages are similar because they have the same mother language while others are similar purely by chance. The following sections give you a quick rundown.

Starting with the same design features: Language universals

Some properties are found in all human languages. Linguists call them *language universals*. For example, all languages have syllables, and though languages differ in the types of syllables they allow, they all organize sounds into syllables based on universal patterns. Similarly, all languages have patterns of word order that appear, despite differences, to follow certain universal organizing principles. See Chapter 11 for more on language universals.

Inheriting family traits: Genetic affiliation

Languages can share features in common with each other because they descend from the same mother language. Linguists call this *genetic affiliation*.

Borrowing from the neighbors: Diffusion

Our neighbors influence us, especially when they're neighboring languages. Sounds, word endings *(suffixes),* word-order, tone, and other linguistic features can spread from one language to another to make otherwise unconnected languages more alike. Linguists call this spreading *linguistic diffusion,* and they call a feature that has diffused in this way an *areal feature.* Here are some examples of areal features created by diffusion:

- In southern Africa, those cool click sounds (which are rare among the world's languages) originated only in the Khoisan languages, which are now endangered. As Bantu (Niger-Congo) languages spread southward, they took on the same sounds. So clicks are an areal feature of southern Africa, even though Khoisan and Niger-Congo languages don't share any historical connection.

- The Pacific Northwest coast of North America includes three language families: Wakashan (6 languages), Salish (23 languages), and Chimakuan (2 languages). Linguists can find no historical connection between the three families, but through many centuries of contact, these languages have come to share a striking number of features:

- They all have the sounds /k/ and /q/ (made at the uvula), as well as some unusual variants of these sounds: rounded lips for /kʷ/ and /qʷ/ and *popped* (ejective) versions (/k', q', kʷ', qʷ'/). *Ejectives* are voiceless consonants that are produced with a simultaneous closure of the glottis.

- They all have word endings (lexical suffixes) that indicate location (of/on/by the hand) or shape (round object).

- They all use verb-initial word order: Instead of *He walks,* they say *Walks he.* And they all use sentence-initial negation, so *not* comes at the start of the sentence: *not walks he.*

How do you know whether a similarity indicates genetic affiliation or just diffusion? Linguists agonize over this question. That's why they're so careful, when applying the comparative method, to only look at words from the basic vocabulary because such words are unlikely to be borrowed.

Leaving it to chance: Resemblance by accident

Languages can come to have the same properties by chance. For example, Bantu languages (spoken in sub-Saharan Africa) and Algonquian languages (spoken in North America) both attach suffixes to the verb to extend the basic meaning of the verb. For example, a *causative* suffix added to the verb 'eat' makes the extended verb 'cause someone to eat something'. Or another suffix indicates that the action is done on behalf of someone — 'eat something for someone'. But even though these two language families are morphologically similar, they're not connected in any way: They resemble each other by accident.

Reconstructing Indo-European

English — the language of the Anglo-Saxons of Merry Old England — and Sanskrit — the language of the priestly caste in India — are part of the same language family! Why do linguists believe this? On the basis of linguistic archeology. In this section, we take you through the comparative method to show how English and Sanskrit are related, and then we give you a peek at how linguists work backward to reconstruct the proto-type ancestral Indo-European language.

Applying the comparative method

Using the three steps of the comparative method — comparing words, finding sound correspondences, finding morphological correspondences — linguists find evidence that the languages of India and Iran share a common ancestor with most of the languages of Europe.

Comparing words in Europe, India, and Persia

At first glance, languages from India and Iran seem very different from European languages. And yet, many words are similar. Some words in Hindi look a lot like Greek words. And some Sanskrit words are like Latin words. In fact, when you look closer, you can see lots of words that are similar in all these languages: Hindi, Bengali, Sanskrit, Latin, Greek, Persian, German, and even English. Words like *father*. Words like *brother*. The numerals are all similar in this group of languages as well. In fact, a large number of words from the basic vocabulary show sound correspondences. The words are a little different in sound, but the differences are systematic. Table 10-2 gives a sample of languages and related words (parentheses indicate that a part of the word is optional). Avestan is the ancient language of the Zoroastrian scriptures.

Table 10-2	**Indo-European Cognates**			
	European		**Indo-Iranian**	
Semantic Field	**English**	**Latin**	**Sanskrit**	**Avestan**
Kinship	mother	māter	mātár-	mātar
	father	pater	pitár-	pitar
Pronouns	me	mē(d)	mā(m)-	mạm
	thou	tū	t(u)vám	tū
Numbers	two	duo	dvā (u)	dva
	seven	septem	saptá	hapta
Body parts	knee	genū	jānu	žnūm
	nose	nāris	nas-	nāh-
Animals	cow	bōs	gáuḥ	gāuš
	mouse	mūs	mūṣ-	muš
Natural features	star	stēlla	tārah	stărəm
	wind	ventus	vātaḥ	vātō

These words are cognates. They're not borrowed. Their similarities are not coincidental: Chinese, Arabic, and other languages of the world have no such similarities with North Indian and European languages. So what's going on? Linguists, starting in the late 1700s, began to explore a startling hypothesis — the languages from Europe, northern India, and Persia descend from the same ancestral proto-language. This hypothesis has now been thoroughly supported by further research.

Using the comparative method, linguists discovered a historical connection that goes back 10,000 years! Linguists call this language Proto-Indo-European, and the people associated with it are called Indo-Europeans. Work on plants and geography suggests that Indo-Europeans lived somewhere in the Caucasus region in Europe, north of Turkey, near the Black Sea. See Figure 10-1 for a plausible — though not certain — map of how the Indo-Europeans spread out from there, probably entering Europe around 4,000 years ago.

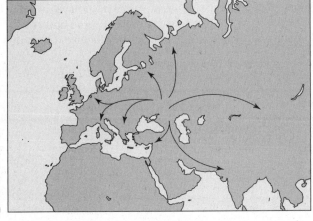

Figure 10-1:
Indo-European language expansion from the Caucasus region.

Cognates are words from different languages that are historically related. For example, English and German were the same language a little more than a thousand years ago, so many cognates exist: *Mann* and *man* are cognates, as are *Schaf* and *sheep, Segel* and *sail,* and *Dieb* and *thief*. As linguists go further back in time, they find it harder to find cognates because so many more sound and meaning shifts have occurred.

Using sound correspondences to uncover sound laws

Today, historical linguists identify most of the modern languages of Europe as descended from proto-Indo-European. Much of the evidence for this is based on the existence of regular and systematic correspondences in the sound systems of the languages — linguists call these *sound laws*. One of the more famous laws was discovered by Jacob Grimm, one of the Grimm brothers who collected many of the famous fairy tales like *Snow White, Hansel and Gretel,* and *Rapunzel.* Jacob (1785–1863) and his brother Wilhelm (1786–1859) Grimm were in fact two hard-core historical linguists who collected those folk tales for linguistic purposes. The Grimms knew about the proto-Indo-European story, and collecting folk tales provided important data about the *Germanic* branch of Indo-European.

Jacob Grimm's discovery, known now as *Grimm's Law,* identified a set of systematic sound changes that the Germanic languages had made to the original proto-Indo-European language:

- ✔ Voiceless stops change into voiceless fricatives: /p/ becomes /t/, /t/ becomes /θ/ (this is the *th* in *teeth*), and /k/ becomes /h/ or /x/.

- ✔ Voiced stops change into voiceless stops: /b/ becomes /p/, /d/ becomes /t/, and /g/ becomes /k/.

- ✔ Voiced aspirated stops change into voiced plain stops: /b^h/ becomes /b/, /d^h/ becomes /d/, and /g^h/ becomes /g/.

Table 10-3 shows the sound shift that Germanic languages (such as Gothic and English) made away from the other Indo-European languages (such as Greek and Latin), illustrating Grimm's Law.

Origins of the proto-Indo-European people

Thousands and thousands of years ago, a single ancient ancestor of all the modern Indo-European languages was spoken somewhere between Europe and India. No one knows what the original people called their language. Linguists call it *proto-Indo-European,* adding *proto-* which is Greek for "first" to the name of the language family: *Indo-European.* Who were the original Indo-Europeans? Where did they live? Here's the best guess, drawn largely from linguistic evidence:

- ✔ **The language family probably emerged within the last 10,000 years along with the spread of agriculture.** Linguists think this because there are many shared words related to agriculture, such as *goat* and *plow.* These words would not have been in use before the dawn of agriculture 10,000 years ago.

- ✔ **They lived in a northern area, most likely between Europe and India.** Linguists know this because they can trace back proto-Indo-European words for northerly phenomena such as *salmon* and *cedar* (the proto-Indo-European word for salmon is similar to *lox*). Indo-Europeans don't have common words for southerly things, like *olive* or *jalapeno pepper.* Some modern Indo-European languages have those words, but cognates for these words are not found throughout the group, which indicates they must have been added after the proto-language split into its daughter languages.

Table 10-3	Indo-European Cognates Reflecting Grimm's Law				
	Indic	*European*			
		Non-Germanic		*Germanic*	
	Sanskrit	*Greek*	*Latin*	*Gothic*	*English*
p > f	pad-	pod-	ped-	fōtus	foot
t > θ	trī	treīs/tría	trēs	θrija	three
k > h/x	svŕan-	kúōn	canis	hunds	hound
b > p	—	—	lūbricus	sliupan	slip
d > t	pad-	pod-	ped-	fōtus	foot
g > k	jŕánás	génos	genus	kun-i	kin
bʰ > b	bhar-	phér-	fer-	baír-an	bear
dʰ > d	vidhŕávā	ē-wíthewos	vidua	widuwo	widow
gʰ > g	hams-ŕá-	khēn	(h)āns-er	Gans [German]	goose

Grimm's Law is pretty cool just in itself, but it also illustrates how language change operates in general. Individual words don't change randomly, one by one — rather, language change is *systematic* in that it affects the entire system. Historical linguists know this, and when they compare languages they look for systematic correspondences. They want to understand the following:

✔ Which sounds change and in what words?

✔ How do the sounds change?

✔ Are the sound changes regular (systematic)?

Most sound changes are regular: They apply automatically and in a completely general fashion. For example, the p>f change of Grimm's Law affects *all* /p/ sounds, changing them into /f/. And so on for the other sounds that are affected by the law: /t, k, b, d, g, bʰ, dʰ, gʰ/. Such historically important sound changes are sometimes called "laws" — as with Grimm's Law — because they apply across an entire language with no (or very few) exceptions.

One of the first phonologists, Ferdinand de Saussure, started out as a *wunderkind* in historical linguistics: In 1879, at the age of 21, he explained a set of previously mysterious sound alternations by arguing for the existence of an additional sound in proto-Indo-European. It took 50 years, but the discovery of Hittite in the early 20th century confirmed de Saussure's claim for this sound, written as * *ḫ*. Linguists found that many words beginning with *a* — for example Greek *anti* 'against', Latin *ante* 'in front of, before', and Sanskrit *ánti* 'near, in the presence of' — correspond to words beginning with *ḫ* in Hittite **ḫants* 'front, face'.

TECHNICAL STUFF

Historical change is also called *diachronic change,* which just means change through time. Voiceless stops changing to voiceless fricatives is an example of *phonological* (sound) *change*. Historical change can affect all parts of the linguistic rule system (grammar), including phonological, morphological, syntactic, semantic, and pragmatic.

Finding morphological correspondences

Comparing word-forms allows linguists to discover *morphological correspondences.* (See Chapter 5 for more on morphology.) Table 10-4 shows correspondences for the verb 'to be' in five Indo-European languages. Notice that the reconstructed proto-Indo-European forms begin with **es-* (again, using the historical linguistics convention of an asterisk for proto-forms) in the singular, but with **s-* in the plural. What's cool for linguists here is that the proto-language form is completely regular but becomes irregular (mixed) in the daughter languages. Latin, Sanskrit, and Gothic each preserve a mixture of the two forms. But Greek and Hittite preserve only the **es-* form.

Table 10-4 The Verb 'To Be' across Indo-European Languages

	Begins with es-		*Begins with s-*
	1st Person Singular	***3rd Person Singular***	***3rd Person Plural***
Proto-Indo-European	*es-mi	*es-ti	*s-enti
Latin	**s**um	**est**	**s**unt
Sanskrit	**as**mi	**ás**ti	**s**ánti
Gothic	**a**m	**ist**	**s**ind
Greek	**ei**mi	**es**ti	**ei**si
Hittite	**e**ʃmi	**e**ʃtsi	**a**ʃantsi

LINGUIST LINGO

An irregular inflectional pattern is a *suppletive paradigm*. If related languages share an unusual morphological property, linguists call this *shared aberrancy*. Because the same irregularity is unlikely to arise independently in two languages, historical linguists use this type of grammatical patterning to reconstruct language families.

Reconstructing the language

By the 1500s, linguists recognized that European languages could be grouped into distinct language families. But they didn't get a clear picture of the historical relationships until the 1700s, and they argued over the nitty-gritty details right into the 1950s. Although the debate continues about a few details, linguists now agree that the proto-Indo-European language branched off into nine groupings.

- **Anatolian** is an extinct language group that was located in Asia Minor, between the Black Sea to the north and the Mediterranean Sea to the south. It's the earliest confirmed branch of Indo-European. Palaic was the first Anatolian language to become extinct, perhaps as early as the 16th century BCE. The last of the Anatolian languages — Lycian and Lydian — survived almost to the end of the first millennium BCE.

- **Tocharian** is an extinct group that was located in Central Asia. Written records of two Tocharian languages (Tocharian A and B) suggest that these languages were spoken from the 3rd to the 9th century CE.

- **Albanian** is its own branch.

- **Italo-Celtic** has two branches: the Italic languages (this includes the Romance languages of Galician, Portuguese, Spanish, Catalan, French, Italian, French, and Romanian) and the Celtic languages (which include Irish and Scots Gaelic, Manx, Welsh, Cornish, and Breton).

- **Germanic** has three branches. The West Germanic branch includes modern-day Dutch, Scots, English, Frisian, Saxon, and German. The North Germanic branch includes Swedish, Danish, Norwegian, Faroese, and Icelandic. The East Germanic branch is extinct: The last language of this group, Crimean Gothic, survived until the 18th century.

- **Greek** is its own branch.

- **Armenian** is its own branch.

- **Balto-Slavic** has two branches: the Baltic languages (which include Lithuanian, Latvian, and Old Prussian) and the Slavic languages (which include Russian, Bulgarian, Serbo-Croatian, Czech, and Slovak).

- **Indo-Iranian** is the easternmost group of surviving Indo-European languages and has two branches. The most widely spoken languages of the Iranian branch are Farsi (spoken in Iran), Pashto (spoken in Afghanistan), Kurdish (spoken in Kurdistan), and Balochi (spoken in Pakistan, Iran, and southern Afghanistan). The Indic languages form the other branch and make up more than half of all Indo-European languages: The most widely spoken languages are Hindi-Urdu, Bengali, Punjabi, Marathi, and Gujarati.

Losing track of your family: Language isolates

Some languages seem to be orphans — with no family members at all! Linguists call these orphan languages *language isolates*. And no, they're not from outer space! Given what linguists have discovered about how languages are related to each other, the best guess is that language isolates are the remnants of a previous historical period. The speech communities using related sister languages are now lost in the mists of time, leaving behind these language orphans. Here are a couple of well-known language isolates:

✔ **Basque:** Hundreds of thousands of Basque people speak this language in northern Spain and France. Basque is not historically related to Spanish or any Romance language, or any other language anyone can find. Some place-name evidence suggests Basque was spoken throughout Europe before the Indo-European languages squeezed it out.

✔ **Ainu:** An indigenous language of northern Japan, Ainu is spoken by about 100 people who are culturally, linguistically, and genetically distinct from modern Japanese folks. Thanks to recent efforts to revitalize use of the language, there may soon be more, but most Ainu people today speak only Japanese.

If linguists class a language as an isolate, it means the evidence for historical connections is weak or tenuous at best. Every language classification is subject to debate and change when new evidence is found. At various times, you'll hear all sorts of stuff: how Basque is related to Albanian, or Haida to Hawaiian, and so on. Remember that the three most reliable indicators of a historical connection are confirmed relations between words, between morphemes, and between sounds. It's possible for groups of people (and their languages) to split apart and wander off in different directions. This is what happened to Yurok and Wiyok, two languages spoken on the northern coast of California — in the 1920s, linguists discovered that they're related to languages of the Algonquian language family, most of which are spoken east of the Rocky Mountains!

Over time, certain branches in a language family can die off (like Anatolian and Tocharian), while other branches may continue to split and diversify (like Romance). See Chapter 12 for a discussion of language birth and death.

Surveying the World's Language Families

Historical linguists have found that the precursor to Old English — they call this *proto-English* — is a language that arrived in England as a result of the migration of Germanic peoples around 200 CE. No written records exist of the languages that were spoken by these Germanic peoples. But by using the tools of linguistic archeology, historical linguists can reconstruct an even older form of the language — *proto-Germanic* — which is the ancestor of proto-English. Linguists don't think proto-Germanic was an actual language or grammar, rather it is a hypothesized reconstruction based on a set of languages that have many grammatical features in common.

And just as linguists reconstruct older stages of English, they reconstruct older stages of other Germanic languages, such as German, Dutch, and Frisian. By combining the results of such a comparison, linguists construct a *family tree,* which shows how individual languages are related both to ancestral languages and to each other.

Figure 10-2 gives the family tree of the Germanic languages. As is conventional for genealogies, the ancestral languages are at the top and their modern descendents are at the bottom.

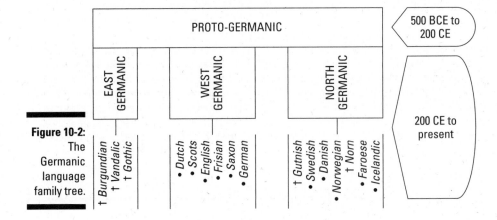

Figure 10-2:
The Germanic language family tree.

A *language family* is a group of historically related languages. In Figure 10-2, West Germanic is the *mother language* of English and a *daughter language* of proto-Germanic. The *sister languages* of English are German, Saxon, Frisian, Scots, and Dutch.

Tallying up family lineages

Linguists have discovered that most of the 6,000 or so languages currently spoken belong to at least 100 different language families. Table 10-5 lists the six largest language families of the world according to how many languages are in each family. Together, these six language families account for two-thirds of the world's languages.

Table 10-5	Major Language Families of the World			
Language Family	**Number of Languages**	**Number of Speakers**	**Geographical Location**	**Most Widely Spoken Languages**
Niger-Congo	1,510 (22%)	350,000,000 (6%)	Sub-Saharan Africa	Yorùbá, Ìgbo, Fula, Shona, Zulu, Swahili
Austro-nesian	1,231 (18%)	350,000,000 (6%)	Islands of SE Asia & Pacific, Madagascar, continental Asia	Tagalog, Indonesian, Cebuano, Malagasy
Trans-New Guinea	475 (7%)	3,000,000 (0.06%)	New Guinea, Nusa Tenggara, Maluku Is.	Melpa, Enga, Western Dani, Ekari
Indo-European	427 (6%)	3,000,000,000 (46%)	Europe, Iranian plateau, South Asia	Spanish, English, Hindi, Portuguese
Sino-Tibetan	445 (6%)	1,200,000,000 (21%)	East Asia, SE Asia, South Asia	Mandarin, Shanghainese, Cantonese, Fukkiense
Afro-Asiatic	353 (5%)	350,000,000 (6%)	M. East, N. Africa, Horn of Africa, Sahel	Arabic, Berber, Amharic, Hausa

The languages families in Table 10-5 are the largest because of the number of languages in each family. This does not mean they are spoken by the largest number of speakers, nor does it mean they have the largest geographic spread.

Locating language families

Linguists have traced back many language families: groups that diverged and evolved from traceable ancestors into multitudes of modern tongues. Here's a whirlwind world tour of these other families by geographical area:

- ✔ In Africa, the majority of languages belong to the Niger-Congo family, which is the largest in terms of area and number of speakers. The Afro-Asiatic language family (which includes all the Semitic languages, like Hebrew, Arabic, and Amharic) is also quite large. But most other language groupings remain uncertain. Of note are the Khoi and the San languages of southern Africa (which probably belong to different language families) — these are the ones with those cool click sounds.

✔ Southern Indian languages form the *Dravidian* family, which includes a language called Kannada (no connection to Canada). If you've never heard of Dravidian, it's time you did: It has 85 languages in the family and more than 200 million speakers.

✔ South Asia is the home of the Sino-Tibetan family, which includes Mandarin Chinese. It's a huge family that includes up to 250 languages and more than a billion speakers.

✔ Australia originally had more than 250 indigenous languages, with most of them (about 150) belonging to one family (the *Pama-Nyungan* family). Today only about 15 of these languages are still fairly strong.

✔ North America once had hundreds of native languages, with as many as 300 languages in the areas that are now Canada and the United States and many more in Mexico and Central America. The Dene family includes all the Athapaskan languages spoken in northern Canada and also a group that went south only fairly recently (in historical terms): Navajo and Apache. The Eskimo-Aleut languages — the name of the language family that includes Inuktitut — are the most recent ones to come to North America.

✔ South American languages — not counting the ones introduced most recently by Spain and Portugal — are a wildly diverse group: around 350 indigenous languages still exist today, but as many as 1,500 languages existed before Pizarro and his gang of *Conquistadors* came along.

Chapter 11

Cataloguing Differences: Linguistic Typology

*A*s a human, you share features in common with the other 7 billion humans on this planet. All humans have one head and two arms and hands and walk upright on two legs. But these features don't show up in exactly the same way in each individual human being. This is because your genetic code interacts with the environment you live in — over time this leads to surface variation in eye, hair, and skin color, as well as body build. So, although modern humans are a single species, there are different types of human beings. Languages work the same way — all human languages have a common set of structural features. They use sound patterns (or gestural patterns for sign languages) to form units of meaning, which combine with each other to make sentences, which in turn combine to make larger utterances. But languages differ in the particular structures they use — in this sense, they fall into different types. Linguists study how the languages of the world systematically differ from each other as well as the limits of these differences. This area of study is called *linguistic typology*. In this chapter, we show you how linguists sort the languages of the world into types according to the systematic differences that they observe in their phonology, morphology, syntax, and semantics.

Just in case you forgot, *phonology* is the study of sound patterns (see Chapter 4). *Morphology* is the study of word formation (see Chapter 5). *Syntax* is the study of sentence structure (see Chapter 6). And *semantics* is the study of meaning (see Chapter 7).

Choosing from the Language Smorgasbord

One way of thinking about how languages differ from each other is in terms of a language smorgasbord. From amongst a large set of dishes, each language selects a unique set of menu items that it serves up to its speakers. Languages that select similar menu items fall into the same language type.

To figure out the menu choices individual languages make, linguists use two strategies: examining surface patterns and looking for underlying patterns:

- **Examining surface patterns:** Imagine you're in a roomful of people and your job is to sort them according to height. The easiest way to do this is to line them up and order them from shortest to tallest. This is classification based on examination of a surface pattern. Same thing for language. Different languages use different word orders in their clauses. While English uses a subject-verb-object order *(The duckling saw the farmer)*, Japanese uses a subject-object-verb order *(The duckling farmer saw)*.

- **Looking for underlying patterns:** Now imagine you're in a roomful of people, and your job is to sort them according to where they were born. This means you have to approach people and ask them "Where were you born?" This is classification based on the detection of an underlying pattern. Same thing for language. For example, English singular count nouns require a determiner: That's why English speakers say ***The duckling*** saw ***the farmer***, but not *****Duckling*** *saw* ***farmer***. But other languages, such as Yorùbá, permit nouns to be used without determiners. And even English permits bare nouns in some circumstances, for example when they are pluralized *(**Ducklings** saw **farmers**)* or when they are mass nouns *(**Oil** doesn't mix with **water**)*.

In looking for underlying patterns, linguists use a combination of positive and negative data. Positive data are those examples that speakers recognize as being part of the language. Negative data are "ungrammatical" examples that speakers don't recognize as being part of the language. Linguists put an asterisk (*) in front of these examples.

For typologists, finding such differences — whether they are surface or underlying patterns — is just the beginning of the story. They then sort through all the languages of the world — or, rather, a representative sample of the languages of the world — to see how such differences are distributed. They're looking to see whether some patterns are more common in some areas of the world, whether the distribution is more or less even across different areas, or whether correlations exist between different patterns.

For cool maps that show how the languages of the world differ from each other, go to the online *World Atlas of Linguistic Structures:* http://wals.info/ and http://wals.info/chapter.

Investigating Sound Patterns

To understand how human languages organize their sound patterns, linguists look for both surface and underlying differences. Surface differences relate to the number of phonemes that a particular language uses. Underlying differences, which are often more subtle, relate to how segments group into larger units such as syllables, which form the basis of rhythmic and melodic patterns.

Phonemes are the minimal contrastive units of sounds that a language has. (See Chapter 4 for more info.)

Adding up sounds

One way linguists type languages is by how many vowels and consonants they have. Every human language uses consonants and vowels, but they differ greatly in how many and which types of vowels and consonants they actually use.

The International Phonetic Association lists over 100 distinctive speech sounds — with about 30 or so different vowels and at least twice as many consonants. See Chapter 1 for a list of the IPA symbols used for consonants and vowels. For details on how you create speech sounds, and how linguists classify consonants and vowels, see Chapter 3.

Counting up the consonants

Most languages have about 20 or so consonants. The smallest number of consonants that any human language has is 6 (Rotokas, spoken in Papua New Guinea) and the largest is 120 (Xóõ, spoken in Botswana). After they tally up the inventories — itself a huge job that wasn't completed until the 1990s — typologists then turn to the question of how consonants are distributed geographically:

✔ **Languages with larger than average inventories** (more than 25 consonants) are found in Africa (especially south of the equator), in the center of Eurasia, and in the northwest of North America. The North American language families that have large inventories aren't related to each other historically — they include Eskimo-Aleut, Na-Dene, Salishan, Tsimshianic, and Wakashan. In contrast, many Bantu languages in southern Africa enlarged their consonant inventories by borrowing click sounds from neighboring Khoisan languages, which already had a huge number of consonants.

✔ **Languages with average consonant inventories** (between 19 and 25 consonants) are found in all areas of the world: the Americas, Europe, Africa, Asia, and Oceania. Typologists interpret this as indicating that this is a typical size of consonant inventory. English, with 24 consonants, has an average size inventory.

✔ **Languages with smaller than average inventories** (less than 19 consonants) are found in the Pacific, in South America, and in the eastern part of North America. Particularly small inventories are found in New Guinea and in the Amazon basin (in South America). For the Pacific region — which includes Australia and New Guinea — the similarity of consonant inventories is a trait that was preserved from the time when Australia and New Guinea were connected via land some 7,000 years ago.

By grouping languages according to the number of consonants they have, typologists can see whether any underlying patterns emerge. One pattern uncovered by Björn Lindblom and Ian Maddieson is that there's a link between inventory size and how consonants are articulated:

✔ Languages with small consonant inventories tend to have consonants that have *basic articulations*. This includes the voiceless stops /p, t, k/, the voiced stops /b, d, g/, the glottal stop /ʔ/, the voiceless fricatives /f, s, h/, the voiceless affricate /tʃ/, and the sonorants /m, n, ŋ, l, r, w, j/.

✔ Languages with average consonant inventories use consonants with basic articulations, but they also add in some that have *elaborated articulations*. This includes those with marked voicing (voiced fricatives, consonants with a breathy and creaky voice), marked manner of release (ejectives, implosives, clicks), marked place of articulation (labiodental, palatoalveolar, retroflex, uvular, pharyngeal), marked secondary articulation (palatalisation, labialisation, pharyngealisation, velarisation), as well as pre- and post- nasalization and pre- and post-aspiration.

✔ Languages with large consonant inventories add in consonants with *complex articulations,* which are combinations of elaborated articulations. For example, Haida combines a marked place of articulation (uvular) with secondary articulation (labialisation) to make the labialized uvular stop /qʷ/.

Tallying up vowels

Most of the world's languages have between five and six vowels. German, which has one of largest vowel inventories, has 14 vowels. And the fewest numbers of vowels that a language has is two, for example Yimas, spoken in

Papua New Guinea. When vowel inventory sizes are compared — according to whether they are small, average, or large — the languages of the world show the following distribution:

- ✔ **Small vowel inventories** (2 to 4 vowels) predominate in Australia and are frequent in the Americas. They also occur in specific language groups, including the Berber languages of northern Africa and the Caucasian languages spoken at the border between Georgia and Russia. In other parts of the world they are rare.

- ✔ **Average vowel inventories** (5 to 6 vowels) are found in most parts of the world. Languages of southern Africa are special in having *only* average-size vowel inventories.

- ✔ **Large vowel inventories** (7 to 14 vowels) predominate across the middle of Africa, between the equator and the Sahara. Languages from this area come from three language families — Niger-Congo, Nilo-Saharan, and Afro-Asiatic. Large vowel inventories are also found throughout Europe, in interior Southeast Asia, southern China, as well as interior New Guinea. Large vowel inventories have two main sources. Vowels can "double up" because of vowel length, so each vowel has a short and a long version. This happens in English, German, and Italian. Or vowels can double up because of vowel harmony, so each vowel is paired off with another according to height, backness, roundness, tongue root position, or nasalisation. This happens a lot with the languages of Africa (which are famous for tongue root harmony), as well as for some European languages such as Finnish and Hungarian (which have backness harmony), and Turkish (which has a combination of fronting and rounding harmony).

Organizing sounds into larger groups

Languages fall into different types according to how they organize sounds into larger units. How languages group sounds together determines how syllables are formed, how melody is deployed, and how rhythm is structured.

Grouping sounds: Syllabification

When classifying syllable types, linguists use the following terms:

- ✔ **Nucleus:** This is the core of the syllable. It's usually a vowel (V), but in some languages can be a sonorant sound like [n], [l], or [r].

- ✔ **Onset:** These are the consonants that begin a syllable. The onset can be a single consonant (C), two consonants (CC), or three consonants (CCC).

- ✔ **Coda:** These are the consonants that end a syllable. The coda can be a single consonant (C), two consonants (CC), or three consonants (CCC).

Different languages have different types of syllables. The CV syllable, which is the simplest type, is found in all languages. More complex syllables — such as CVC or CCVCC — are found only in some languages. Typologists classify the languages of the world according to how complex their syllables are.

✔ **Simple syllable structure:** Some languages limit their syllables to CV or V — examples are languages in equatorial zones in Africa, New Guinea, and South America. (These are the same areas that have relatively small consonant inventories.) Only a few languages have only CV syllables — Hawaiian is a famous example.

✔ **Moderately complex syllable structure:** Some languages add on to the basic CV syllable with a consonant at the end (CV**C**) or the beginning (**C**CV), or both (**C**CV**C**). These languages may also limit the type of consonants that can be used in syllables beginning with two consonants. Most of the languages of the world have moderately complex syllables, but particularly those in Africa, eastern Asia, and most of Australia.

✔ **Complex syllable structure:** Some languages permit additional consonants at the end and beginning of a syllable and have fewer restrictions on consonant combinations at the beginning. For example, English allows **CCCVCCC** in the word *strength* /strɛŋθ/. The northern two-thirds of the northern hemisphere is the home of languages with complex syllable structures; this area includes much of North America and northern Eurasia. There's also a small cluster of languages in northern Australia that have complex syllables.

Singing the melody: Intonation and tone

All languages use *pitch* (the melodic sounds of language that are carried by the syllable nucleus), but they divide into two types according to *how* they use it — some languages are intonational, while others are tonal.

✔ **Intonational languages:** In these languages, pitch distinguishes between utterance meanings in a conversational context. For example, in English, this is the difference between a declarative and interrogative intonation. Declarative intonation is used for making statements, as in *Lucy saw the Queen.* Interrogative intonation is used for asking questions, as in *Lucy saw the Queen?* Intonational languages predominate in western Eurasia, including South Asia, as well as in the southerly regions of South America and the coast areas of northwestern North America.

✔ **Tonal languages:** In tonal languages, each syllable carries a characteristic pitch, which may be a *level tone,* with relatively flat pitch at a particular level, or a *contour tone,* with a pitch rise or fall over the duration of the syllable. Most of the world's languages are tonal languages, and almost all the languages of Africa are tonal. Most tonal languages have level tones, but many languages in East and Southeast Asia have contour tones, as do languages in Mexico and Central America.

The typology of tone and intonation

While both intonational and tonal languages involve systematic variation of pitch, they differ in how they accomplish this:

✔ Intonation is a structural property of syllables and is sensitive to the weight contrast between light (CV) and heavy (CVV, CVC) syllables. Tone is a property of individual vowels and so isn't sensitive to syllable weight.

✔ Tone targets vowels and assigns pitch to both lexical words (like nouns and verbs) and function words (like determiners and conjunctions). Intonation organizes an utterance into phrases and gives lexical words a pitch prominence. It also assigns pitch to individual syllables and assigns phrase accents to entire phrases.

✔ Intonation results from the application of phonologial rules — because all lexical words undergo these rules, they all end up having a pitch prominence. In contrast, tone is a property of individual words — it's part of their lexical representation. This means that it's possible for some words to carry tone — linguists call this *tonal specification* — and for other words to have no tone.

Finding the rhythm: Metrical structure

Languages also fall into three different types based on their rhythmic structure, which is tied to syllable structure:

✔ **Mora-timed:** These languages are sensitive to syllable weight — the light CV syllable has one mora, a heavy CVV syllable has two morae. In such languages, where syllables don't end with consonants, rhythm aligns with the beat of the vowel. Japanese is an example of a mora-timed language.

✔ **Syllable-timed:** In languages that either begin or end a syllable with a consonant, rhythm aligns with the syllable. French is an example of a syllable-timed language.

✔ **Stress-timed:** In languages that both begin and end syllables with consonants, rhythm aligns with the stressed syllable (or the intonationally prominent heavy syllable). Examples include Dutch (which allows CCVCC syllables) and English (which allows CCCVCCC syllables).

A stressed syllable is pronounced with more prominence than an unstressed one. A prominent syllable can be louder, be longer, have a higher pitch, or be associated with a particular vowel quality.

Word size restrictions

Restrictions on word size is another way linguists sort languages. Some languages require that a word be no smaller than a certain size *(minimality restriction)*, while others require that a word be no bigger than a certain size *(maximality restriction)*.

✔ In the Zezuru dialect of Shona, a southern Bantu language spoken in Zimbabwe, words must be at least two syllables. So the noun root [gò] 'wasp' is pronounced with a supporting vowel [i] ìgò. The verb root for 'give', which consists of just the consonant p-, is pronounced with two supporting vowels *ìpá.*

✔ In Koyo, a Bantu language spoken in the Democratic Republic of Congo, verb stems can't be longer than three syllables. So the CVC verb root *kór-* 'see' can occur as *kór-a* 'to tie' and can take the causative *-is* suffix (*kór-is-a* 'to cause to tie') or the reciprocal *-in* suffix (*kór-in-a* 'to tie each other'). But it's not possible for both the reciprocal and causative to combine: **kór-is-in-a, *kór-in-is-a* because this would create a word with four syllables.

Looking at Word Formation

Nineteenth-century German linguists — the brothers Freidrich and August von Schlegel, together with Wilhelm von Humboldt — classified languages according to the complexity of their words. In their system, languages fall into three different morphological types according to how they combine morphemes (the basic unit of meaning in a language) with each other. The three morphological types are *analytic, synthetic,* and *polysynthetic.*

To investigate word formation, the following distinctions are useful. A *free morpheme* can stand by itself; a *bound morpheme* can't. *Derivational morphemes* change meaning and may be category-changing (such as changing a noun into a verb). *Inflectional morphemes* maintain basic meaning and are never category-changing. A *root* is the primary meaning-carrying unit, and a *stem* is the basis for inflection. (See Chapter 5 for details on morphology.)

Keeping separate: Analytic languages

In an analytic language, each morpheme is an independent word. Examples of analytic languages include Mandarin, Vietnamese, Yorùbá, and Haitian Creole. In Haitian Creole, elements that are realized as *inflectional affixes* in a language like English — such as plural *-s* and past tense *-ed* — are separate words. Take a look at the following sentence:

Mari te renmen flè yo.

Marie *past* like flower *plural*

'Marie liked the flowers'

This example uses the format that linguists use for presenting data: The first line is the form in the target language (here, Haitian Creole); the second line is a morpheme-by-morpheme rendering (called a *gloss*); the third line is the translation into English.

Sticking together: Synthetic languages

In a synthetic language, a root combines with several morphemes to form a word. The two kinds of synthetic languages are *agglutinative* and *fusional*.

Keeping clear boundaries: Synthetic-agglutinative languages

In an *agglutinative language,* morpheme boundaries are clearly identifiable, and each morpheme represents only one meaning. And sometimes, a single word can be a whole sentence. Examples of agglutinative languages include Finnish, Korean, Hungarian, Swahili, and Turkish.

In Shona, another agglutinative language spoken in southern Africa, morphemes come in the following shapes: Prefixes are CV, roots are CVC, and suffixes are VC or V. Take a look at the following example. Each morpheme represents only one meaning: *ha-* means 'not', *ti-* means first person plural 'we', *no-* means 'present habitual', *bik-* means 'cook', -*il* means 'for' (called an applicative suffix), -*an* means 'each other' (called a reciprocal suffix), and the final vowel -*a* indicates that the stem is verbal.

hàtínòchíbìkìrànà

hà- tí- nò- chí- bìk- -ìr -àn -à

'We don't often cook for each other'

Shona is a tone language that contrasts high pitch (marked with an acute accent (ˊ)) and low pitch (marked with a grave accent (ˋ)).

Fusing elements together: Synthetic-fusional languages

In a *fusional language,* morpheme boundaries can't be clearly identified because bits of meaning are fused together into a single word or affix. Such languages often have complex morpho-phonological rules (see Chapter 5 for discussion of morpho-phonology). In fact, most Indo-European languages are fusional.

In Modern Greek, words often fuse together several units of meaning. In the following sentence, the boldfaced words are fusional morphemes. Reading from left-to-right, the morphemes line up as follows. *ðen* is fusional and combines 'negation' with the fact that a statement is being made (linguists call this "indicative assertion"). It's followed by *θa,* which marks future tense. Then comes *ton* 'him', which fuses together 'masculine', 'singular', and 'accusative', and marks the direct object of the verb. After that is the verb stem *páte,* which combines three units of meaning: 'go', '2nd person plural', and 'non-past'. The morpheme *sto* fuses 'to' and 'the', and *spiti* is 'house'. And last but not least, *su* 'your' fuses the meanings of '2nd person', 'singular', and 'genitive', which marks the possessor of the noun. So, literally, this sentence says 'Not will him you (plural) take to the house your (singular)'.

> **ðen θa ton páte sto** *spiti* **su**
>
> 'You (plural) won't take him to your (singular) house'

Stringing out sentences: Polysynthetic languages

In a *polysynthetic language,* a word is a complete sentence: A verbal stem combines several different morphemes, some of which mark the *arguments* (the subject and direct object) of the verb. Most of the indigenous languages of the Americas are polysynthetic languages.

Plains Cree, an Algonquian language spoken in the northern Plains of the Americas, is polysynthetic. In the following Plains Cree sentence — which is a single word — the root *kisî-* 'agitate' combines with -*pêk* 'liquid' to get the meaning of 'wash'. This further combines with -*in* 'by hand' to indicate the way washing was done. Then the noun -*ayôwinis* 'clothes' is added to mark the direct object of washing. This is followed by the suffix -*ê* which indicates the subject is animate, and then -*w* further specifies that the subject is third person singular. The boldfaced morphemes mark the subject, while the underlined morpheme marks the object.

> *kisîpêkinayôwinisêw*
>
> *kisî-pêk-in-<u>ayôwinis</u>-ê-**w***
>
> 'He washed his (own) clothes by hand'

More on morphological variation

Two other types of morphological variation, which are called parameters of variation, include:

✔ **Prefix/suffix differences:** Prefixes attach to the beginning of a word; suffixes attach at the end. Linguists have found that these affix types differ in a number of ways. For example, English prefixes more easily bear contrastive stress ("I said UNdo, not REdo"). Many prefixes don't change the category of the word they attach to (*do* and *undo* are both verbs), while most suffixes are category-changing (*do* is a verb, *doer* is a noun). Typological studies have found that suffixes are more frequent than

prefixes. One possible explanation for this is that while suffixes don't interfere with stem recognition, prefixes make it more difficult to identify the beginning of stems, which slows down word recognition.

✔ **Pronoun-drop (pro-drop):** In languages where verbal inflectional morphology on the verb indicates the person and number of the subject — linguists call this *subject agreement* — the subject need not be pronounced. In such languages, 'arrives' means 'S/he arrives'. Languages with this feature are called *pro-drop languages* where *pro* stands for 'pronoun'.

The dividing line between morphological types — analytic, synthetic-agglutinative, synthetic-fusional, and polysynthetic — isn't always clear. However, when you study a language, it's useful to have some idea of where it fits into this broad morphological classification. For example, English has some of the properties of an analytic language (many of its words are single morphemes) and some of the properties of a fusional language (many of its words contain several morphemes which are fused together in complex ways).

In both agglutinative and polysynthetic languages, a single word can be a complete sentence. What distinguishes the two types is how the morphemes combine with each other. The morphemes of agglutinative languages mark the subject and object of the sentence and indicate whether any other argument has been removed (as with passive) or added (as with the causative). Polysynthetic languages go a step further and add morphemes that modify the meaning of the root. The literal translation of the previous Plains Cree example is something like 'he acts on his clothes by agitating liquid by hand', with the root part of the verb stem being *kisî-* 'agitate'.

Observing Sentence Structure

Languages can also be categorized based on whether the three essential elements of a sentence — the subject, verb, and object — have a fixed order or are freely ordered. For example, English uses subject-verb-object order to make sentences like *The dog chased the squirrel.*

Putting words in their place: Fixed word order

In languages with fixed word order, the relative order of subject (S), object (O), and verb (V) is pretty much always the same. Fixed word order languages fall into one of six types according to how they order these three elements, as Table 11-1 shows.

Table 11-1	Examples of Fixed Word Order	
Language/Sentence	*Word Order*	
Japanese	S O	V
'John read the letter'	*John-ga* *tegami-o*	*yon-da.*
	John-subject letter-object	read-past
Mandarin	S V	O
'Zhangsan received a letter'	*Zhāngsān* *shaōudaǎo-le*	*yi-faēng* *xìn.*
	Zhangsan receive-perfective	one-classifier letter
Irish	V S	O
'The priests are reading the books'	*Léan* *na sagairt*	*na leabhair.*
	read-present the priests	the books
Nias	V O	S
'My mother cooked rice'	*Irino* *vakhe*	*ina-gu.*
	cook rice	mother-my

Language/Sentence	Word Order		
Hixkaryana	O	V	S
'The jaguar grabbed the man'	*Toto*	*yahosā-ye*	*kamara.*
	man	grab-distant past	jaguar
Nadëb	O	S	V
'The child sees the jaguar'	*awad*	*kalapéé*	*hapUh.*
	jaguar	child	see

The most frequent of the six word orders is SOV, followed by SVO (which is the order that English has) — most fixed word order languages have one of these two orders. SOV order dominates Asia, Australia, and New Guinea. SVO order dominates sub-Saharan Africa, Europe, and around the Mediterranean, as well as an area extending from China and Southeast Asia into Indonesia and the western Pacific.

The next most common order is VSO, followed by VOS. VSO is found in eastern Africa, North Africa, in the westernmost part of Europe, the Philippines, in the Pacific, in Mesoamerica, and in the Pacific Northwest of North America. As for VOS, though it's less common, it's found pretty much everywhere except mainland Africa or Eurasia.

The most infrequent word orders are OVS and OSV, with OVS languages mostly spoken in South America and OSV languages being very rare.

Letting the chips fall where they may: Free word order

In many languages, the order of words isn't fixed. Such languages have *free word order*. In a sentence with a transitive verb, the verb and its two arguments can appear in any one of six orders: *SVO, OVS, VSO, VOS, SOV,* and *OSV.* Table 11-2 shows the six ways of saying 'A woman is digging yams' in Warlpiri, a free-word-order language spoken in Australia. The only ordering restriction that Warlpiri has is that the auxiliary, here the present auxiliary *ka,* must be the second word of the sentence.

Head-initial versus head-final ordering

Each phrase in a sentence has what linguists call a head: the head of a verb phrase is the verb; the head of a prepositional phrase is the preposition; the head of noun phrase is, guess what, a noun. Many languages with fixed word order fall into one of two types according to whether they position the head as the first or last element of the phrase. For example, while the phrasal constituents of English are consistently head-initial, those of Japanese are consistently head-final:

✔ English is an S[**V**O] head-initial language: The head of a phrase is at the beginning.

[$_{VP}$ **V** NP] as in ***bought*** books

[$_{PP}$ **P** NP] as in ***at*** home

[$_{NP}$ **N** PP] as in ***foot*** of the table

✔ Japanese is an S[O**V**] head-final language: The head of a phrase is at the end.

[$_{VP}$ NP **V**] as in '…books bought' *(hon-o **katta)***

[$_{PP}$ NP **P**] as in '…home at' *(jitaku **de)***

[$_{NP}$ PP **N**] as in '…table of foot' *(tenure no **ashy)***

However, many fixed word order languages mix it up a bit: Dutch, German, and Mandarin use a mixture of head-initial and head-final orders. Investigating head-initial/head-final orders is a lively area of research. The debate centers on whether these ordering patterns reflect structure-building principles specific to syntax or more general information processing principles, or a combination of the two. Stay tuned: The jury's still out!

Table 11-2	Free Word Order in Warlpiri
Word Order	**Examples**
S Aux **V** O	*Karnta-ngku **ka** karla-mi yarla.*
	woman-subject present dig-nonpast yam
O Aux **V** S	*Yarla **ka** karnta-ngku karla-mi.*
	yam present woman-subject dig-nonpast
V Aux S O	*Karla-mi **ka** karnta-ngku yarla.*
	dig-nonpast present woman-subject yam
V Aux O S	*Karla-mi **ka** yarla karnta-ngku.*
	dig-nonpast present yam woman-subject
O Aux S **V**	*Yarla **ka** karnta-ngku karla-mi.*
	yam present woman-subject dig-nonpast
S Aux O **V**	*Karnta-ngku **ka** yarla karla-mi.*
	woman-subject present yam dig-nonpast

Finding Different Ways to Express Meaning

Linguists have a handle on how sentence-level meaning is composed (see Chapter 7), but they've only begun to explore how basic elements of meaning are formed. In particular, they don't understand much about how verb or noun meanings come into existence. But in the course of comparing languages, in the 1980s linguists discovered that languages build verb and noun meanings in different ways called *lexicalization patterns*.

Keeping to the path: Motion verbs

By comparing how motion is described in both English and French, linguists have found a lexicalization pattern. In English, a motion is described by the verb expressing the *manner of motion* (such as *limp* or *run*), followed by a preposition expressing the path the motion follows *(into* or *from)*. To see this, look at the following English sentences:

John **limped across** the room.

    manner   path

The children **ran   from** the room.

    manner path

This *manner-path pattern* is found not only in English but also in all Germanic languages.

Now look at the corresponding French sentences. There's a switcheroo! In French, a motion is described by stating the path before the manner. So it's the verb that expresses the path: *traverser* 'traverse', *quitter* 'leave'. As for the manner of motion, it's expressed by a prepositional manner phrase: *en boîtant* 'by limping', *en courant* 'by running'. This *path-manner* pattern is found in all Romance languages.

Jean a **traversé** *la pièce* **en boîtant**.

Jean has traversed the room in limping

    path   manner

Les enfants ont **quitté** *la salle* **en courant**.

the children have left the room in running

    path   manner

Imposing a limit: Count nouns

In the 1930s, a chemical engineer by the name of Benjamin Lee Whorf started to train as a linguist on the side. His linguistic research, conducted under the supervision of Edward Sapir at Yale, lead him to work on Hopi, a Native American language spoken in Arizona. Whorf noticed that Hopi nouns are organized differently than English nouns with respect to how they express the distinction between singular and plural. Although Whorf didn't know it at the time, what he stumbled into was a difference in the lexicalization patterns of count nouns in English and Hopi.

English nouns divide into two semantic classes. Count nouns describe bodies with definite outlines — for example the nouns *cup* and *lump*. Mass nouns describe "stuff" with no boundaries — for example, the nouns *water* and *sugar*. The two semantic classes pattern differently:

✔ English count nouns have two forms: an unmarked singular form and a marked plural form. Adding the suffix *-s* forms the plural.

- **Unmarked singular:** *cup, lump*

- **Marked plural:** *cup-s, lump-s*

✔ English mass nouns have an unmarked singular form but no plural form. To talk about individual portions of a mass noun, one introduces a container word such as *cup* or a shape word such as *lump*. Whorf called this *invidualization*.

- **Unmarked:** *water, sugar*

- **No plural form:** **water-s, *sugar-s*

- **Individualization:** *cup-s of water, lump-s of sugar*

Hopi nouns show a very different pattern. All Hopi nouns have an individual sense and have both singular and plural forms. Hopi nouns that translate as English mass nouns refer to vague bodies or vaguely bounded extents. For example, the Hopi word *key* corresponds to English 'a water' — it denotes a specific mass of water. In other words, Hopi doesn't seem to have mass nouns. This fits with the fact that Hopi doesn't need to use container or shape words because all Hopi nouns already have an individual sense.

The status of the count/mass distinction in the languages of the world is currently the focus of intense research, with debate between semanticists and syntactictians about where the distinction comes from. This debate can only be resolved by looking at data from a wide range of languages, which is what typologists do.

Chapter 12

Beginning and Ending: Language Birth and Language Death

The language you speak today has an ancestry that dates back, directly or indirectly, to the birth of human language in Africa tens of thousands of years ago. And today, new languages are still being born, in different ways. But you also live at the time of a lot of endings, too — a time when at least half of the world's languages (and possibly many more) will soon be extinct. In this chapter, we show you both sides of the coin: how languages are born and how languages die.

Finding Out How Human Language Got Started

Nothing is more human than language. But did humans always have language? Linguists — working with anthropologists, archeologists, biologists, computer scientists, and psychologists — have pieced together a scenario for how human language emerged. It involves two changes that reinforce each other. One is a change in human anatomy: The human vocal tract became larger and the human brain became bigger. The other is a change in human culture: Tools, technology, social organization, and art all became more complex. And although scientists don't yet understand exactly why or how, language played a key role in both of these changes.

Trying to figure out when, where, how, and why human language first appeared requires understanding how language is structured and what it's for. To gain clues about how language learning, culture, and evolution interact, researchers examine how human children learn a first language and also compare the language and communication systems of early humans with those of modern humans.

Evolutionary linguistics — also called *language phylogeny* or *language phylogenesis* — looks at how the language of early humans *(proto-language)* evolved into the language of current humans. *Historical linguistics* tracks the history of current human languages (see Chapter 10 for more on this topic).

Getting ready to talk

You, along with the many billions of human beings on the planet today, belong to the species *Homo sapiens*. Your genetic roots extend back 200,000 years to the emergence of the first modern humans in Africa. Fossil records indicate humans have been around for 2 million years and that *Homo sapiens* emerged 200,000 years ago.

But speech doesn't leave fossil records, so it's difficult to know where language fits in. Using the methods of *linguistic reconstruction* — which allow linguists to trace how languages change over time — linguists can trace back currently spoken languages to 10,000 years ago (see Chapter 10 for more on how languages have changed over the years). However, they don't know how long language was around before then. What scientists do know is that your ability to talk reflects biological changes in your hominid ancestors that enabled speech.

Growing a bigger brain

Humans need big brains to understand and to produce language, and our brain size has tripled over the course of human evolution. Our early human ancestors of 2 million years ago had a brain size of 500 cubic centimeters, while modern humans have a brain size of about 1300 cubic centimeters. But big brains gobble energy: Your brain is only 2 percent of your body weight, but it uses 20 percent of your oxygen supply and gets 20 percent of your blood flow.

Getting a bigger vocal tract

The anatomy of human breathing and swallowing were reorganized in ways that facilitated speech production. Two developments took place:

✔ **The oral cavity got bigger.** By 200,000 years ago, hominids had cranial bases identical to modern humans. The distance between the spinal column and the mouth had increased, lengthening the oral cavity. You may be thinking: "So what?" This change made the oral cavity better adapted for speech, but these people could still only make a limited number of sounds. At this point, the airstream is still optimized for air to pass through the nose during breathing while food goes through the mouth to the throat.

✔ **The larynx descended.** This development created a new section, called the *pharynx,* of the passageway between the larynx and the mouth — it runs parallel to the spine and is situated at right angles to the oral cavity. The tongue can now rapidly change the shapes of these cavities in a wide range of combinations, making it possible to produce a larger set of distinct sounds. Air can also pass easily through both the nose and the mouth to get out. Figure 12-1 compares the vocal tract of the modern human (right) with that of the chimpanzee.

Figure 12-1:
The human vocal tract (on the right) has changed over time to enable speech.

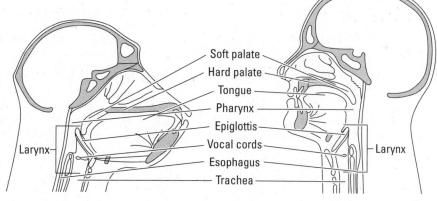

Soft palate
Hard palate
Tongue
Pharynx
Epiglottis
Vocal cords
Esophagus
Trachea
Larynx
Larynx

The changes in human anatomy associated with language also have a down side. Big brains need big heads, making childbirth more difficult and dangerous for human mothers, compared to other primates. A lowered larynx means that it's not possible for humans to swallow and breathe at the same time — they run the risk of choking if food gets stuck in the larynx.

Early humans and modern humans

Humans are part of the *homo* group *(genus)* that spread from Africa — they are characterized by their large brains and their ability to use tools. The traditional view was that humans evolved one after another in a single lineage. Nowadays, most scientists recognize that different species of humans co-existed.

- **Homo habilus** — the "handy man" — had a brain size of around 500 cubic centimeters (cc). One of the earliest members of the human group, they lived in eastern and southern Africa 2.4 to 1.4 million years ago. They were small — averaging 3–4 feet in height and weighing about 70 pounds — and may have used stone tools.

- **Homo rudolfensis** had a brain size of around 700cc and lived in Eastern Africa between 1.9 and 1.8 million years ago. The name *rudolfensis* comes from Lake Rudolf (now called Lake Turkana), which is where the fossils were discovered.

- **Homo erectus** had a brain size of around 900cc and lived between 1.9 million and 143,000 years ago. They're the first species to expand beyond Africa around 2 million years ago, with fossil records being found in western Asia (Dmanisi, Republic of Georgia) and East Asia (China and Indonesia). They were the first to control fire: campfires *(hearths)* occur during this time range, indicating social interaction and food-sharing. These precursors to modern humans are bigger than other early humans: averaging 5–6 feet in height and weighing between 88 and 150 pounds. Soon after the earliest fossil records of Homo erectus (about 1.9 millions years ago), there is evidence for innovation in stone tools (about 1.75 million years ago), including large cutting tools like hand axes and cleavers.

- **Homo heidelbergensis** had a brain size of around 1200cc and lived between 700,000 and 200,000 years ago. They lived in Europe and Africa, and also possibly Asia. They were the first to build shelters and hunt big game. In Europe, they were the ancestors of *Homo neanderthalensis*. In Africa, they were the ancestors to *Homo sapiens*.

- **Homo neanderthalensis** had a brain size of about 1450cc and lived between 200,000 and 28,000 years ago. They lived in Europe and in southwestern and central Asia. Adapted to cold and dry climates, their bodies were shaped for heat conservation, with shorter limb extremities. They are the first early humans to wear clothing, and they may have been the first to have language.

- **Homo floresiensis** had a brain size of about 500cc and lived between 95,000 and 17,000 years ago. They're named after Flores Island, in Indonesia, where the fossils were discovered. Because of their small body size, they carry the nickname "the hobbit." Anatomical features link them to *Homo erectus*, but they co-existed with modern humans.

- **Homo sapiens** (modern humans) have a brain size of around 1350cc and emerged about 200,000 years ago, at a time of climate change in Africa. They hunted and gathered food and were able to adapt to a wide range of climates. Compared to earlier humans, modern humans have a lighter build and larger brains. And although they co-existed with other early humans, they're the only surviving species of humans.

Finding signs of complex language

Clear signs of complex language — or any of the behaviors associated with language — don't emerge until about 60,000 years ago. At that time, there was a profound change in human culture, a change so far-reaching that anthropologists call it a revolution. And because the change occurred during the Upper Paleolithic era — the Stone Age — it's called the *Upper Paleolithic revolution*. With these changes, humans began engaging in activities that created socially shared meaning and that required language.

Changing human culture

Some people believe that language made socially shared meaning possible. And others believe that socially shared meaning gave rise to language. It's a chicken and egg debate. Whichever came first, it's clear that the emergence of more complex social structures and language are linked. Here's what we now know about what happened:

- **Purpose-driven tool-making:** Humans began making tools with a specific purpose: projectile points, engraving tools, knife blades, piercing tools, drilling tools, and so on. This was a change from the very general-purpose tools with no particular form or function that had been the norm before.

- **New technology:** Humans started to use different materials to make tools, such as bone. They also began to use advanced darts and harpoons, along with fishhooks, oil lamps, ropes, and eyed needles.

- **Social organization:** Humans began to move in groups, establish seasonal campsites, exploit different food sources at different times of the year, participate in collective hunting, and store food for future use. Reliable food sources and specialized tools supported more complex social groups. Trading links emerged between groups.

- **Production of artistic work:** The first artistic work dates to this period. Examples include the cave paintings in France (dating to 33,000 BCE). The most recent major discovery is the Venus figurine of Hohel in Germany; nearby a bone flute was found. Both date to 35,000 BCE.

Linking language to culture

What prompted the upheaval of the Upper Paleolithic revolution? Nobody knows for sure, but most agree on three main lines of thought:

- **It reflects a change in human society.** A more temperate climate in Africa, where humans lived at the time, made larger amounts of food available. This triggered rapid population growth, which changed the structure of human society. The need to organize large numbers of people caused language to crystallize as part of a larger social change.

✔ **It reflects a change in human cognition specific to language.** A biological change gave humans the capacity for language. Perhaps a mutation amongst the modern humans of Africa promoted the capacity for rapid, flexible, and highly structured speech, which led to the dramatic changes of the Upper Paleolithic period.

✔ **It reflects gradual change in human cognition.** Perhaps a subtle re-organization of the brain gave rise to the integrated intelligence needed for generalizing and perceiving analogies, which made language possible. For example, making tools and applying them to intricate tasks required long periods of training and apprenticeship. Transferring conceptual and procedural knowledge from one generation to another increased the need for greater working memory and cognitive processes. Over time, this reorganized the brain to handle abstractions, analogy, and elaborate naming and description of the world.

LINGUIST LINGO

Indirect evidence for the emergence of language

Language doesn't leave physical traces — there aren't any linguistic fossils — so research on language evolution relies on indirect evidence. The three approaches linguists use to study the emergence of language are

✔ **The windows approach:** This approach examines phenomena for which direct evidence exists and provides a window on how and when human language may have evolved. This includes looking at fossil skulls, ancestral brains, prehistoric symbols and rituals, prehistoric sea-crossings, parallels between language and song, and parallels between speech and gesture. Researchers also get clues by examining the genetic basis for the language capacity, the development of new human languages, infant-directed speech *(motherese)*, and how children learn a first language. (For more information on the last three, see Chapter 13.)

✔ **The comparative approach:** This approach figures out which features of human language have been inherited from a common primate ancestor, which have undergone minor changes, and which features are new to humans. The features that emerged gradually are compared with sudden leaps of language development in order to try to determine whether language evolved from pre-existing communicative systems or as an adaptive response to advances in numerical reasoning, tool-making, and social complexity. This research area — called *biolinguistics* — has been the focus of intense research over the past decade or so.

✔ **The computational approach:** This approach uses computational models to evaluate theories of language evolution, explore how different mechanisms interact, and demonstrate how particular accounts of language change work.

Seeing New Languages Being Born

New languages, both spoken and signed, pop up all the time. Figure 12-2 shows the three ways that new languages develop — emergence of a *daughter language* from a mother language, emergence of a *creole language* from multiple parent languages, and emergence of language out-of-the-blue. Linguists have studied examples of these three ways to create a new language. What they've found is that kids are central to each type of language creation. Daughter languages arise when small changes introduced by generations of kids reach a tipping point. Creole languages arise when kids, who are exposed to several languages, combine them into a single new language. And in the absence of language input, kids create a new language from scratch!

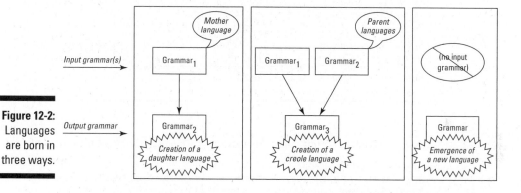

Figure 12-2:
Languages are born in three ways.

Staying in the family: Daughter languages

Over time, language variation and change (see Chapters 9 and 10 for more on these two topics) can lead to a new language. Very small changes add up — and behold! — a new daughter language is born.

Romancing the sisters: The daughter languages of Latin

Modern-day Romance languages — which include Spanish, Portuguese, French, Italian, Romanian, and Catalan — are all daughter languages of Vulgar Latin. This wasn't "rude Latin," but the Latin of common people: the soldiers, settlers, and merchants who worked for the Roman Empire. For 500 years — between 350 BCE and 150 CE — Latin was the dominant language of continental western Europe. After the collapse of the Roman Empire in the fifth century, local varieties of Latin became more isolated and different from each other, quickly evolving into distinct languages. The oldest recorded daughter language is Romanian, which dates back about 1,500 years: It was first mentioned as a language distinct from Latin around 500 CE. Table 12-1 gives the datelines of the other sister languages that are most widely spoken nowadays.

Table 12-1		Dateline of Some Romance Languages
Language	*Date Emerged*	*Earliest Written Record*
Romanian	700 CE	500 CE: reference to a language distinct from Latin
French	800 CE	842 CE: *Oath of Strasbourg* by Charlemagne's grandsons
Italian	900 CE	900 CE: oldest texts published in the form of letters
Catalan	1000 CE	1000 CE: texts of sermons called *Homilies of Organyà*
Spanish	1000 CE	900–1000CE: *Glosas Emilianenses*, list of words and phrases
Portuguese	1200 CE	1290 CE: King Diniz creates Portuguese University in Lisbon

Transplanting French Sign Language to the U.S.: The birth of ASL

Just as spoken languages are grouped into families and share a common ancestor, so too with signed languages: American Sign Language (ASL), a widely used sign language, is a daughter language of French Sign Language (LSF). In the early 1800s, the French educator Laurent Clerc brought LSF to the United States and co-founded (with Thomas Gallaudet) the American School for the Deaf. The deaf community quickly adopted LSF and, through generations of use, the American variety eventually became a separate language.

Crossing family lines: Creole languages

Creole languages pop up when languages bump into each other — they're found everywhere and are an important source of evidence for models of language evolution. How do creoles pop up? It works like this. Communities speaking different languages often come into regular contact with each other. The sensible thing is for everybody to become bilingual. But if large social and economic differences exist between speech communities — for example, in situations of slavery — then nobody learns anyone else's language. So another option is to create a new language by combining features from each language. A dramatic example of European and African languages bumping into each other is the transatlantic slave trade, from the 1600s to the 1800s, which displaced millions of people from Africa to the Caribbean and the

Americas. The linguistic outcome of this process was the creation of several creole languages, such as Haitian Creole and Jamaican Creole. While linguists (strongly!) disagree on how creole languages come into being, they agree that all creoles involve multiple input languages, with one language being the main parent. So while Haitian is a French-based creole, Jamaican is an English-based creole.

Creoles are classified in terms of the language that contributes most of the vocabulary or *lexicon*. Linguists call the main parent language the *lexifier language*. Currently spoken creoles — which number over 70 languages — are based on nine lexifier languages: English (31), French (14), Portuguese (11), Malay (8), Arabic (5), German (2), Spanish (2), Mandarin (1), and Ngbandi (1).

Starting from scratch: Language genesis

A more radical way to create a new language is to start from scratch, which happens when language transmission to the next generation is disrupted. This happens most often with signed language because deaf kids often don't have models to imitate:

- ✔ **Al-Sayyid Bedouin Sign Language** emerged in the 1920s in southern Israel as a result of congenital deafness and is in its third generation of fluent signers. It's at risk of extinction, however, because of the influence of Israeli and Jordanian Sign Languages in school.

- ✔ **Nicaraguan Sign Language** *(Idioma de Señas de Nicaragua)* developed in the 1980s, shortly after two schools for deaf children were established in Managua in 1977 and 1980. By 1983, more than 400 deaf students were enrolled in the two schools. Something amazing happened: The kids began to use a common set of (signed) symbols, which rapidly developed into a full-blown language.

Hearing kids sometimes don't get enough spoken input. This happens in extreme cases of social isolation and is limited to individual cases. See Chapter 13 for how this affects their ability to learn language.

Losing Languages: What's Happening and Why

Although new languages are still being born, older languages are dying out at a much faster rate. In fact, a period of mass extinction of the world's languages is just beginning: Within your children's or your grandchildren's lifetimes, at least 50 percent — and possibly as much as 90 percent — of currently spoken languages will disappear.

In this section we explain what *language death* means, why it happens, and how linguists decide whether a language is safe or endangered.

Losing languages through change

Some language loss isn't necessarily a bad thing. Languages are constantly changing, and over time they turn into new languages (see Chapter 10 for more on language change). For example, English has changed so much in the last 1,000 years that modern speakers can't understand the old form without special training — in fact, only 10 percent of our Modern English words are from Old English! Yet English isn't considered a dead language because it continues to evolve and live on in its new form as a daughter language. Linguists sometimes call this process of normal language change and drift *pseudoextinction* — the older form of the language is gone, but it lives on through its descendants.

A more profound form of language loss is when a language is not passed down at all — when a whole system of words, sounds, and structures disappears. This usually happens slowly, through a gradual process of cultural assimilation. A speech community can lose its language gradually over several generations. At first, most people in a community are bilingual, speaking both their language and the new language. Over time, though, social and economic pressures lead people to use their language in fewer and fewer parts of their lives, until children eventually stop learning it as a mother tongue.

The state of languages today

Languages can't be classified as safe or endangered based on the *number* of living speakers because languages may be perfectly safe with relatively small numbers of speakers, or they may be severely endangered with many speakers still living.

Instead, linguists describe the health of a language based on whether and how many kids are learning the language:

- ✔ **Safe:** The language is being passed on from parents to kids in a natural way, and it looks like this will continue indefinitely. English, Mandarin, and most (though not all) European languages fit into this category. Other examples include the Niger-Congo family of Africa, which includes languages such as Yorùbá or Swahili that are extremely safe. Many linguists estimate that just 10 percent of the world's languages (600 out of roughly 6,000 existing languages) fall into the *safe* class today.

✔ **Endangered:** Some kids are learning the language as their mother tongue but likely won't teach it to their children. Blackfoot, one of the languages of the Great Plains, has around 4,500 speakers and appears to be severely endangered. In Indonesia, some languages have *tens of thousands* of speakers but are endangered by the spread of other, more dominant, languages. Linguists figure that 60 to 80 percent of today's languages are in this *endangered* class (somewhere between 3,600 and 4,800 out of 6,000 languages).

✔ **Moribund:** Some people, mainly older generations, still speak the language, but no kids are learning it. The language will be lost forever when the current adults and elders are gone — maybe in just a few years. The most recently available public survey of Anambé, spoken in Brazil, lists just seven speakers — a number that could drop to zero very quickly. Linguists estimate that, at the very least, 20 percent of the world's languages (around 1,200 out of the 6,000 languages) are moribund. The line between *endangered* and *moribund* is hard to draw, though, and some estimates put this moribund class as high as 50 percent.

✔ **Extinct:** No one speaks the language anymore as a mother tongue. Scholars and adults may learn bits of it, but it's not learned as anyone's native language. Hittite is one ancient example — it went extinct around 1100 BCE. Of course, we don't find out much about these languages unless they were also written languages. The number of recently extinct languages is also growing — one example is the language Aka-Bo, traditionally spoken on an island in the Bay of Bengal (officially part of India). Aka-Bo's last speaker is reported to have died in 2011.

The percentage of languages in these classes is not uniform around the world. For example, around 90 percent of the aboriginal languages of the United States, Canada, and Australia are moribund or already extinct. But linguists estimate that only around 27 percent of the South American languages and only 17 percent of the languages of Central America and Mexico are moribund or extinct. But the overall trend around the world is clear: While hundreds of languages will continue to be spoken in the future, at least 3,000 languages — and probably more — will become extinct in the next century.

Killing language diversity

It is no accident that so many languages are dying or in danger today. Technological change and globalization create conditions that make small speech communities vulnerable.

Let's start with Big Government. Governments since ancient times — especially after a military conquest and colonization — have used their control of the political system to make one language dominant. This serves to create a homogenous culture and weaken opposition because when the non-dominant language stops being used altogether, a disheartening loss of linguistic identity occurs. Governments have done this in two main ways:

- ✔ **Choice of language of government:** Many conquerors impose their language as the language of the public sphere, which means that if you want any influence in politics or business, you need to work in the official language. This, of course, strongly encourages cultural assimilation. This is the reason, for example, that Egyptians today speak Arabic — the Coptic language of Egypt was assimilated after the Arab conquest of Egypt (around 640 CE), when Arabic became the language of government. Similarly, nations typically marginalize dozens of local languages by introducing an official language or *lingua franca,* like Mandarin in China, Portuguese in Brazil, and Bahasa (Malay) in Indonesia.

- ✔ **Choice of the language of education:** Governments, usually led by the dominant culture in a region, often choose their own language as the language of instruction in schools. This does two things. It removes any non-dominant languages from a major part of children's lives. And it adds the prestige of educational approval to the dominant language. (For discussion of the relation between language dominance and the linguistic standard, see Chapter 9.)

Economics, the media, and urbanization also play a huge role in leading people to lose — sometimes willingly — the original languages of their cultures. Three of the biggest factors are:

- ✔ **Predominance of a language of trade:** People need some kind of shared language for trade, and a more globalized trading system functions more smoothly with fewer languages. If your child can get a good job only by learning a language used widely for trade, like Swahili or English, it's easy to see those languages as more valuable and useful than local languages. That affects everyone's linguistic choices, usually to the detriment of local languages.

- ✔ **Media influence:** The economics of the media business dictate that certain languages (the languages of the biggest and richest markets) predominate on TV, on the radio, and in movies and games — you just can't make *Star Wars* in 6,000 different languages (though it would be cool to try). If your kids are seeing only English or some other dominant language in the media they love and respect, then the language of their local speech community is removed from a huge part of their lives, and it's easy for them to think it's not useful or important.

- ✔ **Social mobility:** People today move around more than ever, and this particularly affects small languages spoken only in a limited region. If you speak a language or dialect that is understood only in your little home village, you'll pretty much have to give it up when you move to the big city to get a job — as hundreds of millions of people have done in recent years. Minority languages can be safe in small, stable communities, but there just aren't that many stable communities anymore.

Demoting language in residential schools

The education system can be used to deliberately overwhelm a non-dominant language. This is what happened with the residential schools set up for aboriginal children in the early 1900s, where children were sent to schools a long way from their families and speech communities. The governments of Canada, the United States, and Australia instituted programs that required First Nations/ Aboriginal children to attend boarding schools for most of the year. At these schools, the children were often punished for speaking their own languages. If you want to get a sense of what the residential schools/boarding schools programs were like, check out the Australian movie *Rabbit Proof Fence*, which tells a poignant story of children in such a school. Be prepared to cry. Most of these schools were closed by the 1970s.

These forces are often mutually supporting — economic factors influence government decisions, and government policy influences the media, and so on. In the end, it all adds up to the loss of many languages.

Though many people believe that learning a language spoken only by a small group takes away economic opportunities for their children, that's not true at all because children can grow up bilingual almost effortlessly. Learned from infancy, a child can easily master two or more languages. (See Chapter 13 for info on how kids learn language.)

Debating Diversity: What Dies with a Language?

It's a fact that a lot of human languages are being lost. Some people, including linguists and language speakers themselves, think that such language loss actually doesn't matter that much. Others think it's a terrible tragedy that should be slowed or prevented. In this section, we show you both sides of this debate.

The case for letting languages go

Here are some of the arguments people give to say it doesn't matter when a language dies:

- ✔ **The *speakers don't care* argument:** In some speech communities, the speakers themselves don't care — sometimes they *want* their children to lose their language.

- ✔ **The *economics first* argument:** Giving up the language spoken in your culture may simply be the cost of joining a wealthy modern society — and if so, it's a price that many rural people would willingly pay. Traditions are important, but let's face it: People also need jobs and money.

- ✔ **The *political unity* argument:** In many countries where different ethnic groups have been in conflict, distinct languages can strongly reinforce cultural tensions, sometimes to the point of tearing a country apart (as almost happened in Canada).

- ✔ **The *natural language loss* argument:** Languages always come and go. Even if every language were saved today — an impossible task — those languages would quickly change and adapt into new languages anyway. Why not just let people switch to a widely shared language?

The case for trying to save languages

Many speakers and linguists believe that it's important to save as many endangered languages as possible. Here are a couple of the arguments they put forward:

- ✔ **The *cultural identity* argument:** A shared language strengthens a speech community's cultural identity and gives them a sense of cultural continuity with their ancestors and pride in their culture. It's impossible to put a price on having pride in your culture and who you are, but it makes a measurable difference in people's lives. For example, a Canadian study found that First Nations/Aboriginal children who learn the language of their culture, even to a limited degree, have a lower suicide rate. Pride and cultural identity may be intangible, but they're an important part of succeeding in life.

- ✔ **The *cultural warehouse* argument:** Many people see each language as an intellectual treasure — a rich and complex system that serves as a storehouse for a shared cultural knowledge and offers a particular way of seeing the world.

It is common to hear people — sometimes the speakers themselves — denigrate minority languages as simplistic or bad or ugly. This notion has no place in the debate because there are no bad or simplistic human languages. All languages, including the languages of hunter-gatherer societies, are as rich, complex, and systematic as Latin, Greek, or the Queen's English. It doesn't take city living and schools to have a fully complex and systematic language.

Breathing life into languages

Even for people who think endangered languages deserve to be saved, it can be tough to figure out what — if anything — can actually be done to revitalize a language. Community organization and support, however, are always key to language revitalization because language revitalization means *creating* a speech community where the language can live. The top three community-centered models for language revitalization are

- ✔ **Language nests:** The Maori people of New Zealand have created spaces for some of their native-speaking elders to live and raise children entirely in the language. These language nests are not schools but just spaces for living and interacting in the language, in an area where no English is used. The program has proved highly successful in re-vitalizing Maori and is now being used in more and more communities around the world.

- ✔ **Master-apprentice learning:** Many of the languages of California had been reduced to just a few speakers when community activists working with linguists developed a new method for learning languages. This method pairs one learner (the *apprentice*) with a fluent speaker (the *master*) for several hours each week — just to talk and communicate in the language. This method doesn't have any formal teaching or textbooks — just real interactions in the language. With this method, an apprentice can acquire a basic level of fluency in any language within a year.

- ✔ **Immersion schools:** Immersion learning, where you learn all your school subjects in a certain language, is far and away the best school-based method for kids to become fluent in a language. A growing number of cultures with endangered languages have followed this model for their languages, and through this method they have created entire new generations of highly fluent speakers. For example, in Hawaii, students can now go from kindergarten to university in a program taught entirely in the Hawaiian language — and the kids who go to the Hawaiian immersion schools end up doing great overall academically, including on their English exams!

It is a mistake to think that a linguist can come and save an entire language in some kind of documentary project. The dictionaries and grammars that linguists make give very small windows into a language. Nevertheless, linguists can play a supporting role, especially for the most severely endangered languages, by collecting and sharing certain kinds of materials for the language, such as stories and words from elders who have passed away. Linguists also have a responsibility — one that they are taking increasingly seriously — of promoting public awareness and training community members to do linguistic documentation and research for themselves. Governments can also play a role in helping endangered languages get back on their feet. The strongest positive role for the government to take is to support the use of the language in government and education. Canada learned a lesson from Greenland and made Inuktitut (spoken by the Inuit) the official language of the northern territory of Nunavut. Greenland and Nunavut are both examples of stable, relatively isolated, populations, so this policy decision will help Inuktitut prosper for generations to come.

Hebrew: A world record in revitalization

Hebrew was the ancient language of the Jewish people, but even in Jesus' time many Jews had already switched to another language (Aramaic). By around 200 CE, almost everyone had stopped speaking Hebrew as an everyday language because of emigration to diverse countries and assimilation there.

The Hebrew language continued to exist after that only as a sacred and scholarly language. People used written forms of the language, sometimes reading it out loud in ceremonies, but no one used Hebrew as their home language or for everyday communication. Jewish people in Europe mainly spoke Yiddish (which is similar to German) or other languages such as Ladino (a language derived from an old form of Spanish, but influenced by Hebrew). In the Middle East, many Jewish people spoke forms of Arabic as their native language.

This all changed towards the end of the 19th century with the rise of the Zionist movement. Initially led by a man named Eliezer Ben-Yeduda (1858–1922), early Zionists recognized the importance of language to creating a homeland, and they created what became Israeli Hebrew by organizing schools and forming social groups where young people could use the language in public. Modern Hebrew shows the influence of many languages. It has the morphology of earlier forms of Hebrew — and so is classified as a member of the Semitic language family. But it also bears the imprint of many other languages, including Yiddish, Polish, Ladino, Arabic, and English.

The movement really took off after Jewish refugees settled in Palestine after World War II and created the nation of Israel. The children of these emigrants grew up as native speakers of Hebrew. The effort to revitalize Hebrew in order to promote a common identity among Jews was supported at an official level as well — Hebrew was the language of the state, radio, street signs, and the education system. Organizations strongly encouraged Hebrew to be the language spoken by individuals on the street, shaming people if they spoke Yiddish or one of the languages from their pre-Israel days.

The movement was not just top-down. It was supported by the Israeli people themselves, who understood the important role Hebrew revitalization had to play in what they were doing: forging a nation, uniting the people together with a shared language, and connecting them to their ancient language and culture.

Whatever your take on the nation of Israel, everyone can agree that Hebrew is one of the most successful examples of language revitalization in history — transforming the language from one that had no native speakers to one that has millions. Whether the same model could work elsewhere is hard to know — but it's a clear demonstration of what happens when government and people join together to revitalize a language.

Part IV
Your Brain on Language: Learning and Processing Language

The 5th Wave   By Rich Tennant

"You mean, 'wo,' 'ta,' 'baba,' and 'mama' are all words in Mandarin? My gosh, Alice, our baby's been speaking Chinese the last few weeks!"

In this part . . .

Language is a window into the human mind. Looking at how humans learn language, how they perceive and produce it, and what happens to their brain when they use language — these are some of the ways in which language reveals the workings of the human mind. In this part, we explain what linguists have learned about how humans learn and process language.

Chapter 13

Learning Language

*Y*ou likely don't remember learning your first language. You're not alone: By the time you're able to form memories (by the age of three), you've mastered the essential parts of language. In fact, most children learn their first language — or languages — easily and effortlessly. But if you've ever learned a second language later on in life, you know that it's a hard and slow slog. We show you why language learning is easy for kids, how it's a balancing act between nature and nurture, and why adults find it so hard.

Hitting the Ground Running: Language in the First Year of Life

No matter which language you learned as a child — English, French, Japanese, Swahili, Mandarin, or something else — you drew on your ability to detect patterns in the signals around you. This pattern-detecting ability is not specific to language. But learning a language is possible only if you have the ability to detect patterns and to then organize those patterns in certain ways. All kids, no matter which language they're learning, use similar strategies to decode language and go through a series of age-related stages.

L1 acquisition is the process involved in learning a first language (your *L1*) as a child.

During the first year of life, infants integrate sensory percepts, fine-tune their motor skills, and get the hang of paying attention to other people. This affects all aspects of learning and shapes the timeline for the acquisition of speech, as Figure 13-1 shows. In the figure, ellipses (...) at the beginning of a stage means the onset precedes the timeline shown, and ellipses at the end of a stage means that the process continues after the timeline shown. Notice that sensory learning and speech perception begin before birth!

- **Sensory learning:** The ability to process sensory information — based on what an infant hears, sees, smells, touches, and tastes — kicks in from the get-go. Some senses, in particular hearing, are active before birth.

- **Motor learning:** From birth, infants begin to acquire motor skills that make it possible for them to move more independently. By 3 months, they are beginning to use their vocal tracts to shape speech sounds.

- **Speech perception:** Because sensing precedes doing, speech perception kicks in before speech production. All human infants — independent of the particular language that they're learning — start out with the ability to *discriminate* (perceive whether two sounds are the same or different) all human speech sounds. In some sense, they are natural-born phoneticians. Then, at about the age of 6 months, they home in on the particular language (or languages) of their environment. From that point on, they can only recognize the speech sounds of the target language.

- **Speech production:** Speech production kicks in later. Initially, young infants start out with the ability to produce all human speech sounds. Then, at about the age of 6 months, they start to aim their speech production to the sounds of the target language (or languages).

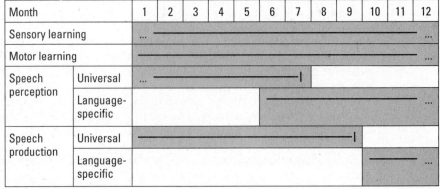

Figure 13-1: Timeline of speech perception and production in the first 12 months of life.

Month		1	2	3	4	5	6	7	8	9	10	11	12
Sensory learning		...											...
Motor learning													...
Speech perception	Universal	...											
	Language-specific												...
Speech production	Universal												
	Language-specific												...

Throughout this chapter, the timelines provided are approximate. For each individual, the actual onset of a particular stage can be earlier or later.

How infants perceive speech

To perceive speech, you have to be able to recognize sound patterns and separate speech sounds from other sounds. This is a tall order for a newborn infant! But you come into the world pre-tuned to perceive speech. About 3 months before birth, you begin sensing sound and draw on this experience from the outset. You begin life with a preference for listening to speech over other complex sounds.

Sussing out segments, phonemes, and languages

How do infants break into the speech stream? They face three challenges:

- ✔ **The segmentation problem:** How do infants figure out that a stream of speech can be segmented into phonemes?

- ✔ **The invariance problem:** How do infants identify a stable set of phonemes from a signal that is chock-full of variation? For example, /p/ is pronounced differently according to whether it appears at the beginning or end of a word: compare ***p**it* (where /p/ is aspirated) to *tip* (where /p/ isn't aspirated). Add to that the fact that each speaker has a slightly different pronunciation, and that even the same speaker doesn't pronounce the same word twice in the same way.

- ✔ **The language problem:** How do infants figure out which set of sounds belong to their target language?

Linguists measure how infants perceive speech by paying attention to what infants pay attention to. In newborns, response is measured by monitoring sucking activity. In older infants, researchers monitor where infants direct their gaze.

Cracking the code

The segmentation, invariance, and language problems are interconnected, and infants go through a series of stages that allow them to solve these problems in a lockstep fashion. By 9 months, they "crack the code" of their language.

Initially young infants can *discriminate* (perceive whether two sounds are the same or different) phonetic sounds from any human language, even ones they haven't been exposed to. That's quite a feat because human languages distinguish hundreds of sounds! They retain this ability until the age of about 8 months, at which point they show a preference for the sounds of their target language. Their attention to the sounds of their target language is based on statistical learning — infants pay more attention to the sounds that are most frequent. Being able to discriminate the sounds of a target language and to identify the most frequent ones are the first steps in solving the segmentation and to language problems. And the fact that infants do this based on input from different speakers means they're also solving the invariance problem.

By 8 months, infants are expert statisticians and keep score of which sounds hang out together. They detect regularities about which sounds are likely to occur with which other sounds, the typical stress patterns on words, and the difference between content words (such as verbs and nouns) and function words (articles such as *the* and auxiliaries such as *be*, *have*, *do*). The ability of infants to detect rhythmic properties such as stress means that they're now solving the segmentation, invariance, and language problem at the word level — this is a prerequisite for them being able to chunk up the speech signal.

By 6 months, infants recognize familiar words, including their own names. By 9 months, they recognize sound patterns for words of their language. The ability to *perceive* words as units lays the foundation for the ability to *produce* single-word utterances. Linguists call this the one-word stage. What's cool about this stage is that even these simple single-word utterances have the same falling pitch that a complete sentence does! Infants' ability to detect sentence-level pitch melodies means that they're now solving the segmentation, invariance, and language problems at the sentence level.

How infants produce speech

In addition to being sensitive to speech sounds, you as an infant seek out social interaction with other human beings. In fact, you're very good at drawing attention to yourself and establishing social relations with adults in your environment.

Calling attention to yourself: Crying

The universal strategy of all babies everywhere is crying. In addition to communicating physical discomfort or hunger, you cry as a dress rehearsal for speech. Crying comes in regular bursts — there are pauses in between, and each soundburst falls in pitch as it goes on. And if the crying isn't immediately responded to, you turn up the volume. These three ingredients — a rhythm of recurring sounds, modulation of pitch, and modulation of volume — lay the groundwork for speech.

Communicating before words: Cooing

You're getting used to the shape of your vocal tract, figuring out where your tongue fits in your mouth, and learning to coordinate breathing and making sound. By 2 months, you've progressed to cooing. You experiment making consonant-like and vowel-like sounds — they're not actual consonants and vowels — and you're soon stringing them together in longer sequences. And somewhere between the ages of 5 and 8 months, your natural ability as a phonetician bursts forth. You can produce all sorts of speech sounds, including ones that are not in your target language.

In a conversational exchange, participants need to coordinate their interaction so they don't talk over each other. Research conducted by Catherine Snow indicates that adults provide turn-taking instructions to young infants. She reports the following interaction between a mother and her infant daughter of 3 months. Notice that the mother's feedback gives her daughter implicit instruction on turn-taking.

> Daughter: (smiles)
>
> Mother: _Oh, what a nice little smile. Yes, isn't that nice? There. There's a nice little smile._
>
> Daughter: (burps)
>
> Mother: _What a nice little wind as well. Yes, that's better, isn't it? Yes._
>
> Daughter: (vocalizes)
>
> Mother: _There's a nice noise._

By the age of 6 months, infants have figured out how to get adult attention through a mixture of vocalizations and gestures. But the adults are still doing all the work to create the conversation, interpreting any sounds the infant makes — from cooing to burping — as a conversational turn.

Zeroing in on the target: Babbling

Next you start to zero in on your target language. By the age of 6 to 7 months, you're babbling away, and the sounds that you are using are getting closer and closer to being the sounds of your language. You repeat similar syllables and sounds over and over again: _ba, ba, bi, bi, bu, bu._

Your ability to detect and produce sound distinctions not found in your language starts to fade away: By 9 months, your speech _perception_ is focused on the sounds of your target language, and by 10 months, your speech _production_ locks onto your target language as well.

The adults around you continue coaching you in turn-taking. For example, when adults interact with you, they don't move on to their turn until you respond by babbling or vocalizing.

From phonemes to syllables to words

Stop consonants (/p, t, k, b, d, g, m, n, n/) and glides (/y, w/) develop early across many languages, by around 7 months. Most children master the vowels in their target language by around 24 months. The last sounds to be acquired are fricatives /s, z/, affricates /ts, dz/, and liquids /r, l/ because the production of these sounds requires fine motor control. For example, for children acquiring English, fricatives pop in at around 30 months and /l/ and /r/ make their appearance at around 36 months.

Until they attain the motor control that allows them to produce all the sounds of their language, kids often omit or substitute sounds. For linguists, such omission and substitution "errors" provide a window into the rule system that the child is developing.

✔ **Substitution:** Kids often voice consonants in initial position, and devoice consonants in the final position. So *pie* comes out as [**b**ay] and *knob* comes out as [nɑ**p**]. And until they figure out how to produce frication, they often substitute a stop for a fricative. So *knife* comes out as [naib], and *bus* comes out as [bʌd]. And because /r/ and /l/ come in so late, kids often substitute those sounds with [y] and [w]. So *rabbit* comes out as [wæbɪt].

✔ **Omission:** Kids often omit the final consonant of a word. So *ball* comes out as [ba], *boot* as [bu]. For words with more than one syllable, kids acquiring English, which has a stress-based intonation, often omit the weak (unstressed) syllable. So **bye**-*bye* comes out as [bab], *he**llo*** comes out as [hwow], **Stev**ie comes out as [iv], and a**way** comes out as [wei]. This also means that they often omit grammatical words such as *the* and *a* (which are almost always unstressed). So a sentence like *He catches the pig* may come out as 'He catches pig.'

In addition to learning the phonemes of their target language, kids also have to figure out how the sounds combine with each other. Kids' first words are often single CV syllables, like [ga], [da], [ba], [ma], and [na]. Then they move onto sequences of CV syllables, then CVC syllables, then syllables with long vowels (CVV, CVVC). And when they start making CVC syllables, they often produce forms where the two consonants have the same place of articulation, for example [tin] (where both [t] and [n] are alveolar) or [pom] (where both [p] and [m] are labial).

Falling Down the Linguistic Rabbit-hole: Language after the First Year of Life

After you get your first words out (at around 12 months), you start combining words with each other (at around 18 months) and then move onto more complex sentences (at around 24 months). By 3 years old, you have a pretty good understanding of how your language forms words *(morphology)* and sentences *(syntax)* and how to use language appropriately *(pragmatics)*. Here are the major developmental stages that you go through.

Getting one word in at a time

By 12 months, you produce your first words! Linguists call this the *one-word stage*. You have a few words, but no sentence structure yet. You say things like *Down!,* for 'Put me down', or *Door!* if someone closes the door. You use differences in pitch — the same kind of pitch changes you were practicing back when you were crying to get attention — to show the difference between a command, *Down!,* and a request, *Down?* What you say depends heavily on context. You can gesture, stand, and wave bye-bye. You understand familiar words and simple orders associated with gestures.

Although you're a ways off from having a full-fledged conversation, you can respond to the adults around you with actual words. You have a limited amount of topics to work with — the exchanges focus on what's in your immediate environment. Here's an example from the same mother-daugher pair (again from research reported by Catherine Snow). Here the daughter is 18 months old and is participating more actively in the exchange. But notice that her utterances are all a single word.

> Daughter: (blowing noises)
>
> Mother: *That's a bit rude.*
>
> Daughter: *Mouth.*
>
> Mother: *Mouth, that's right.*
>
> Daughter: *Face.*
>
> Mother: *Face, yes, mouth is in your face. What else have you got in your face?*
>
> Daughter: *Face* (closing eyes).
>
> Mother: *You're making a face, aren't you?*

Getting two words in at a time

The two-word stage happens between 18 and 24 months. You use pitch now to signal that words group together, and you spread your falling or rising pitches over the whole two-word combination. You know about 50 words, and you use two-word combinations — this is the beginning of syntax. For example, *Doggie bark* for 'The dog is barking' expresses an agent-action semantic relationship and a subject-verb syntactic relationship. And *Daddy hat,* for 'Daddy's hat', expresses a possessor-possessed semantic relationship and a genitive-noun syntactic relationship. By this time, you can walk, feed yourself, and scribble lines with crayons.

Knitting together sound, meaning, and structure

From the age of 24 months onwards, your grammar explodes! There's a rapid vocabulary expansion: At 24 months you know about 400 words, by 30 months you have around 900 words, by 36 months you're at 1,200 words, and by 48 months you're hovering at 1,500 words. There's also a rapid growth of syntax — you now begin to master the forms of words, the rules of word order, the placement of negation, and the forms of passives, questions, and relative clauses.

Learning the forms of words

In early stages of language acquisition, kids leave out grammatical words and word endings, in particular, inflectional suffixes. (See Chapter 5 for info on inflectional morphology.) In an early case study of three kids learning English, Roger Brown reported that they acquired grammatical morphemes in the order given in Table 13-1.

Table 13-1		Order in Which Kids Acquire Grammatical Morphemes		
	Form	*Example*	*Category*	*Meaning*
1	-ing	*I'm eat**ing**.*	Aspect	ongoing process
2	in	*It's **in** the car.*	Preposition	containment
3	on	*It's **on** the table.*	Preposition	support
4	plural -s	*The cows moo.*	Number	plurality
5	*went* (irregular)	*She **went** home.*	Tense	past
6	-'s	*The boy**'s** dog.*	Genitive	possessive
7	was (unreduced) are (unreduced)	***Was** Lucy here?* ***Are** they girls?*	Number/Tense	3rd person singular, past, 3rd person plural, non-past
8	a, the	*Lucy has **a** book.*	Determiner	new/old info.
9	-ed (regular)	*She walk**ed** home.*	Tense	past
10	Verb -s	*She walk**s** home.*	Number/Tense	3rd person singular, non-past
11	has, does	***Does** the cow moo?*	Number/Tense	3rd person singular, non-past

	Form	Example	Category	Meaning
12	is, were	*Is she coming?*	Number/Tense	3rd person singular, non-past
13	-'s (reduced)	*That's her.*	Number/Tense	3rd person singular, non-past
14	-re (reduced)	*They're here.*	Number/Tense	3rd person plural, non-past

What determines which morphemes are acquired first? It seems to be a combination of two factors: semantic complexity and formal complexity. Notice that the morphemes 1 to 6 aren't semantically complex, nor are the forms complex. But morphemes 7 to 14 are either semantically or formally complex (or both). *Semantic complexity* fuses number and tense, as well as the articles *a/the,* which requires kids to understand the difference between new and old information. *Formal complexity* includes morphemes that contrast unreduced and reduced forms (as with the helping verbs *was, are, 's, 're*), as well as those that contrast regular and irregular forms (as with the past tense).

Linguists are cautious not to over-interpret child language data. While it seems that children's use of past tense forms really means *past,* it's harder to tell whether the present tense forms that children use really mean *present* — that's why linguists use the term *non-past* to describe such forms.

Since the publication of Roger Brown's 1973 study, other studies have looked at how children acquire grammatical morphemes in other languages. The details differ from language to language, but each language shows a particular sequence of acquisition. What seems to drive the relative order of acquisition in all languages is a combination of semantic and formal complexity.

Figuring out word order

Between 24 and 30 months, you figure out the rules for basic sentences. You use the subject-predicate pattern, for example, *I good boy* for 'I'm a good boy'. You also use the subject-verb-object pattern (*Daddy like book* for 'Daddy likes the book'), which you embellish on with an adverb (*Man ride bus today* for 'The man rode the bus today').

Going from active to passive

By the age of two, kids start to use the passive-live sentence, but they don't fully master the passive construction until they're three. Eve Clark reports the following sentences:

Adult models:

My temperature was taken by the doctor.

I want to see my bottle getting fixed.

Child's version (26 months):

I took my temperature from the doctor.

I want see my bottle getting fix.

In an active sentence the subject does the action, as in ***The dog*** *chased the squirrel;* the subject 'the dog' is doing the chasing. In a passive sentence the subject is getting the action done to it; in the passive sentence, ***The squirrel** was chased by the dog,* the subject 'the squirrel' is the one being chased.

Asking questions

Children need to master different kinds of questions — questions that can be answered by 'yes' or 'no' and questions that can be answered by a content word. For both question types, kids learning English need to learn the helping verbs, which include *be, do, can,* and *will.* As documented by Edward Klima and Ursula Bellugi, children progress in their mastery of both yes/no questions and content-questions in the following way:

Stage 1: *see hole?* and *where kitty?*

Stage 2: *you want eat?* and *where my mitten?*

Stage 3: *will you help me?* and *where the other Joe will drive?*

Forming relative clauses

By the age of two, kids unpack relative clauses into their component clauses. Dan Slobin and Charles Welsh report the following relative clauses produced by a 26-month-old child. It will take another two years for kids to master the *form* of relative clauses, but by the age of four they match the adult model.

Adult model:

The owl who eats candy runs fast.

The man who I saw yesterday got wet.

Child's version (26 months):

Owl eat candy and he run fast.

I saw the man and he got wet.

A *relative clause* modifies a main clause. In the sentence *The owl who eats candy runs fast,* the main clause is *The owl runs fast;* the relative clause is *who eats candy.* In the sentence *The man who I saw yesterday got wet,* the main clause is *The man got wet;* the relative clause is *who I saw yesterday.*

Acquiring signed language

Children acquiring signed language go through the same stages as children acquiring spoken language. Within the first 18 months, they go from a signed babbling stage to a signed one-word stage to a signed two-word stage. Older signing kids show the same error patterns as speaking kids with respect to mastering the fine details of morphology and syntax. Bilingual signing-speaking kids who are exposed to both languages from birth acquire the signed and spoken languages in the same way as kids who acquire two spoken languages. And hearing kids who are exposed only to signed language from birth acquire it as their first language, just as effortlessly and seamlessly as hearing kids acquire spoken language.

Achieving a basic grammar

By the age of five, you've mastered the basics of your grammar. You can use language to talk about language, you can define words, and you can correct yourself. The rest is fine-tuning — your vocabulary continues to increase (at a slower rate), and you become more sensitive to stylistic variation.

Linguists give names to some of the stages that kids go through. The *one-word stage* (12 to 18 months) is also called the *holophrastic* or whole sentence stage. It's followed by the *two-word stage* (18 to 24 months) and then the *telegraphic speech stage* (24 to 30 months).

Kids' ability to understand language outstrips their ability to produce it. For example, when two-year-olds are tested on their ability to understand and produce a certain set of verbs and nouns, they *understand* roughly 75 percent of the verbs and 60 percent of the nouns. But they *produce* only about 20 percent of the verbs and 40 percent of the nouns. This difference between comprehension and production is found with adults as well, but is less dramatic.

Balancing Nature and Nurture

Learning a first language is a balancing act. Biology — nature — determines the presence of neural structures that support language. The environment — nurture — determines whether the input is there at the right time.

Constraining first language acquisition

Everyone agrees that first language acquisition is constrained in some way. Some researchers believe that nature (biology) is the primary force constraining language, others believe that nurture (environment) is. After more than 50 years of research on first language acquisition, the consensus is that some aspects of language acquisition are constrained by nature, others by nurture.

Nature drives language acquisition

The *innateness hypothesis* (also known as *nativism*) claims nature drives language acquisition. In this view, your built-in linguistic nature helps you learn and shapes how and what you learn. In this hypothesis, which is associated with Noam Chomsky's concept of universal grammar, a child's language faculty — the built-in universal grammar — creates linguistic knowledge by reacting to language input. One reason for thinking that some aspects of L1 acquisition are determined by the language faculty is that children's output doesn't reflect the input available to them. Linguists point to two aspects of child language that support this view: over-generalization and structure-sensitivity.

Making over-generalizations

Kids make generalizations — often incorrect ones — about the rule system that they're acquiring. These over-generalizations indicate that kids are working with a rule system that's not driven by what they're exposed to. For example, in learning the English past tense, kids first go through a state where they correctly produce regular and irregular foms of the past tense *(walked* and *went),* and then they go through a period where they over-generalize the use of the regular past tense and say things like *goed* (instead of 'went') and *seed* (instead of 'saw'). But forms such as *goed* and *seed* are not in the input, so the only way kids can be making them is if they have internalized the regular past tense rule of English that adds *-ed* to the end of a verb and have overgeneralized the rule to *all* past tense verbs. But because irregular verbs are the most frequent ones, kids eventually get the hang of which verbs do what, and at a later stage start to produce the adult target forms of the irregular verbs.

The stages that kids go through in learning the English past tense are an example of *U-shaped learning.* Initially kids get the past tense right on a word-by-word basis. Then they figure out the rule for regular verbs, and over-apply it — that's the bottom of the "U". Then they learn the exceptions to the rule.

Being sensitive to structure

Kids never make certain types of errors. For example, all human languages have rules that move words or phrases from one position to another in sentences, and it turns out that kids are sensitive to the structure of such sentences. (See Chapter 6 for discussion of movement rules.) In English yes/no questions, for example, an auxiliary element is placed at the beginning of the sentence — a statement like *Smoky is here* is transformed into a question by moving *is* to the beginning of the sentence *Is Smoky here?* This rule is structure-sensitive. To apply it correctly, you have to know that the auxiliary *is* skips over a *phrasal constituent* that can contain one or more words, as in *Is **Smoky** here?* or *Is **the dog** here?* or *Is **the big dog** here?* When kids learn the rule for yes/no questions, they never move the auxiliary to a position that interrupts the phrasal constituent — so they don't make errors like *****The** is *dog here?* or **The is big dog here?* or **The big is dog here?* Linguists take the *absence* of such errors in child language to indicate that the rule system of children is structure-sensitive, which is a property of universal grammar.

Nurture drives language acquisition

The *general learning hypothesis* claims nurture drives language acquisition. In this view, language acquisition results from our interactions with other people *and* from our general thinking processes. This approach is used to explain how kids acquire concepts necessary for vocabulary learning.

The problem that kids face in learning new words is that they often can't tell from the context what the word means. And this problem isn't just a problem for kids. The philosopher Willard Quine talked about a situation where a linguist is trying to figure out the word for 'rabbit' in another language. The linguist points to a rabbit in the hopes that the language consultant will say the word for 'rabbit'. The consultant says 'gavagai'. But the linguist has no way of knowing whether *gavagai* means the entire rabbit, the rabbit-leg, its tail, or the hopping motion of the rabbit. Many researchers think that kids solve this problem by using learning *biases* that push them to prefer certain kinds of meanings. Some widely discussed learning biases include:

- **Whole-object bias:** Expect that the first word that you hear as a name for the object applies to the whole object and not part of the object. So kids assume that the word *gavagai* applies to the whole rabbit.

- **Taxonomic bias:** Assume that a new word applies to other objects of the same kind. So the word *gavagai* applies not only to the salient rabbit in the context but to any other rabbit that they encounter.

- **Mutual exclusivity bias:** Assume that an object has only one name. If kids are presented with two objects and they already know the name for one of them, they assume that the new word refers to the object whose name isn't known.

- **Count noun bias:** Assume that a count noun is the name of an object. By the age of 30 months, kids assume that words that occur in count noun context, for example after the indefinite determiner *a (a rabbit)* are names of objects. This sensitivity to count nouns seems to be universal. Kids aren't sensitive to other categories such as adjectives, mass nouns, or verbs until later on.

Being exposed to language at the right time

To be successful, language acquisition needs to happen between birth and puberty. This window of time when neural functioning for language is most sensitive to external input is biologically determined.

Statistical learning

According to the *general learning hypothesis*, your ability to learn language is constrained by general learning principles that aren't specific to language. These are the strategies you use for any input-driven learning: You detect patterns, you use your knowledge, and you pay attention. But you need to have some way of figuring out which combinations of sounds, morphemes, or words are more likely than others — the fancy term for this is *probabilistic decision-making*. Probabilistic models claim that infants track two kinds of information:

✔ **Frequency:** How often a surface pattern occurs.

✔ **Correlation:** How consistently one element occurs with another.

While some researchers claim that *all* L1 acquisition is probabilistic, it's more likely that only *some* aspects of L1 learning are based on statistical probability — especially the initial steps of breaking up the continuous stream of speech into words and the learning of the native language sounds and sound patterns. Other more abstract structural properties — like embedding sentences within sentences — reflect properties of universal grammar.

Statistical learning also explains how older learners acquire a second language (L2). For L2 acquisition, some researchers assume that all aspects of the first language transfer to the second language. The L2 learner initially uses the statistical patterns of their first language to decode the patterns of the second language. Sometimes this works, and sometimes it doesn't. Through trial and error, the L2 learner figures out the statistical patterns for the second L2. But L2 learners make mistakes that aren't always due to the influence of their L1. That's why some linguists believe that, in addition to statistical learning (which is input driven), L2 learners are also guided by the principles of universal grammar.

The window for learning the building blocks of syntax and phonology begins at birth and ends at puberty — the building blocks must be in place by puberty in order for the rule system to be fully acquired. After puberty, you continue to learn new grammatical patterns (syntax), and you can make adjustments to your dialect (phonology), but only if the building blocks are already in place. The window for learning vocabulary is optimally between birth and puberty, but you continue to learn new words throughout your life.

If the beginning *(onset)* and end *(offset)* of the window are abrupt and fixed, it's called a *critical period*. If the onset and offset are gradual and variable, it's called an *optimal period* or a *sensitive period*.

Wiring the brain for language

By puberty, the left hemisphere of most people's brains is specialized for language. If you suffer damage to the left hemisphere before puberty, your language functions probably won't be permanently damaged — your neural structures can be re-programmed. If you suffer similar damage after puberty, it usually results in permanent loss of language functions — this is called *aphasia*. (For a discussion of language functions and the brain, see Chapter 16.)

The special brain structures that support rapid language acquisition shut down at puberty. After that language is learned through general-purpose learning mechanisms. One consequence of this is that accent-free second-language acquisition can occur until the age of puberty, but rarely beyond.

Factoring in the environment

The environment (nurture) is also key to language development. For example, children learn to conduct conversations by paying attention to what those around them are paying attention to by tracking eye gaze, body posture, and physical orientation. Psychologists call this *joint attention*. Infants make extensive use of joint attention both to learn words and to navigate conversation:

- **Performing speech acts:** Even before infants are able to speak, they are making statements and issuing requests. From around the age of 10 months, infants point to objects that they're interested in with their index finger. Around this age, they also use a reaching gesture to indicate things that they want. These early communicative gestures are ways of making assertions (by pointing) and requests (by reaching).

- **Taking their turn in a conversation:** By the age of 2, children can answer questions as well as join in and contribute to conversations with family members. They also interrupt and intrude into conversations.

- **Tracking information flow:** Young children know how to be overhearerers and can keep track of conversations they're not directly participating in. (Adults sometimes forget this, often much to their dismay, when a young toddler loudly and proudly repeats an embarassing snippet of an overheard conversation.)

- **Being informative:** At the two-word stage (between 18 and 24 months) and beyond, children mention given information first, and then they follow up with new information. This is a principle of information structure found in all languages: People remind their listeners of things they already know (given information) before telling them something new. And by the age of two, kids take into account what the person they're speaking to knows. (They are using rules of inference, presupposition, and common ground. See Chapter 8 for a discusson of these terms.)

The cooing and babbling that infants do in the presence of caregivers — innocent as it may seem — is an infant's first step towards acquiring *pragmatic competence*. It lays the groundwork for the ability to use language appropriately in cooperation with other conversational participants across a broad range of contexts. For more info on pragmatics, see Chapter 8.

Is there a gene for language?

In the late 1990s, researchers became aware of a family living in the United Kingdom — known as the KE family — who had an inherited language disorder that was the result of a defect in a single gene. The family spans three generations and about half the members of the family suffer from the disorder. They can't control fine coordinated movement sequences of the mouth, tongue, lips, and soft palate, which interferes with their ability to make speech sounds. In addition, in both their written and spoken languages, they have a hard time putting words together to express thoughts cohesively,

and they also have difficulties understanding language. The defective gene in the KE family was called FOXP2 — it's located on chromosome 7, and its mutation causes severe speech and language disorders. For this reason, FOXP2 is sometimes called a "language gene." Versions of FOXP2 also exist in distantly related vertebrates, and it seems to be important for modulating plasticity in neural circuits. While FOXP2 is linked to language in humans, to song-learning in birds, and to echolation in bats, it is only one piece of a complex genetic structure that results in human language use.

Mastering Language Later in Life: Slow and Hard

Learning your first language as a kid is remarkable when it *doesn't* happen. Without much muss or fuss kids acquire grammar and master phonology, morphology, syntax, semantics, and pragmatics. But learning a second language as an adult is remarkable when it *does* happen. In formal learning situations, most L2 (second language) learners don't reach a level of fluency that makes the target language useful to them. By some estimates, 80 percent of students of English as a second language are beginners — this means that only 20 percent go onto higher levels.

Learning a second language is a tug-of-war between the language learner, the *target language* (the language you're learning), and the *source language* (the language you already know). Linguists who study constraints on learning a second language look at whether and how L2 acquisition reflects the properties of universal grammar (nature) or of the linguistic environment (nurture) and at the stages that L2 learners go through.

A *native speaker* of a language is someone who learns that language as a first language (from birth). *Native fluency* is the level of fluency that native speakers have. Many second-language learners achieve *near-native fluency;* very few achieve native fluency.

Everybody agrees that L1 acquisition starts at birth (or perhaps before). But what about L2 acquisition? Some researchers define L2 acquisition as being any language that's not acquired from birth onwards. Other researchers define L2 acquisition as the process involved in learning a second language after puberty. But however it's defined, L2 acquisition always refers to *later* learning of a *second* language.

Getting in the way or giving a hand: How a first language affects the second

Your *source language* — the language that you learn as a first language — affects how you learn a *target language* (the language that you're learning) in a number of different ways:

Making transfer errors

You can mistakenly apply the sound system, sentence patterns, and conversation strategies of your source language to your target language. The following examples show the error patterns of different advanced adult L2 learners of English. Learner A, whose source language is Russian, leaves out the determiner *the* — in Russian, you don't *have* to use determiners. Learner B, whose source language is Italian, uses the infinitive 'to verb' instead of the gerundive 'verb-ing' because Italian would use an infinitive in this context.

> Learner A (source language: Russian)
>
> Target sentence: *To the victor belong the spoils.*
>
> L2 speaker: To **victor** belong **spoils**.
>
> Learner B (source language: Italian)
>
> Target sentence: We won't take it lying down.
>
> L2 speaker: We won't take it **to lie** down.

If the source and target language are of a similar type — French and Spanish, for example — then more from the source language transfers to the target language. (See Chapter 11 to see how linguists study language typology.) And even if languages aren't related, if the learner perceives similarities between the two languages, then transfer is more likely to occur.

Making performance errors

The errors of L2 learners are different in different contexts. The more complex the communicative task, the more likely you are to fall back on your knowledge of your source language. This means that even though you can do well on a classroom quiz (identifying the correct forms of a yes/no question, for example), you may flounder when you try to have an open-ended conversation and say things like *Do you bought this too?,* which would be the way you would say it in your native language, instead of *Did you buy this too?,* which, of course, would be the right answer on your quiz!

Language transfer is the influence that a source language has on a target language. *Interlanguage* is the grammar that results from the language learning process; it's created from the speaker's combined knowledge of the source and target languages. *Fossilization* refers to a situation where someone stops learning the target language before they achieve native fluency.

Turning to mother nature: Accessing universal grammar

According to the *universal grammar hypothesis,* acquiring a second language is constrained by principles of universal grammar that are specific to human language — those same principles that guide L1 learning. This hypothesis is compatible with two scenarios: full access to universal grammar with or without transfer.

Full access to universal grammar with no transfer

Only universal grammar principles guide L2 learners. The idea is that L2 language learning is constrained by all the same principles that constrain L1 learning. For example, L2 learners of Italian should go through the same stages as L1 learners of Italian, and the grammar and vocabulary of their L1 should have no influence on the acquisition of L2.

Most L2 researchers reject this scenario because L2 learners start out with something that infants lack, namely a *first* language (L1)! This gives them a leg up, but it also means that the errors of L2 learners are *not* the same as those of L1 learners. For example, children acquiring English have trouble understanding that reflexive pronouns like *herself,* when used in object position, must refer to the subject. So, many young children interpret a sentence like *Mama Bear saw herself* as *Mama Bear saw her*. But Mandarin speakers acquiring L2 English show a different error pattern. They correctly interpret *Lucy saw herself*, but when presented with a sentence like *Lucy thinks Mary saw herself*, they interpret the reflexive pronoun *herself* as referring to Lucy. They make this sort of mistake because in a sentence like this in Mandarin, *herself* CAN refer to *Lucy.*

Full access to universal grammar with transfer

L2 learners have access to universal grammar *and* to their L1. Many researchers believe that older second-language learners combine their knowledge of universal grammar with their knowledge of their L1, which makes it important to distinguish universal grammar effects from language transfer effects. Researchers tease them apart by looking at how learners acquire L2 features that aren't present in their L1.

Finding transfer errors: The three ways

Linguists have figured out a pretty good way of detecting whether a language learner has transferred a property of their source language to the target language. If all three of the following patterns are found, then it's likely that a transfer error has occurred. (This method isn't foolproof, but it's pretty reliable.)

✔ **Parallelism:** The learner speaks the second language with patterns found in his source language. For example, speakers of Egyptian Arabic regularly insert the vowel [i] between consonants in their L2 English forms. Egyptian speakers do this because their source language doesn't permit such consonant sequences: This is an example of how the phonotactic restrictions of the L1 source language affect the learner's L2 language. For example, *floor* becomes *filoor* and *three* becomes *thiree*.

✔ **Homogeneity:** Learners of a particular target language who also have the same source language all make the same error.

For example, learners of English who have Egyptian Arabic as their source language show the same error pattern: They all break up consonant clusters with the vowel [i].

✔ **Heterogeneity:** Learners with different source languages should exhibit different error patterns. For example, learners of English who have Egyptian Arabic as their source language have a different pattern of errors than learners who have Iraqi Arabic their source language. (Because these languages are both called "Arabic," it seems like they should be the "same" language, but in fact, they are so different that a speaker of one can't really understand a speaker of the other.) While Egyptian speakers insert the vowel [i] *between* consonants in their L2 English forms, Iraqi speakers insert the vowel [i] *before* consonant clusters. So *floor* becomes *ifloor* and *three* becomes *ithree*.

For example, Japanese speakers who learn English as an L2 must figure out how to form content-questions such as *Who did Mary see?* In Japanese, such questions are formed by simply adding a question particle at the end of the sentence — nothing else in the sentence changes. But in English, the question word appears at the beginning of the sentence, an example of a *movement rule*. One property of movement rules — which many linguists believe is a universal grammar property — is that they apply only to sentences that have a particular kind of structure — linguists call this *structure dependency*. Linguists have found that, when learning English content-questions, L2 English learners who have Japanese as their L1 correctly apply the principle of structure dependency. This can't be explained as the effect of transferring their knowledge of L1 to L2 because Japanese doesn't use a movement rule in these contexts. So linguists conclude that the L2 learners are using the universal grammar principle of structure-dependency.

Focusing on the target: What you must learn

All second-language learners go through a series of stages, no matter which language is learned. These stages take them from the rudimentary knowledge needed to exchange greetings and buy something at the store to the extensive knowledge needed to participate in conversations and watch a movie.

The logical problem of language acquisition

Language learners (L1 or L2) must come up with a grammar for the language being acquired based on the input they get. However, the input doesn't give learners enough information to work out all the properties of language that they eventually come to know. This is called the *poverty-of-the-stimulus problem*. More specifically, the input has two problems:

✔ **Under-determination:** The input underdetermines the grammar. This means that language learners hear utterances that are ambiguous or contain speech errors. Ambiguous sentences are a problem because learners have to work out the correct meaning. And utterances with speech errors — mispronunciations, false starts, interruptions, incomplete sentences — are a problem because learners have to work out the correct form.

✔ **Absence of negative evidence:** The input provides the learner only with positive evidence. Certain types of linguistic knowledge require abstract rules to be internalized, for example, understanding how to use pronouns correctly — *Lucy said that Bill saw **her*** but not **Lucy said that Bill saw **herself*** — or knowing how to form content questions correctly. The question *Who did Lucy say that she saw__ had eaten the peanuts?* can be formed from

Lucy said that she saw <u>Bill</u> had eaten the peanuts. But the sentence **Who did Lucy say that she saw the peanuts that __ had eaten* can't be formed from *Lucy said that she saw the peanuts that Bill had eaten.*

The poverty-of-stimulus problem divides the nature/nurture camp. For the nature folks, universal grammar guides the acquisition of language. If, even in the absence of all the necessary evidence, learners come to know the properties of the target language — be it L1 or L2 — the nature folks conclude that universal grammar must be helping out in language acquisition. For the nurture folks, the poverty-of-stimulus problem is solved not by universal grammar but by continued exposure to the language over time. In this view, the fact that a speaker is able to judge certain forms as ungrammatical doesn't indicate they have unconscious knowledge of universal grammar; it simply indicates that such sentences are infrequent.

It's hard to find data that clearly indicates that it's nature (universal grammar) or nurture (statistical learning) that allows language learners to solve the poverty-of-stimulus problem. But the problem has forced researchers on both sides of the nature/nurture debate to look more carefully at how L1 and L2 learners acquire language.

Overcoming the first stumbling block: Figuring out the sound system

In the first stage of learning a second language, you're not doing much talking, but you're doing a lot of listening. It takes a few weeks for your ears to get used to the different sounds that the target language uses. And it may take even longer for you to get the hang of producing those sounds.

The silent period that second language learners go through before they begin talking is called the *pre-production stage*.

There's always a time lag between your ability to perceive and your ability to produce language. This holds for both L1 and L2 acquisition.

Clearing the second hurdle: Recognizing words

Within a couple of months, you recognize a vocabulary of about 500 words. In a formal language teaching situation, your teacher at this stage focuses on exercises that build vocabulary. And if you're learning in a context where the language is spoken around you all day long — for example, if you've moved to a place that uses a different language — you feel exhausted just from the effort of listening to unfamiliar sounds all day long. That's natural: You're processing a lot of information, and that's hard work for your brain.

The *receptive vocabulary* of language learners contains words that they can recognize. The *active vocabulary* contains words that they can use.

Getting through the third barrier: Producing simple phrases

Within six months, you recognize and use about 1,000 words. You can form simple phrases and use short language chunks that you've learned by heart. At this point, you can negotiate simple face-to-face transactions like buying groceries or getting a bus ticket. If you're in a language class, then your teacher encourages you to talk more, all the while building your receptive vocabulary through more complex listening activities. At this stage, simple forms of written language can be used to reinforce oral language learning.

Clearing the fourth obstacle: Stringing sentences together

Within a year, you recognize and use about 3,000 words, make simple sentences, and have short conversations. If you stick with it, soon after that, you'll be up to 6,000 words, making more complex sentences and having extended conversations with your buddies.

Passing to the other side: Dreaming and joking in a second language

Fast forward 4 to 10 years and you're pretty fluent in the second language of your choice. You now understand and tell jokes in your second language; you even dream in that language! You know enough vocabulary items to express yourself fully, and your control of sentence structure allows you to say complicated things. But there's a lag between your comprehension and your production. In terms of comprehension, you can understand anything that anyone throws at you. In terms of production, you still get tripped up on minor points of grammar and pronunciation.

The ideal second-language learner

The following factors make a positive contribution to second-language learning later in life:

✓ **Your linguistic knowledge:** Knowing linguistics allows you to understand how languages differ. For example, languages have different sound systems, different ways of making words and sentences and constructing meanings, and different ways of responding in different social contexts. Knowing about these things won't make it easier for you to actually master these differences, but it makes a big difference in your attitude. A basic knowledge of linguistics allows you to understand (and accept) that different languages use different rules.

✓ **Your cultural knowledge:** Language is part of a larger cultural system. The more you understand about the culture of the second language that you're learning, the more you can appreciate the subtleties of its linguistic system.

✓ **Your language aptitude:** Just as some people are natural athletes, some people are natural language learners. Research has found that about 4 percent of the population can learn a second language and acquire the fluency of a native speaker. These language superstars learn a second language faster than other ordinary mortals, and they achieve a higher level of fluency. If you're not a language superstar, don't fret. Just sit down with your friends and learn those verb paradigms by heart!

✓ **Your motivation and attitude:** Your motivation for learning a second language and the attitude you bring to it are key. The stronger your motivation, and the more comfortable you are getting out and using what you know — even if it is only a little, and even if it is full of mistakes at first — the better and faster you learn.

Chapter 14

Perceiving Language

*U*nderstanding what that guy sitting next to you is saying may seem like a pretty simple thing to do, but the process of *perceiving* speech is very complex. Perception of the sound reaching your ears involves constructing sound patterns, drawing on linguistic knowledge, and paying attention to speech.

In this chapter, we show you how you process information related to speaking — both auditory and visual — and we present the challenges that arise when the perception of sound doesn't function normally.

Speech perception is *multisensory* — getting a complete picture of neural processing of sensory information during speech perception means looking at the brain structures of three sensory systems — sound, sight, and touch — and understanding how they're interconnected.

Getting Speech to the Brain

In order for you to perceive speech — for you to hear anything — sound needs to get from your ears to your brain. You do this by transforming sound into nerve impulses, which then become part of a flow of information to and from the *brain cortex* (the wrinkled layer of neural tissue that covers the surface of the brain). Figure 14-1 gives you a visual of the following steps:

1. **Your eardrum vibrates.** Speech sounds arrive at your ear and cause your eardrum to vibrate. The vibration is transmitted to the *basilar membrane,* a long membrane coiled inside the cochlea. Different sound frequencies hit different parts of the membrane and vibrate tiny hairs (hair cells). Each hair cell has a nerve attached to it that fires when vibrated. The bundle of frequency-specific nerve fibers becomes the *auditory nerve.*

2. **You measure pitch and loudness.** The auditory nerve goes from the cochlea to the cochlear nucleus in the brain stem, which contains organized arrays of neurons. Each neuron array is assigned to a specific *pitch* (sound frequency) or loudness (sound amplitude), allowing them to be measured.

3. **You synchronize timing and loudness.** From the cochlear nucleus, information about sound frequency and sound amplitude moves upstream to the *lateral lemniscus*. This brain-stem nucleus first synchronizes sound information from the two ears and then distributes auditory information to the two hemispheres (left and right) of the brain.

4. **You process pitch and loudness.** From brainstem nuclei like the lateral lemniscus and *superior olivary nucleus,* sound information moves upstream to the *inferior colliculus* and *medial geniculate body.* These mid-brain nuclei analyze which sound frequencies go together at what amplitudes.

5. **You categorize pitch and loudness.** The last step is to go from the inferior colliculus and medial geniculate body to the *primary auditory cortex* — this is a small part of the cortex located on the left temporal lobe of the brain. The auditory cortex does a lot, like lets you *hear* the sound. It also sends information back to the mid-brain and peripheral nuclei to fine-tune the processing of the incoming sound information.

6. **You identify the sound as speech.** Auditory information about speech sounds interacts with knowledge, attention, and pattern. No one knows exactly how this happens, but various areas of the cortex must interact, including areas related to short-term memory, word-retrieval, temporal patterning, and speech production.

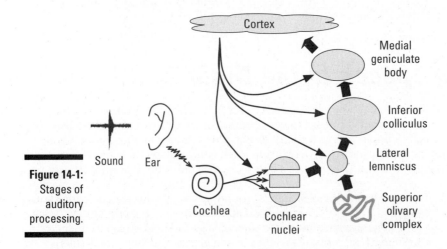

Figure 14-1: Stages of auditory processing.

TECHNICAL STUFF

Is speech special?

One remarkable aspect of human speech is the high rate of information transmitted and received during spoken communication: about 12 *bits* per second. (A bit is a minimum unit of digital information, kind of like a speech segment; sequences of bits combine into multitudes of *bytes,* like words.) In the 1960s, Eric Lenneberg, a neurologist and linguist, was interested in whether humans have an innate capacity for language. In other words, whether the human language capacity has the four biological criteria for *heritable traits,* the stuff about you that comes from the genetic code of your parents:

✔ The entire species has the trait at the same time: The trait is *species typical.*

✔ The species typical trait persists unchanged by training and experience.

✔ The trait isn't learned.

✔ The trait follows a rigid development schedule in the individual: There's a *critical period.*

Language meets the biological criteria for innateness: It's species typical because all humans can learn to speak, speech hangs around as people get older, people are born with the ability to learn language, and there's a critical period during early childhood when exposure to language is necessary for that learning to occur. But there continues to be a debate about the innateness of language because scientists disagree about how innateness interacts with the capacity to learn from experience. Alvin Liberman and Ignatius Mattingly of Haskins Laboratories related the innateness of language to the existence of specialized cognitive structures *(modules)* responsible for identifying and categorizing linguistic structure from the ever-changing stream of behavior through time. In the *Motor Theory of Speech Perception,* which was initially formulated in the 1950s by Liberman, Franklin Cooper, and other colleagues at Haskins, the objects of perception are the movements of the vocal tract, called *gestures,* that shape the speech. Modules are hypothetical structures specialized for processing gradient (continuously changing) speech signals and recovering the produced gestures via *categorical perception.*

Perceiving Spoken Language

In perceiving speech, you rely on three processes:

✔ **You construct sound patterns.** Your brain is tuned to extract patterns from sensory stimulation, and you do this from the get-go. Within a few hours of being born, you discriminate between speech and non-speech sounds. Later on, this ability allows you to detect the difference between *there's a **mom** in the kitchen* and *there's a **bomb** in the kitchen.*

- ✔ **You draw on linguistic knowledge.** About three months before you're born, you begin sensing sounds, so you come into the world equipped with auditory knowledge. With experience, you acquire knowledge of speech patterns (by 6 months), the sounds of your language (by 12 months), and the basic rules of your grammar (by 18 months).

- ✔ **You pay attention to speech.** You separate speech from other sounds in the environment. This is more than simple discrimination because, in a noisy environment, you pay attention to speech-related sounds by tuning out other sounds.

Linguists call any sound that hits your ears an *auditory stream* or an *acoustic signal*. The sounds produced in spoken language are called the *speech stream* or *speech signal*.

Constructing sound patterns

You, as a language perceiver, are able to break a continuous speech stream into identifiable bits. But how do you know what the identifiable bits are? And how does your perceptual system extract them from the speech stream? First, your brain has to break the sound stream into pieces that it can detect and distinguish from other pieces. At the same time, these pieces have to be small enough to store in memory while your brain processes the contents. For these reasons, the syllable functions as the basic unit of speech perception and production.

A basic unit of speech production is the syllable

Producing a speech sound requires an open vocal tract and airflow. This is what vowels (like *a, e, i, o, u*) do — that's why any vowel can be a syllable by itself. Consonants (like *p, t, k, s, d*) constrict the vocal tract and typically can't be heard on their own. So it's no wonder the most common syllable in the world's languages is the consonant plus vowel (CV) combination that gives us words like *so, be, tea, too.*

Nasals *(m, n)* and liquids *(l, r)* are special consonants because they can also be syllabic. Nasals are produced via the nasal airway (when the oral cavity is closed). Liquids can be syllabic because they are made without closing the oral cavity all the way.

A basic unit of speech perception is the syllable

Sequencing CV syllables like *pa pa pa pa* causes a *modulation* (rising and falling) of loudness as the vocal tract opens for vowels and closes for consonants. Your auditory system is sensitive to the loudness changes associated with the transitions between consonants and vowels, so this modulation helps you break the sound stream into syllables. Two tests identify the syllable as basic:

- ✔ **Tapping test:** People, tapping along to repeated syllables, tap almost exactly when the vowel sound begins, right where the sound suddenly gets louder.

- ✔ ***Minimal pair test:*** Linguists use the *minimal pair test* to identify minimal differences in sound that change meaning. By this test, ***pat, bat, mat, sat,*** and ***rat*** differ only in their initial sounds, even though each is also a different syllable. In fact, the initial sound isn't all that changes. The vowel following and even the final consonant also differ for these different minimal pairs. (For a discussion of such effects on production, see Chapters 4 and 15.) From the perspective of perception then, the entire syllable carries fine-grained phonetic information about these different sounds, making your ability to discriminate sound segments dependent on your ability to discriminate syllables!

Syllable perception is universal

The ability to perceive syllables is universal — everyone can do it without any special training. For example, try tapping your finger on a table as you say the sentence *there's no business like show business.* One thing you may notice immediately is that you only tap twice for the word *business.* Well, that's correct because, despite the way it is spelled, *business* has only two syllables when you say it, transcribed phonetically as [bɪz.nɨs]. (For details on phonetic transcription, see Chapter 3.)

Syllables are the basic units of rhythm

Rhythm is the musical patterning of speech and combines melody, timing, and loudness. Infants at the babbling stage (six to seven months) have syllables (and rhythm) and by the time they're able to say single words, they're pros.

Extracting meaning works better with syllables

When speech engineers try to program computers to extract meaningful bits of speech, the systems do much better when the basic unit is a sequence of at least two sound segments like the *ba* and *at* in *bat* — which can be a syllable or part of a syllable.

Being the basic unit of *physical processing* does not mean the syllable is the smallest unit of *linguistic analysis.* The *phoneme* is considered the most basic unit of speech by most linguists. Phonemes are segments that change meaning when used in the same position — like the final sound in *tin* and *tip.* In combination, phonemes form larger chunks like syllables, words, and phrases.

Drawing on linguistic knowledge

Your linguistic knowledge helps you to perceive speech quickly and accurately. This is part of the *chunking problem* — the challenge of having to divide up the incoming stream of speech into smaller bits and pieces. On the one hand, experience teaches you how sounds group together. But it also goes the other way: Knowing how sounds group together helps you identify sounds during perception. Here we focus on how phonological knowledge of sound patterns and syntactic knowledge of how words are grouped into meaningful phrases assist speech perception.

Categorizing speech sounds with phonological knowledge

Perception of speech depends on categorization. Traditionally, a *category* is a grouping according to a feature that every member of the group shares and which distinguishes that group from other groups. For example, *apple* and *orange* belong to the category of *fruit,* and *fruit* itself is a category of food that's distinct from the categories of *vegetable* and *meat.* Your knowledge of phonology provides a list of your language's sound categories, such as vowels or fricatives or nasals (see Chapter 4 for more on categorizing sounds).

You also need to know under which circumstances these sound categories may change. For example, technically a tomato is a fruit, but it's treated as a vegetable when talking about food categories. Applying this to speech perception, *phonological categories* also have variable tendencies. For example, in most languages, vowels can stand alone as a syllable, but consonants typically cannot. But languages make different decisions about which consonants can be syllabic. English allows nasal /m, n/ and liquid /l, r/ consonants to be syllabic in special cases, but never /s/. Blackfoot, a language spoken in Montana (United States) and southern Alberta (Canada), does use /s/ syllabically. Thus, defining a phonological category depends on identifying similarities among sounds that apply to a certain set of circumstances.

Filling in the blanks with syntactic knowledge

Just as you can visualize a car from a brief glimpse of only its fender and front bumper, you can identify a sound sequence even when one or more segments is missing or masked. This is possible because you already know how sounds go together to make syllables and words, and you use that knowledge to fill in gaps in the speech stream. Filling in missing sound segments is called *phoneme restoration.* You can do this for almost any sound in a sequence, so long as the overall duration of the sequence doesn't change — that is, the span of time corresponding to the missing or masked sound provides the information necessary for the restoration to work. So you can replace a vowel with noise or a simple tone. For example, if you hear *pick up the b+noise+t and hit the ball,* you know to pick up the *bat.* You use your knowledge of baseball to perceive *bat,* allowing you to restore the missing vowel.

Phonemes, syllables, and perception

Phonology differentiates /p/ and /b/ by the presence or absence of *voicing* — caused by vibrating your vocal cords (see Chapter 3 for more on vocal fold vibration). But your ability to discriminate voiceless /p/ from voiced /b/ depends on events related to the presence or absence of vocal fold vibration:

✔ **Aspiration:** The voiceless /p/ of *pat* has a puff of air (called *aspiration*), written phonetically as [p^h]. This air puff event helps you perceive the difference between the /p/ of *pat* and the /b/ of *bat*. In English, the /b/ is also usually voiceless at the beginning of words like *bat,* so aspiration is critical here. But aspiration doesn't help you to perceive the difference between *tap* and *tab,* when the final *p* has no air puff. In this case, the final /b/ usually has vocal fold vibration, which helps you distinguish the two.

✔ **Vowel length:** English words with the same syllable structure take the same amount of time to say. The puff of air for /p/ eats into the vowel, making the vowel of *pat* shorter than it is for *bat*. This vowel length difference is another way to perceptually distinguish the voiceless /p/ of *pat* from the voiced /b/ of *bat*. A similar effect on vowel length is seen for *tap* and *tab* because the lips close faster for voiceless /p/, making the preceding vowel end sooner than for voiced /b/.

Your phonological knowledge tells you that these events are related, that each event is *phonetically predictable*. But in order for an event to be phonetically predictable, you have to know how your language structures syllables and which sounds appear in which position. How a language structures syllables is called *syllable phonotactics* or *syllable structure constraints*.

Attending to speech

Every time you speak, you produce a unique speech signal — you simply can't produce the same signal twice, ever — and you produce the signal in a noisy environment. This lack of signal *constancy* (or repeatability) and the presence of environmental noise pose real challenges to speech perception. To overcome these challenges, you draw on your extensive experience with sound streams of all sorts to separate and identify the stream of speech coming your way.

Recovering speech from a noisy environment

The sound stream entering your ear at any given time contains sounds from various sources. In addition to someone talking to you, you may be hearing a door closing or a washing machine running. If you're listening attentively to someone, you may not notice that other sounds are occurring at the same time.

This ability to tune in to speech means that you're really good at recovering speech in noise. If you're at a party where people are all talking at once, you can still hear the person talking to you. It's as if you can zero in on the person talking to you and turn the others off. But you don't turn the volume off, you rearrange the sound stream so that sounds of interest stand out: You'll still be able to pick out when someone in another group starts talking about you! This is called *auditory scene analysis* — you create a soundscape whose structure helps you focus your attention on certain sounds, bringing them to the *foreground,* by putting all the other sounds in the *background.* For example, your physical orientation by a lakeside places the sound of a motorboat off to one side and the sounds of birds singing off to the other side. With these sounds in their proper places, you can then pay better attention to the sound of your friend talking to you, just behind you.

Recovering speech from an inconstant signal

You can't say the same thing twice and make the exact same sounds. Every time someone says *hello* to you, you're dealing with a unique event that happens just once in the history of the universe. In addition, each person you talk to forms their sounds in slightly different ways. The uniqueness of people's voices sets up an interesting problem. On the one hand, you need to hear these differences to identify who's talking — imagine how difficult it would be to tell people's voices apart if everyone sounded the same. On the other hand, you are able to extract the same linguistic information — for example, *how do I get to the train station* — from almost any speaker who asks you. Speech scientists don't know exactly how this works but they have a name for the process — *speaker normalization* — that leads to *perceptual constancy.*

Of course, you use all kinds of knowledge to help you figure out what people are saying to you. For example, your knowledge that people on the street usually begin an interaction with *hello* or *excuse me* helps you "hear" what comes next because it gives you a sample of the way a particular person's sound pattern links to a linguistic message. As an experienced perceiver, this is enough for you to quickly throw together a model of what the speaker sounds like and then predict how specific sound sequences will be shaped. The better you know the speaker, the better your ability to predict the sound patterns.

You may not notice this within your own community of speakers, but it's really obvious when you first encounter speech that's really different from what you're used to. For example, if you're from North Dakota and have to speak with someone on the phone from Alabama, odds are you'll each have trouble understanding the speech of the other. But your knowledge about the topic of conversation, the typical syntactic form of English, and the words that are likely to get used help you work up a reasonable model of how this person's sound system works, so that before you know it you're conversing normally.

When attending to speech hits a wall

Your ability to attend to the speech stream hits a wall when you start learning a new language. The first problem confronting you is perception. When you hear a language that you don't know, the sounds all blur together. That's because you don't know how to chunk the sound stream and find the syllables, which may pattern differently than in your own language. The trick is to figure out the rules of the new language, especially the ones for sounds and syllables.

Until you acquire this basic knowledge of the new language, you can't help but apply your knowledge of your own language to guide the process. This has good and bad points. For example, your first language has taught you which syllables are used to create words and sentences. This knowledge leads you to predict what you'll hear, but the predictions are wrong for the new language and will be until you can put together a new set of predictions based on different rules of combination. Luckily, people are good at this and begin perceiving and producing the sounds of a new language pretty fast.

Perceiving sound distinctions of the new language: Learning the sound system of a new language can be difficult when the sounds used by the new language are unfamiliar to you. But learning can really be frustrating when the language uses familiar sounds differently. In this case, you have to put aside the distinctions predicted by the sound system of your first language in order to learn the distinctive sound system of a second language. That is, when

faced with a new language, you readily hear sounds that are *distinctive* (make meaningful contrasts) in your own language, but this does not mean these sounds are distinctive in the new language, at least not in the same way. (For more on distinctive sound contrasts, see Chapter 4.)

For example, English and Japanese both make distinctive /r/ sounds. So, if you hear these sounds used, you are likely to think that English and Japanese treat /r/ the same way and use them in the same phonetic contexts; but you would be wrong. For example, when Japanese /r/ precedes /i/, as in the woman's name *Kaori*, it sounds to the English ear like the /d/ of *deep*, which would lead you to think her name is *Kaodi*. This makes sense to your English ear, because /r/ and /d/ are distinctive and both are used before /i/ in English. But, in fact, the Japanese never produce /d/ before /i/. What they do instead is pronounce the /d/ with a [j] sound as in *Daimonji*.

Producing sound distinctions of the new language: You must also change the tuning of your production system to prevent it from interfering with the production of new sound sequences. For example, as you get the idea that the Japanese /r/ isn't really a /d/ when it occurs before /i/, your production changes. To make Japanese /ri/, you bring the tongue further forward than usual, whereas to make English /di/, your tongue tip goes to the same place it goes for making other sounds with /d/, like /da/, /de/, /do/.

Hearing Language Is Seeing Language

When you speak, you move — you move your face and head, your body sways, you shift your weight, you move your hands and arms. Many such movements are unconnected to speech: While talking, you can scratch your head because it itches. At other times, these same movements are connected to speech: Scratching your head emphasizes your puzzled state when you say *I wonder where I put my keys?* Linguists call these movements *gestures*. You're generally unaware of your own gestures and may not notice that you do them even when you talk on the phone! However, when you communicate face to face, you present perceivers with linguistically relevant information from two sensory streams — sight and sound — at the same time. We show you how speech and gesture work together in *audiovisual* perception.

Gestures that influence perception fall into two categories: those that are simply a physical result of producing the speech stream and those that help create meaning.

Matching gestures with speech rhythm

Some visible gestures supplement information that's already in the speech signal. This is especially true of rhythmic face and head motion, which is linked to the vocal tract and respiratory actions that produce speech. Visual signals that reinforce acoustics are useful — if for some reason you have trouble hearing what's being said, you can use the visual stream as a fallback to more accurately perceive speech.

✔ **Rhythmic face motion:** Seeing a talking face tells you where in the mouth a consonant is produced and how it's produced. Vowels in English can be identified visually because the shape of and separation between the lips tells you a lot. To see this, try saying the vowels /i/, /u/, and /a/ in front of a mirror.

✔ **Rhythmic head motion:** When you speak, your head moves constantly in ways that match changes in vocal pitch and loudness, changes that contribute to the songlike quality of your speech. For example, head motion becomes more pronounced when you speak louder. The flip side of this is that, if your head motion is severely restricted, the loudness of your voice and the range of pitches you use both drop drastically. This restricts the *intonation* of your voice, which is critical to conveying meaning. (For more on intonation, see Chapter 4.) This type of head motion is independent of other things you do with your head in a conversation, such as nodding affirmation or shaking your head in negation.

The face conveys information about sounds, such as the place and manner of articulation for consonants, that involve rapid acoustic transitions caused by changes of vocal tract configuration. But the face doesn't convey much information about slow changes such as voicing, except at the lips where their visible shape and motion help perceivers distinguish between voiceless /p/, voiced /b/, and nasal (and voiced) /m/.

When hearing and seeing don't match up

Back in the mid-1970s, a psychologist named Harry McGurk had his assistant prepare videos for a study of audiovisual speech perception. This was back in the days where you had to rewind the audio tape to the right place and then dub it onto the sound track of the video. When Harry screened the final video, he thought the assistant had mistakenly put the utterance /ada/ on the tape, instead of an instance of /aga/. There was indeed a mistake, but an unexpected one: the *sound* of /aba/ had been dubbed onto the *video* of /aga/ — a combination that caused him to *perceive* /ada/.

Thus was born one of the most famous illusions in modern speech science: the McGurk Effect or the *fusion illusion*. The illusion is robust: About 70 percent of the population hears /ada/ or /aða/ when the sound /aba/ is dubbed on the video for /aga/. Your perceptual processing system expects multi-sensory information about speech to be congruent and treats the multi-sensory information as coming from a single source. This shows that, if you see and hear, you can't help but perceive speech as an integrated audiovisual unit — the visual stream is not an add-on.

Creating meaning with gesture

Many gestures that accompany speech make their own contributions to the meaning of what the speaker is saying. The following list gives you the major types of gestures that carry meaning:

- **Regulator gestures** help you figure out when the speaker is holding the floor and when it's your turn to start talking. For example, speakers may raise their arms when they're getting ready to speak and lower them at the end of a speaking turn.

- **Affect displays** convey the mood of the person talking. For example, a smile produced at the end of a harsh reprimand reduces the severity of the words.

- **Iconic gestures** give you information about the size, shape, or location of concrete objects. For example, drawing the size and shape of an object in the air augments the spoken description and is closely timed to the verbal reference to the object.

- **Metaphoric gestures** give shape and action to concepts. For example, the metaphor of time *rolling along* can be depicted by a sweeping sequence of circular motions of the hand and arm or even the two hands just in front of the body. Metaphoric gestures usually combine simpler iconic gestures into the more complex structures needed to represent the metaphor.

- **Beat gestures** punctuate or emphasize what you're saying. You use your hands, head, and torso to make movements that are timed to what you say — what form the gesture takes can vary from one instance to the next, or several forms can be used interchangeably within the same conversation. For example, you may repeatedly tilt your upper body forward and back rapidly to emphasize that this is the important point of some story. Or, in a more drawn out scenario, you may switch from torso movement to keeping time with your hands.

Gesture combines with speech to create meaning in one of three ways:

- **Speech is basic, gesture is additive.** Gesture supplements speech; it's an add-on. This is the most common type of gesturing.

- **Gesture is basic, speech is additive.** Here, speech supplements the gesture. For example, this happens when you point at something and then say *Look! Here! This is the one I want you to watch*.

- **Gesture is equal to speech.** Sometimes neither gesture nor speech conveys the meaning by itself. For example, Plains Cree, a language of the northern plains in Canada, has no words to describe playing a video game. So a Cree speaker can use the word for *play* along with a hand motion gesture that resembles thumb twiddling, and the perceiver knows immediately what's being said.

The coupling of speech and gesture

The psychologist David McNeill, a pioneer of gesture analysis from the University of Chicago, has identified important connections between speech and gesture:

- **Temporal structure:** They happen at the same time. Gestures and speech are congruent, and some gestures occur only during speech.

- **Functionality:** Gestures and speech do the same thing. They express the same range of semantic and pragmatic distinctions.

- **Acquisition:** Gestures and speech develop in parallel. Just as children acquire a vocabulary of words like *milk* and *mama* that are concrete and of immediate importance to them before moving on to more general, abstract words like *lunch* and *family*, they also acquire concrete gestures before more abstract gestures. For example, at first an infant pushes something away that it doesn't want, but later discovers that a shake of the

head, meaning "no," conveys the same information and can be used for almost anything (a major component of the "terrible twos" period of child development).

- **Neurology:** Gestures and speech are similarly targeted by *aphasia* (language deficits usually associated with damage to the left temporal lobe of the brain). Broca's aphasia preserves linguistic content and simple grammatical structure, but it disrupts and slows down production: Telegraphic speech (truncated utterances like *Take bath?* short for *May I take my bath now?*) and iconic gestures dominate. Wernicke's aphasia retains grammatical structure and fluency of production but does not preserve meaningful linguistic content — speech often sounds like fluent gibberish, and metaphoric and beat gestures dominate. (See Chapter 16 for more on aphasias.)

When Seeing Is All There Is: The Challenge of Deafness

Imagine for a moment that you're deaf. All around you people are using spoken language, but you're unable to perceive it. How do you go about figuring out what they're saying if you can't hear them? People trying to solve this problem adopt one of three approaches: They make spoken language perceivable in some way, they devise an alternative language, or they create the perception of sound.

Recasting speech into other sensory modalities

The primary sensory mode for language is auditory, but if you can't hear, then you need to find a workaround. One option is to make spoken language visible and, where appropriate, tactile as well:

- **Visible speech:** The deaf can learn spoken language via sight and touch. In the 1860s, Alexander Melville Bell (the father of the guy who invented the telephone) came up with one of the earliest systems of this sort, called *Bell's Visible Speech*. It's simple: While you speak, the deaf person places her hands on your face and throat. Visual and tactile contact with the face allows deaf people to perceive movement gestures that accompany speech, and contact with your throat allows them to perceive vocal fold vibrations (another kind of movement gesture) that accompany voiced sounds.

- **Speechreading:** Another way to learn spoken language is to watch the facial movements that accompany speech. But this is difficult because the visual stream conveys only a small part of the richness of human speech. Very few people become really good at speechreading, and the reasons for their success are not easy to identify: Good training helps, some residual hearing helps, and some people just may have more of a talent for processing visual information as speech.

   The older term for speechreading is *lipreading*. Deaf people were trained to pay attention to the lip movements that accompany speech. But good lipreaders also take in visual information from glimpses of the tongue tip and deformations of the lower face caused by jaw movements; so the training technique was changed as was its name.

- **Hand-signing of spoken language:** Another solution is to develop a language that uses gestural signs to re-create the alphabets of spoken languages. Hand-sign systems are used for transcribing languages like French and English by spelling out words and phrases in a visual alphabet. Because this requires both parties in a conversation to be trained, it limits the deaf person's ability to interact with the world at large.

Making language visible

In the late 1700s, students in a French school for the deaf were taught a signing system — without any finger spelling of spoken words — and were encouraged to adapt it. What happened? It took off! The original group of kids quickly expanded the language's capability — it was never based on spoken French — and each successive class of kids changed it. The language, called *signed language,* was exported to North America in the early 1800s where it flourished. The language is entirely visible and involves the upper body area: facial expressions, head movements, and hand gestures. The language works just like spoken language in that it combines small gestural elements into larger ones for conveying whatever meaning the speaker wishes. The language has rhythm, and timing is a critical component to constructing meaning, just as intonation is in speech. Communities of deaf signers have grown to the point that the members can fully communicate with each other using signs.

Creating the perception of sound

In the 1970s, researchers in Australia developed a neuro-electronic system for converting external sounds (via a microphone) to neural impulses directly to the cochlear nucleus. These devices — called *cochlear implants* — are surgically implanted in the skull behind the ear. They divide the sound stream into a small number of frequency bands, and electric signals for each band are delivered to different parts of the cochlear nucleus. They work well if they're implanted early (by the age of two), and they work especially well if the implantee is born with hearing and has been exposed to spoken language.

To get a sense of the sound signal that a cochlear implant generates, look at these two links of what this kind of speech sounds like:

- ✔ https://mustelid.physiol.ox.ac.uk/ drupal/?q=prosthetics/noise_ vocoded_speech
- ✔ https://mustelid.physiol.ox.ac.uk/ drupal/?q=prosthetics/music

Chapter 15

Producing Language

*I*n order to say something, no matter how important or trivial it is, you first have to decide to speak. This *intention to speak* sits at the border that separates thought from action. Most formal linguists — the ones who focus on phonology, morphology, syntax, and semantics — stay on the thought side of the border. Folks interested in actions, and specifically in the production of speech — engineers, computer scientists, psychologists, speech pathologists, and phoneticians — stay mostly on the action side of the border. In their world, the behavior associated with executing instructions takes center stage. In this chapter, we show you how you put your thoughts into words, how you coordinate your physiological systems to produce speech, and how you supplement your speech with gesturing. We also introduce you to the two main approaches linguists use to model speech production.

Saying What You Mean: Planning Complex Motor Tasks

How do you actually say what you intend to say? Speech production involves two activities — planning motor tasks and then executing them. Although speech scientists disagree on exactly what's involved in these activities, they agree that planning and execution depend on one another. Producing speech is like an orchestra producing music. An orchestra consists of groups of musicians — strings, wind instruments, percussion — all performing specialized tasks, but coordinated and in concert. Where speech production and orchestral music differ is in planning. Orchestras have conductors who use a musical score, which is the plan for the entire piece of music, to guide the orchestra from start to finish. Speech planning works in much the same way, except that your performance isn't planned in advance on such a grand scale. Rather it evolves in small chunks, with sizes varying according to the situation.

Linguists detect the effects of speech planning in different ways, but the following three stand out: the timing of when you breathe in more deeply, the kinds of speech errors that you make, and how you break up your speech.

Breathing in more deeply

When you plan to talk for a long time, you inhale more air into your lungs to let you talk longer (or louder). Taking in a larger breath doesn't mean you know which words you're going to use. But it does mean that you've chosen your topic and made decisions about its complexity. For example, if someone asks you to explain how a radio works, you'll probably take a deep breath before answering. This allows you to generate a long stream of speech; it also lets your listener know that your answer will take a while.

Making speech errors

Certain types of speech errors — called *slips of the tongue* — show that speech is planned. The Reverend Spooner is famous for slips of the tongue — he reportedly said **queer old dean** when he meant to say **dear old queen** — which involve substituting one sound for another. Spooner switched the [d] and the [kw] from different words, suggesting he'd already planned to say *dear old queen* and messed up on the execution. Linguists call such substitution errors *spoonerisms*. Spoonerisms don't always result in reconfigurations that make sense — for example, you can say **dost mefinitely** when you meant to say **most definitely**. Notice that these, and indeed most, speech errors operate on sound segments or syllables, not on the larger syntactic phrasing. Thus, the shape and meaning of words may change, but not the grammar, even when the result is meaningless.

Breaking your speech at syntactic boundaries

Your need to breathe forces you to break up your speech. Speakers make a virtue out of this necessity, and they pause to breathe at major syntactic boundaries. For example, in reporting the list of items you bought at the store, you may say either of the first two sentences listed below. If you did say the second sentence, you likely launched into your shopping report only to realize that you can't remember exactly what you bought, and so you introduced a pause to stall for time. But pauses can't be introduced at whim, which is why you probably wouldn't say the third sentence, with a pause between *the* and *store*.

I went to the store and bought milk, eggs, and cheese. [pause] [breath]

I went to the store and bought [pause] [breath] *milk, eggs, and cheese.*

#I went to the [pause] *store and bought milk, eggs, and cheese.* [breath]

These examples suggest that planning occurs over different spans of speech — sentences, phrases, and words. In some cases, you know exactly what you want to say and say it. In other cases, such as the second sentence, you may know the topic and even the syntactic form you'll use, but you may not know exactly what your shopping list is going to look like until you stop midway through the sentence and remember the items you bought. In such cases, the syntactic form helps fill gaps in your memory because you know, for example, that what follows the verb *bought* must be a list of nouns that are possible things to buy. Syntactic structure is a bridge between your intention to speak and the need to smoothly start, stop, and start speaking again.

Executing Complex Motor Tasks

Producing speech requires you to execute complex *motor tasks*. We take a look at the three systems that you coordinate to perform speech: how your breathing takes a lead in speaking, how your vocal tract orchestrates the performance, and what you do to make speech not only audible, but also visible and touchable.

Speech production and speech perception are intricately connected: To communicate, the speech you produce must be perceptible to others. See Chapter 14 for more on how you perceive speech.

Coordinating the lungs, larynx, and vocal tract

To produce speech, you have to coordinate your lungs, your larynx, and your vocal tract. However, as Table 15-1 shows, each of these subsystems has a primary function other than speech, and these functions have to be coordinated with each other and with speech.

Table 15-1	Speech and Non-speech Functions of Lungs, Larynx, and Vocal Tract	
System	*Speech Function*	*Non-Speech Function*
Lungs	Provide airflow for speech.	Brings oxygen into blood stream and regulates heat.
Larynx	Uses airflow from lungs to vibrate vocal folds and make voicing for vowels and many consonants.	Makes non-linguistic noises (vocalizations) like grunts and murmurs. This scares away enemies and attracts friends. Grunting while lifting a heavy object is a side effect of closing off the lungs. Closing off the airway also prevents choking.
Vocal tract	Shapes speech sounds by positioning lips, jaw, tongue, and uvula.	Chews and swallows food to nourish the body.

Speech scientists who study these three subsystems that produce speech have found that

✔ **How you coordinate the subsystems is elaborate.** You can't swallow food and breathe at the same time. Nor can you breathe normally and talk at the same time. But, provided you don't try to talk for too long between breaths, breathing and talking work well together: You fill your lungs with air and, while your lungs absorb the fresh oxygen you need, you can let the air out slowly as you speak. This is why most speech sounds are produced while air is exiting the lungs (these are called *egressive sounds* and you can read more about them in Chapter 4).

The time frame of the cycle that joins breath and speech has consequences for how you organize what you say. You were probably taught in school that a sentence expresses a complete thought, but a better description of a sentence may be that a sentence is whatever fits into a breath cycle.

✔ **What you do with each subsystem is sophisticated.** Whether you're chewing, swallowing, or speaking, the tongue executes sophisticated maneuvers involving

   • **Coordinated action** of dozens of muscles to change the shape and position of the tongue. For example, to channel the jet of air needed to produce [s], you precisely position the front of the tongue near the roof (palate) of the mouth and then rapidly bring the middle part of the tongue up against the palate further back.

• **Interaction with the rigid structures** of your teeth, alveolar ridge, and hard palate. By positioning your tongue against them in different ways, you produce sounds like the [θ] of *thigh* and the [ð] of *thy* (tongue blade in contact with teeth), [t] and [d] (tongue tip in contact with alveolar ridge), and [ʃ] of *ship* (tongue body in contact with hard palate).

Breathing takes the lead in syllables

To produce audible speech, you need airflow. You can check this out for yourself by trying the following:

1. **Say the word *happy* with your hand in front of your mouth.** You can probably feel the air hitting your fingers, especially as you make the *p* sound.

2. **Whisper *happy* with your hand in front of your mouth.** This time you should feel even more air hitting your fingers.

3. **Move your mouth the way you would if you were saying the word *happy*, without actually whispering or speaking.** Nothing happens, right? You don't feel any airflow against your hand, nor do you hear any sound remotely resembling the word *happy*.

When you say *happy* normally as in Step 1, air flows through the larynx which is partially open for the [h], closed and vibrating for the [æ], open for the [p], and closed and vibrating again for the final [ɪ]. Even though air flows through the larynx for the [p], there's no sound because the vocal tract is closed at the lips. This is just one example of how you coordinate the lungs, larynx, and vocal tract to make sound. In what follows, we show you some other ways this coordination creates, modulates, and organizes the speech stream.

Modulating your voice

Your speech depends on airflow, but it also depends on regularly changing, or *modulating,* the sound of your voice. Is this a physical necessity? No, you can imagine your sound stream consisting of just a continuous sound: for example, a vowel like [a] or [u] or a continuously sustainable consonant like [s]. It would be boring and your set of possible utterances would be limited to a small number of vowels and consonants, but it wouldn't be physically impossible. You can even imagine a language that combines continuous sounds — the question *Where were you* consists entirely of continuous sounds. But no language relies entirely on continuous sounds either singly or in combination. There are two good reasons for this:

✔ **Vowels are a lot of work.** Vowels require a lot of airflow from the lungs. Using consonants that stop or reduce airflow helps conserve your air supply, much like turning your car off in a traffic jam saves gas.

✔ **Vowels are in short supply.** Your vocal tract can't make that many vowel sounds, certainly not enough to make all the distinct sound combinations you need for linguistic expression. That's why all human languages use a combination of vowels and consonants.

All human languages achieve modulation by combining consonant-like events, which restrict the flow of air (and sound) from the vocal tract, and vowel-like events, which let air and sound flow fairly freely. This makes more efficient use of limited air supply by producing alternating sequences of consonants and vowels, where consonant constrictions of the vocal tract stop, or at least substantially slow, the flow of air out of the lungs. These consonant-vowel sequences correspond to successive closures (consonants) and openings (vowels) of the vocal tract. The more open the tract is, the louder a sound can be. This adds to the *modulation* of the sound stream by alternating between louder vocalic events and softer, less audible, consonantal events.

Producing continuous sequences of syllables

Vocal modulation is not specific to humans — birds and other primates also do this. Listening to a bird song, you can hear elaborate melodies composed of syllable-like sequences. Human speech also modulates sound by stringing together syllables, but what makes humans special is their ability to produce many syllables on a single breath of air. Most animals can vocalize only one syllable per breath of air (*cetaceans* — porpoises and whales — are an exception). For example, the *pant hoot* of the chimpanzee involves one loud sound per breath, as does the chirp of a bird. Try saying the word *portable* with a breath between each syllable:

por [breath] *ta* [breath] *ble* [breath]

You can imagine how difficult it would be to get through even a single sentence this way. Your ability to produce continuous sequences of syllables makes linguistic communication possible — it allows you to produce sound streams of sufficient complexity, variety, and speed. You develop this ability early on, while you're lying around with nothing much else to do. One day you're making cooing sounds on a single breath and soon after, at about six or seven months old, you get the idea that you don't need to breathe every time you produce a sound. Voilà, the onset of babbling! To get a feel for how this works, take in a breath of air and say the following string of syllables:

ba, di, ba, da, di, di, du, da, di, da, di, du…

Syllables: The basic unit of speech production

Although the phoneme is considered the smallest unit of language (certainly of linguistic analysis), the syllable may be the most basic unit that your vocal tract and its partners can produce. There are several reasons for this:

✔ **Physiology:** Speech is produced in syllables characteristically involving a transition between an open and closed (or at least less open) vocal tract.

✔ **Production-perception coupling:** The smallest audible unit of speech is syllabic: If you produce a /p/ just by closing your lips, you hear nothing; if you make the /p/ audible by releasing a puff of air so you can hear it, that air puff has vowel-like qualities that make the production syllabic. Our perceptual systems are tuned to hear transitions in sound — specifically, when sounds start and stop and other changes in frequency and amplitude. These transitions are syllabic (see Chapter 14).

✔ **Language processing:** Syllables make it possible to encode language at speeds that the auditory system can handle, given limits imposed by memory and neural processing (see Chapter 16).

✔ **Language acquisition:** Syllable production, as in crying, predates acquisition of smaller, phoneme-sized segments, which must be learned along with the ability to decouple syllable production from the breath cycle. Newborns do not need to learn to coordinate the larynx and lungs to cry. However, they do need to learn the more complicated maneuver of letting the air out of the lungs slowly and in a controlled way while opening and closing the vocal tract. This happens somewhere between cooing and babbling, at around six months of age. (See Chapter 13 for more on how kids learn to speak.)

✔ **Language typology:** Different languages have different syllable structures. A language's way of building syllables — its *phonotactics* — determines which sound combinations make up a syllable, the structure of morphemes and words, the rhythm of spoken language, and speech rate. (For more information on different syllable types, see Chapter 11.)

How many syllables you can produce in one breath of air? Quite a few, right? The need for speed in speech production is no joke. Rapidly producing continuous sequences of syllables conserves air, saves motion, and allows complex configurations — such as words and meaningful phrases — to be coded in short spans of time. Speed of speech production is also important for speech perception — if you take too long to say something, your listener will forget the beginning of the sentence before you get to the end of it. Perceivers must process speech signals and do linguistic decoding within the short time limits of *working memory,* only about 15 seconds or so. (For more on working memory, see Chapter 16.)

How often you breathe in and out depends on how much oxygen your body needs for metabolism, and that depends on what you're doing. You breathe more when you run than when walking or standing still. This metabolic need for oxygen is non-negotiable, so speech must work out its dependency on airflow within strict limitations. Because speech sounds are produced while the lungs are full of air, speaking can get away with slight lengthening of the breath cycle (so long as you're not doing anything else). This arrangement facilitates speech planning and is a lot more efficient than if speech were produced ingressively by taking air into the lungs. Minimally, you'd need to breathe more often to produce the same number of syllables. Other disadvantages would be less efficient sound transmission, reduced pitch range, reduced effectiveness of a configurable vocal tract, and severe limitations on how fast you can transmit information.

Sequencing sounds

Speed is important in producing speech because you have a lot to say and your listener can't make sense of information that comes too slowly. Producing continuous sequences of syllables during a single breath is a huge step forward because you can produce lots of different sounds quickly by making simple and rapid changes in your vocal tract shape. For example, an articulator you just used — the tongue, say — is already in position for the next sound, as in the sequence [st] in *stop,* where repositioning the tongue blade for the [t] occurs rapidly just by raising the tongue tip to touch the alveolar ridge. This is a simple example of how your knowledge of vocal tract resources gets applied to a specific speech goal.

In fact, your bag of tricks for producing sound sequences quickly is impressive. People who study speech production, including phoneticians (see Chapter 3 for more on phonetics), call this elegant manipulation of sound sequences *coarticulation.* Coarticulation simply means doing two articulatory things at once, but it makes a difference whether the coarticulation involves two independent articulators, like the tongue and lips, or one articulator or linked structure like the tongue and jaw. Coarticulation of independent articulators is called *co-production* and occurs when one articulator moves into position earlier than necessary thus overlapping another articulator's action. The other type of coarticulation, called *blending,* occurs when the same articulator doesn't have enough time to get from one place to the next.

Here is an example of co-production that may be familiar to you. Chances are that you pronounce the word *input* as [ɪmpʌt], where the /n/ changes its *place of articulation* from *alveolar* (/t, d, s, r, n, …/) to *labial* (/p, b, m/). Based on the word's spelling, if the two syllables *in* and *put* are separated by a breath (or even a long pause), no simplification occurs. But here's what happens when they occur in the same sound stream:

1. **You raise your tongue and jaw for the vowel /ɪ/.**

2. **You open the velum in anticipation of /n/ as you produce the vowel /ɪ/.**

3. **You can do one of two things to make the consonant /n/:**

   • **You raise the tip of your tongue to touch the alveolar ridge to make /n/.**

   • **You do not raise the tip of your tongue to make /n/.**

4. **You close your lips in anticipation of the /p/ as you make the /n/.** Because your velum is open, this produces an [m] sound. You then close your velum before releasing your lips for the /p/.

5. **Your tongue and jaw are in neutral position for the vowel /ʌ/.**

6. **You raise the tip of your tongue to the alveolar ridge for /t/ and close the velum.**

Opening the velum allows sounds to be nasalized: Sound goes into the nasal cavity and bounces around. This is what makes the /n/ sound and also turns the /ɪ/ into a partially nasalized vowel.

Step 3 is interesting because, when speakers first encounter *input,* they often raise their tongues for the /n/ even though it occurs at the same time as the early closure of the lips in Step 4. But after using the word several times in a conversation, they simplify the process by not raising the tongue at all. You can check whether speakers have made the shift by asking them to say *input* slowly — if they say *im-put,* then you can be sure they've made the shift to the second step.

Because sounds do affect one another so much, linguists call this process of making adjacent sounds more similar to one another *assimilation. Input* exemplifies *partial* rather than *total assimilation* because the /n/ changes its *place of articulation,* but not its *nasality* or *voicing* — /n/ is a *voiced* alveolar *nasal* stop, whereas /p/ is a *voiceless* labial *oral* stop. A more complex example of assimilation is what happens to the negative prefix *in-* when it is added to different words: In front of vowels, it doesn't change — *in-accurate.* But in front of a labial /p/, alveolar /n/ becomes a labial /m/ — *im-possible.* And in front of the alveolar liquids /l, r/, it changes to match those sounds completely — *il-logical, ir-reparable.* Assimilation is so powerful that it can even change how words are spelled over time!

The effects of blending coarticulation are harder to notice because they are more prevalent in fast speech. For example, the top of your tongue touches the roof of your mouth much further forward when you produce the [k] of *a key* compared to the [k] of *a car.* The [i] vowel for *key* is produced further forward in the mouth, and because it doesn't matter as much where the [k] is produced, it moves forward. Actually, if you compared the articulator position of the [k] for *cut* with those of *car* and *key,* you would see the [k] moves back for the [a] and forward for the [i].

Shaping speech with the vocal tract

If you have enough air in your lungs, you can turn the production of sound on or off with your larynx, as you do when you make a glottal stop /ʔ/. But it's the vocal tract above the larynx that shapes the sound flow. Looking at different levels of detail reveals that

✔ At a broad level, opening the vocal tract to create vowels and closing it to create consonants while passing air through the tract accounts for the basic modulation of sound.

✔ At a more fine-grained level, positioning the articulators — tongue, jaw, lips, and velum — at different times and in different combinations changes the shape of the vocal tract. The coordinated acts of positioning the articulators — not specific vocal tract shapes — are called *articulatory gestures*.

  • For consonants, this means constricting the vocal tract so that it's closed, or nearly closed, at one or more locations.

  • For vowels, this means narrowing the vocal tract less and in different configurations than for consonants.

Getting your act together: Managing multiple components

In order to say a word like *palm,* which for many English speakers is a single syllable containing three phonemes [pɑm], you have to

✔ Identify which articulators you need.

✔ Group the articulators by function — for example, the lips (and jaw) coordinate to produce an opening between them.

✔ Assign them an activation schedule (when to act and for how long).

To see how this works, look at Figure 15-1. This action scheme, or *gestural score,* highlights the tasks required for the vocal tract and larynx to achieve the right configuration, at the right time, to produce *palm* [pʰɑm]. (If you're wondering where the 'l' in *palm* is, we're pretending you're from somewhere like New York and don't pronounce it.)

Each panel of Figure 15-1 shows the action (indicated by rectangular boxes) of one articulatory gesture and the effects of that action (indicated by curved lines) over time (horizontal axis).

✔ **Velum:** Velum opens to allow air to flow through the nasal cavity to produce [m].

✔ **Pharynx:** The root of the tongue is retracted, narrowing the *pharynx* — the vertical portion of the vocal tract between your larynx and your *velum* (your throat) — to shape the airflow for the vowel [ɑ].

✔ **Lips:** The upper and lower lips act together to close for [p] and [m], but are open for the vowel [ɑ].

✔ **Glottis:** The glottis is open (vocal folds are apart) when the lips close for [p], but then closes as [p] is released and stays that way for the rest of the utterance.

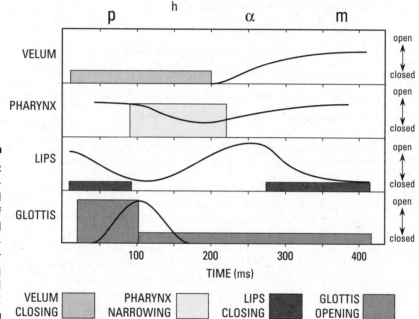

Figure 15-1: The activation and motion of the vocal tract articulators for producing the word *palm* [pʰɑm].

 Multiple components cooperate to produce a sound. To make [pʰ] your glottis is open, your lips are closed (with help from your jaw), and your tongue doesn't block the vocal tract. The action of articulators also doesn't necessarily line up with where you think the sound segments are. For example, the velum can open anytime after the release of [pʰ] — that's why many people's vowels are nasalized before a nasal consonant.

 Each articulatory activation shown in Figure 15-1 has a certain size or strength. Activation strength affects how quickly an articulator changes its position or configuration. This way of modeling speech production as a coordinated set of tasks was pioneered by a group of scientists — psychologists, linguists, and mathematicians — at Haskins Laboratories in New Haven, Connecticut. In the 1980s, this work launched *the revised motor theory* of speech perception, task dynamics, configurable articulatory synthesis (CASY), and what is now known as *articulatory phonology*.

Timing is everything: Banana, bad data, bandana, and bad nana

The order in which certain articulators engage relative to one another greatly affects the sounds you make. Figure 15-2 shows how changing the timing of velar opening results in four completely different productions: *banana, bandana, bad nana,* and *bad data,* even though all four productions have the same sequence of articulatory movements:

1. **Close your lips for the initial [b].**
2. **Open your lips for the first vowel [æ].**
3. **Raise your tongue tip (and jaw) to touch the alveolar ridge.**
4. **Lower your tongue tip (and jaw) for the second vowel [æ].**
5. **Raise your tongue tip again, making contact with the alveolar ridge.**
6. **Lower your tongue for the final vowel [ə].**

Across the top of Figure 15-2 is a row of schematic vocal tracts (larynx at bottom, lips at upper right), one for each step in the sequence.

No sound is identified for the two instances of alveolar contact — Steps 3 and 5 — because touching the tongue tip against the alveolar ridge alone doesn't determine which alveolar consonant is made. For Figure 15-2, assume that there's vocal fold vibration during these consonant closures — that means these are voiced alveolar sounds. But even this isn't enough information to identify the consonant: You need to know what your velum is doing. You can produce four different word sequences that have very different speech acoustics, just by controlling when you open and close the velum!

- ✔ *banana:* If your velum opens just after the release of [b] and stays open, then both times the tongue is raised to the alveolar ridge, you produce the nasal consonant [n].

- ✔ *bandana:* If your velum is open just before the first alveolar contact, closes in the middle of it, and then opens again during the second [a], you produce [n], then [d], then [n].

- ✔ *bad nana:* If your velum is closed and then opens during the first alveolar closure and stays open, then you produce [d], then [n], and then another [n].

- ✔ *bad data:* If your velum never opens, then the alveolar consonants are both variants of /d/. (Note, the short duration of the second alveolar of *data* produces a flap sound [ɾ] that is indistinguishable for /d/ and /t/.)

Philip Rubin of Haskins Laboratories and creator of the Haskins articulatory synthesis programs (ASY and CASY) uses the example in Figure 15-2 to show how simple changes in articulation — here the timing of velar opening — changes the perceived identity of words. The simplicity of the gestural score in Figure 15-2 may suggest that planning and execution of motor tasks are based solely on articulation. But speech planning and motor execution incorporate both speech production (articulation) and speech perception (acoustics). Because people are speakers *and* hearers, articulation and acoustics reinforce each other — people tune their production to match what they perceive, and vice versa.

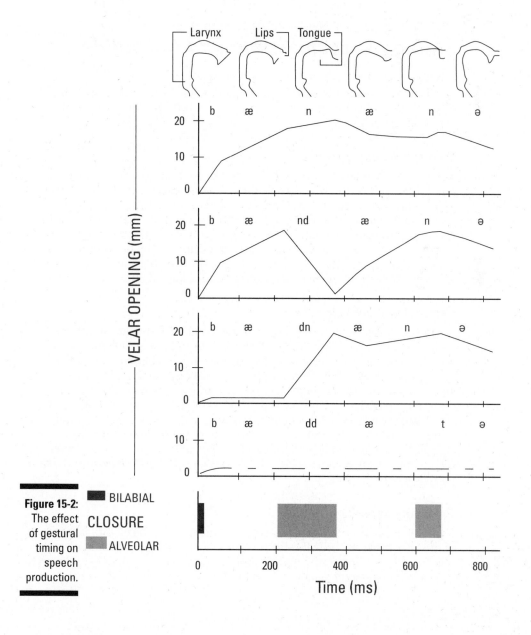

Figure 15-2:
The effect of gestural timing on speech production.

If you want a closer look at the workings of the vocal tract during speech, go to Kevin Munhall's (Queen's University, Canada) website for cool X-ray movies of people talking: `http://psyc.queensu.ca/~munhallk/05_ database.htm`. For more on articulatory synthesis, check out the Haskins Laboratories website for ASY: `www.haskins.yale.edu/facilities/ asy-demo.html`.

Making speech visible and touchable

Producing speech involves a lot of moving parts — the lungs, larynx, and vocal tract — the results of which are audible, of course, but also visible and even touchable. This section gives you a quick rundown of how speech is visible and touchable.

Creating visible speech

You may have difficulty seeing the motion of the lungs or vocal folds, but you don't need an X-ray to see what's going on in the vocal tract. You can see a lot of what's going on in people's vocal tracts right on their faces. Why? For one thing, the lips, a major articulator of the vocal tract, are entirely visible. Also, the jaw, which is coordinated with the tongue and lips, changes the shape of your face continually as it moves to support the production of consonants and vowels. The moving tongue tip is visible some of the time, and some folks think seeing the throat provides information.

Fashioning touchable speech

When you speak, a lot of the sound energy comes out of your mouth, but some of it gets transmitted through skin tissue and bone. This means that someone can feel the vibrations of your voice by touching the skin of your face or neck. A vibration signal such as this isn't as rich and detailed as a sound signal, but it can still be useful. With training, people can pick up patterns of modulated vibration corresponding to consonants and vowels, and in some cases even tell which consonants and vowels are being produced. In the special case of speakers who are deaf and blind, touch becomes critical. *TADOMA* is a method that allows *deafblind* people to "read" speech by touching the lips and jaw line of the speaker. (Tad and Oma were the first two TADOMA students.)

Producing speech amodally

Signals that occur in multiple *modalities* — sounds from the mouth, movements of the face or hands, and vibrations you can feel — can be *multimodal* or *amodal*. *Amodal signals* all originate from the same activity and just happen to broadcast on different sensory channels. For example, the visible changes in lip shape and face deformations due to jaw movement result from shaping the vocal tract to produce audible speech. Researchers consider these signals to be *amodal* (without a specific intended modality) in terms of their production even though perception processes them through multiple sensory channels. Amodal signals don't involve extra planning or additional neural and motor resources.

Producing speech amodally means that the signals in each sensory channel have a lot of shared structure and convey the same or, at least, related information. Perceivers take advantage of this when they process speech through multiple sensory channels. For example, it's easier to understand people face to face — when you can see them — than on the telephone. And if someone is deaf, being able to see how the movement of the lips, jaw, and even the tongue change the shape of the face can be critical for perception. This is a form of *speechreading* that everyone does to some extent without special training. (For more on speechreading and multisensory perception, see Chapter 14.)

Producing speech in different modes

Multimodal signals result when you produce speech sounds along with signals produced in other modalities — for example, smiling or gesturing while you speak. Multi-modal signals require extra planning and involve more neural and motor activity.

When you speak, you do a lot more than move your mouth as part of the process of shaping sounds. Your head moves, your eyebrows arch or narrow, you smile or frown as you speak, your shoulders rise, and you move your hands and wave your arms. You may even stamp your foot. You do some of these things consciously, perhaps for dramatic effect, but most of the time you do these things without any particular awareness of what you're doing. These are commonly called gestures, and their importance in communicative interaction — especially gestures that go beyond simple expression of emotion (like smiles or frowns) — has become an area of intense research interest, although mainly from the perspective of perception (see Chapter 14). Multimodal production of speech and gesture is much more complicated than amodal production. Gesture production has (at least) two very interesting features:

- Gestures are produced independently of speech and usually involve different physical sub-systems like the arms, but they're obviously coordinated with speech production.
- Each person has his or her own set of gestures and unique way of putting them together with speech, but perceivers seem to have no problem processing and interpreting these unique gesture-speech configurations.

How signals carry information

Speech production can create signals in three modalities that all flow from the same act. Each medium — sound through air, reflected light, and vibration and movement of tissue — imposes restrictions on the information carried by each signal. Speech scientists study how these signals differ by looking at

✔ **What perceivers get from the signals:** Lynne Bernstein of Georgetown University (United States) and others have studied how much speech information is available to deaf perceivers in the signals they can touch and see. In general, perceivers get more useful information from the combination of sight and touch than from either signal alone. The visual medium gives perceivers information about where sounds are produced in the mouth (the place of articulation) and what type of sounds they are (the manner of articulation). But perceivers also need to feel the vibration to know whether a sound is voiced or not.

✔ **What's in the signals:** In the mid-1990s, Hani Yehia, Takaaki Kuratate, and colleagues at Advanced Telecommunications Research (ATR) International in Japan began to analyze the production of audiovisual speech signals. They measured how the motions of the vocal tract and the visible (face motion) and acoustic signals that result from those vocal tract motions all fit together so well that they could predict one set of signals from another. For example, they were able to synthesize intelligible speech acoustics from the visible motions of the face and head. It was even easier to synthesize visible speech, or *talking heads*, from audible speech. (For more on talking heads, see the Talking Heads website at www.haskins.yale.edu/featured/heads/heads.html, hosted by Haskins Laboratories.)

Being Adaptable and Predictable

Language production combines two opposite traits: It's adaptable *and* predictable.

✔ **The adaptability of speech production:** Adaptability allows you to respond rapidly to changing conditions in your physical environment, both internally and externally. In conversation, you don't always get to say what you expect or want to say. You may even find yourself saying things you never intended to say. To meet these challenges, you have to be able to plan and execute speech from scratch, beginning with figuring out what you want to say and then how you want to say it.

✔ **The predictability of speech production:** Predictability allows you to go on autopilot when external conditions are predictable. Speech production is a highly *over-learned* skill. How many thousands of times have you greeted someone with *hello?* Just as you can find a familiar light switch in the dark, you produce a lot of speech on autopilot, without detailed planning.

Scripting what you say

The predictability of speech production suggests that a lot of human speech is generated from *scripts* or *templates*. A script is a set of instructions that, when followed, produce a specific result. For example, you pass an acquaintance on the street who says, "*Hi, harya doin,*" and for the zillionth time in your life you play back the "*Fine*" tape and walk on. This is an example of an entire discourse that's automated.

You probably have scripts for lots of things you say often, certainly the hundreds and hundreds of words you use in everyday conversation and the dozens of idiomatic expressions like *give me a break, you're joking.* Phrases you use to set up a piece of discourse, like *On the one hand, . . . On the other hand,* are part of the large inventory of partially specified plans or templates that people carry around and flesh out on the fly. These templates aren't specific to you — they reflect the influences of your dialectal region, education, and socio-economic status.

Getting from scripts to speech planning

Linguists disagree on how detailed scripts have to be for speech planning and how scripts are implemented in speaking situations like loud parties where you have to adjust everything you do just to be heard. Opinions and approaches differ widely:

- **Linguistic models of speech planning:** Many linguists think of producing speech as simply a matter of implementing an intention to speak. This intention follows a series of steps from large thought-like units — meaningfully organized groups of words — to smaller elements like words and morphemes, which consist of the smallest linguistically relevant bits, phonemes. For some linguists, it's just a matter of stringing these bits together in time and making them detectable to a perceiver. But recent studies of the brain show that this can't be the whole story. Skilled behaviors like swinging a bat or producing speech are not processes where the smallest imaginable bits, say the phoneme, are executed one after the other. This is true even when actions are novel and have not achieved script status.

- **Dual-process models of speech planning:** Speech production interacts with planning and execution, adapting rapidly to sudden changes in the physical environment, but otherwise following a plan. For example, when the room you're in suddenly gets noisy, you raise your voice and maybe even choose different words that you think are easier to hear in all the noise, but you don't change more than you have to. Scripts streamline this process and resemble the orchestration of gestural scores we mention earlier in this chapter, but they do it on a massive scale that incorporates all levels of linguistic knowledge, including the knowledge of sound patterns, words and meanings, grammar, conventions for their use, and the physical conditions that can affect production of the utterance. After all, all these things have to hold together in order for you communicate intelligibly.

Brain studies suggest that scripts differ from novel language in the way they're learned, stored in memory, and accessed in the future. It may be, as Diana van Lancker Sidtis of New York University suggests, that humans have a *dual process* model for language — one for novel speech production and one for scripted speech production. However, novel language and scripts probably sit on widely separated parts of a language-processing continuum that is still largely uncharted by research.

✔ **Computational models of speech planning:** Beginning in the 1980s and early 1990s, researchers approached questions about speech planning computationally. They tried to use large computers to connect what neurophysiologists and psychologists know about brains and cognition with linguists' observations about language behavior. To make a long story short, the cleverest folks working with the biggest computers couldn't make this work. A basic problem with this approach, which still faces us today, is that there's a (huge!) mismatch between how the brain organizes and plans behavior and what linguists and others see as the result.

Chapter 16

Locating Language in the Brain: Neurolinguistics

*P*roducing and perceiving speech requires your brain to do a lot of work. Hundreds of thousands, even millions, of nerves have to kick into action to receive, process, and send signals to other parts of the brain and to the various parts of the body involved with talking and listening. The study of what your brain does when you produce or perceive language is called *neurolinguistics*.

Neurolinguists measure your brain activity while you use your language ability — speaking, listening to speech, reading, and even thinking about speaking. They do this so they can find out which parts of your brain are active and how the various parts interact during specific *tasks* (speaking, listening, and so on). Neurolinguists also study special cases of language loss and impairment due to aging, disease, or trauma to the brain and situations like deafness where language has to work a different way.

This chapter gives you a quick rundown of how neurolinguists measure brain activity, what they know about how language lives in the brain, what happens when the brain is damaged, and the special tasks they use to uncover language-related brain activity.

Looking at Language and the Normal Brain

You can't tell much about how the brain works just by looking at it, at least, not the way you can look at the fingers on your hand and know what each one does and how it's connected to the others. So neurolinguists and neuroscientists find out how the brain works by watching what it does when you perform specific tasks, like counting backwards from ten to one, listening to odd sentence constructions, or reading a newspaper. By comparing what the brain does during different tasks, neurolinguists identify the correspondences between language tasks and brain activity. (For more on the technology used to study the brain, see the sidebar "Modernizing the mapping: Living brains" later in this chapter.) However, the more neurolinguists look at what the brain does during language processing, the more impressed they are by how complicated both language and the brain are. In this section, we show you the key language areas in the brain and how they interact.

Brain structure in grey and white

If you cut into the brain, you'll find two distinct types of tissue: grey matter and white matter.

✔ Grey matter covers the surface of the brain. You may hear people talk about the cerebral cortex (that's all those wrinkles you see when you look at a photograph of the brain) and the *cerebellar cortex* (which sits underneath the cerebrum and looks more like a set of horizontal bands). These are grey matter areas. Grey matter is also found in various places inside the brain and on the spinal cord. Grey matter consists of many *neurons* (microscopic processors of information), which are connected to neural fibers coming mostly from deeper regions of the brain. When cortical neurons are firing away doing their job, neurolinguists call that *cortical activation*.

✔ White matter is what lies underneath the cortical grey matter and makes up most of your spinal cord and the nerves that go to the various parts of your body, such as your face and hands and down your legs. It looks different from grey matter because it consists of long nerve fibers that carry electrochemical nerve impulses quickly and efficiently to and from different neurons in the grey matter and over long distances to and from everywhere else in your body. White matter makes billions and billions of connections with close to 100,000 miles of nerve fiber.

One way to think of the difference between grey matter and white matter is that grey matter is where information is processed and white matter is the cable system that brings information to the cortex from other parts of the cortex or from various parts of the body. The neural fibers of the white matter are also what the brain uses to send information to the body, for example, telling your fingers and toes to move, and telling your auditory system to tune in to some sounds rather than others.

Comparing human brains to each other

No two brains work the same way. This makes it tough to connect language with specific neural structures. One of the things that neurolinguists have discovered in their quest to locate language on a brain map is that brain activation patterns actually vary for different people doing the same task.

Suppose a neurolinguist wants to understand the relation between reading and language. Everyone knows there's a relation between them, but the neurolinguist wants to know how that difference plays out in the brain when, for example, you read a sentence compared to when you hear that same sentence. If two language tasks — such as reading and listening — activate different areas of the brain, then this means that language probably doesn't have one specific location in the brain. And for different people, the active brain areas for reading and listening may be the same, partially different, or entirely different. To make matters more complicated, the same person may exhibit different brain activity on different days for the same task!

Locating language in the brain

Language doesn't have a specific physical location in the brain — it happens all over the brain. Neurolinguistic research connects every brain area identified in Figure 16-1 to language, especially in the left hemisphere (where language functions are concentrated), but also in the right hemisphere. Here, however, are a few of the most important areas of the brain for language:

✔ Frontal lobe areas are associated with planning and emotion and influence what you want to say and how you feel about it.

✔ The perception of speech is multisensory: It involves visual and tactile sensory input in addition to the auditory information you associate with hearing. (For more on perception, see Chapter 14.) This means that, when you see and hear someone speak, the areas of the brain associated with hearing, vision (seeing and visual memory, shown in Figure 16-1), and multisensory processing interact with one another.

✔ One of the most important brain areas for language is Wernicke's area. It is crucial for multisensory processing and for communicating between sensory and motor systems.

Wernicke's area is named after Carl Wernicke, the German neurologist who first described its importance in speech comprehension in 1874.

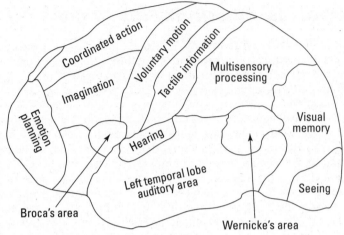

Figure 16-1:
Map of left hemisphere brain functions related to language.

Taking sides in the brain

Although the physical brain structures look the same for the right hemisphere and the left — well, mirror-reversed — they contribute to language processing differently. Strong evidence exists for *hemispherical lateralization,* where certain aspects of language processing happen more on one side of the brain or the other.

  ✔ **Left-hemisphere specialization:** Lexical, syntactic, and semantic processes seem to be associated with the left hemisphere.

  ✔ **Right hemisphere specialization:** Phonetics, phonology, emotional, and motor-sensory processes associated with producing and perceiving speech seem to be associated with the right hemisphere.

  ✔ **Interaction between the hemispheres:** fMRI and other techniques show that the two hemispheres interact for all aspects of utterance formation. For example, intonation, which gives speech its songlike rhythm, is controlled primarily by the right hemisphere, while semantic processing is controlled by the left hemisphere. Thus both hemispheres must be active to distinguish the statement *You went to the store* (with falling intonation) from the question *You went to the store?* (with rising intonation).

So, while it's important to determine whether individual components of language processing occur in the left hemisphere, the right, or both, the more important message is that language makes extensive use of both sides of the brain.

Storing language in the brain

Language depends on complex reasoning, extensive memory, and all the machinery for producing and perceiving linguistic information. Processing and coordinating information from different sources takes time, and the brain buys time by storing relevant data in memory where it can get to it easily when needed. There are many theories about how memory works, how and where memory is located, and how many kinds of memory there are. For neurolinguistics, the following three types are the most important:

✔ **Short-term memory** stores sensory data such as sights and sounds in "raw" form until the information is processed by all the cortical components that need to make use of it. Short-term memory is located in each sensory cortex at or near where sensory signals arrive from each sensory transmission system — for the auditory system, for example, this would be where sound data arrive from the *inferior colliculus* and *medial geniculate body* (see Figure 14-1 in Chapter 14 for an illustration of this system).

✔ **Working memory** stores processed information for use by other areas for short periods of time, usually 15 seconds or less. This includes multisensory processing of auditory, tactile, and visual information during speech. Working memory is located in the frontal (left portion of Figure 16-1) and parietal (center top of Figure 16-1) cortex, as well as other cortex areas not shown here.

✔ **Long-term memory** stores permanent information such as the phonological forms of words and contributes to utterance processing. How items are stored in long-term memory, and where, isn't clear. Some scientists believe that components of a single item may be stored in various cortical areas, depending on how they were stored initially and how a particular person uses them.

Processing language places particularly intense demands on memory. First, it takes time to process information that arrives at different times from different sensory sources. For example, auditory signals reach the cortex sooner than visual signals. Second, speech occurs through time so you can't wait until the signals stop coming in before you process them. So at any given moment in time, your brain has to simultaneously process language information at various levels. For example, suppose you hear the sentence,

> *The next bus doesn't stop here, so you'll have to wait until the one at 10 o'clock.*

The following list gives you an approximation of how your brain handles this utterance (the exact details of the process are the subject of intense study by neurolinguists). Our purpose is to demonstrate that your brain operates simultaneously on signals and on the information derived from processing them in ways that require memory to act on some aspects of the process immediately and on other aspects over longer periods of time.

- ✔ **Storing the signal in short-term memory:** Your auditory system (starting with your ears) transmits the sound signal for the first syllable, the word *the,* to the auditory cortex (left temporal lobe), where it goes into short-term memory.

- ✔ **Analyzing the signal:** After the signal is in short-term memory, your brain begins to analyze it. The first task is to identify the signal as speech, so that all the processes specific to language can kick into gear.

- ✔ **Moving the signal to working memory:** While your brain identifies the first part of the sound stream as speech, more signal is arriving in short-term memory. Your brain needs this additional signal information to identify the first part of the signal as an example of the word *the.* Why? Without a larger signal stream, the brain can't *chunk up* the signal into relevant pieces. In particular, your brain stores phonological knowledge that helps it quickly divide the signal into discrete syllables. The phonological information for the first syllable goes into short-term/ working memory and is part of what Alan Baddeley has called the *phonological loop:* This loop connects working memory to Wernicke's area and the *inferior parietal lobe* (close to Wernicke's area, but inside the *multisensory processing* area shown in Figure 16-1) and is essential for integrating different levels of auditory, phonological, and lexical information.

- ✔ **Accessing long-term memory:** As more signal arrives at the cortex, it goes into short-term memory and gets phonologically processed. Your brain now uses the results of the phonological analysis — syllables in sequence — stored in working memory to retrieve word forms from long-term memory that fit those syllable sequences. These word forms are stored in long-term memory with information about their phonological form, their grammatical status (whether they are a noun, verb, or adjective), and their meaning.

The brain needs to hold even more signal in working memory in order to identify the grammatical structure and overall meaning of the utterance. Your brain can't dismiss the phrase *the next bus* as soon as it figures out its structure and meaning, because it now needs to figure out what *the next bus* is doing — *doesn't stop here* — and, even more importantly, your brain needs to hold on to this phrase in order to know that the word *one,* almost at the very end of the sentence, means another *bus.* This means your brain can't just forget words as soon as it identifies them — you'd never be able to understand the complete utterance.

Activating speech and non-speech areas

Language doesn't play alone — it also involves gestures and expressions of emotion. This means that both speech and non-speech motor areas of the brain have to be active. Motor areas associated with speech production include Broca's area and other frontal areas responsible for *coordinated action* and *voluntary motion* (see Figure 16-1). Again, no one knows exactly how this works, so we won't attempt to take you through a hypothetical set of steps for producing an utterance. (Check out Chapter 15 for information on speech production.) By now you can appreciate how complex a process it must be to organize the neuromotor commands going to the different subsystems — the lungs, larynx, and vocal tract — to ensure that they coordinate properly to produce the necessary conditions for generating sounds with the correct amounts of airflow, vocal fold vibration, and vocal tract shaping at the right times.

To make matters more complicated, the brain doesn't completely separate the processes of speech production and perception. For example, even when you are just listening to what someone is saying to you, you still activate parts of your motor cortex — the frontal lobe areas shown in Figure 16-1, including Broca's area. Obviously, you don't activate these areas the same way you do when you are talking, but they are still active.

A phonological loop connects auditory and acoustic information about sounds-in-sequence with articulator information about how you would produce them if you were talking. For example, Broca's area, which was long thought to be active only during production, shows weak activation during speech perception as well. There is at least a three-way interaction between activation in Broca's area, in response to processing in Wernicke's area, mediated by Geschwind's territory — the lower part of inferior parietal lobe (the low end of the multisensory processing area in Figure 16-1). The simultaneous activation of motor and sensory areas of the brain has generated a lot of interest because it seems as if the motor areas mirror the reactions of the sensory areas during speech perception.

Geschwind's territory was named in honor of Norman Geschwind, whose work in Boston in the 1960s and 1970s launched the field of *behavioral neurology*. Because Geschwind's territory sits at the critical junction between auditory, visual, and other sensory processing areas, Geschwind predicted that the inferior parietal lobe would be important in processing language signals in whatever form they are perceived — as multisensory signals corresponding to sounds and visible motions, in symbolic written form, or even in the symbolic movements used in signed language.

Mirror neurons and silent speech

When you read, you also activate the muscles in your larynx that control vocal fold vibration. You wouldn't necessarily notice this phenomenon, known as *silent speech* — after all, you aren't talking as you read — but you may have noticed after reading for a long time that your throat feels tired or a bit sore. Careful study of silent speech has shown that the laryngeal muscles are active while you read and inactive when you pause or stop reading.

For many years, silent speech remained an interesting curiosity about language processing; no one gave any thought to the possibility that the perception of specific acts may activate neural structures in the motor systems related to producing those acts. That situation changed drastically in the mid-1990s when Italian researcher Giacomo Rizzolatti showed that monkeys doing a perception task activated neural structures in motor areas of the brain corresponding to the actions being perceived. For example, if you show a monkey a video of another monkey reaching for a banana, there is activation in the part of the watching monkey's brain that would be active if the watching monkey herself were reaching for the banana. The neuronal recordings made by Rizzolatti and hundreds of other researchers since 1995 have established this mirror neuron link between action and the perception of action.

The existence of mirror neurons in human brains has to be inferred because scientists don't stick electrodes into human brains with as much experimental aplomb as they stick them into monkeys' brains.

Changing the structure of the brain

Neuroscientists often talk about *neural plasticity* in relation to the brain's continued ability to learn new things and to use different neural structure to achieve the same function. Your neural plasticity is how you continue to learn new words and expressions throughout your life, as well as how you recover language abilities lost due to injury and stroke.

Learning changes the brain

Learning a new word or memorizing a poem requires neural plasticity because committing these structures to long-term memory means organizing (or reorganizing) some amount of neural structure. You can think of plasticity as changes in the functional groupings of neurons.

Injury changes the brain

Larger scale changes occur when one part of the brain no longer does what it did before. For example, there are many documented cases of severe brain injury where what was previously done on the left side of the brain now has to be done on the right side, including the processing of language. That is, even though certain parts of language processing are usually *lateralized* to one side or the other, they can switch sides when they have to. Processing may not be as good as before, but it works. The younger the brain, the more successful the switch.

Deafness changes the brain

Neural plasticity allows people to master an alternative way to perceive and produce language if they've lost the primary sensory modality for language. Deaf people, for example, use visible gestures of the hands, face, and body for face-to-face communication. Even though deaf people may receive little or no auditory speech information, many regions of their brain that would normally be processing only auditory signals actively respond to the visual signals produced by signing! For example, Broca's area is active during sign production and Wernicke's area is active during sign perception and comprehension.

This brings out an interesting fact about neural plasticity: It appears that the same brain structures get organized for language processing regardless of the actual signal (auditory, visual, or tactile) used. This shows neural rigidity at the functional level — Broca's area is for speech production, even if it is sign language. But there's plasticity at the signal level because it doesn't matter which sensory channel is used.

Uncovering Effects of Brain Damage on Language

The brain is pretty well protected, but severe knocks on the head, bomb blasts, stroke, disease, and even certain infections can damage parts of the brain, disrupting its normal function. If there's damage right in the vicinity of the left temporal lobe (see Figure 16-1), then language is disrupted. Disruptions of language production or perception are called *aphasias* — derived from the Greek work *a-phanai,* which literally means "without speech" or "speechless." There are many types of aphasia, such as *alexic anomia* (also known as *visual aphasia* or *word blindness*), which is literally a loss of the ability to recognize written words. But the two most famous aphasias — the two that have been studied the longest — are Broca's and Wernicke's aphasias.

Broca's aphasia

Broca's aphasia is caused by damage, or *lesions,* in the Broca's area. It causes people's speech to be slow and ponderous, but leaves the meaning of what is said (the *semantics*) intact. Broca's aphasics (people with Broca's aphasia) also typically use simplified grammar. They may not add plurals or alter the form of verbs as in *I ... er... buy seven ... ha ... apple* instead of *I bought seven apples.*

It makes sense that this aphasia affects speech production rather than speech perception and comprehension when you realize that Broca's area is on the border between the temporal lobe, which is heavily involved in language processing, and the motor cortex that you need to control actions (see Figure 16-1). Because Broca's aphasia is primarily a production disorder with little effect on comprehension, Broca's asphasics are aware they have difficulty speaking.

Wernicke's aphasia

Wernicke's aphasia, also known as *fluent aphasia,* has almost the reverse effect of Broca's aphasia. Wernicke's aphasics have trouble understanding speech, but their speech production is often fluent and may even be grammatical for short phrases. On the other hand, it sounds like gibberish because they don't combine words into appropriate meanings. For example, a Wernicke's aphasic may say *Well this is .... Dad is gone here working his work out o'here to get him better.* Wernicke's area, as you can see in Figure 16-1, is at the opposite end of the temporal lobe from Broca's area, right up against the vision area and the inferior parietal lobe, where so much multisensory perceptual processing occurs. Wernicke's aphasics are often unaware of their language deficit.

Damage to either of these areas — the temporal lobe or the inferior parietal lobe — has fairly predictable and often permanent effects (especially in older patients). There's little treatment for these conditions, although some techniques — such as sound imitation or singing instead of saying their utterances — have limited success for Broca's aphasics.

Other types of brain injury

Some types of brain injury are less permanent than the aphasias. Stroke, tumors, and fluid build-up that put pressure on a specific part of the brain surface can all disrupt language. For example, strokes in a frontal area on the left side of the brain may temporarily affect a bunch of motor behaviors, including speech production, much like Broca's aphasia.

Dyspraxia, from the Greek *dus* + *praxis* meaning "bad action," is a neurological disorder whose cause or origin is unknown even though it's fairly common. Dyspraxia causes people to have difficulty speaking, but it isn't an aphasia because it has no relation to brain damage.

Using neurosurgery and autopsies to map the brain

Before modern brain-mapping technology, it was hard to study the brain of someone who was still in a condition to speak. One notable option was pioneered during the 1940s and 1950s. Just before conducting brain surgery to treat severe types of epilepsy, Wilder Penfield and his colleague Herbert Jasper at McGill University would conduct experiments to help them avoid damaging areas of the brain related to motor skills such as speaking and manipulating the hands. Known as the Montreal procedure, Penfield and Jasper applied very small electrical charges directly to the cortical surface and observed the effect on the patient. The patient's ability to report the effects that they sensed helped the surgeon determine where not to cut into the brain. (Brain surgery is still conducted on awake patients for exactly this reason.)

Autopsies provided another source of knowledge about language and the brain. This is how two critical language areas in the left hemisphere — Broca's and Wernicke's areas — were first identified in the 19th century. Paul Broca (1824–1880) and Carl Wernicke (1848–1905) pioneered the study of the brain areas named for them by conducting extensive case studies of patients who had problems producing or understanding language. These early researchers didn't run rigorous experiments, but they did keep detailed notes on each patient. To identify which part of the brain was responsible for a patient's language difficulty, or deficit, they performed an autopsy after the patient died to determine the size and location of the brain lesion (damaged area). A major limitation of these studies was that each patient was a unique case; each patient had his own particular language deficit corresponding to a particular brain lesion. From these individual case studies, it was difficult to attain a general understanding of the link between brain structure and language function.

One other particularly important post mortem technique involved injecting a chemical stain in one part of the brain, which over time (24 hours or so) would spread to other parts of the brain neurally connected to the injection site. A widely used stain was horseradish peroxidase (HRP), an enzyme extracted from (no surprise) horseradish. Researchers still use HRP to distinguish different tissue types, but most folks now use fMRI and other modern methods for determining the functional, rather than physical, connections between neural structures.

Getting the Brain to React to Language

With modern technology, neurolinguists can now ask questions about the active links between language and the brain and quantify the answers. Techniques such as electroencephalography and functional magnetic resonance imaging let researchers measure the neural responses of healthy, awake people (see the sidebar "Modernizing the mapping: Living brains" for more on these technologies). There are plenty of people willing to participate in experiments, so neurolinguists can run large studies — with lots of subjects and lots of data collected for each subject — that show how people's brains process different aspects of language. This allows them to accurately measure how grammatical, semantic, lexical, phonological, and phonetic factors — as well as social and environmental factors — are related to brain activity.

Why is it so important to run large studies? Because every brain works differently from every other, and each brain works differently from one moment to the next, even though the task may be the same. But, with enough data, and with statistical methods that reveal consistent patterns of brain activity, neurolinguists can discover which features of brain activity are more or less the same for everybody. More importantly, they've designed tasks that show them how the brain responds to events it expects as well as to surprises.

Electroencephalography (EEG) and magnetic encephalography (MEG) studies look at the timing and location of subjects' cortical responses to contrasting word forms or other language tasks the researcher is examining.

Responding to oddball paradigms

A fundamental component of survival is to be alert to changes in the environment. It stands to reason that your brain has developed sensitive ways of detecting sudden changes in what it senses — be it something you hear, see, smell, taste, or touch. For example, when something new appears in your visual field, especially off to the side, it's important that you catch it in case it turns out to be something that is going to cause trouble. Neuroscientists want to know how your brain does this for all sorts of things. Neurolinguists want to know how sensitive you are to unexpected linguistic events, and they have created experimental tasks that lull you into expecting one thing and then present you with something unexpected — an oddball. What they've found is that your brain reacts in a predictable, consistent way when you're presented with something you don't expect — maybe it's a verb slipped into a long list of nouns, or a two-syllable word in a string of one-syllable words, or the occasional nonsense word in a list of real ones.

Because your brain responds quickly to oddballs, usually in a fraction of a second, the best measurement devices are those that can measure quick changes. EEG and MEG measure neural activity indirectly by measuring the electrical (EEG) and magnetic (MEG) effects near the surface of the cortex. (Remember these devices detect weak signals from outside your skull, so they have to be really sensitive to detect differences in cortical activation!)

Mismatch negativity

Mismatch negativity (MMN) is one of your brain's responses to an oddball paradigm, occurring really fast in response to very low-level differences in a stimulus. Suppose you're in an EEG study and you hear the string of sounds: s s s s s s s s s s d s s s. The *d* sound is not nearly as loud as the *s* sound and is shorter in duration. It takes your brain only 150 milliseconds (ms) to react to this tiny difference by changing its electrical activity. This is only about 100 ms after the auditory signal reaches your brain.

TECHNICAL STUFF

Modernizing the mapping: Living brains

In the 1980s an array of new techniques became available for studying living brains. They weren't overly invasive and in many cases could be used for both human and animal studies. This reduced scientific dependence on animal research alone and made it possible to do real cross-species comparisons. Two primary types of technology have revolutionized neuroscience in general and neurolinguistics in particular:

✔ **Electroencephalography (EEG)** measures electrical activity in the brain and on the brain surface, the *cortex*. EEG is good at telling you when things happen, but it's not as good at telling you exactly where they happen. For example, EEG can tell you the moment your brain reacts to a specific linguistic event such as hearing a French word in a list of English words. Magnetic encephalography (MEG) and near infrared spectroscopy (NIRS) are also used for similar functions.

✔ **functional Magnetic Resonance Imaging (fMRI)** shows which parts of the brain are active by measuring changes in the amount of the brain's blood supply while you perform a certain activity. It's good at telling where things happen in the brain. For example, fMRI shows an increase in activity in a certain area of the brain if you read a newspaper, but it shows no increase when you just imagine holding the newspaper. Researchers interpret the result as evidence that your brain uses that area to read. Magnetic resonance imaging (MRI), which can build detailed 3D models of soft tissue (brains, muscles), serves a similar function.

Because language processing is an activity that occurs in time, you need to know when something happens in the brain in order to connect it with the relevant bit of linguistic behavior. One of the most common uses of EEG is to measure a subject's neural response to a stimulus. Neural activity is chemical, but when neurons generate a nerve impulse, there's also a tiny electrical charge. When many neurons are firing more or less at the same time, the electrical charges produce wave patterns, which can be picked up by sensors on the scalp. When a subject hears a word or sees it written, large groups of neurons respond and the EEG system is able to monitor the resulting electrical waves, which neuroscientists call the *event-related potential* (ERP). MEG measures something similar to ERP, called the *event-related field* (ERF). ERPs and other events of interest are measured from weak electric (EEG) or electromagnetic (MEG) signals generated by the brain in response to some stimulus or cognitive task, such as counting backwards from ten.

In the case of NIRS, cortical activation heats up the tissue close to the surface of the brain. Heat emits infrared light, so NIRS can measure it. All these systems measure very weak signals originating in the brain, but that can be detected from outside the skull. This means that measures can't be made for anything that is farther away from the skull than the cortex and in some cases can be made only for the most superficial layers of the cortex. Because the signals are the weak byproducts of neural activity generated by millions of neurons, they are highly variable. This means many samples have to be recorded and averaged for each experimental condition. For example, if you want to compare the brain's response to a word like *pout* to its response to a non-word like *mout*, you need to repeat each word dozens of times and average the responses to see whether the brain detects the difference.

The lower graph in Figure 16-2a shows an example of a mismatch negativity response to the oddball non-word *ko* tucked into a list of real words. The acoustic signal at the top of the figure shows the sudden onset of sound for the vowel /o/ after the release of the consonant /k/. It's the vowel that tells your brain that this is an oddball. The vertical line connecting the two graphs marks the moment when your brain detects the difference between *ko* and the other words in the list — your brain responds with a negative change of voltage (the mismatch negativity) 150 ms later.

You may be used to plotting negative numbers below the zero line, but event-related potentials (ERP), of which mismatch negativity is a component, are plotted the opposite way. This is because so many of the brain's responses to oddball events are electrically negative.

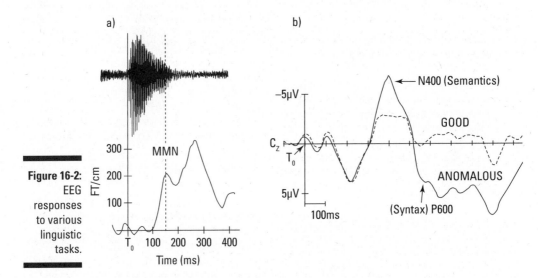

Figure 16-2: EEG responses to various linguistic tasks.

The vertical scales for Figure 16-2 refer to different, but related, electrical measures: femtofarads/centimeter (FT/cm) is a measure of how easily very small electrical currents pass through brain tissue (this is also known as resistance). Voltage (V) measures the strength of the electric field picked up by one or more of the sensors.

Mismatch negativity is used to probe lexical, phonological, and syntactic processing. Interestingly, its effects are easier to get when the subject is being distracted by another task, such as watching a video or reading.

Semantic and syntactic anomalies

Neurolinguists use unexpected stimuli in other ways to find out how your brain responds when the grammatical form (syntax) or meaning (semantics) isn't quite what you expected. For example, there's nothing wrong with the sentence *The cow won't eat.* But *The cow won't teach* is definitely odd because teaching is not something you normally associate with cows. This is an example of anomalous *(wrong)* meaning. Take another sentence, *The cow won't eating.* This is grammatically weird because you never add *-ing* to the verb in sentences like this. In *The cow won't teaching,* both the grammar *(-ing)* and the meaning *(teach)* are wrong.

Lee Osterhout and colleagues at the University of Washington used EEG to measure event-related potentials — the amount of electrical energy your brain generates as it works to process what you are hearing — for sentences like the four just given — normal syntax and semantics, semantically anomalous, syntactically anomalous, and semantically and syntactically anomalous. Figure 16-2b shows that your brain responds to both semantic and syntactic anomalies, but that the responses occur at different times and with different voltage polarities (positive or negative).

In the figure, the solid line represents the event-related potential for a sentence like *The cow won't teaching.* The dashed line represents a normal sentence like *The cow won't eat.* If you compare the two lines, you can see distinct responses to both the semantic anomaly and the syntactic anomaly. About 400 ms after the subject hears a word like *teach,* the brain responds to the semantic anomaly by suddenly increasing the negative voltage — measured in microvolts (μV — millionths of a volt). This response is called the N400 where N stands for, you guessed it, negative, and the 400 represents how long it took the brain to react — 400 ms. Osterhout and others have shown again and again that this is when and how the brain responds to semantic anomalies.

A little later, 600 ms after the last word of the sentence, the brain responds to the syntactic anomaly. This is called the P600 and corresponds to the brain's positive response to the grammatical anomaly caused by adding *-ing* to the verb *teach.* Why the polarity (positive or negative voltage) is different for the two responses is not important. What is important is the indication that brains, just like linguists, distinguish between semantic and syntactic processing. However, you have to be careful how you interpret these results. Just because the syntactic effect (P600) occurs later than the semantic one (N400) does not mean that syntax is processed slower than semantics. Why? Because these responses may indicate intermediate stages of syntactic and semantic processing that just happened to show up in the event-related potentials.

Priming the brain

Priming the brain is a testing technique that helps neurolinguists determine the organization and accessibility of words in the mental lexicon — how words are related by meaning, frequency of use, and similarity of phonological structure. These issues are closely related to questions about how long-term memory works, how items get stored in long-term memory, and what happens to them as you age, to name but a few.

The way priming works is like this: An experimenter presents you with a word and then follows it with another word that is either related to the first one or not. If the second word is related to the first, it should be easier for you to process than the first word was. That is, the first stimulus primes you for the second one. For example, suppose an experimenter presents a list of words to you that all relate to writing: pen, ink, eraser, notebook, and so on. This list is your prime. Your task is to decide whether the next word you hear is a real word or not. If the test word is *pencil,* it should be easier for you to decide that pencil is a real word than if the test word is *doughnut,* which has nothing to do with writing.

What does easier mean? For years, psycholinguists have used reaction time to demonstrate priming effects (in our example, you'd be faster to decide about *pencil* than about *doughnut*). Nowadays, neurolinguists can use the size of the N400 in much the same way; a bigger N400 indicates less familiarity with a word and corresponds to a slower reaction time in a psycholinguistic task.

Making use of the whole brain

Attention defines your relation with the world. When you're awake, you attend to at least some of what your senses tell you — whether you want to or not. Many neuroscientists study attention and its role in managing sensory data. What goes into working memory — that is, how and what sensory data are processed — is an act of attention. To hear the sound of a bird out on the street, your brain has to selectively tune in the bird and tune out, or at least reduce, the other sounds. The same is true with linguistic events. In an fMRI study, for example, the experimenter may tell the subject to pay attention at first to grammatical differences between utterances — this generates activation predominately in the left temporal lobe. Then, she may tell the subject to pay attention to differences in *prosody* (the melodic quality of speech) — in this case, the right temporal lobe activates (for perception of rhythm) as well as the left temporal lobe.

That attention can have such profound effects on your brain's activity is great, but it's also a cause for concern: Your attention wanders when you perform a task again and again and this can affect the experimental results. For example, while responding to an oddball word in a list, you may also be thinking about how your elbow is beginning to itch or you may be fighting to stay awake. Such attentional tidbits affect your brain activity, adding variability to the experimental results and making it even harder for neurolinguists to interpret their results. One way experimenters try to keep their subjects' attention focused is to present them with engaging or difficult tasks. Another approach is to use subjects who have better conscious control of their attention. Evan Thompson (University of Toronto) and others argue that subjects with extensive Buddhist meditation and mindfulness training perform more reliably in fMRI studies of various cognitive tasks.

Part V
Getting from Speaking to Writing

The 5th Wave   By Rich Tennant

©RICHTENNANT

Cartoon English
☆ Yikes! POW
6☆#!ℳ

"Remember, it's 6 before ☆ except after ℳ."

In this part . . .

Of the 6,000 or so human languages on this planet, only a very few are written down. Writing is a technology that changes society in profound ways. In this part, we explain how writing systems come into existence and how writing changes the way you think and even the way you use language.

Chapter 17

Writing Down Language

• •

In This Chapter

▶ Finding out what makes writing possible

▶ Tracing the story of the alphabet

▶ Writing in other cultures and other systems

• •

You text, check e-mail, surf the Internet, read. Writing is everywhere, and because it's everywhere, the concept behind writing may seem obvious. Use marks to represent language? Duh. And yet, the idea of writing isn't obvious — for millennia, it never occurred to our ancestors to write. And when writing was invented about 10,000 years ago, it was a big deal. In fact, it's one of the most important human technological breakthroughs. In this chapter, we tell you how writing got off the ground and where the alphabet you use comes from, and then we take you on a tour of writing around the world.

Writing Is a Technological Achievement

Writing is a technology: It has a design and a purpose. The design: using symbols to represent spoken language. The purpose: keeping records and communicating over long-distances. But the world wasn't always this way.

About 50,000 to 100,000 years ago, in Africa, humans began developing the ability to speak language, to make pictures, and to interpret symbols — the skills that are essential precursors to writing. Surprisingly, humans had these skills for all of 40 millennia — making symbolic pictures and using language — without ever thinking of *using* their symbolic pictures to represent specifically the sounds or words in any language.

The switch to developing true writing systems began only around 8000 BCE (around 10,000 years ago), as part of the transition to agricultural society, and only developed into a full writing system thousands of years later, around 3200 BCE (around 5,200 years ago), with the development of nation states.

Farming leads to writing

Writing was invented only three times: in the ancient Middle East, in China, and in Mesoamerica. And every time writing was invented, it coincided with agriculture. What gives? Agriculture leads to trade, which leads to accounting, which leads to writing. Agricultural societies can feed armies and often have kings and emperors who need to be in contact with their troops and record their exploits — writing makes this possible. Agriculture also leads to calendars because farmers need detailed calendars with notes on which crops to plant at which date — another incentive to use and improve on writing systems in mass-agricultural societies.

In the rest of this chapter, we'll tell you the story of how the switch happened, how writing developed from its earliest origins, and how the social changes connect with these developments.

If someone asks *Is it writing?* ask yourself *Does it represent language?* Drawings tell stories, but this isn't writing. It's writing only if symbols are related specifically to things like sounds, words, and other elements of human speech. With a small sample, it's not easy to decide whether marks are writing — that's why it's hard to date the precise start of writing.

Tracing the Origins of the Alphabet

The alphabet you use — the *Roman alphabet* (Alert: the Romans didn't invent it) — is the fruit of steps taken by ordinary people to solve everyday problems, spread over many centuries and civilizations. This alphabet evolved out of the very first writing system, through a series of four innovations:

- **8000 BCE:** Accounting on clay tokens in the ancient Middle East

- **3200 BCE:** Sounding out words *(rebus writing)* in Mesopotamia and Egypt

- **1900 BCE:** Sound-based writing of consonants *(abjad)* in the Sinai Desert

- **1000 BCE:** Adding in sound-based writing of vowels in Greece

Writing is any system that uses symbols to represent language. Alphabets are a particular kind of writing system: systems that represent the basic sounds *(phonemes)* in a language. Not all writing systems represent sounds, so not all are alphabets. Our writing system (a, b, c, . . ., z) is an alphabet because the symbols, however imperfectly, represent the distinct consonant and vowels of our language. Chinese writing is *not* an alphabet because, though it has some sound components, it largely represents whole words as a single symbol. Ancient Greek was the first true alphabetic system because it represented each speech sound (vowels as well as consonants), and the Roman alphabet is a borrowing from that.

Accounting in Mesopotamia: 8000 BCE

If you jump back to the ancient Middle East around 8000 BCE, a special chain of events was taking place that established a correspondence between written symbols and spoken language:

- **Agriculture:** Humans perfected the first systems of agriculture and could produce much more food on their land.

- **Large numbers of soldiers and workers:** With more food, they could support large numbers of soldiers and workers.

- **Cities and trade goods:** These soldiers and workers built cities and made lots of trade goods. These were the first civilizations.

- **Accounting:** With more stuff being made, there was more stuff to keep track of. And so was born the profession of accounting.

Accountants can't do without writing: They need weigh-bills, bills of lading, inventories, credit slips, and receipts. In a hunter-gatherer society, you remember such things in your head and use witnessing ceremonies to seal the deal. In a citified culture, you keep score by keeping books, and you can't have books without writing. In those early days, accountants used clay tokens to begin keeping track of accounts. If you needed to give someone credit for 10 oxen, you'd give him 10 tokens. The accountants then started carving little pictures into the clay tokens. Need a token for an ox? Draw a little picture of an ox. Need a token for grain? Draw a little picture of grain.

These markings on the tokens represent aspects of speech, including:

- Symbols for names
- Symbols for numerals and units of measure
- Symbols for adjectives

This was a crucial transition. From using marks to record numbers, humans now used symbols to represent spoken language. There's no turning back: For the first time, symbolic marks were used to stand for a word. This is *logographic writing:* It's limited — only some parts of language could be represented, and paper and pens weren't around yet — but it's writing.

The *logogram* for one-word symbols comes from Greek *logos+gram = word+written*. If you want to see some examples of logograms today, just look at the top row of your keyboard: !@#$%& are all logograms as are the numerals 1 to 10. Notice how these logogram symbols — unlike sound-based letters — can represent totally different-sounding words in different languages. For example, the logogram 1 can represent English *one*, but also German *eins*, French *un*, or Japanese *ichi*.

Sounding out words: 3200 BCE

The next breakthrough in developing an alphabet occurred about 3200 BCE, still in the Middle East. Agriculture had taken hold, and two major civilizations — the Sumerians in what is present day Iraq and the Egyptians along the Nile — had established cities, temples, taxes, and big government. These two separate areas were about to take the next big step in the development of writing.

Each group had a long-established writing system of using word-symbols. But a system built on word-symbols was becoming a drag for two reasons:

- ✔ **You need a separate symbol for each word.** A typical language has thousands and thousands of words, so you need thousands and thousands of different symbols — it's hard to keep track of them all.

- ✔ **You can't find pictures for abstract concepts.** If you use pictures to represent words — as the Sumerians and the Egyptians did — you find that while drawing a picture for *arrow* is easy (↑), it's hard to draw something abstract like *life*.

Both the Sumerians and Egyptians needed to expand their writing beyond basic word-symbols. But how? Again, necessity was the mother of invention. The scribes discovered a trick that's still used to this day. To see how it works, try reading the following sentence: 👁 **8 π**. If you guessed *I ate pie*, you'd be good at reading ancient scripts. This is how scribes squeezed extra meaning from symbols: If a word-symbol sounded like another word, they'd use the same symbol for both. Here are a couple of examples from Sumerian:

- ✔ **The reed symbol ⟨ goes with /gi/:** The Sumerian words for *reed* and *reimburse* are both /gi/. To get mileage out of the existing reed symbol, scribes start to use the reed-mark also for *reimburse*.

- ✔ **The arrow symbol ⚡ goes with /ti/:** The Sumerian words for *arrow* and *life* are both /ti/. It's easy to draw an arrow, but it's hard to draw a life, so scribes started to use the arrow symbol for *life* as well.

Using the sound-the-same trick, Sumerian and Egyptian scribes progressed quickly — they didn't need as many symbols because they could recycle them. And now they could represent abstract words — like *reimburse* or *life* — with existing symbols. This is *rebus writing* and is a major step towards sound-based writing. By moving the meaning of the symbol to the sound of a syllable, a line has been crossed. For the first time, humans were representing the sounds — in this case syllable-sounds — of language.

Sounding out the first consonant

Another way to get mileage out of logograms is to use the first-consonant principle, which linguists call *acrophonic writing.* For example, suppose you use the pictogram ♨ for the word spider. If you want to write the s-sound, you could use ♨. Now try identifying the following word: ✎ ♨ ♨ ♨ ♨ ☎. If you guess *psssst* — from pencil, spider, and telephone — then scribehood is an excellent career choice. The scribes used this trick in both Egypt and Sumeria. The Egyptians found it so handy that they developed signs for all 24 of their consonants, making for a more flexible system and getting close to a full alphabet.

If anyone asks you which kind of writing system is most *efficient,* you can answer: a sound-based system. When you start using symbols to represent sounds, the writing system can get by with far fewer symbols because you only need enough symbols to represent each sound in the language (a fairly small set). In logographic systems, with a symbol for each word, you need huge numbers of symbols.

Getting stuck with too many symbols

The Sumerians and Egyptians got to the point where an individual symbol could represent one of three things: a concept, syllable, or a consonant. The writing system was hard to decipher and took years to master. Writing and reading were slow and laborious and in the hands of a small, skilled elite. And the scribes were probably making writing more complicated on purpose: A system that's hard to read provided them with job security.

In order to help them figure out which word a symbol was referring to, Egyptian and Sumerian writing used extra symbols — called *determinatives* — that didn't represent words or sounds but were clues to help the reader interpret other symbols. For example, Egyptian determinatives indicated 'this next part is about gods', or 'I'm talking about a body part here', or 'this word here is a plant word'.

Egyptian writing on papyrus and wood continued until around 400 CE, at which point everyone forgot what the symbols meant. Linguists had a hard time deciphering the Egyptian system — it was picture-like, so they mistakenly thought it was purely logographic. It wasn't deciphered until the 19th century, with a key clue coming from a stone that Napoleon's troops found in the Egyptian desert in 1799, called the *Rosetta Stone.* The Rosetta Stone had Egyptian hieroglyphs with translations into two other languages; the French linguist Jean-François Champollion cracked the code in 1822. If you're ever in London, England, stop by the British Museum and check out the Rosetta Stone.

The fate of the first writing systems

Sumerian writing developed from pictures into a stylized system called *cuneiform*, written in straight lines by sticking wedges into clay tablets. A number of other cultures in the region adapted Sumerian cuneiform, including the Semitic Akkadian and Hittite cultures. But eventually the whole approach died out around 200 CE. You can see an example of the evolution of a cuneiform symbol (the logogram for *ox*) in the following figure.

Concentrating on consonants: 1900 BCE

By 1900 BCE, writing had spread all over the Middle East, and lots of people in the Sinai — in northern Egypt — had borrowed and adapted Egyptian hieroglyphs. These desert folks made a key improvement: They simplified the system. Word-symbols? No thanks. Syllable symbols? Nope. They kept only the symbols for consonants. Everything else, they tossed in the sand.

Writing only consonants: Abjadic writing

A consonant-only system is more effective: You no longer spend years learning hundreds or thousands of symbols. Assuming you're okay ignoring the vowels, as everyone did anyway at the time, you only need about 24 symbols to write down a language. That's something anyone can learn easily and quickly. Linguists call such consonant-only writing systems *abjads* — these systems don't have distinct symbols for the vowels, except for optional markers, called *diacritics*. We don't know who the first consonant-only folks were, but the oldest surviving examples are at Turquoise Mine in the Sinai and at Serabit el-Khadem in modern Egypt. The funny thing is the examples are graffiti carved into the rock walls of the mine. All of which reinforces two important life lessons. First, sometimes to improve a system you need to simplify it. Second, graffiti-artists really do leave works of lasting historical significance.

Spreading the word: What the Phoenicians did

Phoenician culture flourished around 1500 BCE in what is today Lebanon and Syria. These folks were not innovative with writing — they simply borrowed from the Sinai desert-dwellers. But what they lacked in originality, they made up for in public relations — the Phoenicians loved to travel. They traded all over the Mediterranean region, and, everywhere they went, they showed off their cool new sound-based (though still consonant-only) alphabet. Their trading and sharing is a key reason why you're reading these letters today.

The advantages of a sound-based system were obvious to most of the people the Phoenicians traded with, and their system was borrowed and adapted many times. Several of the world's writing systems descend from this system. If you check out Phoenician writing, you'll find that most of the characters are related to our capital letters, though often turned in different directions or with modified shapes. For example:

- ✔ *B* comes from the Phoenician symbol ⌐, the logogram for house, which in Phoenician is *beth* /bɛθ/.

- ✔ *K* comes from the Phoenician symbol ≯, the logogram for palm of a hand, which in Phoenician is *kaph* /kæf/.

- ✔ Many vowel symbols (including *A, E*) and many consonant symbols (including *Z, K, R, T, W, M, H, D*) are recognizable in Phoenician writing.

In Phoenician, *A* and *E* stand for consonants: *A* represents a glottal stop and *E* represents the consonant sound /h/. Figure 17-1 shows you how *A* evolved from the older Egyptian pictogram.

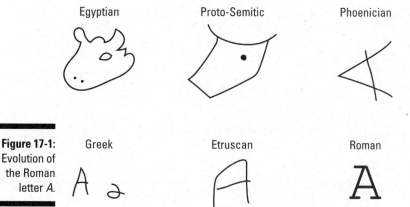

Egyptian   Proto-Semitic   Phoenician

Figure 17-1: Evolution of the Roman letter *A*.

Greek   Etruscan   Roman

Putting in vowels: 1000 BCE

Around 1000 to 900 BCE, the Greeks, impressed by the Phoenicians' consonant-based writing system, borrowed the system and adapted it to their language. And that — by a happy accident — led to the first fully phonetic alphabet. Greek belongs to a different language family than Phoenician does, which means that the Greeks have a different sound-system. In particular, they don't have the same consonants that the Phoenicians do. For example, they don't have a glottal stop, which frees up the *A* symbol for another sound. At first, it must have seemed like one of those not-so-exciting problems: What do we do with the leftovers? But then, just as great recipes are discovered by people trying to use up their doggy-bags, the Greeks discovered that there was something, after all, they could do with the *A* and other unused symbols — hey, we can use these for the vowel sounds!

Consonant-only writing systems

Arabs and Jews borrowed their writing systems — that's the Arabic script and the Hebrew writing system — from the Phoenicians via another language, Aramaic. All these Middle Eastern systems are *abjads:* Only consonant sounds are written down. You have to wonder why the desert-living graffiti artists in the Sinai (and others later in the region) only cared about consonants. It's related to the linguistic properties of their languages. Egyptian, Phoenician, Hebrew, Arabic, and most of the other languages spoken in the Middle East are part of the Semitic language family (itself part of the Afro-Asiatic family — see Chapter 10 for more info on language families). Semitic languages have meaningful units (morphemes) that consist only of consonants (see Chapter 5 for more info on these kinds of consonant-only units). For example, in modern Arabic, the consonantal root /k...t...b/ is related to anything having to do with writing and books. Vowels supply other meaningful units to build words: *kataba* 'he wrote', *kutub* 'books', *kutubii* 'bookdealer'.

So, after 7,000 years of writing, the first fully sound-based writing system, and the first true alphabet, were born. It's proven to be the most successful alphabet in history: easy to use, easy to learn, and capable of representing all of a language simply and effectively. This new phonetic alphabet was something everyone could master and fast — the Volkswagen of writing systems. From Greece it spread to the Etruscans (an ancient Italian people), who adapted it. The Romans borrowed it, adapted it some more, and then modestly renamed it the *Roman alphabet*. It spread widely, with adaptations and adjustments, through their empire, including, when the Romans conquered England, us.

Cyrillic and runic writing

Around 860 CE, Saint Cyril, a missionary to the Slavs, borrowed a bunch of symbols from the Greek alphabet, threw in a few of his own, and started spreading this alphabet among the Slavic people. For example, he used A for Roman A, but he used Д for D. This system was originally called the *Glagolitic alphabet*, but it was adapted into what became the modern *Cyrillic alphabet*. Cyrillic writing is what you see in Russian writing, like on those posters for *Borat*. Major users include Russians, Bulgarians, Serbians, Ukrainians, and Macedonians. Some non-Slavic folks use it too, including Mongolians, Romani, and Tajiks.

Runes or runic writing started among Germanic and Scandinavian tribes around 150 CE, based on some old alphabets (not the Roman alphabet, but also ultimately derived from Greek) that had been in use in Italy. This system of runic writing lasted until about 1100 CE, at which point the burly Christianized Norsemen switched over to the Roman alphabet.

Writing Around the World

Writing systems have been invented from scratch only three times in history — once in the Middle East, once in China, and once in Mesoamerica. All other writing systems have either been re-invented based on contact with writing in other cultures or by borrowing, which is the most common way of getting a writing system.

Writing gets around: From Mesopotamia to Egypt to Rome

Archeologists have a hard time determining whether Mesopotamians or Egyptians had the earliest system of writing and how the two systems are connected. The best guess is that the Mesopotamians were first and that they shared their idea with the Egyptians through trade. But the Egyptian system is distinct, and nobody has yet found a direct connection between the systems. These ancient systems led to the Roman alphabet you now use and which is the most borrowed from or re-invented alphabet around.

Writing an empire into existence

The Roman alphabet is the oldest and most widespread writing system. Some historians think that, rather than the Romans spreading the alphabet, it's the alphabet that spread Rome. Writing is a key tool for allowing a centralized power to communicate with a widespread and complex empire. How else are you going to send orders from Rome to Scotland and back? Phonetic writing — with a small number of symbols and its adaptability to different words and languages — was as necessary as the well-drilled Roman legions.

Borrowing an alphabet

The Roman alphabet is the most-borrowed writing system in history: It's been adapted to the largest number of languages and is used by the largest number of speakers. Languages have different inventories of consonants and vowels and that means that almost every case of borrowing results in either leftover characters or not enough characters. Leftover characters are easy to toss or adapt for other sounds, but what do you do if you don't have enough characters?

- ✔ **Add new symbols:** For example, linguists use the symbol [β] for the voiced bilabial fricative sound found in Ewe, a language spoken in Ghana.

- ✔ **Add digraphs:** Combine two characters to represent a sound. For example, English uses *sh* to represent the sound [ʃ], as in *ship*.

- ✔ **Add diacritics:** For example, rather than using two letters for one sound, the Czech alphabet adds a mark over *c* to make *č* to represent the sound in English at the start of *church*.

Using symbols for syllables and words: Out of China

The Chinese are the second group to invent writing from scratch. Their system — which was up and running by 1300 BCE and standardized by 220 BCE — follows a familiar pattern of development:

- ✓ **Agriculture:** The start of Chinese writing coincides with the development of mass agriculture, in their case rice.

- ✓ **Accounting, calendars, and government:** The symbols are first used for accounting, calendars, and Big Government.

- ✓ **Stylization:** The symbols start out as pictograms, but over time they become stylized and more abstract.

- ✓ **Specialization:** As with all logographic systems, the number of symbols is huge and requires years of learning and specialized skills to master. In modern Chinese, a well-educated person learns up to 4,000 logograms.

But the system doesn't remain purely logographic. Over time, Chinese scribes improved the system and introduced the following:

- ✓ **Syllabic writing:** They interpreted some symbols as the sound of a syllable and used it whenever that syllable occurs.

- ✓ **Disambiguating symbols:** They added extra symbols — Chinese scholars call them *radicals* — to give clues about other symbols: 氵 'this is something about water'; 木 'this is something about the eye'.

- ✓ **Combinations of symbols:** They combined symbols that add up logically. For example, the symbol for 'tree' is 木; doubling the symbol 林 means 'grove'; and tripling it 森 means 'forest'.

Some linguists call Chinese a *logosyllabic* writing system because it has both logograms (word-symbols) and symbols used for syllables.

Re-inventing an alphabet: Korean hangul

In 1440 CE, King Sejong of Korea — who liked to go by *Sejong the Great* — was unhappy with his kingdom's writing system, an unwieldy syllabic script called *hanja,* based on Chinese logograms. It was hard to learn, complicated to use, and had a huge number of symbols. It made Sejong feel like a Mac-user with a PC-loaner, so he ordered that a new writing system be built. So what did his team of advisors do? Without having seen a single consonant or vowel symbol, they developed a phonetic alphabet that represented every individual sound: every vowel, every consonant! Koreans called their alphabet *hangul,* and every year on October 9th they celebrate *hangul day* to remind themselves how cool they are to be the sort of people who invent an alphabetic system out of non-alphabetic characters. Strangely, South Korean kids still learn the 1800 characters of the old *hanja,* maybe to remind themselves how lucky they are to be writing phonetically the rest of their lives. The *hangul* is a singular intellectual achievement: In one fell swoop, Korean scholars achieved what took the Western World 2,000 years. However impressive, the *hangul* doesn't count as a writing system that was invented from scratch. That's because the Koreans already had the syllabic *hanja* system (itself borrowed from Chinese) before they developed the alphabetic *hangul* system.

Writing by syllables

Instead of writing down the individual sounds of a language, another approach to writing is to write down the syllables of language. This is called *syllabic writing*.

Using syllabic writing for languages with simple syllables

With syllabic writing, there's one symbol for each syllable, so words like *bi, bip, bo,* and *bom* each have a symbol. This works well with simple syllables, but goes haywire for complex syllables. Here's why:

- ✔ **Simple syllables:** If your language has only a relatively small number of different syllables, then syllabic writing can work fairly well. For example, if your language has only syllables of the shape CV *(ha)* or V *(Oh!),* then 5 vowels and 20 consonants would require not too many syllables — around 105 (5 x 20 for all the possible CV syllables, plus 5 for just the V-types).

- ✔ **Complex syllables:** But if your language has complex syllables, like CCVCC *(spuds)* or CCCVCCC *(sprints),* you'll quickly get into trouble with syllabic writing. You'd need hundreds, more likely thousands, of symbols to cover all the possible syllables. For example, if your language has again just 5 vowels and 20 consonants, then writing all the possible CCCVCCC syllables would require 320,000,000 (20 X 20 X 20 X 5 X 20 x 20 x 20) symbols! Of course, not all logically possible syllable shapes are found in a given language, so you could probably get by with thousands — rather than millions — of symbols. But that's still a lot of symbols.

Inventing a syllabic script in Mesoamerica

The Mayans, in what is today Mexico and Guatemala, started writing around 300 BCE (or perhaps earlier) — they are the third group to invent writing. The Mayan system — which they painted on ceramics, walls, and bark-paper — is a mixture of logographic and syllabic writing. For example, the symbol 𝕒 for 'fish, fin', pronounced /ka/, was eventually used for the sound /ka/. Knowledge of the system was lost, and linguists got fooled for many years by the picture-like quality of the symbols and mistakenly thought it was logographic. They deciphered the script only when they realized that it was partly syllabic.

Reinventing syllabic writing in Arkansas

Sequoyah, a Cherokee blacksmith living in Arkansas in the early 1800s, never spoke English and never learned to read or write English. Observing white people using marks on paper, he figured out that these symbols represented language. Sequoyah thought this was cool: He manned up and, without asking for help, invented a syllabic writing system from scratch. This is how he did it:

- **Marks represent transactions:** Sequoyah started using marks to keep track of his business transactions. He was a blacksmith, remember.

- **Symbols represent words:** He then developed a logographic system, but soon realized that it sucked. Like every other logographic system, it quickly got out of hand, requiring hundreds, then thousands, of symbols.

- **Symbols represent syllables:** Realizing that it's more efficient to represent sounds, on his second try, Sequoyah linked each symbol to a syllable: **S** represents /sa/; **b** represents /si/; **4** represents /se/.

Many of Sequoya's symbols are borrowed and adapted from the Roman alphabet. Cherokee uses a syllabic writing system, so the values of the symbols are unrelated to how you sound out the same symbols. The system was adapted for printing in 1828 and remains in use. Today, just as Sequoya intended, this efficient, sound-based system helps to support the language and the cultural identity of the Cherokee people.

One writing system for many languages?

Sound-based writing is efficient, but systems based on word-symbols, such as Chinese, are also portable. For example, the symbol ♀ works for English and French, even though the words differ: *man* versus *homme*. In fact, Chinese isn't a language: It includes Mandarin and Cantonese, which aren't mutually intelligible, and about 20 other languages. And even though Cantonese and Mandarin speakers use the same characters, they can't necessarily read each other's writing, largely because of the non-logographic extensions of the Chinese system. So if you hear that the Chinese writing system is used for many languages, you should take that with a grain of salt.

On the other hand, Japanese uses four writing systems: logographic *kanji*; syllabic *hiragana* (invented by the Japanese for regular words); syllabic *katakana* (used for loanwords and onomatopoeia and words that imitate sounds, like English *buzz*); and *romaji* (alphabetic characters used for computing and advertising). By 57 CE, the Japanese had borrowed and adapted Chinese logographic characters. With updates every 700 years or so, these *kanji* characters are still in use. The Japanese also introduced symbols for syllables, inventing the *hiragana* syllabic writing system. When writing, they combine the systems: They often write a word-root with the Chinese-derived *kanji* symbol and write affixes and grammatical markers in the syllabic *hiragana*.

Chapter 18

Writing Changes You

*W*riting changes you mentally, physically, and socially by making new connections between your brain, your language, and your social world. That's a lot of change, but there's more. Because writing enables communication across distances, writing changes the world. This chapter gives you a look at how writing shapes your language, how you use writing to connect socially and understand the world, and how fast electronic writing is shaping the future.

Writing Changes Your Language

Writing uses a different medium for linguistic expression than speaking does. When you speak, the sound of what you say exists for a moment and then is gone. In most situations you say whatever comes to mind without much planning — unless you're in court trying not to get tripped up by your testimony. By contrast, writing proceeds more slowly than speech or thought, and you have to use your hands or, in the case of dictation, someone else's hands to write or type the words. And after you write something down, it may last forever. The relative permanence of writing lets you review and edit what you write — you can compare what you are writing now with what you wrote a month ago. This allows you to craft complex grammatical structures that are rich enough in meaning to stand on their own without further explanation. The *aesthetics* (what's conventionally considered to be cool) of writing are different from those of speaking.

These properties of writing that distinguish it from speech — grammar, permanence, independence, and visual aesthetics — have profound effects on your language and what you do with it. E-mailing and texting, however, are narrowing the gap between writing and speaking, while changing both.

Handwriting is slower than typing, and both of these are slower than speaking. Handwriting averages about 30 words per minute while a fast typist can type 120 words per minute. Fast talkers, like auctioneers, can produce 400 to 500 words per minute (about what's on this page) — about 15 times the speed of handwriting!

Writing changes your grammar

The context or situation has a huge effect on how you use words. Just as you can't write the way you speak, you can get in trouble for speaking the way you write. If you use elaborate vocabulary when you speak, people may complain that you sound like a dictionary. Learning how to use words properly in these different contexts depends on learning which word-grammar combinations are better suited for speaking and which are better suited for writing. For example, you get in trouble if you don't write complete sentences or change topics from one sentence to the next. But you rarely hear a complete sentence in spoken conversation because people often change topics in mid-sentence and leave the old one hanging. (For more on context and the medium of language, see Chapter 8.)

The permanence of writing reduces the load on memory — neither the reader nor the writer needs to hold everything in memory all at once. As a result, writing can be bigger than speech: It allows for bigger words, bigger phrases, bigger sentences, and bigger topical groups like paragraphs. To see what we're talking about, take a look at the following phrases:

in the park or *on the other side of the street*

Both phrases are common to both spoken and written language, but you would never hear the following phrases in a conversation:

that somber, otherworldly demeanor, characteristic of the abraded relics of prolonged conflict

Using multiple adjectives — *somber, otherworldly* — to modify a noun is possible in speaking, but not nearly so common as it is in writing. The use of elaborate clauses to modify a previous phrase is even less common in spoken language. You would be more likely to say something short like

that gone look, typical of war victims

Long sentences are rare in speaking, but they're rampant in most writing, like the one taken from the earlier paragraph:

Related to permanence and its usefulness to memory, writing tends to be bigger than speech: It allows for bigger words, bigger phrases, bigger sentences, and bigger topical groups like paragraphs.

In general, written language is simply less urgent. The time it takes to write is *independent* of the time it takes to read. The persistence of the written word on the page or screen allows you, the reader, to review with your eyes, rather than with your memory. As you read you visually scan back and forth between what has come earlier and what is coming next. This languid approach to telling a story or explaining an idea allows larger units such as paragraphs, sections, and chapters. The writer uses this expanded structure to make sure that what gets said is thorough and clear because there'll be no chance for the reader to ask for clarification along the way. As a reader, you are not forced to process language at a fixed rate, the way you have to when you listen to someone, so you can pace yourself to the complexity of what is written, to your level of interest, and to other factors that influence how quickly you can or want to read what is written.

Learning grammar can also influence writing. Because writing is a visually guided language medium, it is easier to become aware of certain grammatical structures in their written form. A good example of this are *inflections* like the *-s* marking the plural of *cat-s* or the *-ed* that marks the past tense in *walk-ed*. In the late 1970s, Karl Zeigler of Indiana University was working with students with poor writing skills and discovered that their writing improved impressively when they learned German inflectional endings (the endings attached to nouns, adjectives, and verbs), determiners equivalent to English *a* and *the,* and the two irregular verbs *haben* and *sein* that correspond to English *have* and *be*. Oddly, this exposure did not help them learn German or any other foreign language. But learning these grammatical forms made them more aware of how writing is put together.

Writing changes your spoken language

Writing (and reading) greatly affects your spoken language, but not always in socially acceptable ways. For example, you may sound *bookish* if you use a more extensive vocabulary than usual in conversation, which can lead to unfortunate stereotypes. Real men, for example, are not expected to know works like *fuchsia* (bright purplish red). People typically use just 500 to 1,000 words in daily conversation, but reading and writing increase the size of your extended vocabulary, which hovers around 20,000 words for a college graduate. Words you read more frequently can enter your working vocabulary and bring along their stylized use. So new vocabulary brings new grammatical forms into your speech.

Writing also affects the way you introduce information, which can influence your speech. When you speak, you need to hold your listener's attention. In spoken English, grammatical word order tends to be straightforward, and information gets introduced piecemeal. Compare the two simple spoken sentences with the more complex written sentence:

Form: Subject + Verb + Object [+ Indirect Object]

Spoken 1: *George (S) sold (V) the farm (O).*

Spoken 2: *He (S) got (V) two million (O) [for it] (IO).*

Written: *George (S) got (V) two million (O) [for the farm he sold] (IO).*

The two spoken sentences introduce key information in a natural progression from *what got sold* to *for how much*. The written sentence, however, makes the listener wait a long time to find out *what he got two million for*. The more complex structure of writing also changes the rhythm of the language.

Because writing is usually read silently and often written one word or short phrase at a time, it does not necessarily follow the same rhythmic patterns typical of your speech. In fact, our university students often complain that reading assignments are hard to understand because they are not written in a style they are "used to hearing." In particular, it is the organization of the information — the way it is introduced — rather than the vocabulary that causes the written form to be so difficult for them. Some modern writers try to use spoken language to change the written form by writing in a more conversational style. There's a problem with this though — spoken language changes constantly, but a book's written style lasts until you throw away the book.

Writing changes your comprehension

Writing introduces a new dimension to the way language shapes our experience of the world and of ourselves. Spoken language happens so fast that you have no real chance to analyze what you say. Of course, you know when an interaction goes well — you succeed in getting your point across or you feel good about a conversation. But you can't see how your language use both reflects and shapes your thoughts and guides your experience of the world. Writing, on the other hand, removes the damaging effects of time on memory and shapes the link between your thinking, your language, and your communicative purpose, changing each of them. Writing changes your comprehension with consequences for the way your brain organizes and processes language. Writing also helps you figure out what you think.

Writing provides a sketchpad for thought

For most folks, writing is a better medium than speaking for developing complex thoughts. When you're talking, by the time you get all the pieces together for some hint of a big idea, you've begun to forget how the earlier pieces fit together. Writing, on the other hand, provides a sketchpad where you can develop your thinking about something. Writing lets you shape and record pieces of an idea, allowing you to set out a logical sequence of conditions and consequences. And while you're trying to get the right combination and sequence of pieces to fit together, you don't have to worry about forgetting what came before — it's right there on the page or computer screen. Writing, whether it's a book like this or an entry in a private journal — allows people to explore their thoughts and hone their ability to think, including creating rational arguments, artistic expression, and detailed descriptive sequences.

Writing doesn't match the flow of thought

Many people master the art of speaking at what must be close to their rate of thought, allowing them — for better or worse — to talk "without thinking." However, most people can't come close to this in writing. For one thing, they can't write (or type) fast enough to keep pace with their thinking. In addition, the flow of thought itself doesn't quite fit the grammatical frame of writing. Have you ever had the experience where you "hear" what you're thinking in your head, but no matter how hard you try, you can't quite write it down that way? This is an instance where your writing has to re-write your thinking.

Writing can be revised

Writing changes how you think and talk about things. You can organize your writing spatially — for example, by printing out the term paper you are writing for school, you can set the pages side by side and examine the way the contents are organized. In the days before word processors, reorganizing your text involved cutting and pasting your writing with scissors and paste. Of course, this process is almost effortless now, but it has the same effect — you can organize your writing in mobile, independent chunks, group these chunks thematically, and even group themes to address some general topic from a number of different perspectives. This grouping of groups, often referred to as *hierarchical organization,* aids your thinking substantially. You can build bigger ideas from smaller ones or, going the other way, generate a bunch of small ideas from a bigger one. Neither of these processes works very well in spoken communication — it puts too much load on you, the speaker, and your listener.

Writing shows you who you are

Writing can also reveal the unexpected. This happens in journal writing, poetry, and intimate correspondence. It's where you start with a mere glimpse of an idea and suddenly, as you write, ideas and opinions emerge that you didn't know you had! Something similar can happen when you carry on a silent, speech-like, internal dialogue, but again writing provides a broader canvas to work with. In writing a journal entry or a personal letter, it is the structure of the idea that expands. In writing poetry, you use the form of the poem — the choice of particular words and grammatical conventions — to evoke a sense of the idea, story, or emotions that the phrases convey.

Writing electronically streamlines your language

The advent of electronic writing brought about a huge change in the way people write and the way they use writing to communicate. When people first began to use e-mail and electronic bulletin boards extensively in the 1980s, they used the same formalities they had used in traditional correspondence. However, several factors have led to more relaxed grammatical rules and less concern for semantic consistency: the potential for immediate turnaround between correspondents, the increased number of correspondences, and increased anonymity among correspondents.

Streamlining grammar

E-mail and text conversations can take place almost instantaneously when both correspondents are online. This makes these electronic exchanges much more conversational. Because typing is slower than speech, people reduce or drop time-consuming formalities such as salutations — no more *Dear So and So*, just *Hi, Hey,* or nothing at all. As in spoken conversations, thoughts are often not fully expressed. For example, you may be explaining why you are late to meet someone and begin your list of delays with one delay such as *went to the store, the bank, . . . ,* where the ellipses indicate a longer list, but you spare your reader the agony of having to read them all. Other shortcuts abound: Words get shortened, and common phrases and emotive expressions get abbreviated, like *LOL* for "laugh out loud," or represented by *emoticons* such as J or simple text character versions such :) or :(. *Are you* becomes *r u, talk to you* becomes *t2u,* and your name becomes *E* for "Eric," *R-M* for "Rose-Marie," and so on.

Streamlining zeros in on key information at the expense of traditional sentence structure. For example, if you are answering a question about yourself and your reader knows that's what you're doing, then why refer to yourself? In response to *what're ya doin,* you're likely to say things like

- ✔ *sittin around* — instead of *I'm just sitting around.*
- ✔ *homework* — instead of *I'm doing my homework.*

These examples show reduction of the sentence subject, *I,* and the auxiliary verb, *am,* and even simplification of spelling, *sittin* for "sitting." What makes these reductions work communicatively, even when novel, is that they strip away contextual information, not content, in ways that are predictable from the common knowledge you and your reader have about your language.

Minimizing content

Conversational content also becomes streamlined. Reference to content, once established, may not be revisited in subsequent exchanges. For example, if an e-mail exchange began with a question about a specific person, *Charlie,* chances are *Charlie* won't get mentioned by name again — rather *Charlie* is replaced by pronoun forms such as *he, him,* or *his.*

Message content is stripped to the bare essentials, especially when correspondents know each other. For example, if someone is preparing a phonology lecture, they may send out the following e-mail to a colleague that they know well:

Hey, need to teach phonology. Have refs? Thanks.

Writing gizmos

If you've spent any time on the computer, you have probably used software tools designed to help you write. Most common are tools that check your spelling and grammar and that auto-complete partially typed words and common phrases. What makes these interesting is that each depends on some aspect of written language remaining relatively constant: dictionaries and spelling, the rules of written grammar, and certain forms of phrasal expression.

✔ **Spellcheckers** search for words in a document and check them against an electronic dictionary, indicating words it cannot match against entries in the dictionary. If the stored dictionary is large and gets updated every now and then to include new words, then the spellchecker mainly finds misspelled rather than unknown words. Spellcheckers are the most widely used electronic aid to writing because they work and save you the effort of checking your spelling, either while you type or later when you check your work.

✔ **Grammar checkers** depend on a complex electronic dictionary and a fairly elaborate model of written grammar to judge whether what you write is grammatical. The dictionary contains word spellings and grammatical classifications: noun, verb, adjective, and so on. Words with multiple meanings or grammatical uses, like *lead,* require more than one entry. Verbs in particular have to be indexed by what can follow them grammatically — for example, *transitive*

verbs can take a *direct object,* as in *I read **the book,*** while *intransitive* verbs cannot: *I looked **for him**.* Using sentence punctuation to mark the boundaries of the grammar check, the checker then tries to fit the string of words to a grammatical template for an acceptable sentence such as *subject + verb (transitive) + object.* To do a reasonable job, the grammar checker needs to predict tens of thousands of sentences, using numerous grammatical templates that allow for active and passive sentences and inclusion of prepositional phrases. The bad news is that this is nowhere near good enough and many people turn the grammar checker off.

✔ **Auto-completion** completes words by fitting whatever you have typed so far to a dictionary of possible words. For example, you type *Cinci* and it suggests *Cincinnati* — correctly spelled. Because the goal is to find the right expansion for what you type, not present you with a bunch of choices, the auto-completion system needs to limit the possible answers. The most common way to do this is by word frequency. Some word dictionaries index each entry by frequency. So, if you type *stam,* the system may choose high-frequency *stamp* instead of *stamina, stampede,* or *stammer* as the most likely completion. But, if you live in Calgary, home of the Calgary Stampede, *stampede* and *stamina* may be more frequent than *stamp.* A smart auto-completion system "learns" your word and phrase preferences based on how often you use them.

A traditional letter of request, on the other hand, may contain a lot of important information about the relationship between the correspondents, how urgent the request is, and a more indirect approach to the question, so the reader feels more obligated to comply. Streamlined writing often makes people more blunt about asking for something, but that same bluntness makes it easier for the other person to say *no*. In the phonology example, the request is made with four short phrases that fit on one line of text. Neither the sender nor the receiver is identified in the text; there's no need, because the e-mail *header* tells the reader who the sender is. The message does give a minimal greeting, *hey,* which is now more common than *hi* when used alone (*hi* has replaced *dear* in salutations with names). After the salutation is a concise, but general, request for reference materials on phonology. The sender assumes the reader will ask for more information, if necessary. Thus, the reader may respond with a request for more details or may answer: *sorry, too busy.*

Writing Changes Your Brain

Just as you can't think for very long about speech production without thinking about its counterpart, speech perception, you can't really understand writing without considering reading, which is the perception of writing. Most studies of neural processing focus on perception of writing for the simple reason that the existing technology can't make reliable measurements when the subject moves — writing involves physical motion, whereas perception doesn't. Therefore, little research literature exists on how writing, independent of reading, changes the brain. Someday, neurolinguists will have the tools to distinguish between how writing and reading skills affect brain organization. For now, we show you how certain neural disorders and brain damage can affect one, the other, or both reading and writing.

Literacy impacts brain function

Because literacy is so new to human history, neurolinguists don't think it has caused any substantial changes to brain structure. However, learning to read and write uses brain structure and takes over some of the brain's processing power, so the question to ask is *How does literacy interact with older processes and functions?* The answer is good and bad — literacy can help existing neural processes but also steal neural resources from other functions.

Literacy improves brain function: Dexterous reaching

Processing written language requires that you use both sides of the brain. A lot of the functions specific to language processing are *hemispherically lateralized* — located on one side of the brain or the other. For example, much of language comprehension is done in the left hemisphere in *Wernicke's area* and the *inferior parietal lobe.* (For a map of different functional brain structures for language processing, see Chapter 16.) However, you use your visual system to read and write — moving your eyes, processing visual information, combining visuomotor and somatosensory information for eye-hand coordination, especially for the finely detailed characteristics of text. This means a lot of information has to move back and forth between the two sides of the brain and be combined. This is called *bihemispheric integration,* which becomes highly developed in learning to read and write. As a result, literate people can reach objects faster in certain parts of their visual field than non-literate people.

Literacy hinders brain function: See faces or see words

Reading makes extensive use of your visual system. And there's pretty good evidence that your literacy interferes with your ability to process other important visual information such as faces. The particular area of the brain affected is the visual word form area (VWFA), also called the *Brain's letterbox* by Stanislas Dehaene of France. The VWFA is specific to written language because it actively responds only to reading — there's no response during perception of spoken language and there's no response in the brains of people who can't read when shown the same words. However, the linguistic bias in the names for this brain area may be unfortunate because the VWFA also responds to faces, especially in people who don't read. In other words, the presumably more ancient function of the VWFA has something to do with face processing, but literacy has caused this function to be reduced.

The buck stops at the angular gyrus

The *angular gyrus* is a cortical structure that sits about halfway between Wernicke's area and the visual cortex on the *occipital lobe* (towards the back of the brain on top). When this little area gets damaged, it causes a lot of reading and writing problems — notably, the inability to read *(alexia)* and to write *(dysgraphia).* It also shows functional abnormalities in *dyslexia* (difficulty reading). Its location on the edge of the inferior parietal lobe, where so much of the processing related to comprehension occurs, suggests that damage to the angular gyrus interferes with understanding the visual information, but that the visual information itself is not affected.

Writing improves word memory

Reading and writing change the way you learn and store words in the brain. Neurolinguists have compared the time it takes to recall words like *ball,* which is pronounced identically with *bawl,* and words like *tall,* which does not have spelling alternatives. The idea is that if there is only one spelling, the word is likely to be identified faster than if there are multiple spellings, which would indicate that your brain has to look up the written form of the word. Sure enough, spoken words with multiple spelled forms are retrieved more slowly from memory.

Putting a dent in literacy: Television

Television took post–World War II America by storm. Where radio shows could follow you around the house as you did your chores, the full effect of TV, namely sound and picture, rooted viewers to one location and left little option to do anything else at the same time, exercising and ironing being two notable exceptions. Approximately two generations of North Americans, beginning with the post-war *baby boomers,* grew up watching increasing amounts of TV every day. TV time was time not spent reading, writing, playing games, or running around outside. As a result, TV got the rap for reduced literacy and poorer mental and physical health.

The situation improved somewhat for the third post-war generation. Home video game systems improved rapidly and provided an interactive skilled activity that honed eye-hand coordination and manual dexterity. While playing video games may not have anything directly to do with writing, the manual dexterity required to play video games and the social context of their use prepared kids for the full-scale onslaught of electronic writing.

Dyslexia bites the apple

One reason to be optimistic about the role of computers in developing new modes of written expression comes from the special case of *dyslexics,* folks who have problems processing written language. Common attributes of dyslexia are difficulty reading and spelling, including confusion of reversible letters such as *b* with *d* and *ε* with *3.* Terrible handwriting, or *dysgraphia*, is also common — a dyslexic's handwriting is often totally illegible to them and to everyone else.

Oddly, until the Apple Macintosh computer appeared in the mid-1980s, many specialists were inclined to explain dyslexic writing problems as the combined inability to compose and execute written language — that is, some combination of cognitive organization, neuro-motor execution, and possibly defective visual feedback. Working with dyslexic teenagers, Richard Wanderman, Laurel Fais, and their colleagues at the Forman School in Connecticut showed that putting dyslexic students on a Macintosh bridged a critical gap in the writing process by taking the students' handwriting out of the feedback loop between execution and perception. Students would type and the computer would display streams of beautifully crafted words on the screen. Very quickly, these educators determined that the thematic and grammatical composition skills of these students were about what you would expect of anyone who had spent so little time writing. This success story quickly gained the attention of researchers, but it really got the attention of the students whose writing, for the first time ever, *looked* just like anyone else's. The computer leveled the playing field and enabled these and many more students like them to find ways to work with their disability and eventually succeed alongside other students.

Contrasting Forms of Communication

Writing allows you to participate in communication whenever you want to — even when the folks you're communicating with aren't around. In fact, throughout the history of writing, the separation between sender and receiver in both distance and time has enhanced communication tremendously. However, while the permanence of written records has certainly benefited later generations, the historical record of the past two centuries suggests that people would much rather have their communication now than wait for it. To understand the impact writing has had on communication, it's useful to contrast the different forms of communication — both oral and written — that characterize recent human history. The following subsections show the evolution of communication — illustrated in Figure 18-1 — focusing on the following factors:

- ✔ Face-to-face versus long-distance interaction
- ✔ Instantaneous interaction versus delayed interaction
- ✔ One-to-one versus one-to-many interaction

Communicating face-to-face

Face-to-face communication occurs in real time and in the same space: It includes conversation (one-to-one communication) and public speaking (one-to-many). For most of human history, communication has been limited to people talking in the present and in close proximity to each other. Conversations finish, leaving no record other than rapidly fading memories. However, face-to-face communication is interactive, you can repair misunderstandings when they arise, and you can tailor what you say during the conversation to responses you get along the way. Face-to-face communication may have had its roots in group hunting activities, but it remains a cornerstone of collaborative interaction.

Communicating pen-to-paper

Written communication has a delayed response and can cross any space: It includes letters (one-to-one) and newspapers and books (one-to-many). Written communication allows people to process large amounts of information, and the impact isn't necessarily immediate. For example, if you trade someone a pair of shoes for a sheep, why keep a record? On the other hand, if you eventually have to account to someone else, like a tax collector, for every trade you make, then it helps to keep records of your transactions.

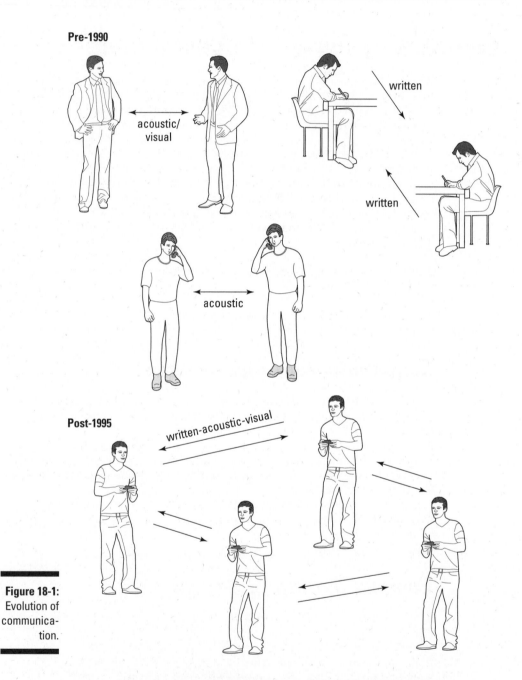

Figure 18-1:
Evolution of communica-
tion.

Communicating pen-to-ear (wait, what?)

Until the advent of electronic communication in 1838, a man on a horse was the fastest means of conveying written communication. Samuel Morse changed all that with his elegant *Morse Code*. Suddenly, messages could be transmitted at the speed of light anywhere that could be connected by a wire cable. Morse Code lies between *written communication* and *ear-to-ear communication* in Figure 18-1 — coding was slow, but transmission was nearly instantaneous over any distance.

Communicating ear-to-ear

Ear-to-ear communication occurs in real time and across any space: It includes one-to-one telephone conversations and one-to-many radio broadcasts. For close to 100 years, from the 1880s to the 1980s, the telephone provided the nearly perfect extension of *face-to-face conversation. Ear-to-ear conversation* made real-time interaction via spoken communication possible on a global scale. Guglielmo Marconi's invention of the wireless radio in 1895 extended the instantaneous link to masses of people all over the globe.

Communicating finger-to-keyboard

E-mail rapidly eclipsed the electronic bulletin boards of the early 1980s as the primary form of electronic communication among all levels of society. However, it is the cell phone that, over the past 15 years, has reshaped electronic communication and the social fabric of society, particularly for the young, who were the principal group targeted by the telecommunications companies. For older users, the cell phone affords full-scale mobility to an otherwise unchanged electronic communication tool, the telephone. But for younger users, the cell phone is a nexus for social interaction that does not rely much on its telephonic capability.

Literacy as a form of power

Historically, the most important role of writing was the power it gave the select few who could read and write. The great religions were transmitted to the people through the tight valve of literacy. This enabled the Church to dominate European society for 1,200 years. Illiterate rulers and literate clergy provided balance between the sword and the pen. The literate elite perpetuated their power by controlling the supply of written materials. The invention of the printing press in the 14th century weakened the power base by reducing the cost and increasing the rate of information flow. This didn't lead to education of the masses, but it did standardize language use for a wider range of people and fueled the demand for more diverse materials.

Among cell phone users, *texting* has replaced talking with mixed effects on mental and social health. *Texters* form close-knit circles who are perpetually in text contact. However, despite the much greater openness about sharing personal information with fellow members, texters are often more lonely and socially anxious than comparable groups of people interconnected solely by cell phone.

As texting vastly expands the number of people doing writing, teachers at all levels of the education system report the radical effects that electronic writing has had on academic writing assignments: the use of abbreviations and acronyms in formal (classroom) writing and shorter, choppier sentences that are unsuitable for written assignments. Teachers fear, correctly, that many of these changes to writing style are inevitable and will soon become the norm for various types of formal writing.

So long as texting is the dominant mode for the majority of a target group of users, it has obvious appeal in political and commercial campaigns where customers can engage interactively. These campaigns can operate globally, generating business revenue through the interactive use of texting to weigh in on news issues, donate to charities, and vote on TV show contestants. Politicians are now only a *Policlick* away from constituents and prospective voters via Facebook and Twitter. Organizations like Avaaz, a "global web movement" addressing a wide variety of current political and social issues, say forms of communication, like electronic petitions, are effective because they are far easier than signing a paper petition taken door-to-door or writing a letter to your government official.

Globalization of literacy

Industrialization and the globalization of trade throughout the 19th and 20th centuries brought prosperity to industrial nations that were able finally to effect universal public education, which resulted in nearly universal literacy. This had a snowball effect on reading and writing: Literacy led to discovery and innovation, which increased prosperity in industrial nations and their non-industrial colonies and trading partners. Education and higher literacy spread to the less-developed nations (which resulted rather naturally in a lot of colonies then becoming non-colonies). Widespread education and literacy accelerated the growth of written interpersonal communication and created mass markets for books and other one-to-many publications such as scientific and popular journals, and regional, national, and international newspapers.

Part VI
The Part of Tens

The 5th Wave

By Rich Tennant

"Your buddy says the two of you were peripheral to the incident in question. You just said you were superficial to the incident. Now which is it, peripheral or superficial?!"

In this part . . .

*L*anguage is a vehicle for communication, and what linguists do is look under the hood to see what makes language work. Curious about what they've figured out? Look at ten myths about language busted by linguists. Want to know what continues to stump linguists? Look at ten unsolved problems in linguistics. Ready to dive into a linguistics career? Look at ten jobs that linguists do.

Chapter 19

Ten Myths about Language Busted by Linguistics

- -

*Y*ou know a lot about language, because you use it all the time, every single day, and so does everyone else. Language is so universally important that people have come up with their own notions about how it all works. A lot of what people think about language is true, but sometimes people get it wrong. This chapter looks at some common misconceptions about language.

Myth 1: Slang Is Bad

Slang words are "bad." Everybody says so — everybody that is, except linguists! When linguists look at who uses slang and whether it affects the quality of language, what they find is quite the opposite. A healthy language is one where there's a lot of variation among speakers. Slang is a normal part of that variation and is one of the ways that you, as a speaker, use language to broadcast your social identity. The way you talk — including the slang words that you use — reflects your personal style, where you grew up, how old you are, and the people you hang out with. And yesterday's "bad" slang often becomes tomorrow's "good language" — this is part of the normal course of language change. A language without slang is a language in trouble: It means that, for whatever reason, speakers aren't playing with their language anymore.

The idea that slang is "bad" reflects a judgment based on social norms. A linguistic norm is an expected pattern of usage. Slang falls outside the norm because it departs from the expected pattern. But that doesn't make slang inherently "bad." Slang simply is: deal. (For more on language variation and linguistic norms, see Chapter 9. For info on how languages change over time, see Chapter 10.)

Myth 2: Only Other Folks Have Accents

Some people sound funny to you — they have an accent. But if you think of it from their point of view, you sound funny to them. That means that you have an accent. But does this mean that everyone has an accent? Yup. No two speakers produce speech sounds in exactly the same way. If there's quite a bit of overlap between the way you make your speech sounds and the way someone else makes theirs, you'll both perceive yourselves as speaking with the same accent. You can mimic someone else's accent: This involves you shifting to a different mode of production. And you can work with a voice coach to learn to drop an old accent and learn a new one.

Teasing out the exact differences between accents involves knowing how individual sounds are articulated (see Chapter 3) and also understanding how speech is perceived and produced (see Chapters 14 and 15).

Myth 3: Bilingual Kids Have a Hard Time at School

Some parents think it's better if their children speak only one language because they think that speaking two (or more) languages slows kids down at school. Linguistic research has shown that kids who speak more than one language don't do any worse at school than kids who speak just one language. In fact, quite the opposite is true. Speaking two languages is good for the brain: It increases neural pathways and improves memory and attention. And this is a life-long advantage. A bilingual (or multilingual) brain ages more gracefully — it resists the inevitable decline in memory and other cognitive functions related to problem solving, verbal reasoning, and attention. In fact, being bilingual (or multilingual) is so beneficial that psycholinguists call it the *bilingual advantage*.

Some studies have claimed that bilingual kids have smaller vocabularies in each language and are slower to process words than monolingual kids. But what's happening is that different bilinguals perform differently on these tasks according to how balanced their bilingualism is. If they use both languages across a wide range of social contexts, they'll learn the vocabulary items for those contexts. But if they use one language at home and another language at school, then, over time, the vocabulary items that they learn in each language will reflect these differences in social context. And as for longer processing time, this is the case only for tasks that require a bilingual to monitor both languages at the same time. In such bilingual contexts, monolinguals don't pay attention to the other language (because for them, it's just noise), while a bilingual pays attention to both languages. So bilinguals take longer to process the information because they're processing more information. (For additional info on how children learn languages, see Chapter 13.)

Myth 4: Language Decays Over Time

If you're an older speaker, you may feel that the young people around you or on TV just don't speak properly anymore. And school teachers seem to agree, judging by the following quotation:

> *"The vocabularies of the majority of high-school pupils are amazingly small. I always try to use simple English, and yet I have talked to classes when quite a minority of the pupils did not comprehend more than half of what I said."*

But is English — or any other language for that matter — really getting worse? Well, to put things in perspective, this quotation is from 1889, in a book by M. W. Smith called *Methods of Study in English*. If we take such comments seriously, this would mean that English has been decaying for more than 120 years. That means that you young folk can blame your great-grandparents for ruining English. Or can you? Not if you're a linguist. That's because linguists know that the language change that occurs from one generation to the next is healthy and inevitable. All human languages are rule-governed, ordered, and logical — they don't improve or get worse over time, they simply change. Differences between groups of speakers, including variation between generations of speakers, are a normal and predictable part of language variation. In addition, individual speakers themselves use a variety of forms and styles in different social situations. Of course, that doesn't stop people from having opinions — sometimes very strong ones — about how the language is changing. But these opinions are based on social rather than linguistic factors. (For info on the ways in which language can vary, see Chapter 9. For discussion on how language can change over time, see Chapter 10.)

Myth 5: Some Languages Are Primitive

Are some languages more primitive than others? Most linguists would answer "no" to that question. All human languages have a system of symbols — spoken languages use sounds, signed languages use gestures — words, and sentences that can communicate the full range of concrete and abstract ideas. For this reason, linguists believe that all human languages are equally expressive — this is called *linguistic egalitarianism*. In particular, there seems to be no correlation between linguistic complexity and the technological level of a society. Every language can create new words to describe new situations and objects, and every language changes over time. Even relatively new languages, such as the *creoles* that emerge when languages come in contact, are fully expressive. The same thing can be said about dialects. All dialects of a language are equally expressive. Although non-standard dialects may be viewed in a negative way, this judgment is based on their social value, not on their linguistic expressiveness. So just as there are no primitive languages, there are no deficient dialects.

But not all linguists believe in the principle of linguistic egalitarianism. The anthropological linguist Dan Everett has challenged this principle, arguing that Pirahã, a language spoken in Brazil, might be less expressive than other human languages. The case has garnered a lot of media attention and is being debated in the halls of academe. In particular, Everett says that Pirahã can't build compound sentences and can't refer to past and future events. But other linguists who've looked carefully at the Pirahã data haven't found any evidence in support of Everett's claim.

Another challenge to linguistic egalitarianism comes from linguist John MacWhorter, who believes that creoles have a simpler grammar. But because no one can agree on how to measure the overall complexity of a language, it's impossible to give individual languages a complexity score. The most one can do is compare features of languages to each other. It is clear that languages differ in the numbers of phonemes they have, or in how big their syllables are, or in how complicated their word forms are — but this doesn't mean that one language is less complex than another. (For info on the ways in which languages can differ from each other, see Chapter 11.)

Myth 6: Signed Languages Aren't Real Languages

If you've ever seen deaf people use sign language, you know that they happily gab away with their hands. But are the signs that they use the same thing as real language? The short answer is "yes." The longer answer requires looking more closely at signed languages as systems of communication. An obvious difference between spoken and signed language is the modality used: Spoken languages use an auditory modality; signed languages use a visual modality. But other than this difference in modality, signed languages walk and talk like spoken languages.

Signed languages have the same expressive capacity, the same grammatical regularities, and the same structures as spoken languages. Just as spoken languages have rules for combining basic sound units, signed languages have rules for combining basic gestural units — likewise for rules of word-formation, sentence-formation, semantic composition, and conversational interaction.

Signed languages vary across individual speakers, change over time, and fall into different types, as do spoken languages. In particular, there is no single signed language used by all deaf people. Just as there are families of spoken languages that are related to each other, there are families of signed languages.

Sign language isn't the poor cousin of spoken language: Children acquiring sign language go through the same stages as children acquiring spoken language. At about the same ages, babies "babble" with their hands, go through a single-sign stage and then a two-sign stage. As they acquire the grammatical patterns of their signed language, they make mistakes producing the signs and sign patterns just as speaking kids do with words and word patterns. Kids acquiring both signed and spoken languages from birth go through the same developmental stages as kids learning two spoken languages. And whether the learner is hearing or deaf makes no difference to how they learn sign language; hearing kids who have been exposed only to sign language learn it as easily as they learn spoken language. (For info on how auditory and visual modalities are used in language production and perception, see Chapters 14 and 15.)

Myth 7: Women Talk Too Much

A lot of guys think women talk more than men do. The curious thing about this is that women don't talk more — in fact, all things being equal, men actually talk more than women do. Study after study has shown that, if you put women and men in the same room — and they talk to each other — gals do more of the listening and guys do more of the talking. Yet guys still have the impression that women talk more. What's going on? Well, it's complicated. The *impression* that women talk more — which, remember, is an impression that *guys* have — is based on expectations reflecting a larger social reality: Men (on the whole) command more economic and social power than women do (on the whole). And people who run the show expect to be listened to. So if a man is in conversation with a woman, and she talks as much as he does — in other words, she behaves like an equal — the guy will walk away with the impression that she talked more than he did. What actually happened is that she talked more than he *expected* her to. (For examples of how women and men use language differently, see Chapter 9.)

Myth 8: Languages with Writing Systems Are More Developed

Most of the 6,000 or so languages spoken on the planet aren't written down, which just goes to show that, between humans, spoken language is the primary form of communication.

Writing itself was invented relatively recently in the history of humankind, and even the best writing system can't represent the richness of spoken language. Think of how much tone of voice, timing, and gesturing all contribute to the meaning of an utterance: Written language simply doesn't have the same expressive range that spoken language does.

Even so, some people believe that written language is somehow superior to spoken language. There's no denying that written language is handy: It permits communication across long distances and through time. That's something that spoken language just can't do. But that doesn't mean that written language is superior to spoken language or that languages with writing systems are superior to languages that aren't written down. Written language and spoken language simply have different uses.

Writing is a form of technology: It's useful for some things (like recording scientific discoveries), but not so good for others (having an argument over e-mail!). A written language can outlive its speakers — this is what happened to Latin. But a language is a *living language* only if a community of speakers uses it. So what keeps a language alive is the spoken form, not the written form.

For info on how writing developed as a form of technology, see Chapter 17. For discussion of how writing and language influence each other, see Chapter 18.

Myth 9: Human Language Isn't Logical

In logic, two negatives cancel each other out. So, to a logician, *"Lucy did **not not** eat the whole cake by herself"* means "Lucy ate the whole cake by herself." But many speakers don't use negation in the way that a logician would expect. For example, you'll hear some speakers of English say: *"I have**n't** never owed **nothing** to **nobody**."* If you count, there are four negatives in this sentence. If we apply the rules of logic, these negatives should cancel each other out, and the sentence should mean "I have sometimes owed something to somebody." But even if you yourself don't speak a variety of English that uses multiple negatives, you'd understand that the person who said this sentence is claiming that they have never owed anything to anybody. Does this mean English is illogical? No. What linguists have found is that some varieties of English, along with many other languages, use multiple negatives — linguists call this *negative concord*. Languages that use negative concord include Afrikaans, Bavarian, Finnish, Greek, Hungarian, Portuguese, French, Romanian, Serbian, Spanish, Persian, and Welsh. And although negative concord is frowned upon in written English, it shows up in many spoken varieties of English, including Southern American English, African American English, and most British regional dialects.

Another way in which speakers' everyday use of negation parts company with the logic of logicians is when double negatives are used to create the stylistic effect of understatement. For example, if you ask an ill friend how she's feeling, she might reply *"I'm not feeling unwell today."* When you hear your friend say this, you'd infer that her condition has improved, but that she's still not in tip-top shape. This is called a *scalar implicature:* If the speaker were feeling well, then she would say *"I'm feeling well today."* In using a double negative, the speaker's utterance implies that the simple affirmative isn't true. From this, the hearer infers that the speaker hasn't fully recovered yet. This is different from the logic of logicians, but it's just as logical: The philosopher Paul Grice, who drew attention to this aspect of conversation, calls it the *logic of conversation.*

For info on different kinds of language variation, and the difference between standard and non-standard varieties of a languages, see Chapter 9. For discussion of Grice's conversational maxims, see Chapter 8.

Myth 10: Some Languages Are Easier to Learn

Linguists believe that all human languages are equally easy to learn based on how kids learn a first language. Linguists call this *first language acquisition* or *L1 acquisition.* Kids learn the language they hear around them. Put them in a context where their caretakers speak Spanish, and, surprise surprise, they become fluent in Spanish. If their caretakers speak Mandarin, they become fluent in Mandarin. L1 acquisition of every language goes through the same stages. They first start out by practicing the sounds of the language: This is the babbling stage. They then move on to one-word and two-word utterances, and by the age of three they've nailed down the grammar.

But what about learning a second language later on in life? Linguists call this second language acquisition or *L2 acquisition.* You, as an English speaker, may think that learning German is much easier than learning Japanese, but this is only because German and English share many properties, including a shared vocabulary. Japanese seems more challenging because English and Japanese have different sound systems, different vocabularies, and different rules of syntax. Similarly, a speaker of Shona, a Bantu language spoken in Zimbabwe, will find it easier to learn another Bantu language, such as Swahili, but more difficult to learn English.

So what makes a language relatively easy to learn is not a property of the language itself. Rather the previous linguistic experience of the language learner, in particular the degree to which their L1 shares properties with their L2, determines whether they experience L2 learning as easy or hard. (For more info on the difference between L1 and L2 learning, see Chapter 13.)

Chapter 20

Ten Unsolved Problems in Linguistics

. . . .

*L*inguists know lots about language, but there are still plenty of unsolved problems in the field — enough to keep us busy for many years to come. Key questions that remain open include questions about the origin and evolution of language, about the relation of language to communication and to thought, and about the universality of language and linguistic units like *word* and *sentence* and *noun*. In this chapter we give you an overview of what we consider the ten most important unsolved problems for future generations of linguists to resolve.

What Is the Origin of Language?

Most linguists agree about roughly where and when humans first started speaking language: Based on archeological evidence about changes in society and culture, we think it was almost certainly in eastern Africa, somewhere around 60,000 years ago. But what linguists do *not* know is whether all modern spoken human languages can be traced back to just *one* original language.

Maybe there was just one first language, and this "proto-human" language gradually evolved into all the modern ones. That is certainly a possible scenario, given the fact that languages constantly drift and change in different directions.

But it is also possible that, after a certain evolutionary shift made language possible, language emerged spontaneously in several different groups of humans, in different places. These separate eruptions of chatty folks would have all been based on a similar evolutionary change and taken place at around the same time, but this would mean some modern languages descend from one group's first stab at language, and others from another. It's also quite possible that some groups made up entirely new languages (as we see in sign languages) at certain points in history, ignoring what their ancestors had done before.

How Are Human and Animal Communication Related?

Some linguists will tell you that language is a unique cognitive ability — almost like there's a special machine for manipulating symbols built into our brains — that only we humans have. They see language as a special mental faculty that evolved only in us. See Chapter 1 of this book for more discussion of the ideas and evidence behind this approach.

Other linguists will tell you that it's more a matter of degree: Almost all animals (and even plants) communicate, and all of these communication systems share a number of important features. To these linguists, human language is not unique in *kind* — it evolved out of animal communication systems, and though it advances on them in some ways, human communication is still quite similar to animal communication and can be understood using one general theory of communication. See Chapter 2 of this book for more info on communication and more discussion of this issue.

Is Language Adaptive or Exaptive?

Let's assume — as most linguists do — that language is an evolved ability: Somewhere there was a genetic mutation that rewired our brains and gave us the gift of language. Okay, but *how* exactly did this language evolution happen?

One scenario is the familiar Darwinian "survival of the fittest" scenario: People who happened to be born with the mutated language gene were more successful than other people — they could communicate better for things like hunting and gathering. So the folks with the gene had more offspring and spread their genes. This is the familiar evolutionary model that people call an *adaptive* hypothesis. The term comes from the notion that the mutations that led to language helped us adapt to our environment, so we evolved in that direction over many generations.

But other linguists (including Noam Chomsky) think we had a change in our brains quite unrelated to communication or communicative ability — something just happened, maybe a little switch in the wiring, for reasons totally unrelated to communication. For example, maybe we had a mutation that allowed us to have recursion (a kind of looping that lets us extend our sentences) in stringing units together in our minds. There was no actual process of selection *for* language — it was just a happy coincidence that something changed for other reasons, and this feature then turned out to be useful for communication. This is called the *exaptive* model of language evolution — exaptation being a kind of evolution in which a feature ends up getting used for something it was not originally selected for (the term comes from "ex" plus "adaptation").

Is There a Universal Grammar?

Obviously languages are not all the same: There is tremendous variation in the sounds, words, word order, and other aspects of the linguistic systems around the world. But if you look beneath the surface of all the world's languages, you start to see lots of stuff that is the *same* about languages. The sound systems vary, for example, but they also share common features, strategies, and organizing principles. For example, sounds in all languages are ordered into words in only a few particular ways. Similar underlying principles — with only superficial variation — can be seen in word-building processes, sentence-building processes, and other key aspects of how languages all around the world work. Some linguists believe strongly that these underlying structural similarities are proof of a *universal grammar* — a built-in set of principles that determine how we structure our languages, whatever language we speak.

Not everyone believes this, though. Languages have some similarities, sure — but there are an awful lot of differences, too. And even where there are similarities, there may well be alternative explanations besides some built-in universal basis that all languages share — maybe the similarities arise because languages have similar practical needs. For example, you need certain linguistic features in order to communicate effectively or because of general facts about how our brains organize information (not specific to language), in which case you'd expect the languages to share these features because of superficial practical needs, not some deep universal shared structure specific to language. And maybe we structure our languages the same way not because of a "universal grammar," but for more general cognitive reasons (general principles of how our brains work, now specific to language).

Is Language Innate or Learned?

Closely related to the debate about universal grammar is a debate about how kids acquire language. One camp thinks kids learn language using general learning strategies like the ability to see patterns, to memorize, and to make connections. Language-learning is not built into our brains — we just have a general ability to learn stuff, and we use it to learn language and lots of other things.

The other camp thinks that kids are born with an innate ability to learn language. Now, obviously you're not born speaking Finnish or Swahili — you do need to learn some arbitrary aspects of language, including the vocabulary and the precise sounds. But the innateness theorists think you don't just learn from generalizing from patterns you hear — you are *born* knowing certain things about language, such as that words will be structured in only a limited range of possible ways.

What's the Relation of Language to Thought?

Some linguists have argued that the structure and form of your language can strongly influence your thinking and, through this, your whole worldview — how you perceive the world, how you analyze it, and how you act in it. For example, if your language has a certain set of color terms, this might affect how you classify objects based on color; if your language has a certain tense system, this might shape your view of time; or if your language has grammatical gender, so that certain objects are classed as male or female, it might even influence how you think about those objects. The idea that language shapes thought is often called the *Sapir-Whorf hypothesis*.

The Sapir-Whorf hypothesis has been extremely influential, but not all linguists think it really pans out into that much. Forms of language such as color terms, tense, and noun-classification systems may have just superficial effects on our worldview — or none at all.

Is Language a Bunch of Probabilities or a Set of Rules?

Many linguists think language is a set of absolute rules: A certain sound or word or sentence pattern is either good or bad, in or out, right or wrong. This is your English teacher who said you could never end a sentence with a preposition.

But not all linguists buy this. Language, as we actually speak it, is in fact *not* rigid: There are many tendencies *towards* a certain pattern, without any fixed rule that tells you that you must use that pattern. There are many sentences that speakers will find sort of okay, but that are not clearly part of the grammar. And there are many facts about how language is structured that can be expressed as statistical probabilities, without being necessarily present 100 percent of the time. Linguists who focus on these aspects of language believe that statistics and statements about probability are useful tools for describing key features of language.

Work on language-based statistical probabilities has gotten a big boost in recent generations from the growing power of computers and the ability to access and machine-analyze large collections of language on the Internet; however some rule-based linguists dismiss this "statistical revolution" as being about as interesting as doing physics by videotaping the street outside your office for days on end and then running statistical analyses programs to predict what will happen next.

Is There a Universal Definition of "Word"?

A common linguistic definition for *word* goes like this: a meaningful unit that can stand by itself. For example, *dog* is a word because it has a meaning and it can stand alone as a separate unit; but the plural ending *-s* is not a word because, though it has a meaning, *-s* can only be used attached to another unit, as in *dogs*. Thus we say *dog* is a word, but *-s* is not (it's just a suffix).

The trouble is, it's not all that clear what *stand alone* really means — and whether it means the same thing in different languages. You certainly separate word-units when you write by putting spaces between them, but this may not be the best guide. Writing systems are not necessarily perfect reflections of linguistic structure and can have historical relics and sometimes arbitrary conventions. And listening for pauses between the units won't help that much: You may think you hear them that way, but words are *not* normally pronounced with pauses in between them in natural speech. So in what sense do words stand alone?

Linguists focused on English do see important reasons to recognize word units within the language. For example, in English (and many related languages), words pattern as units with respect to stress assignment — each of these units will have primary stress (emphasis) on one syllable in a predictable position. But these and the other criteria that lead linguists to recognize word units in English may not work well, or at all, for all other languages in the world — the case is still open.

Is There a Universal Definition of "Sentence"?

When you talk, a string of words comes out of your mouth as an uninterrupted stream — until you stop, of course. This uninterrupted stream, from start to stop, is what linguists call an *utterance*.

Now, it's easy to spot an utterance. But a *sentence* can't be defined the same way as an utterance. After all, you might utter 2, 3, or 20 sentences before you pause for breath. And you might change your mind in mid-utterance and — well, you get the idea. So sentences are linguistic units that are more abstract than just strings of words that you say together.

So what defines this *sentence* unit, and is it the same across all languages? Because we can't just look at where the pauses are, linguists have to look for much more subtle cues, like intonation contours (the up and down pitch of your voice as you make a sentence) or structural definitions like *a verb with a subject and/or object (and modifiers)*. And even if we define the sentence-unit for one language, we can't just assume that other languages group their words into sentences using the same criteria and based on the same cues.

Is There a Universal Set of Lexical Categories?

English has nouns, verbs, adjectives, and a few other classes of words that linguists call *lexical categories.* Each lexical category can appear only in certain parts of a sentence, for example, in English, a verb will not start a declarative sentence, so we say *Bill walked,* not **Walked Bill.*

Different languages have different orders for their nouns and verbs — some languages put the verb first in a sentence, for example. But do all languages even *have* verbs? Or do they distinguish adjectives from adverbs? And is it possible, conversely, that some languages might divide their words up into *more* lexical categories, ones that we don't even have in English? This is part of the broader question of whether there is an underlying universal grammar, but we think it's worth isolating as a specific debate because of its importance to the field of syntax (a key area of linguistics), for which lexical categories like *noun* and *verb* are absolutely essential.

Some linguists have indeed specifically argued that certain languages, specifically the Salish group of languages (spoken in Canada), indeed do *not* have any distinction between nouns and verbs, in which case those lexical categories cannot be universal. But other linguists have questioned that claim about Salish, based on more subtle understanding of how the languages work — they think if you look harder, you will find good evidence for nouns and verbs even in Salish. So it is possible that there is an underlying set of universal lexical categories that languages pick and choose from, but it is also possible that there is no fixed universal base.

Chapter 21

Top 10 Jobs for Linguists

*L*anguage connects with everything. So if you're interested in a career in linguistics — which is the study of language — then you're in luck. You can do "pure research" or more practical things. But no matter which linguistics path you decide to follow, you'll find it an ear-stretching, eye-opening, mind-enlarging experience!

Theoretical Linguist

Typical career goals: Understanding language by developing formal theories based on language data. The data that theoretical linguists look at includes sounds, words, phrases, or stories that they collect from fluent speakers. Over the course of their career, theoretical linguists publish books or research papers in academic journals that focus on aspects of language structure or on the mathematical properties of the theories they work with. Theoretical linguists also train graduate students, who go on to become professional linguists.

Works for: Universities or publicly funded research institutes.

Daily grind can include: Working with language speakers to elicit data, transcribing and analysing data, developing theories, writing papers, books, and reviews, supervising students, and collaborating with other researchers at seminars and conferences.

Skills, aptitude, and training: Normally requires a PhD in theoretical linguistics and an appetite for working with complex symbolic systems.

Experimental Linguist

Typical career goals: Uncovering the structure of human language with experiments that probe how we produce speech, perceive it, acquire it, and process it cognitively and neurally. Experimental linguists publish papers and books that focus on language behavior and brain function.

Works for: Universities or research institutes. Experimental research institutes are sometimes public, but private corporations involved in telecommunications, such as the famous IBM-Watson and the ATT-Bell Labs, also depend on basic research on language. They need experimental linguists to help them understand how human beings produce and perceive speech so they can build systems for transmitting speech signals — that's what telephones do.

Daily grind can include: Running experiments on how fast speakers recognize words or how different parts of their brain respond to language-related tasks; analyzing data from experiments; writing papers and books; teaching and supervising students; bidding for and administering research funds; setting up and running lab facilities.

Skills, aptitude, and training: Normally requires a PhD in experimental linguistics or psychology and may also require joint or additional training in engineering, computer science, and neuroscience. This is a great job if you enjoy a combination of linguistics, experimental psychology, and computer science.

Sociolinguist/Dialectologist

Typical career goals: Mapping the varieties of a language and correlating language variation with education, social class, gender, region, and context of use. Sociolinguists publish books and research papers based on their research. Dialectologists are a kind of sociolinguist: They focus on the regional variations — dialects — of a language.

Works for: Universities, civil government agencies, and private or NGO research and development programs.

Daily grind can include: Organizing large surveys of different populations, asking speakers of different dialects to read passages or tell stories; analyzing data quantitatively to try and understand social variation in language use across groups and contexts. Many sociolinguists focus on issues relating to language and gender.

Skills, aptitude, and training: Normally requires advanced degrees in linguistics or sociology and a combination of interests in language, society, and (for quantitative sociolinguistic studies) statistical analysis.

Language Documentation Specialist

Typical career goals: Collect large samples of a language, including dictionaries, grammars, word-lists, and stories. A major documentation project can take many months or even years to complete and may be geared towards future linguistic analysis, language revitalization, posterity, or (ideally) a combination of those.

Works for: Universities, government agencies, or community and tribal organizations.

Daily grind can include: Working with fluent speakers to record words, phrases, and stories; transcribing and formatting the collection; annotating, transcribing, and translating the documentary collection; indexing and archiving the collection; working with community and tribal organizations to share the collection.

Skills, aptitude, and training: Enjoy working with the elderly (because many endangered languages are only spoken by people in their 70s and older) and diverse cultures; highly organized and committed to language documentation and preservation; trained in general linguistics as well as database design, audio recording, and archiving.

Speech Scientist

Typical career goals: Speech scientists fall into two groups: *speech language pathologists* (who focus on speech problems) and *audiologists* (who focus on hearing). Some speech scientists focus on research, but many are therapists, applying speech science knowledge to help people with speech, hearing, and language disorders.

Works for: Hospitals, clinics, universities, schools, or private therapy practices.

Daily grind can include: Helping people with stuttering, delayed language, and neurologically impaired speech. They also work on voice and swallowing disorders and are often part of sex-change therapy. Audiologists diagnose and treat issues in hearing loss, hearing aids, cochlear implants, and speech and language issues related to hearing loss.

Skills, aptitude, and training: Usually requires undergraduate work in linguistics and then an MA or PhD degree in some aspect of speech science. This is a well-paid, high-demand job. Training involves a combination of academic coursework, clinical training in hospitals, and diagnostic training in schools. The only way to enter the field is through training positions, which are very competitive.

Forensic Linguist

Typical career goals: Helping catch criminals of all types using linguistic analysis or serving as an expert witness and consultant in criminal and civil cases.

Works for: Law firms, prosecutor's office, or private consulting firms.

Daily grind can include: Working on voice identification in an audio recording; looking for linguistic clues in a ransom note; helping immigration officials verify a refugee's claim based on dialect analysis; testifying about the usage history of words in trademark or land-claims cases; analyzing recorded conversations to determine which participant first suggested the idea that may have lead to a crime being committed (this is especially relevant in conspiracy cases).

Skills, aptitude, and training: Requires at least undergraduate level training in linguistics, as well as specialized training in technology and law.

Voice Coach

Typical career goals: Training public personalities — actors, politicians, business people — to either lose or gain the mannerisms and dialect of a specific region. For example, Julia Roberts' speech coach helped her lose her southern accent early in her career. And then later, for the film *Steel Magnolias,* he helped her get it back again.

Works for: Movie industry, politicians, large corporations, or private clients.

Daily grind can include: Helping an Australian actor sound American, or an American actress sound British. Helping someone who must deal with a wide variety of clients acquire a more standard style of speaking. Using phonetic drills that target vowel quality, syllabification, and intonation, voice coaches help their clients learn new dialects.

Skills, aptitude, and training: Excellent social skills, patience and tact, a good ear for dialects, and a strong background in practical phonetics.

Computational Linguist

Typical career goals: Helping program machines to do various language-processing tasks such as automatic speech recognition, machine translation, and speech synthesis. In addition, they develop information processing and retrieving systems, which are applied to text, audio, and image data.

Works for: Universities, military and defence (government and industrial), search engine corporations such as Google, business sector, and research institutes.

Daily grind can include: Working with engineers, computer scientists, and information scientists. Tasks involve developing statistical tools for analyzing spoken language, searching the Web or automatically tagging data based on semantic networks, or modeling how human speech production and perception work.

Skills, aptitude, and training: Advanced training in linguistics, applied mathematics, and computer science; ability to work collaboratively with other scientists and engineers.

Lexicographer (Dictionary-writer)

Typical career goals: Helping create dictionaries and tracking the development and progress of words in a language.

Works for: Publisher or university.

Daily grind can include: Searching large databases to study the different ways a particular word is used; organizing and defining words based on this usage and adding information about word history *(etymology)*, pronunciation, and other grammatical information.

Skills, aptitude, and training: At least some undergraduate-level training in linguistics is very helpful, including historical linguistics; love of words; expertise in a particular research area.

Product-Namer & Advertiser

Typical career goals: Create new names for products and services, taking into account both pronunciation and the emotional and cultural associations of each word, often in multi-lingual markets. Develop advertising language for the purpose of marketing a product.

Works for: Advertising firm or private consultant.

Daily grind can include: Finding a name for a product that is appealing and pronounceable in different languages, while avoiding negative associations. Conducting surveys and studies that measure the emotional response of potential buyers to different words, sounds, letters, phrases, voices, and dialects.

Skills, aptitude, and training: A strong background in linguistics, such as an undergraduate or advanced degree, is very helpful for this and other work in advertising. Other relevant skills include familiarity with many languages; familiarity with government and legislative process; an openness and sensitivity to other cultures.

Index

• G •

• U •

• V •

• Y •

• Z •